T. S. Eliot and Christian Tradition

T. S. Eliot and Christian Tradition

Edited by Benjamin G. Lockerd

FAIRLEIGH DICKINSON UNIVERSITY PRESS
Madison • Teaneck

Published by Fairleigh Dickinson University Press
Copublished with Rowman & Littlefield
4501 Forbes Boulevard, Suite 200, Lanham, Maryland 20706
www.rowman.com

10 Thornbury Road, Plymouth PL6 7PP, United Kingdom

British Library Cataloguing in Publication Information Available

Library of Congress Cataloging-in-Publication Data
T. S. Eliot and Christian Tradition / edited by Benjamin G. Lockerd.
pages cm.
Includes bibliographical references and index.
ISBN 978-1-61147-611-8 (cloth) -- ISBN 978-1-61147-612-5 (electronic)
1. Eliot, T. S. (Thomas Stearns), 1888-1965--Religion. 2. Christianity and literature. I. Lockerd, Benjamin G., 1950- editor of compilation.
PS3509.L43Z872456 2014
821'.912--dc23

2014005185

ISBN 978-1-61147-713-9 (pbk)
∞™

Contents

IV: Culture and Religion

V: Contemporaries

Acknowledgments

Several of the essays in this collection were first presented at a conference on T. S. Eliot held at my school, Grand Valley State University, and at the Russell Kirk Center. I am grateful to GVSU for its sponsorship of that conference and to Annette Kirk, president of the Russell Kirk Center, for co-hosting. *Eliot and His Age*, Russell Kirk's critical biography, has had, as the reader will see, a marked influence on many of the contributors to this volume. Certainly that book has been central to my own understanding of Eliot. Mrs. Kirk has furthered her late husband's intellectual legacy by making it possible for many visiting scholars to do research and writing in the richly conducive atmosphere of the Kirk Center.

I thank the contributors to this volume, who have shown the virtues of patience and hope over the years it has taken for the book to be published. I am fortunate to have worked with this remarkable group of scholars, some of them still in graduate school when they submitted their contributions and others long-established critics. Particular thanks must be given to the elder statesman of the group, Professor William Blissett, the author of the lead essay, which serves to define Anglo-Catholicism and adumbrate the religious milieu in which Eliot immersed himself. I was fortunate to be a student of Blissett's at the University of Toronto—as were two of the other contributors, Thomas Dilworth and Paul Robichaud—so he has had an influence on a whole generation (or two) of scholars. At the other end of the timeline are younger writers who are already making their voices heard with striking authority.

I have been fortunate in editing this volume to have the assistance of several graduate assistants, who made my work much easier and more pleasurable: Jonathan Whitmer, Noelle Kasa, Karie Luidens, and Sarah Slachter. Many, many thanks.

Several of my colleagues at GVSU have been a great help to me in the process of editing this book. I want to thank in particular William Morison and Robert Franciosi.

This project would never have been achieved without the encouragement and inspiration of my wife, Micheline Lockerd. Everything around her comes to life.

—BGL

****

The editor gratefully acknowledges permission to quote from the following works:

Excerpts from *Poems* by C. S. Lewis, copyright © C. S. Lewis Pte. Ltd. 1964, renewed 1992, reprinted by permission of The C. S. Lewis Company and Houghton Mifflin Publishing Company. All rights reserved.

Excerpts from *The Complete Poems and Plays, 1909-1962* by T. S. Eliot, copyright © 1950 by T. S. Eliot, renewed 1978 by Esme Valerie Eliot, used by permission of Houghton Mifflin Harcourt Publishing Company and Faber and Faber Ltd. All rights reserved.

Excerpts from *Inventions of the March Hare: Poems 1909-1917* by T. S. Eliot, copyright © 1996 by Valerie Eliot, used by permission of Houghton Mifflin Harcourt Publishing Company and Faber and Faber Ltd. All rights reserved.

Excerpts from *Christianity and Culture* by T. S. Eliot, copyright © 1939, 1948 by T. S. Eliot, renewed 1967, 1976 by Esme Valerie Eliot, used by permission of Houghton Mifflin Harcourt Publishing Company and Faber and Faber Ltd. All rights reserved.

Excerpts from *Religion and Culture, Beyond Politics, Progress and Religion,* and *Religion and the Modern State* by Christopher Dawson reprinted by permission of The Catholic University of America Press.

Excerpts from the letters of David Jones reprinted by permission of the trustees of the David Jones Estate.

Excerpts from *The Divine Comedy* by Dante Alighieri, translated by Allen Mandelbaum, copyright © 1980 by Allen Mandelbaum, used by permission of Bantam Books, a division of Random House, Inc. Any third party use of this material, outside of this publication, is prohibited. Interested parties must apply directly to Random House, Inc. for permission.

Excerpts from *All Hallows' Eve* by Charles Williams reprinted by permission of the David Higham Agency.

Excerpt from "Letter to Lord Byron" by W. H. Auden, copyright © 1937 by W. H. Auden and Louis MacNeice, renewed, reprinted by permission of Curtis Brown, Ltd.

Introduction

Benjamin G. Lockerd

In the summer of 1926, T. S. Eliot visited Rome with his wife, his brother, and his sister-in-law. As they entered the Basilica of St. Peter and saw the *Pietà*, the poet suddenly fell to his knees, to the surprise of his family.[1] If his closest family were astonished by his Christian belief, his friends and the literary world at large were understandably taken almost completely unawares when, less than a year later (June, 1927), Eliot was received into the Church of England. He made his religious commitment fully public the next year in the preface to a short book entitled *For Lancelot Andrewes*, in which he declared himself a classicist, a royalist, and an Anglo-Catholic. Many were not only surprised but shocked and even dismayed, for they regarded Eliot's avant-garde poetry as a herald of their modern secular worldview. His conversion seemed to them not only incredible but treacherous. According to Tony Sharp, "As Eliot's personal development began to be reflected in his writing and his public career, there were those amongst his devotees who were caught unprepared by his conversion, which had the appearance of suddenness to them."[2] In reaction to his conversion, Virginia Woolf wrote to her sister, "Poor dear Tom Eliot . . . may be called dead to us from this day forward."[3] Right down to the present, many readers of Eliot have continued to respond to his Christian conversion with disbelief or disapproval, and that response is reflected in much critical writing, which has often ignored Eliot's faith, frequently misunderstood it, and sometimes attempted to explain it away by arguing that his Anglo-Catholicism was not a genuine religious belief but rather a sham adopted to serve his aesthetic program or his political commitments. However, there have also been more considered and judicious responses from many scholars, and several critics (often, but not exclusively, Christian believers themselves) have written sympathetically about Eliot's religious beliefs and the way they affected his writing. A consensus has begun to form on the subject, one of the primary tenets of which is that Eliot's conversion was not nearly as sudden as has been assumed. Another is that his religious beliefs were of a piece with his ideas about literature, politics, and culture—but without being determined by them. This developing consensus about Eliot's Christian convictions is absolutely essential to understanding Eliot's poetry, plays, and prose. By explaining his beliefs and the influence those beliefs had on his writing, the contributors to this volume enable us to read the works more intelligently and perceptively, and to understand the complex life and times of the writer more fully.

This new formulation (like most new ideas) is not actually so very new. Much of what has been said about Eliot's religion was well expressed, for example, by Russell Kirk in his book *Eliot and His Age* (1971).[4] In his own recent book on Eliot and Christianity, Barry Spurr calls Kirk's "one of the best books" written on Eliot, and he frequently cites Kirk on key issues.[5] As Kevin Dettmar points out, Lyndall Gordon's biography is another book that expresses "sympathy with Eliot's religious quest," as does Ronald Schuchard's *Eliot's Dark Angel*.[6] Dettmar's article is itself a significant contribution to the new appraisal of this central element in Eliot's life and art. Another thoughtful and knowledgeable essay on the topic is by Cleo McNelly Kearns.[7] In *Words Alone*, Denis Donoghue writes of Eliot but also of his own experience as a Catholic critic in a fundamentally anti-Christian scholarly world. Toward the end of the book, he says, "Eliot's conversion to the Anglican communion has been the object of such intemperate comment that a protest is in order. It is apparently necessary to say that Eliot's right to become a Christian is as clear as anyone else's right not to. I don't understand why his Christian belief attracts more aggressive attention than any other writer's agnosticism."[8] These and other sympathetic critics have laid the groundwork on which scholars today, including those represented in this volume, could build.

Spurr's book, published in 2010, is the full-length study that has been needed, and it is a major achievement. He gives us a rich description of the historical development of Anglo-Catholicism, placing Eliot in a particular phase of that history; he carefully explains Anglo-Catholic theology, custom, and practice; and he shows how Eliot's Anglo-Catholic beliefs and practices inform his writings. This work is the definitive introduction to the topic of Eliot's religion. It may be said to set the stage for the chapters in this book, which explore in greater detail particular aspects of the subject that Spurr introduces and contextualizes but upon which he does not have space to elaborate.

The present volume begins with a concise reevaluation of Eliot's Anglo-Catholicism by the Anglo-Catholic Canadian scholar William Blissett. A little-known document produced by a committee of which Eliot was a member is the starting point for Blissett's analysis of Eliot's Anglo-Catholicism. In 1947 a committee of distinguished theologians and clerics, along with one poet, produced a pamphlet entitled *Catholicity*, an attempt to address the primary strains of thought in the contemporary Christian world: Protestant, Catholic, and Liberal Modernist. Blissett ranges widely from this point of departure: identifying some of the key members of the committee, such as Austin Farrer, Dom Gregory Dix, and

Canon V. A. Demant; defining the prime tenets of Anglo-Catholicism; considering Eliot's decision for Canterbury rather than Rome; clarifying his allegiance to Charles Maurras (and its limits); describing the life of the newly baptized Eliot; and examining the Christian sociology that informs his cultural criticism. Much of this material is new to those who have read only the existing biographies and commentaries, and Blissett describes, *inter alia*, the textures of Anglo-Catholic thought and life in Eliot's time. One of his many interesting observations that complicate our understanding of the Anglo-Catholic movement: Anglo-Catholic priests were not typically given comfortable preferments (the church hierarchy being generally lower church) and were often assigned instead to new churches in slum parishes in the big cities, with the result that the traditionalist priests and parishes often became deeply involved in addressing the needs of the urban poor.[9] Therefore, liturgical and doctrinal traditionalism was often combined with a kind of social activism: for instance, Demant, an acknowledged influence on Eliot's cultural thought, was a lifelong socialist. Blissett offers a richly textured and nuanced description of the religious world in which Eliot drew breath, contextualizing the chapters to follow.

ANTAGONISTIC CRITICS

It is surprising to find that it took nearly half a century for a comprehensive and sympathetic book to be written on Eliot's religious beliefs, but many critics during the decades following the poet's death either were content to underestimate the role of religion in his writing or were determined to find some fault with his faith. As Dettmar puts it, "Eliot criticism was for its first five decades characterized by a widespread unwillingness to engage seriously with Eliot's religious convictions and commitment."[10] The antagonistic response took several different tacks, all of which have a germ of truth to them and are thus superficially convincing. One was to assert that Eliot's conversion was just part of his attempt to cease being a foreigner from Missouri and become more English than any Englishman. The psychological approach asserted that Christianity was a refuge for a neurotic man who could not deal with the tensions and dilemmas of real life and had to cling to something absolutely certain. A variation on that theme was a kind of existentialist critique that found Eliot lacking in the courage it takes to live in the freedom and pain of Heideggerian Thrown-ness into Being. Eliot's conversion began as an intellectual and philosophical one, and some critics have contended that it never went beyond the intellectual level to heartfelt belief. Yet another response claimed that Eliot was never really converted to belief in Christian dogmas but employed the richness of the Christian narrative for aesthetic purposes.

A relatively friendly essay by Donald Davie in 1973, "Anglican Eliot," nevertheless sees his conversion as subordinate to his desire to Anglicize himself. Davie says, ". . . there is some reason to doubt whether Eliot would have joined the Church of England, if it had not been the *established* church."[11] While Eliot's desire for British citizenship was certainly intertwined with his conversion (he became a British subject in the same year in which he joined the church), this essay implies that the religious conversion was subject to the change of national allegiance. Davie hastens to say that he does not mean to "impugn the sincerity of Eliot's conversion" (which, as we will see, others have indeed done), but he concludes that "when it came to deciding what Christian sect he should join, it was of the utmost importance to him that he choose what should seem to be not a sect at all but a national norm."[12] This overstates the case and implies that the nationality of the sect was the most important issue. On the contrary, Eliot gave the utmost importance, not to the national standing of the church, but to its doctrinal orthodoxy and connection to sacred tradition. If there had been no Anglo-Catholic movement within the Church of England, it is reasonable to suppose, based on what is brought to light in the present book, that he would have become a Roman Catholic.

A more antagonistic analysis is given by Eugene Goodheart in *The Failure of Criticism* (1978). Goodheart is primarily interested in Eliot's cultural theory, which he sees as reflecting Eliot's withdrawal from the real world into Catholic dogmatism. He claims that in Eliot's cultural criticism "there is no dialectical interplay between Christianity and the modern world" because Eliot "rejects the alternative open to him of trying 'to adapt Christian social ideals' to the modern world," insisting instead that Christianity "remains . . . an institution ideally able to transform and save the world."[13] Of course that is exactly what orthodox Christians believe, and they know full well that the oft-repeated call for them to adapt to modernity is nothing short of a demand for capitulation. Goodheart quotes approvingly William Chace's statement that "Eliot's political interests lay neither in disposing human energy toward the solution of social problems . . . nor in liberating human energy from social confines, but in showing how men failed to achieve a society in which certain religious values could be appreciated."[14] Now, whether or not one agrees with Eliot's political views, one must grant that he hopes what he envisions would solve social problems by creating a healthy society. In speaking of "liberating human energy from social confines," Chace expresses just the sort of romantic faith in unfettered individual freedom (inspired by Rousseau and others) that Eliot learned to distrust very early under the tutelage of Irving Babbitt. To accuse Eliot of not desiring such liberation is merely to assert fundamentally different assumptions—yet his rhetoric assumes that this liberation is self-evidently good. Chace is proclaiming a doctrine, not making an argument. Goodheart uses other rhetorical ploys, such as accusing Eliot of "rigidity of purpose," of being "quixotic," and (using the standard Marxist-inspired critique of traditionalists) of being "nostalgic."[15] These are simply slurs from the lexicon of the modern secularists.

Somewhat more cogently, Goodheart maintains that Eliot's writing on social issues expresses a "sentiment of resignation, verging on hopelessness," a feeling that is, he claims, "characteristic of the modern Catholic imagination."[16] Probably most readers of Eliot would agree that there is often a tone of resignation, but does it really verge on hopelessness? Eliot did not expect a thoroughgoing transformation of modern culture to occur, but he expected some spiritual renewal of that culture to be achieved. His resignation was permeated by hope. In his essay on F. H. Bradley, he says (in relation to Arnold's efforts at cultural renewal), "If we take the widest and wisest view of a Cause, there is no such thing as a Lost Cause because there is no such thing as a Gained Cause."[17] The Christian social critic expects no total victory, but neither does he expect total defeat. Goodheart entitles his chapter "The Reality of Disillusion in T. S. Eliot" and suggests that this disillusion is destructive, but Eliot goes on to say in the Bradley essay that "skepticism and disillusion are a useful equipment for religious understanding," indicating that he was quite conscious of the disillusion in his religious worldview and thought it an important and healthy element. It seems that Goodheart believes he has shown a great weakness in modern Catholic thinking when he finds this disillusionment, but the Catholic thinker never did expect complete victory in what Augustine called the "City of Man," so the disillusionment is not a surprise and may even engender humility—in contrast to the secular idealogue's confidence in utopian schemes.

Goodheart sees Eliot withdrawing from an "unredeemable temporal order" into an ineffectual asceticism that rejects the temporal order completely.[18] He would turn the tables on the orthodox believer, accusing him of a "Manichaean" heresy, a "self-impoverishing split between spirit and the world." His evidence is the "absurdly quixotic" martyrdom of Celia in *The Cocktail Party*.[19] One wonders what martyrdom would not seem absurdly quixotic to the thoroughly secularized mind. Now, there is no doubt that Eliot had an ascetic leaning, but his writing is full of his efforts to glimpse the "point of intersection of the timeless / With time," and his mind constantly comes to rest in the doctrine of the Incarnation, where "the impossible union / Of spheres of existence is actual" (*Dry Salvages* V). The charge of Manichaeism will not stand up to scrutiny. Goodheart continues to barrage Eliot with slurs, accusing him of "nihilism" and (again with Marxist undertones) of "bad faith."[20] My aim is not so much to offer a rebuttal of Goodheart, who acknowledges in the end that he has presented a one-sided view, but rather to point out that his fundamental assumptions make it simply impossible for him to take Eliot's Catholic social thought on it own terms, or to take it seriously at all, except as an affront to what he calls "the radical estrangement of modern consciousness from the possibility of transcendence."[21] Assuming that the estrangement is nearly complete and is irreversible, he proposes that the church step aside and allow a more appropriate institution to dominate modern culture: "The university in a democratic society, one of the principal institutions of humanism, has an active diffusive power at least as effective as the contemporary church and perhaps more inventive and more inspiring in its 'message.'"[22] This notion that the secularized university should take the place of the church is one of which the Harvard-educated Eliot was well aware, and one against which he argued. Following Coleridge's critique of the new secularist and materialist educational leadership replacing what he called the "clerisy," Eliot spoke against "the clericalism of secularism."[23] It is precisely those who regard themselves as the new humanist clergy who are most likely to attack Eliot's religious convictions.

The reluctance of many critics to accept that Eliot really believed is exemplified by William Skaff's 1986 book, *The Philosophy of T. S. Eliot*. Skaff very ably elucidates the various philosophical influences on Eliot's thinking up to 1927, but he refuses to credit Eliot's faith, asserting that "the true nature of Eliot's religious experience was *not* a literal belief in Christian dogma, as has often been assumed, but a more complex psychological state."[24] He claims that " . . . Eliot will never speak of an afterlife, or even of God as a personal being."[25] Anyone who has read Eliot attentively will easily think of passages that contradict this extraordinary assertion. Here is one that comes to mind: "If you will not have God (and He is a jealous God) you should pay your respects to Hitler or Stalin."[26] Surely this refers to God as a personal being. The "mythic method" spoken of by Eliot in relation to Joyce's *Ulysses* became, according to Skaff, a way in which "the mythology of the Judeo-Christian religion, no longer believed in literally, could nevertheless still serve the religious needs of modern man." Actually, there is no such thing as "the Judeo-Christian religion," but this kind of loose reasoning allows Skaff to say that in poetry "modern man can once again find a satisfactory expression for his religious impulses."[27] This is merely an updated version of Matthew Arnold's attempts to have the cultural benefits of Christianity without the awkward beliefs. Eliot quoted a somewhat similar statement made by Arnold and commented on it: "'The power of Christianity has been in the immense emotion which it has excited,' he says; not realizing at all that this is a counsel to get all the emotional kick out of Christianity one can, without the bother of believing it. . . ."[28] And there is also Eliot's famous response when I. A. Richards took up Arnold's cry "poetry will save us": "it is like saying that the wall-paper will save us when the walls have crumbled."[29] Eliot had long ago anticipated Skaff's objection with a spirited rejoinder.

Once he is committed to this line of approach, Skaff must advance at all costs. He goes so far as to say that "literal belief, the intellectual acceptance of the surface story of a myth, can only hinder religious experience," making his poetical experience of religious feelings superior to that of the simple believer.[30] Even the faith of the Middle Ages must fit this mold: "In keeping with his conception of religious experience as mythic consciousness, Eliot perceives this age of faith as utilizing the mythic method rather than embracing literal belief."[31] Thus Dante himself—whose allegorical method is somehow seen as similar to the mythic method—is brought into the fold of the non-literal believers. This book shows the absurdities critics must embrace eventually if they begin with such equivocations. A far more reasonable conclusion is reached by Kearns: "There is no doubt that he [Eliot] came to believe wholeheartedly and without revisionism not only in hell and damnation, but in the more salvific doctrines, in what he called the 'fact of incarnation' and the atonement and in what he took to be their corollary, the virgin birth."[32]

Another book published in the same year as Skaff's (1986) takes a slightly different approach to explaining away Eliot's faith. Instead of seeing Eliot's religion as an aesthetic concern, C. K. Stead sees it as essentially political—a more thorough-going version of Davie's analysis. "I am not sure whether Eliot's acceptance into the Anglican faith in 1928 is properly called a 'conversion,'" Stead writes (getting the date wrong). It was, he asserts, "something very like a political decision."[33] This is a tempting position to take because Eliot's religious conversion was indeed connected with his political ideas, as he himself affirmed in his tripartite declaration. However, to say that Eliot's becoming an Anglican was fundamentally a political rather than a religious decision is an unwarranted simplification. Stead's analysis seems to be tinged with Marxist ideology: "Sharing with men like Hulme, Maurras and Babbitt that middle-class fear of the emancipation and enfranchisement of the people, he had concluded that Maurras was right in working towards a return of the institutions of the monarchy and the church."[34] Stead apparently cannot conceive of any political philosophy that argues for structures of external authority as being motivated by anything but "middle-class fear," and he also cannot imagine a religious faith that is not driven by the same fear.

Stead's chapter on Eliot degenerates quickly into manifestations of anti-Christian bias. For instance, he asserts that in *Four Quartets* Eliot is prevented from writing good poetry by "a particularly life-denying form of Christian asceticism"—the assumption being that all Christian asceticism is life-denying but this one particularly so. Eliot's focus on the transcendent experience establishes, Stead avers, a measure by which "human kind is found contemptible, human desire deluding, human affections unclean."[35] Such statements reflect, not Eliot's inability to embrace the mundane, but the critic's unwillingness to imagine the intersec-

tion of the eternal and the temporal (the way up and the way down) that
Eliot seeks to glimpse in the poem.

One might expect that as time went by and more information about
Eliot's life and thought became available, understanding of Eliot's faith
would become clearer and such attempts to deny the reality of that faith
would diminish, but in some cases more recent critical works have
merely become more insistent and more malicious. For instance, Alfred
Kazin's chapter on Eliot in *God and the American Writer* (1997) is a bitter
diatribe. Like Stead, Kazin resorts to the assumption that religious belief
is always motivated by fear. His Eliot is "a man susceptible to terror," a
man "psychologically fractured," for whom "the Church was authority,
orthodoxy, a safe bastion." For Kazin, only psychological illness and fear
can account for belief, and to these he adds the requisite comment about
class consciousness: "The world became sordid and pressed its meaninglessness on him to the point where only authority, hierarchy, some absolute never to be doubted, promised to relieve him of the sense of his own
oddity in the democratic mass world."[36] The combination of neurotic
terror and middle-class fear suffice to explain Eliot's conversion for Kazin, who is angry at Eliot's rejection of "the open, democratic, hopeful
America."[37] Playing his trump card, Kazin notes Eliot's supposed "preference for fascism."[38] As is customary among antagonistic critics, the
charge of fascism is made without evidence by a writer who has clearly
not read Eliot's published statements on the subject. Eliot's actual views
on fascism are clarified in this volume by the chapters in the section on
"Culture and Religion."

Kazin finds fault with Eliot's statement that he had been raised "outside the Christian fold," criticizing Eliot for his insistence that without
belief in the dogma of the Incarnation one could not be considered a
Christian. It seems Kazin would not be so offended by Eliot's Christianity
if it did not include a belief in Christ's divinity. He goes on to complain
that Eliot "rejected as well everything open and tolerant in his grandfather's rock-rooted belief that God was more than the Church."[39] By this
point Kazin is completely carried away by his own rhetoric: Eliot
certainly believed that God was more than the Church—it's just that he
also believed the Gospels when they say that Christ did establish a
church and give authority to the leaders of his church (Matthew 16:18;
John 20:23). Kazin is primarily intent on accusing Eliot of a catalogue of
sins that offend modern secularist belief. He fails, as a result, to give a fair
and accurate representation of Eliot's own religious convictions.

The genuineness of Eliot's faith is sometimes questioned by Christian
readers as well, the best example being the 1995 essay "What T. S. Eliot
Almost Believed," by the Catholic writer Joseph Bottum, a normally
sound commentator. Bottum begins by acknowledging the fact that he
cannot know what transpired in Eliot's heart, but he argues that the
public expression of that spirituality in the poems and plays "seems

merely weak and strange" and that it is so because "his self-conscious spirituality ends only in paralysis."[40] He goes on to say that "What we encounter in his late poetry . . . is not about faith's wait for God but about the hollow man's wait for faith."[41] Eliot does speak of waiting in *Four Quartets*, and he speaks of waiting for God, echoing the mystical *Cloud of Unknowing*: "I said to my soul, be still, and let the dark come upon you / Which shall be the darkness of God" (*East Coker* III). This is indeed a self-conscious way of speaking, but Eliot here gives voice to the faith of the mystic *via negativa*, expressing patience, not paralysis—expectation, not uncertainty. Bottum ends his essay with a quotation from this section of the poem, which continues to speak of waiting: "the faith and love and hope are all in the waiting." He argues that these lines show Eliot "has confused his own waiting for faith with the faithful's waiting for God."[42] But this passage follows from the command to wait for the darkness of God and is thus explicitly a waiting for God, not for faith. There is something Bottum does not like about Eliot's poetic expression of belief, but he has not identified the source of annoyance accurately, and he misreads the poem to make it fit his notion of Eliot's "delicate, aesthetic, self-conscious almost-spirituality." This is simply not the impression left on most readers of *Four Quartets*, and it reveals some personal animus not accounted for in Bottum's essay. Is he perhaps seeking for the kind of ruddy-cheeked, meat-and-potatoes Catholic faith to be found in the writings of G. K. Chesterton? The spirituality of *Four Quartets* is certainly subtle and in some way tentative; there is something of the philosophical and personal skepticism that was habitual in Eliot. He favors here, as he commonly did, the negative way. But the poem presents a challenging, difficult spiritual quest, not a delicate one.

I would like to close this review of antagonistic criticism with an anecdote. I recently had a conversation with a retired colleague that turned toward Eliot. He began with a reminiscence of his graduate school days in the 1960s, when, he said, everything revolved around Eliot. "You could be taking a course in Old Norse," he remarked, "and somehow Eliot would be a significant part of it." He revealed that he doesn't like Eliot much, primarily because "Eliot thought he knew the truth about everything." I offered a corrective to this view, saying that Eliot believed mankind collectively, through the gradual accumulation of traditional wisdom, knew some truths about some important things. My colleague acknowledged that this was a more just description, and the conversation moved on. But the topic evidently bothered him, for a few days later I received a letter from him renewing the discussion and identifying the pebble in his shoe as the religious question. "The history of religion is one damned atrocity after another," he declared, and therefore "I am afraid of believers." It is Eliot's religious beliefs that rankle my colleague, leading him to conclude (impausibly) that "As a poet, Eliot lacks irony, or even humor." I record this exchange as a raw, unfiltered version of the black feelings that bubble up in a good deal of Eliot criticism. Probably many critics will continue to react negatively to Eliot's Christian faith, but in this volume we seek to offer (I believe without going to the other extreme of Eliot-adulation) careful consideration of what his beliefs really were and of how they affected his writing in several genres.

A GRADUAL INTELLECTUAL CONVERSION

It is no wonder that Henry Ware Eliot Jr. was surprised by his younger brother's gesture of piety in Rome: even though they were very close and their letters to each other were long, personal, and affectionate, Tom never told Henry (or anyone else that I know of) that he was thinking about being baptized. It seems to me likely that he was not definitely planning to join the church very long before he did. Nevertheless, there is mounting evidence that the process of his conversion was a lengthy one, beginning as early as his college days. It also seems clear now that it was initially an intellectual conversion. Where Eliot scholars previously emphasized a dramatic break between the pre-conversion and post-conversion man, we now see a significant continuity in his life and writing.[43] We also see considerable integration of his religious beliefs with his literary, cultural, and political views (but without reducing his Christianity to politics or aesthetics as the antagonistic critics have done). This is the consensus that is forming today.

Though he was reticent about the longings of his soul, even with his closest friends and family, Eliot sometimes revealed the motives of his conversion in essays written after the fact. Many readers find something self-revelatory, for instance, in his introduction to Pascal's *Pensées* in 1931:

> The Christian thinker—and I mean the man who is trying consciously and conscientiously to explain to himself the sequence which culminates in faith, rather than the public apologist—proceeds by rejection and elimination. He finds the world to be so and so; he finds its character inexplicable by any non-religious theory: among religions he finds Christianity, and Catholic Christianity, to account most satisfactorily for the world and especially for the moral world within; and thus, by what Newman calls "powerful and concurrent" reasons, he finds himself inexorably committed to the dogma of the Incarnation. (*SE* 360)

This, he concludes, was Pascal's (and Newman's) way, but many readers have had the impression that he is describing what was his own way, as well. He came to religion and to Christianity through philosophical contemplation. Yet his choice of Pascal as a model for intellectual conversion is significant, for that great scientific Catholic also had a mystical disposition and experienced at least once a mystical transport. As Eliot puts it later in the introduction, "It is just the combination of the scientist, the *honnête homme*, and the religious nature with a passionate craving for

God that makes Pascal unique." Eliot then calls attention to Pascal's maxim about *le coeur* and *la raison,* saying, "The heart, in Pascal's terminology,
is itself truly rational if it is truly the heart" (*SE* 367). It was such an
integration of thought and feeling that Eliot consistently sought. Another
comment in the Pascal piece is likely also self-referential:

> . . . every man who thinks and lives by thought must have his own
> scepticism, that which stops at the question, that which ends in denial,
> or that which leads to faith and which is somehow integrated into the
> faith which transcends it. And Pascal, as the type of one kind of relig-
> ious believer, which is highly passionate and ardent, but passionate
> only through a powerful and regulated intellect, is in the first sections
> of his unfinished Apology for Christianity facing unflinchingly the de-
> mon of doubt which is inseparable from the spirit of belief. (*SE* 363)

Eliot's mind had always a strong skeptical tendency. In his 1917 piece
"Eeldrop and Appleplex," the character named Eeldrop, who apparently
represents the author, is described as "a sceptic, with a taste for mysticism."[44] Donald Childs begins with this quotation in his book *T. S. Eliot:
Mystic, Son and Lover* and says that "There is neither a briefer nor a more
accurate way of describing Eliot's own religious and philosophical point
of view—whether in 1917 or in the 1940s. . . ."[45] It is perhaps this strong
admixture of skepticism and doubt with faith that makes Eliot's faith
seem tentative or even unreal to Bottum and other readers. But he himself
considered it to be a natural and healthy element in the spiritual life of
the intelligent believer, as it was in that of Pascal.

The year after his baptism, in "Second Thoughts about Humanism,"
Eliot anticipates those critics who suppose that religious belief is always
motivated by a fearful longing for the comfort of reassuring dogmas and
the beauty of ancient rituals. Taking his cue from T. E. Hulme, he says,

> Most people suppose that some people, because they enjoy the luxury
> of Christian sentiments and the excitement of Christian ritual, swallow
> or pretend to swallow incredible dogma. For some the process is
> exactly opposite. Rational assent may arrive late, intellectual conviction
> may come slowly, but they come inevitably without violence to hones-
> ty and nature. To put the sentiments in order is a later and an immense-
> ly difficult task: intellectual freedom is earlier and easier than complete
> spiritual freedom. (*SE* 438)

One feels immediately that this is not merely an abstract argument but a
personal response to people who were saying just such things about
Eliot's recent conversion. It may also serve as his response to those more
recent critics who similarly impugn the motives and authenticity of Eliot's conversion. It does seem that Eliot's conversion was as described
here: a slow, gradual movement toward intellectual conviction, followed
by a lifelong effort to order his emotions so as to attain spiritual liberation. He had come to the conclusion, as he says in his 1932 essay on

"Modern Education," that "There are two and only two finally tenable hypotheses about life: the Catholic and the materialistic" (*SE* 458), and he found the Catholic hypothesis the more compelling. However, enacting that hypothesis as a way of life—giving himself over to it body, heart, and soul—would take time and effort and would be impossible to achieve entirely, as it is for anyone. In a letter to Paul Elmer More shortly after his conversion, Eliot complains that "Most critics appear to think that my catholicism is merely an escape or an evasion, certainly a defeat. . . . But it [is] rather trying to be supposed to have settled oneself in an easy chair, when one has just begun a long journey afoot."[46]

STAGES IN THE PILGRIMAGE

Let us consider the stages of Eliot's gradual intellectual conversion to Christianity. Perhaps the first major influence (apart from that of his Irish Catholic nanny, Annie Dunne) was a non-Christian one that nevertheless impelled him a good way in that direction. In 1909 Eliot was coming of age at Harvard and studying under Irving Babbitt, who introduced him to a critique of the modern attitude of romantic individualism. Though Eliot later turned from Babbitt's humanism, his anti-Romanticism became a lifelong commitment for Eliot, one that gave the initial impetus toward tradition and ultimately orthodoxy. Babbitt also introduced his student to the works of Charles Maurras, who would become another major influence, and one somewhat more committed to Catholicism (if only as a cultural force).

At about the same time, Eliot began to develop an interest in mystical experience that grew throughout his life. Indeed, one of his early poems, "Silence," describes a mystical experience:

> The seas of experience
> That were so broad and deep,
> So immediate and steep,
> Are suddenly still.
> You may say what you will,
> At such peace I am terrified.[47]

Christopher Ricks dates this poem June 1910. Some critics believe it describes an experience of Eliot's; others say it is an imaginary description. In any case, the poem certainly tells of a spiritual ecstasy. It is echoed three decades later in *The Dry Salvages*, when Eliot, having spoken of the "Ardour and selflessness and self-surrender" of the saint, says,

> For most of us, there is only the unattended
> Moment, the moment in and out of time,
> The distraction fit, lost in a shaft of sunlight,
> The wild thyme unseen, or the winter lightning
> Or the waterfall, or music heard so deeply

That it is not heard at all, but you are the music
While the music lasts. (*DS* ,V)

This momentary experience of transcendence was one Eliot attempted to describe both early and late, providing one of the main elements of continuity in his poetry. In the early poem his tendency toward the negative way of mysticism is evident, for the profound peace is terrifying; in the later poem he describes at last the positive way, in which the beauty of the created world suddenly reveals the love of the Creator. I think it likely that Eliot is speaking from personal experience in these poems. In his 1948 Introduction to *All Hallows' Eve* by Charles Williams, Eliot says that Williams "knew, and could put into words, states of consciousness of a mystical kind, and the sort of elusive experience which many people have once or twice in a life-time."[48] Probably Eliot had such quasi-mystical experiences himself.

Eliot spent the 1910–1911 academic year in Paris, living in a *pension* near the Sorbonne (where he met his friend Jean Verdenal) and attending some of Henri Bergson's lectures at the Collège de France. In the past, scholars associated this Parisian year almost exclusively with the French poets who exercised a profound influence on his verse at that time—as well as with the ideas of Bergson and Maurras. These influences were indeed highly important, but we have more recently become aware of the fact that during that year Eliot made profoundly important connections with the group of writers allied with the *Nouvelle Revue Française*. John Morgenstern, in the chapter included here, demonstrates that this group was deeply committed to a revival of Catholic thought. He shows that the *Nouvelle Revue Française* was presented by its editors as a response to Remy de Gourmont's well-established journal, the *Mercure de France*, with its Symbolist commitments. Through his French tutor, Alain-Fournier, Eliot became acquainted with the *NRF* group, which included André Gide and Paul Claudel. One hero of this group of Catholic writers was none other than Charles-Louis Philippe, author of *Bubu de Montparnasse*, a novel about prostitution that has routinely been said to have provided Eliot with images of urban degradation for his poems of this period. Indeed it did, but Morgenstern shows us that the novel had a profoundly moral and religious tenor—and that it was read in this way by the *NRF* group. Eliot also read in this year another Christian novel involving prostitution in an urban wasteland, Dostoevsky's *Crime and Punishment*. Morgenstern's work will bring about a dramatic reassessment of Eliot's Parisian year. It is clear now that he was immersed in the works of Catholic writers and critics during the entire year, and that their influence was long-lasting.

So much critical attention has been devoted to speculation about a homoerotic relationship between Eliot and Verdenal that the intensely spiritual themes of their conversation have been occluded. In July of 1911, while Eliot was traveling in Germany, Verdenal wrote him a long letter in which he deprecates a tendency he sees among the Parisian working class to follow the upper class in rejecting religious belief in favor of faith in science and reason, resulting in a vulgar materialism. He speaks of a countermovement toward Christian belief on the part of many writers (Verlaine, Péguy, Claudel, and others), noting that while these writers are quite different from each other and must be sorted out, "the main thing is to say, in the case of each, *how far he can influence our inner life towards the knowledge of the supreme good.*"[49] His letter to his friend on December 26, 1912, ends with this prayer: "Bring good upon me, O Lord, whether I ask for it or not, and remove evil from me, even though I ask for it" (*Letters* 1, 37). We must now incline to think that his year in Paris planted many seeds of Catholic belief in the young Eliot.

The one French writer of the time whose influence has been most strongly emphasized in Eliot criticism is Charles Maurras, and indeed Maurras exerted a powerful influence on Eliot, who later acknowledged that the French thinker led him toward Christian belief. It is essential to note, however, that the Catholic Church was, for Maurras, strictly an institution that promoted cultural order. He himself was an atheist. The Vatican became increasingly concerned over Maurras's use of Catholicism for political purposes, and Pope Pius XI finally condemned the *Action Française* in 1926, then placed the writings of Maurras on the Index in 1927. The role played by Maurras in Eliot's thought has sometimes been exaggerated and oversimplified, particularly by antagonistic critics, who find Eliot guilty of unsavory political views by virtue of his association with Maurras. This type of tenuous (and dubious) connection between the political thought of Maurras and Eliot is exemplified in the work of Kenneth Asher, which asserts that Maurras was the main source of Eliot's political ideas and continued to be so to the end. As evidence of Eliot's continuing loyalty later in life, Asher quotes Eliot's 1948 statement calling Maurras "a sort of Virgil who led us to the gates of the temple"—failing to see that as a Virgil figure Maurras could lead Eliot only to the steps of the temple, where he was left behind when the disciple went in, just as Virgil must suddenly disappear near the end of the *Purgatorio.*[50] Russell Kirk long before offered a more judicious treatment of the subject, noting that Maurras did influence Eliot's political thought for quite some time but pointing out Eliot's oft-expressed reservations about Maurras's thought. Kirk maintains that "on most points, Babbitt's *Democracy and Leadership* is closer to Eliot than any of Maurras' writings."[51] Several chapters in this book present evidence that other writers became more important influences than Maurras on Eliot's social thought after the mid-1920s.

William Marx, a French critic who has written extensively on Eliot, offers us here a surprising and fascinating perspective on Eliot and Maurras. He notes first of all that the various avant-garde groups in France in the early twentieth century spoke of a "re-founding," finding that only in the past could they discover what was really new. Maurras, along with the *NRF* writers, turned to classicism as a way of countering the preceding generation, the Symbolists (here Marx and Morgenstern are in agreement). Marx points, however, to a paradox in the neoclassicism of Maurras, who proclaimed a classicism of universal truths, yet wanted to emphasize the particularity of French culture. Eliot's classicism, Marx argues, was quite different from that of Maurras, being heavily influenced by Babbitt and Hulme. As Marx points out, Eliot explicitly distances himself from the classical movement in France in an essay on "Hulme and Classicism" in *The Criterion* in 1924. In addition, Eliot's triple declaration in 1928 is actually (and surprisingly) traceable more directly to writings of Albert Thibaudet, particularly to his 1913 article in the *NRF*, "L'Esthetique des trois traditions," than to the works of Maurras. Marx concludes that the transformation of French neoclassicism into Eliot's "analogical classicism" was parallel to the transformation of Catholicism into Anglo-Catholicism, emphasizing the nuances and limits of Eliot's debt to Maurras.

In "T. S. Eliot, the *Action Française*, and Neo-Scholasticism," Father Shun'ichi Takayanagi, S.J., gives us a carefully researched and thoughtfully considered overview of Eliot's intellectual relationship with Maurras. Takayanagi does what few other Eliot scholars have been troubled to do: he actually reads Maurras. He also traces the response to Maurras in France, in Rome, and in England, giving us the contexts we need. His chapter examines the Vatican's concerns over Maurras's use of Catholicism as a cultural and political token, and the eventual proscription of his ideas by Pope Pius XI in 1926. He shows that Jacques Maritain, who was originally sympathetic, wrote in strong support of Rome's judgment; he notices the critique of Maurras put forward by another French writer who strongly influenced Eliot's political views, Julien Benda; and he examines the discussion carried out in the pages of *The Criterion* between Eliot and Leo Ward on the subject (noting that Eliot's defense is carefully qualified and that after this brief exchange Eliot drops the matter and does not mention Maurras in the journal again). Father Takayanagi points to other writers whose political ideas were ultimately more important to Eliot, including S. T. Coleridge, Christopher Dawson, and Maritain. Anyone who wants to think seriously about Eliot and Maurras must read this chapter.

Even as he distanced himself from Maurras, we can now see, Eliot allied himself increasingly with Jacques Maritain. In his chapter here, James Matthew Wilson explores the intellectual relationship between Eliot and Maritain, one which has heretofore barely been mentioned by critics. In his Clark Lectures of 1926, Eliot honors medieval scholasticism as the philosophical unity that made *The Divine Comedy* possible, and he mentions as one prominent source of his thinking Maritain's *Réflexions sur l'intelligence*. The next year, in a *Criterion* Commentary, Eliot called Maritain "the most conspicuous figure, and probably the most powerful force, in contemporary French philosophy."[52] In his 1928 response to Leo Ward in *The Criterion*, Eliot acknowledges that some have called the journal "an organ for a 'Frenchified' doctrine called neo-Thomism."[53] It is a criticism whose substance he does not deny, tacitly admitting that neo-Thomism, of which Maritain was the most prominent expositor, was indeed central to the philosophy of his journal. As Wilson points out, what Eliot found in Maritain's exposition of Aquinas was a Christian philosophy based on Aristotelian realism that gave a cogent response to the subjectivist metaphysics of Descartes, Kant, and virtually all modern philosophers. On his side, Maritain praised Eliot's critical writing. In the 1930s the two found themselves offering similar analyses of cultural and political questions. On the other hand, as Wilson also shows, Eliot had some reservations about Maritain, thinking his explanations of Thomism somewhat emotional, romantic, and even Bergsonian. In time, Wilson suggests, Eliot took more of his understanding of Christian philosophy from other sources, including Étienne Gilson, Paul Elmer More, and Josef Pieper, which meant a greater consideration for a more Platonic approach. Nevertheless, it becomes clear that Eliot's thinking was influenced profoundly by Maritain and Thomistic philosophy in the years immediately before and after his conversion.

When Eliot returned (in 1911) to Harvard from Paris, his mind was full of Catholic ideas from his encounters, both personal and literary, with French Catholic writers. As he pursued his graduate studies in philosophy, he read and took notes on a number of books having to do with mysticism and religious experiences. As Spurr points out, he took particularly extensive notes on Evelyn Underhill's *Mysticism*, an orthodox Christian account of the subject by an Anglo-Catholic writer.[54] His extracurricular readings during this early period contributed to his ascetic ideas and his belief that true mysticism is supported by true doctrine, that it must be theologically sound and intellectually grounded.

At the outset of World War I, having retreated from Germany to England in 1914, Eliot encountered not only Ezra Pound, who famously helped launch his career as a modern poet, but also the writings of T. E. Hulme, which reinforced his belief in hierarchical authority structures in politics, literature, and religion. Hulme's philosophical writings, *Speculations*, were published posthumously in 1924, but, as Ronald Schuchard has shown, some of his most significant pieces were published much earlier, and in journals with which Eliot was involved, as well. Hulme's triple declaration (influenced partly by Maurras) of belief in original sin, anti-romanticism, and Tory politics appeared as early as 1912, and he was publishing his ideas in *New Age* in 1915–1916, when Eliot became connected with that journal.[55] As Schuchard further demonstrates, Eliot explicitly adopted Hulme's definition of classicism in his lecture entitled

"The Reaction against Romanticism," one of his Extension lectures that year, in which he states that "A classicist in art and literature will be likely to adhere to a monarchical form of government, and to the Catholic Church."[56] Clearly, Eliot had fully adopted this point of view more than ten years before his reception into the Church of England and his well-known declaration in *For Lancelot Andrewes* (1928).

By 1920, Eliot was deploring the lack of a traditional theology in the work of Blake: "What his genius required, and what it sadly lacked, was a framework of accepted and traditional ideas which would have prevented him from indulging in a philosophy of his own. . . " (*SE*, 279). A year later, writing about Marvell, Eliot speaks of the integrated awareness of the English poets before the dissociation of sensibility, marked by a "wisdom" that "leads toward, and is only completed by, the religious comprehension" (*SE*, 256). Then, in the running battle of classicism versus romanticism carried out in opposition to his friend John Middleton Murry in the 1920s, Eliot acknowledges his Catholic commitment.[57] In "The Function of Criticism" (1923), Eliot quotes Murry's statement that "Catholicism stands for the principle of unquestioned spiritual authority outside the individual; that is also the principle of Classicism in literature." Pressed by Murry, he agrees, though he expresses the idea in a more positive way: "Those of us who find ourselves supporting what Mr. Murry calls Classicism believe that men cannot get on without giving allegiance to something outside themselves. . . . If, then, a man's interest is political, he must, I presume, profess an allegiance to principles, or to a form of government, or to a monarch; and if he is interested in religion, and has one, to a Church; and if he happens to be interested in literature, he must acknowledge, it seems to me, just that sort of allegiance which I endeavoured to put forth in the preceding section" (*SE*, 15). This is not as pithy and definitive as the proclamation that he will make five years later, but it is consistent with it and with his earlier, less public, statements. Politics, literature, and religion are analogous and interrelated; in all three domains he will accept the necessity of an authority outside himself. Murry performs a valuable function in forcing the issue, proclaiming that "The English writer, the English divine, the English statesman, inherit no rules from their forbears; they inherit only this: a sense that in the last resort they must depend upon the inner voice." In responding, Eliot allies himself momentarily with Matthew Arnold: "The inner voice, in fact, sounds remarkably like an old principle which has been formulated by an elder critic in the now familiar phrase of 'doing as one likes.' The possessors of the inner voice ride ten to a compartment to a football match at Swansea, listening to the inner voice, which breathes the eternal message of vanity, fear, and lust" (*SE*, 16). There is no going back. In a letter of October 1, 1923, to Stanley Rice, who had written to propose an article for *The Criterion*, Eliot declares that "the standpoint of the *Criterion* is distinctly Aristotelian and in a sense Orthodox" (*Letters* II, 230).

Thus in the years leading up to his baptism, Eliot expressed his tendency toward belief in an increasingly overt manner. When Frederic Manning proposed something for the *Criterion* on Père Hyacinthe, who preached a non-sectarian Christianity, Eliot responded (28 January 1924), "Were le Père Hyacinthe representative of something for which the *Criterion* definitely stood, I should jump at the opportunity. But my own position toward modernist movements in the Catholic Church is at best one of neutrality, as never having been a member of that Church I cannot adopt a more positive attitude. I was myself brought up in a strong atmosphere of the most liberal Liberal theology and I cannot but regard such tendencies as unsuitable to the needs of the time" (*Letters* II, 301–2). In a humorous letter to Virginia Woolf (7 May 1924), he suggests extending his forthcoming visit to twenty hours but warns her that she would likely "expire of boredom. . . . But if you sent me to Divine Service on Sunday Morning, and to walk with the Curate on Sunday afternoon, could you endure me a little longer?" (*Letters* II, 413). Though this is all in a jocular vein, it does sound as if attending Sunday morning service is something he has been known to do. Writing to Herbert Read in October of the same year, Eliot says that he wishes "to get as homogenous a group as possible" writing for his journal but insists that "it cannot be reduced to a creed of numbered capitals. I do *not* expect everyone to subscribe to all the articles of my own faith, or to read Arnold, Newman, Bradley, or Maurras with my eyes" (*Letters* II, 514). It seems as if by this time his faith is one that a close friend like Read is expected to be well aware of. Perhaps his reception into the church was not such a surprise to his closer friends as we have supposed.

Eliot also speaks of his interest in Thomism in a letter to Read in July of 1925, insisting he knows little about the subject but is somewhat qualified to understand it by his study of Aristotle: "Beyond this I have nothing more at present than an instinct. Of course the religious difficulty is the great one and it is impossible to tell what one's solution will be. All that one can do at present is conscientiously to avoid anticipating the conclusions to which one may come five or ten years hence" (*Letters* II, 695). Here his discussion of the intellectual topic of Thomism elides into a frank admission that he is struggling with a decision about religion. He is endeavoring to live with the tension rather than deciding precipitously one way or the other, and he expects not to reach a conclusion for five or even ten years, but he makes no secret to Read that he needs must make some decision. In the event, he reached his conclusion in two years.

In August of 1925, Eliot wrote a telling letter to his friendly antagonist Murry: "You see I happened to be brought up in the most 'liberal' of 'Christian' creeds—Unitarianism: I may therefore be excused for seeing the dangers of what you propose, more clearly than I see the vices of what you attack. If one discards dogma, it should be for a more celestial garment, not for nakedness" (*Letters* II, 734). Though he concedes that there are probably vices in orthodox religion, there is no question of turning back. Again in December of that year he wrote quite openly to Read, speaking of some disappointment he felt with Maritain's *Réflexions sur l'intelligence*: "If he had made it part of a thorough historical defense of thomism or of the Church—to show that *any* philosophy except that of the church leads to heresies which ordinary common sense condemns—it would be more permanent (this is what I should attempt if I put myself in his place)" (*Letters* II, 796). Here his understanding of orthodoxy and heresy is already a settled conviction. Six months later, he would fall to his knees at St. Peter's Basilica in Rome.

CATHOLIC TRADITION

As we have seen, Eliot was committed from a very early time to the idea of tradition, the sense that we should be guided to a large extent by the collective wisdom passed on to us by human beings in the past—what Chesterton called "the democracy of the dead." This concept received definitive expression in the 1919 essay that was to become Eliot's most famous piece of prose, "Tradition and the Individual Talent." Our consideration of Eliot's engagement with Catholic tradition begins with that essay, and with a philosophical claim Eliot seems to make in passing when he says, "The point of view which I am struggling to attack is perhaps related to the metaphysical theory of the substantial unity of the soul. . ." (*Sacred Wood*, 56). At the head of the short final section of the piece, he quotes a line from Aristotle, without citation or translation, only to say that he will "halt at the frontier of metaphysics" (*SW*, 59). Old Possum seems to be teasing us, and for the most part we have simply ignored these bits, or we have been satisfied by a footnote that tells us the quotation is from the *De Anima* and translates, "The mind is, no doubt, something more divine and impassible"—without attempting to explain what that has to do with the rest of the essay. Now William Charron has explicated this idea, and it turns out to be crucial to a proper understanding of the whole essay. His piece is densely argued and difficult to summarize, but it has to do with a long-standing debate, with Aquinas on one side and Averroes on the other, about whether Aristotle believed that the mind was one of the faculties in a substantially unified soul or a separate entity. Charron shows that the three categories Eliot talks about—the "man who suffers," the "mind which creates," and the collective "mind of Europe"—correspond to three types of mind defined by Aristotle, clarified by Averroes, and spoken of by Dante in his *De Monarchia* (where he follows Averroes, not Aquinas). The third type of mind, the "possible intellect," is a collective mind of all humanity, common to all. It gathers significant ideas as time passes, just as the relationship among the monuments of literature in Eliot's metaphor shifts ever so slightly when a truly new work appears. In Charron's chapter, we finally have a coherent explication of the philosophical and theological tradition informing the central ideas in Eliot's "Tradition and the Individual Talent."

A significant contribution to the study of Eliot's ideas concerning the Christian tradition in relation to the literary tradition is a chapter on "The Ignatian Interlude" in Schuchard's book *Eliot's Dark Angel* (1999). There Schuchard carefully examines Eliot's changing attitudes toward St. Ignatius of Loyola, his *Spiritual Exercises*, and the order he founded, the Society of Jesus—and he shows how those attitudes align with Eliot's changing view of Donne. Eliot famously names Donne as an exemplar of an undissociated sensibility in his essay on the Metaphysical poets in 1921, but by 1926, when he was delivering the Clark Lectures at Cambridge, he had decided that Donne was actually part of the dissociation. In these lectures, Schuchard points out, Eliot identifies St. Ignatius as a major influence on Donne and calls it an essentially "romantic" one. However, an American Jesuit priest who attended the lectures wrote to Eliot offering a mild corrective, which led him to read the original text of the *Spiritual Exercises* and reevaluate them. Subsequently, Eliot spoke more positively of Ignatius, and in 1929 grouped him (though in a qualified way) with Richard of St. Victor and John of the Cross. Still, Eliot finally considered Ignatius to be an emotional sort of mystic. Schuchard concludes, "The gradual diminishment of Donne's importance to Eliot was hastened by his study of Ignatius, and by the mid-1930s both had essentially disappeared from the center of Eliot's critical consciousness."[58]

Eliot's response to another towering figure in the Christian tradition, first an Anglo-Catholic and then a Roman Catholic, is the subject of Lee Oser's chapter, which begins from the observation that Eliot never devoted an essay to John Henry Cardinal Newman and mentions him only in passing and ambiguously. Yet Newman seems to have been on his mind a great deal, beginning at least as early as 1916, when Eliot featured both the *Apologia pro Vita Sua* and *The Idea of a University* in his Extension course on "Modern English Literature." Oser suggests that Eliot saw Newman as antipodal to Emerson. He also shows that Eliot placed Newman over against Pascal, finding the latter to be a greater aid to believers who doubt. Newman did not share the skepticism that was always a concomitant of belief in Eliot. And of course Eliot kept his distance from Newman simply because he had not chosen to follow him all the way to Rome—and, as Oser suggests, did not want to engage with him and try to explain why he thought Newman was wrong to take that path. Oser closes with a fascinating suggestion, namely that Geoffrey Faber exercised a powerful influence over Eliot just as the latter was converting. Faber wrote a book on the Oxford Movement in which he sides strongly with Edward Pusey (the leader of the movement who remained in the

Church of England) and criticizes Newman harshly. Quite possibly Faber's influence on his new junior colleague (who began to work for him in the crucial year of 1925) was indeed a significant factor. In any case, Oser demonstrates that Eliot's muted responses to Newman say much about his choice of Anglo-Catholicism.

The definitive book on Eliot and Dante was written by Dominic Manganiello, who returns to the subject here in examining the way Charles Williams influenced Eliot's later contemplation of Dante's theology of love. Eliot's introduction to Williams's final novel, *All Hallows' Eve* (published in 1948), expresses his profound respect for the man and his art. Manganiello examines the fiction of Williams in relation to his theological and critical writings (especially his work on Dante, *The Figure of Beatrice*, 1942) and shows that Eliot adopts a very similar point of view in his later works, especially *The Cocktail Party* and *The Elder Statesman*. Under the influence of Williams and Dante, Eliot emphasizes the affirmative way of human love and the sanctity of the ordinary. In particular, the way the married couple, Lester and Richard, in *All Hallows' Eve* learn to love each other is reflected in the way Edward and Lavinia begin to learn love in *The Cocktail Party*. Eliot does not deny the negative way (the way of Celia's martyrdom), but he sees the positive way of human love leading toward divine love as complementary to it.

The final chapter in this section turns to Eliot's interest in the Christian architectural tradition. Hazel Atkins takes note of Eliot's abiding interest in church architecture, from his early visits to two churches in the City (one designed by Christopher Wren, and the other by his follower Nicholas Hawksmoor), both mentioned in *The Waste Land*; to his involvement in campaigns to preserve such historic churches; through his meditations on the church building for *The Rock* (his pageant-play that assisted in raising funds to build new churches in the suburbs); and culminating in his use of the cathedral setting of *Murder in the Cathedral*. No scholar has previously taken account of Eliot's interest in the work of the architect and art historian W. R. Lethaby, whom Eliot called "our greatest living authority on architecture," and this connection greatly assists us in understanding Eliot's ideas about sacred architecture. Atkins shows that Lethaby, like Eliot, was deeply influenced by Sir James Frazer and his school, with their emphasis on the connection between art and ritual in ancient times. Lethaby stressed the notion that "all architecture is one," in that new developments are always elaborations of what was found in buildings in the past, and Atkins shows the similarity between his thinking and that of Eliot in "Tradition and the Individual Talent." In both literature and church architecture, there is a historical development "which abandons nothing *en route*."

RELIGION AND CULTURE

It is well known that Eliot's cultural criticism—expressed in his Commentaries in *The Criterion*, in a variety of essays and talks, and in two books (*The Idea of a Christian Society* and *Notes towards the Definition of Culture*)—is profoundly affected by his religious beliefs. Two critical studies published in 1971 surveyed this topic well: *T. S. Eliot's Social Criticism*, by Roger Kojecký, and *Eliot and His Age*, by Russell Kirk.[59] Since that time, however, most of what has been written about Eliot's cultural ideas has ignored what is found in those books and has been antagonistic to Eliot, more interested in accusing him of elitism, fascism, and anti-Semitism than in attempting to understand his ideas and explore the sources of those ideas (except for Maurras). A chapter on "A Christian State" in Spurr's book is a large step in a more positive direction.[60] The chapters in this section of the present book are largely in agreement with Spurr's approach, while they explore particular aspects of the issue and major influences on Eliot's social thought in greater detail.

To begin, Christopher McVey traces the development of Eliot's social thought through the course of his career, showing that his ideas were not monolithic or unvarying, either before or after the conversion. McVey identifies three major influences: Charles Maurras, Christopher Dawson, and Jacques Maritain. Like other writers in this volume, he argues that the influence of Maurras decreased after the late 1920s, as Eliot came increasingly under the influence of Maritain and Dawson. He points out that these two agreed in important matters but differed in their theology: Maritain was a neo-Thomist, which meant emphasizing the role of reason, while Dawson was an Augustinian, which meant emphasizing the limitations of reason. Both were converts to Roman Catholicism. Maritain was at first a follower of Maurras but became a critic after the Vatican condemnation in 1926. Dawson was critical, not only of fascism and communism but also of modern industrial capitalism: he spoke of the "disaffection of the wage laborer," in language that would have sounded familiar and agreeable to Marxists. Thus Dawson had an effect on Eliot's similar critique of the materialist underpinnings of the western industrial economies. The Catholic publishing company Sheed and Ward produced a series of books entitled Essays in Order in the 1930s, with contributions by both Maritain (*Religion and Culture*) and Dawson (*Christianity and the New Age*). McVey argues that the ideas of these two Catholic writers came together in Eliot's cultural thought in the late 1930s. He warns against seeing Eliot's ideas as fixed, contending that "Eliot continued to reformulate his ideas over the course of the 30s and 40s."

In his contribution to this volume, Anderson Araujo examines the delicate balance Eliot conceived between secular and religious hierarchies. He notes that Eliot was already affirming orthodox Christian dogma as early as 1917 in a little-known review of R. G. Collingwood's *Religion and Philosophy*. He also quotes a passage in *After Strange Gods* that has received little attention, one in which Eliot warns of "the danger of suggesting to outsiders that the Faith is a political principle or a literary fashion"—another response to those who insist that his own faith was one or the other. As Araujo argues, though Eliot saw analogies between aesthetics and religion or politics and religion, he also insisted on distinctions. In particular, Eliot was deeply aware of the danger inherent in an alliance of church and state. This awareness motivated Eliot to reject what Emilio Gentile calls the "political religion" of Mussolini's fascist state.[61] In the ideal Christian society, there would be a creative friction between secular and clerical hierarchies, not a subordination of either one to the other. This concern about a union of church and state was also part of what led Eliot to distance himself from Maurras, and Araujo points out that as early as 1919 Eliot wrote of Maurras's "intemperate and fanatical spirit."

As I pointed out earlier, some antagonistic critics see Eliot's membership in the Church of England as essentially part of his political commitment, which was itself part of his desire to become English. Paul Robichaud presents an analysis of Eliot's thinking on the relationship between religion and nationalism that corrects such mistaken views. As Robichaud shows, Eliot was consistently opposed to extreme nationalism, whether it was fascism, Nazism, or any other variety. The primary mission of *The Criterion* was indeed to foster "the mind of Europe," a common, transcultural awareness. In this, Eliot was in agreement with Christopher Dawson, who hoped to see a renewal of a common Christian culture similar to what had existed in the Middle Ages, when local allegiances were subordinate to a sense of belonging to Christendom. The ultimate failure of intellectual and political leaders to foster a sufficient sense of cultural unity across Europe is what caused Eliot to cease publishing *The Criterion* in 1939, as the European nations went to war against each other again. Robichaud shows that Eliot saw in the totalitarian regimes an attempt on the part of those nations to arrogate to themselves the emotional value of religion. At the same time, Eliot saw the liberal nations attempting to create a completely secular public square, pushing religion to the margins of public life. Both trends were, he believed, dangerous. The ideal Eliot envisioned, as Robichaud describes it, was a common European culture, informed by the Christian tradition, and at the same time a diversity of national and local cultures. As Robichaud concludes, " . . . Eliot's vision of diverse European cultures drawing sustenance from the same Christian spring challenges the virulent nationalism of the 1930s."

The astute reader will have noticed that several of the writers in this volume mention as a major influence on Eliot someone who has very rarely been mentioned in previous studies, the Roman Catholic historian

Christopher Dawson. It is surprising that so little has been written on Dawson, since Eliot explicitly acknowledges his influence in the prefaces to both *The Idea of a Christian Society* and *Notes towards the Definition of Culture*, and since Russell Kirk long ago stated that "Of social thinkers in his own time, none influenced Eliot more than Dawson."[62] Nevertheless, such has been the case. My own contribution to this collection focuses on their collaboration, beginning in the late 1920s and continuing through the 1940s. They reached similar conclusions: religion is integral to culture, which cannot be healthy without a religious center; in a fully secularized state there will inevitably be an ideology substituting for religion, with disastrous results; a secular humanism such as Babbitt's is inadequate to replace religion at the heart of a culture; a renewal of the Christian sources of European culture is needed; at the same time, this renewal cannot be a simple return to the forms of the past. Dawson and Eliot further agreed that a theocratic merging of secular and religious authorities is undesirable—rather, there should be a dynamic tension between political and religious leaders. I contend that Dawson exercised a sane and wise influence over Eliot's mature cultural thought.

Collectively, the chapters in this section present a dramatic revision of the received ideas about the intellectual and religious milieu in which Eliot elaborated and clarified his social and political ideas.

CONTEMPORARIES

In this final section of the book, the reader will find chapters on some of Eliot's contemporaries—older and younger. We begin with George Santayana, one of Eliot's most famous professors at Harvard but one whose influence on him has not been examined previously because Eliot never spoke highly of him after and rarely spoke of him at all. James Seaton shows, nevertheless, that there are strong points of agreement between teacher and student, though Eliot ultimately chose another path. For one thing, Santayana expressed a concept very similar to Eliot's "objective correlative," when he said in *Interpretations of Poetry and Religion* (1900) that the poet's "glorious emotions . . . must at all hazards find or feign their correlative objects." Moreover, Santayana wrote an introduction to *Hamlet* in 1908 in which he is quite critical of the play. Seaton thus demonstrates that Eliot follows Santayana in criticizing *Hamlet*, in considering Shakespeare somewhat romantic and hence slightly inferior to Dante, and in speaking of the need for "correlative objects." He further notes that Santayana spoke of a divorce between life and faith in the seventeenth century, quite similar to Eliot's later concept of a dissociation of sensibility in the same era. Santayana also criticized the non-religious humanism of his colleague Irving Babbitt, in terms quite similar to the ones Eliot would later adopt. Eliot did not acknowledge any of these debts, and he might have been unconscious of them. He probably distanced himself from Santayana because his teacher was not a believer and saw the value of Catholic teaching only as an aesthetic and moral force, while rejecting the central doctrines of the Church.

Another philosopher of the older generation with whom Eliot's spiritual quest was intertwined is Paul Elmer More (1864–1937), who was born in St. Louis, attended Washington University, and taught for a time at Smith Academy (where Tom's older brother Henry was his student), before going on to Harvard. David Huisman examines the parallel paths Eliot and More took toward the Anglican Church, noting that Eliot found in More's life "an analogy with my own journey," a pilgrimage "more like my own, so far as I can see, than that of any human being I have known." Little has been said about the connections between the two writers, and Huisman's chapter rectifies that omission. He observes that More, like Eliot, reacted to the drift of his ancestors in New England away from orthodoxy, criticizing Emerson much as Eliot did. More assisted Babbitt in developing the New Humanism, and Eliot was first introduced to More's writing in Babbitt's course. Eliot later identified in More's literary criticism a moral strain that was instructive to him as he attempted to think through the relations between moral truth and literary value. He and More also held, Huisman shows, the same view of orthodoxy, as two truths held in tension, with an overemphasis on one or the other constituting heresy. Eliot spoke to More of his desire to see a combination of the intellectual and the devotional in the Christian intellectual. Though his philosophical studies led him to the Anglican Church, however, More finally stopped short of full participation—ironically, declining to take Communion, as Emerson had. In their correspondence during the final years of More's life, the two traded accusations of heresy, in a tone of friendly and familiar banter, but with the effect of clarifying for Eliot the nature and depth of his own convictions. Eliot's intellectual and personal interactions with More form another important chapter in the story of his life as a Christian thinker.

Perhaps the two most famous Anglican literary figures of their generation were T. S. Eliot and C. S. Lewis (who was ten years younger). The word in the halls of academe has been that they did not like each other, but more careful research has produced a more complete narrative, one which is told here by Charles Huttar. The two writers lived in somewhat separate worlds, Oxford and London, and did not meet until Charles Williams brought them together for lunch in 1945. Only near the end of their lives, when they worked together on a commission to revise the Psalter, did they finally form a friendship. Lewis, who aspired first of all to be a poet, tended to be critical of Eliot's poetry, and in his literary criticism engaged Eliot in some public disputes. Lewis came back to Christian belief in 1930, and in the years immediately following he was quite critical of Eliot, but Huttar shows that by the late 1930s he emphasized their points of agreement. In his 1941 lectures on Milton, Lewis challenged Eliot's critique of that poet, but he made it clear that he and Eliot were fundamentally allies: "I agree with him about matters of such moment that all literary questions are, in comparison, trivial." And in a friendly letter to Eliot two years later he says that his disagreements should be taken as a compliment because Eliot states his ideas so clearly that he is naturally the one whose views Lewis must attack. Huttar suggests that Eliot was partly influenced by Lewis when he softened his view of Milton. It is significant that at their meeting Eliot said he thought *A Preface to "Paradise Lost"* Lewis's best book. Huttar also argues that Lewis's distaste for Eliot's poetry has been exaggerated. He demonstrates that Lewis admired many of Eliot's poems, and he observes echoes of "Prufrock" in *The Great Divorce* (1946). In this chapter we have at last a comprehensive account of the relationship between these two, and one that details its complexities. Huttar concludes that "on the whole, [Lewis's] attitude toward Eliot and his work was quite favorable."

David Jones (1895–1974) was only slightly younger than Eliot, who was firmly established by the time Jones began writing poetry as an extension of his visual art. Thomas Dilworth recounts the story of their interactions, beginning with their first meeting in 1930. Jones was raised Anglican but converted to Roman Catholicism in 1921. When, in 1936, he finished his long poem about World War I, *In Parenthesis*, he submitted it to Faber, where Eliot read it and strongly recommended publication. After that he met Eliot with some frequency to discuss common interests and concerns. Dilworth notes, for instance, that Jones thought of the Mass as a great work of art and shared with Eliot an admiration for *The Shape of the Liturgy* by Dom Gregory Dix (one of Eliot's fellow members in the committee that produced the pamphlet on Catholicity). Jones and Eliot agreed on much in their discussions of culture, and Jones celebrated the publication of *Notes towards the Definition of Culture*. Like Eliot, Jones formed his ideas about culture partly under the influence of Dawson, whom he often met at meetings of the so-called Chelsea Group. With Eliot, Jones feared the advent of a new Dark Age. Jones also agreed with Eliot's original critique of Milton and regretted the later moderation of Eliot's views. Jones had his own theory of objective art, which accorded with the idea of impersonal art in "Tradition and the Individual Talent." Eliot also championed the publication of Jones's second long poem, *The Anathemata*. Jones did have his differences with Eliot, as Dilworth shows. He thought *Four Quartets* somewhat lacking in concreteness, and he noted what he thought Puritanical and Platonic tendencies in Eliot, which he disliked. Yet they remained allies and friends—and Dilworth tells us that Jones was sometimes invited to lunch, and once to Christmas dinner, at the Eliots' Kensington flat. We can now see that David Jones was an important part of the Catholic intellectual, cultural, and spiritual world Eliot inhabited.

CANTERBURY AND ROME

Given that Eliot fell to his knees at St. Peter's in 1926, and given his experience of Roman Catholicism in France, and given his constant emphasis on the Catholic tradition inseparable from the Mind of Europe, it seems natural to ask—as many have done—why he joined the Church of England the following year. I think Barry Spurr is right in suggesting that if Eliot had ended up living in France he would have become a Roman Catholic, but that since he lived in England and believed that religion and culture were bound to each other, it seemed right and good to belong to what he regarded as the Catholic Church in England.[63] His convictions on this question are perhaps best expressed in his response to the report of the conference of Anglican bishops at Lambeth in 1930. He writes, "I believe that in spite of the apparently insoluble problems with which it has to deal, the Church of England is strengthening its position as a branch of the Catholic Church, the Catholic Church in England."[64] Anglo-Catholics at that time hoped for an eventual reunion with Rome, and that was clearly Eliot's wish.

In 1926, the year before his baptism, Eliot wrote an essay on the early Anglican bishop Lancelot Andrewes that opens up his uncertainty. He writes that "The English Church has no literary monument equal to that of Dante, no intellectual monument equal to that of St. Thomas, no devotional monument equal to that of St. John of the Cross, no building so beautiful as the Cathedral of Modena or the basilica of St. Zeno in Verona" (*SE*, 300). In this passage he reverts to the language of "Tradition and the Individual Talent," speaking of "monuments" and making it clear that he desires connection to the full Christian tradition. But he immediately adds that the churches in London are, for some, as precious as those of Rome, and he claims that "the English devotional verse of the seventeenth century [is] finer than that of any other country or religious communion at that time." Next, he notes that the theological writings of Richard Hooker and Lancelot Andrewes "came to complete the structure of the English Church," making "the English Church more worthy of intellectual assent" (*SE*, 301). Had it not been for these intellectual achievements, it seems clear that Eliot would not have become a member of the Church of England, but the works of Hooker and Andrewes "elevate their Church above the position of a local heretical sect." They do so by enunciating a profoundly Catholic theology. Bishop Latimer was "merely a Protestant," but "the voice of Andrewes is the voice of a man who has a formed visible Church behind him, who speaks with the old authority and the new culture." In other words, he speaks with the full authority of the Catholic apostolic tradition, but in a manner cultivated by the new Renaissance humanist English culture. Andrewes embodies, then, the Elizabethan *via media*; he is, Eliot concludes, "the first great preacher of the English Catholic Church" (*SE,* 301–02). In this pivotal essay, we can practically see Eliot making his choice for Canterbury.

There was likely another factor at work in this decision, one addressed by several of the contributors. Though Eliot always spoke respectfully of the Roman Catholic Church and even of papal authority, there was a skeptical turn in his thinking that made some of the pronouncements of the Holy See difficult for him to accept, while the Anglican *via media* seemed to fit well with his idea that truth was usually a balance of opposing principles. This tendency of Eliot's is visible in his 1931 essay "Thoughts after Lambeth." The Lambeth Conference of 1930 was the first time in the history of Christianity that any group of bishops had agreed to consider contraceptive practices to be morally permissible in some circumstances, and this historic decision made Eliot pause and consider. He says that many readers of the conference report who are not Anglicans will look to find on this issue and others "the clear hard and fast distinctions and decisions of a Papal Encyclical," but "to those who hope for the voice of absoluteness and the words of hard precision, the recommendations and pious hopes will be disappointing" (*SE,* 320–21). Much as he looked to a traditional authority for answers, Eliot was constitutionally leery of "the voice of absoluteness," and even though he criticizes some of the waffling, evasive language of the report, he concludes that "The admission of inconsistencies, sometimes ridiculed as indifference to logic and coherence, of which the English mind is often accused, may be largely the admission of inconsistencies inherent in life itself, and of the impossibility of overcoming them by the imposition of a uniformity greater than life will bear" (*SE,* 332). On certain questions, he finds that the Church of England "is quite properly and conscientiously facing-both-ways . . ." (*SE,* 335). Perhaps it was Eliot's propensity to face both ways that finally made the Church of England more congenial to him than the Roman Catholic Church.

Eliot's time appeared to be one of waning faith, particularly among the intellectuals, but it was also a time of conversions and returns to Christian belief, when many writers who had lost the religious faith of their childhood came back to it. In many cases these intellectual converts were drawn to a more traditional, orthodox church, whether Roman Catholic or High Anglican, or Anglo-Catholic. In France there was a revival of belief among a large group of Catholic writers, and Maritain himself was a convert. In England, there were many Anglicans who crossed the Tiber, including Newman, Hopkins, Chesterton, Dawson, Jones, and Waugh. There were others such as Lewis who grew up in a Low Church setting, drifted away from religion, and became relatively High Church Anglicans upon their return. Paul Elmer More followed a similar path, though he was finally more Platonist than Anglican. And then there was Eliot, who came a long distance indeed from the Unitarian congregation in St. Louis to full participation in the Anglo-Catholic wing of the Church of England. This milieu of dramatic conversions and returns is the one we must continue to study if we wish to understand Eliot's religious beliefs and their expression in his works.

NOTES

1. This incident is recounted in an unpublished piece by Eliot's Anglican friend George Every. See Lyndall Gordon, *T. S. Eliot: An Imperfect Life* (New York: Norton, 1998), 192; Barry Spurr, *"Anglo-Catholic in Religion": T. S. Eliot and Christianity* (Cambridge: Lutterworth, 2010), 43.
2. Tony Sharp, *T. S. Eliot: A Literary Life* (New York: St. Martin's, 1991), 103.
3. Quoted by Kevin J. H. Dettmar, "'An Occupation for the Saint': Eliot as a Religious Thinker," in *A Companion to T. S. Eliot*, ed. David E. Chinitz (Chichester: Wiley-Blackwell, 2009), 363. Of course in actuality Virginia Woolf continued to be a good friend to Eliot after his conversion.
4. Russell Kirk, *Eliot and His Age: T. S. Eliot's Moral Imagination in the Twentieth Century*, 1971; second ed. Wilmington, DE: ISI Books, 2008.
5. Barry Spurr, *"Anglo-Catholic in Religion": T. S. Eliot and Christianity* (Cambridge: Lutterworth, 2010), xii.
6. Dettmar, 374. Schuchard, *Eliot's Dark Angel: Intersections of Life and Art* (New York: Oxford University Press, 1999.
7. Cleo McNelly Kearns, "Religion, Literature, and Society in the Work of T. S. Eliot," in *The Cambridge Companion to T. S. Eliot*, ed. A. David Moody (Cambridge: Cambridge University Press, 1994).
8. Denis Donoghue, *Words Alone: The Poet T. S. Eliot* (New Haven: Yale University Press, 2000), 271.
9. Cf. Spurr, 174–75.
10. Dettmar, 374.
11. Donald Davie, "Anglican Eliot," in *Eliot in His Time: Essays on the Occasion of the Fiftieth Anniversary of "The Waste Land,"* ed. A. Walton Litz (Princeton: Princeton University Press, 1973), 184.
12. Davie, 186.
13. Eugene Goodheart, *The Failure of Criticism* (Cambridge: Harvard University Press, 1978), 51–52.
14. Quoted by Goodheart, 52.
15. Goodheart, 52–53.
16. Goodheart, 53.
17. T. S. Eliot, "Francis Herbert Bradley," in *Selected Essays* (New York: Harcourt, 1950), 399. Cited hereafter as *SE*.
18. Goodheart, 62.
19. Goodheart, 65.
20. Goodheart, 65, 66.
21. Goodheart, 60.
22. Goodheart, 57.
23. T. S. Eliot, *The Idea of a Christian Society* (London: Faber, 1939), 41.
24. William Skaff, *The Philosophy of T. S. Eliot: From Skepticism to a Surrealist Poetic 1909–1927* (Philadelphia: University of Pennsylvania Press, 1986), 7.
25. Skaff, 38.
26. Eliot, *Idea of a Christian Society*, 63.
27. Skaff, 120.
28. T. S. Eliot, "Arnold and Pater," *Selected Essays*, 385.
29. Eliot, "Literature, Science, and Dogma," *Dial*, 82 (1927): 243.
30. Skaff, 121.
31. Skaff, 123.

32. Kearns, 89.

33. C. K. Stead, *Pound, Yeats, Eliot and the Modernist Movement* (New Brunswick, NJ: Rutgers University Press, 1986), 207.

34. Stead, 223.

35. Stead, 229–30.

36. Alfred Kazin, *God and the American Writer* (New York: Knopf, 1997), 195.

37. Kazin, 199.

38. Kazin, 200.

39. Kazin, 202.

40. Joseph Bottum, "What T. S. Eliot Almost Believed," *First Things* no. 55 (1995): 25.

41. Bottum, 27.

42. Bottum, 30.

43. See, for example, Steve Ellis, *T. S. Eliot: A Guide for the Perplexed* (London: Continuum, 2009), 4; Gordon, 87; Schuchard, 27–28.

44. T. S. Eliot, "Eeldrop and Appleplex, I," *Little Review* 4, no. 1 (May 1917): 8.

45. Donald Childs, *T. S. Eliot: Mystic, Son and Lover* (New York: St. Martin's, 1997), 1.

46. Letter from Eliot to More, August 1929, quoted in Roger Kojecký, *T. S. Eliot's Social Criticism* (New York: Farrar, 1971), 74.

47. T. S. Eliot, *Inventions of the March Hare: Poems 1909–1917*, ed. Christopher Ricks (New York: Harcourt, 1996), 18.

48. T. S. Eliot, Introduction to *All Hallows Eve,* by Charles Williams (1948; reprint Grand Rapids, MI: Eerdmans, 1981), xvii.

49. *The Letters of T. S. Eliot*, volume 1, second edition, edited by Valerie Eliot (New York: Harcourt, 2009), 22–24. Verdenal's emphasis.

50. Kenneth Asher, *T. S. Eliot and Ideology* (Cambridge: Cambridge University Press, 1995). "T. S. Eliot and Charles Maurras," *ANQ* 11, 3 (1998): 20–30. Eliot's statement about Maurras is from "L'Hommage de l'étranger," *Aspects de la France et du Monde* (25 April 1948): 6.

51. Kirk, 88.

52. T. S. Eliot, A Commentary, *The Criterion* 5, no. 1 (January 1927): 3.

53. T. S. Eliot, "A Reply to Mr. Ward," *The Criterion* 7, no. 4 (June 1928): 376.

54. Spurr, 23–24.

55. Schuchard, 55–57.

56. Quoted by Schuchard, 61. Cf. Dettmar, 369.

57. See David Goldie, *A Critical Difference: T. S. Eliot and John Middleton Murry in English Literary Criticism, 1919–1928* (Oxford: Oxford University Press, 1998).

58. Schuchard, 172.

59. Roger Kojecký, *T. S. Eliot's Social Criticism* (London: Faber, 1971).

60. Spurr, 174–202.

61. Emilio Gentile, "Fascism as Political Religion," *Journal of Contemporary History* 25 (May–June 1990): 229–251.

62. Kirk, 253.

63. Spurr, 195–201.

64. T. S. Eliot, "Thoughts After Lambeth," *Selected Essays,* 339.

I

Eliot and Anglo-Catholicism

ONE

T. S. Eliot and Catholicity

William Blissett

In 1947 there appeared a report of some fifty-six pages presented to the Archbishop of Canterbury by fourteen notable members of the Catholic persuasion in the Anglican communion. Well-produced and publicly circulated by the Dacre Press, it deals in an irenical spirit but with theological exactitude (qualities found again on a larger scale in the Documents of Vatican II) with the apparent deadlock of Protestant and Catholic opinion, within and beyond Anglicanism, and expands the discussion to include a third term, liberal modernism. A Liberal Church as distinct from High (Catholic) and Low (Evangelical) goes back as far as the Latitudinarians of the seventeenth century and was well established in the Victorian figures of Thomas and Matthew Arnold, and so the widening of the terms of reference is well justified.[1]

T. S. ELIOT, ESQ.

The list of signatories is distinguished. It includes, as one might expect, members of the church hierarchy—a bishop, four canons (one of the future Archbishops of Canterbury, Michael Ramsey), five holders of chairs in theology, and three members of religious orders. In their midst, occupying a line to himself as the others with longer titles do, is placed the name of T. S. Eliot, Esq. We are told in the preface that the report was unanimous and that it was a hardworking committee: "during 1946 three sessions of the group were held, two of which lasted for three consecutive days, and there has been much interchange of papers and memoranda."

Few students of Eliot have taken notice of this. No part of the report being identifiable as Eliot's own composition, it is excluded from Donald Gallup's *Bibliography*. A more decisive reason for neglect may be that Eliot's churchmanship of almost forty years is of small interest to the literary, the political, and the journalistic mind. Yet we may safely assume that he gave his full attention to it and did not simply lend his name, by that time a famous name. Who were these signatories, and how does T. S. Eliot, Esq. belong among them?

Eight of the fourteen are of sufficient eminence to have entered the *Oxford Dictionary of National Biography*. Two that have not entered are nevertheless remarkable figures and of special interest in their connection with Eliot. Fr. Gabriel Hebert, of the Society of the Sacred Mission, edited a highly influential collection of essays on *The Parish Communion* (1939, 1961), which introduced to the English world the ideas of the Continental Liturgical Movement, a major force at Vatican II. It exerted itself to make the mass with communion the norm for Sunday worship, largely replacing the old Catholic pattern of communion of the few at an early "low mass" followed by a solemn choral celebration by the many, at which the celebrant was the only communicant. The average Anglican pattern was similar: communion as the main service once a month and many receiving communion only once or twice a year. The strong new emphasis on the frequent communion of all the faithful led to a relaxation of the law of fasting, for it is difficult to fast from midnight till past noon without either complaining or boasting about it. Father Hebert wrote well-regarded books, including two on the relation of the Old Testament to the New, all published by Faber and Faber when Eliot was responsible not only for the poetry list but for books on religion in its wider definition.[2] Canon C. H. Smyth, a Cambridge don and the friend and executor of the great New Testament scholar, Sir Edwyn Hoskyns (also a Faber writer), contributed some forty reviews to the *Criterion*. It may be noted that Canon V. A. Demant (who is in the *ODNB*) also appeared in the *Criterion* and was for years a leading figure in the discussion of the social bearings of Christian thought and practice. He was very close to the Eliot of *The Idea of a Christian Society*, where his influence is acknowledged.

Two others demand special mention here though their association with Eliot is largely undocumented. Eliot, to his friend William Turner Levy, once expressed a "warm feeling" for the Benedictine monk, Dom Gregory Dix, the convener and leading figure of the group and one of its secretaries. In 1945 he had published his long-awaited treatise on *The Shape of the Liturgy*. Its success was immediate and lasting: many a student of liturgical development from antiquity to the present, approaching it with trepidation, has followed its argument and rejoiced in its wit for more than seven hundred pages. If Eliot had been worried about "the question of Anglican orders," he would have found a short book of that title by Dom Gregory reassuring. They were both exercised about the

"South India scheme" of combining Anglican and non-conformist ordi-
nation, and that may have brought them more closely together.[3]

Austin Farrer, whom Archbishop Rowan Williams has called "perhaps the greatest Anglican mind of the twentieth century," was near the
beginning of his career in 1947, but he had established himself as a philosophical theologian with his *Finite and Infinite*, maintaining a strong
Christian presence in the Oxford of Gilbert Ryle. *The Glass of Vision*, with
its probing and imaginative treatment of analogy and metaphor in poetry
and scripture, was in process of writing, and the great studies of the
Apocalypse and St. Mark's Gospel lay just ahead. The short essays and
sermons, superbly crafted, were many of them to be posthumously published and are still very much in circulation. I mention him especially
because as a writer he stands out even in this company and for a second
reason. The young Eliot seemed destined for philosophy, predestined to
a calling in philosophy, to a chair in philosophy equivalent to a major
pulpit. He was plucked from this like a brand from the burning. A poet
he was born, but he turned decisively in full maturity and for the rest of
his life and became a man of business and Anglican layman, a British
subject—and not a philosopher, though he continued to live the life of the
mind. He never looked back, lest he turn to a pillar of salt. His eminent
contemporaries, Wittgenstein and Heidegger, do not appear in his wide-
ranging discussions of ethics and politics in their bearing on religion;
neither does Austin Farrer, whom we might have expected Eliot to greet
as an ally.[4]

I must now ask how the other signatories could have seen Eliot as
belonging in their company. He was, of course, by that time a literary
celebrity of the first magnitude and an acknowledged adherent to their
way of thinking. These would be good reasons for bringing him in for
decoration, in an honorary capacity. But this is a working committee. Can
Eliot be expected to work? The answer, I think, is an emphatic yes. *The
Rock* (1934) in origin and achievement is a work of specifically ecclesiastical piety. So, for all its great literary and dramatic artistry, is *Murder in the
Cathedral* (1935). His *Thoughts After Lambeth* (1931), *The Idea of a Christian
Society* (1939), and *Reunion by Destruction* (1943) show his close attention
to church issues; and his mysterious (and surely risky) journey to Stockholm in 1942, the darkest days of the War, seems to underline his dedica-
tion to Christendom, already shown in his attendance and active participation in church-related conferences. These activities, added to his editorship of the *Criterion* (1922–1939) and his work as a publisher, all contribute to earn him a presence in the councils of the Church based on
more than literary fame. This side of Eliot is hardly more than mentioned
in the huge library or haystack of commentary, not even, very much, by
Russell Kirk, who must have understood it better than most of his fellows.[5]

The following pages may be called notes toward a study of Eliot's churchmanship. I do not venture to plumb the depths of his religious experience: rather, I try to enter into his concern with Christian doctrine as stated and implied in *Catholicity*, the religion Eliot professed, to which he subscribed (literally, signed his name to), and with Catholic life in the Church of England as lived day by day, Sunday by Sunday, church year by church year. Even of this limited field a full study cannot at present be made. What will be needed, if they can be found, are Eliot's personal and editorial correspondence, his diaries and engagement books, and records of his attendance at vestry and parish meetings, at Church conferences and discussion groups. Meanwhile, with the evidence at hand, one can make a start in understanding him as a Catholic Anglican layman, first by watching him catch up, then by seeing him fit in.

CATCHING UP

T. S. Eliot did not begin from the religious state of many adult converts, so eloquently described as "nothing." His Unitarian family was serious, religious in their seriousness, deeply concerned with civic, educational, and religious institutions and their duties, rightly and admirably so concerned, as he was later to assert, looking back.[6] Unitarianism is, like Judaism and Islam, an ethical monotheism, but unlike them it is an ethical monotheism with a sincere, non-liturgical bow to Christianity. From this mooring he drifted away, at Harvard and more decisively in Paris, and, after contracting his unhappy marriage, he underwent the suffering so vividly conveyed to all readers of his poetry. A scene begins to present itself. Working in Lloyds Bank in the City of London, he would sometimes take refuge from the world of business and from his tribulations in churches: St. Mary Woolnoth perhaps, St. Magnus Martyr almost certainly. In *The Waste Land* he evokes the exterior of the one, the interior of the other. He recalls, "A visible church, whether it assembles five hundred worshippers or only one passing penitent who has saved a few minutes from his lunch hour, is still a church: in this it differs from a theatre, which if it cannot attract large enough audiences to pay, is no better than a barn."[7] A glimpse of the obvious? Rather, a drowning man's glimpse of a lifebelt. On entering a church, it is normal for a visitor to say a prayer, if he knows how, or at least with Philip Larkin, to think seriously of the people who have erected and maintained the building as something apart from the world. Entering a church with the reserved Sacrament, a sacring light burning near it, and seeing other visitors genuflecting, may prompt some to kneel and open their hearts for a minute, or longer.

I mention St. Magnus because Eliot does and because of all the Wren churches it was the most "advanced" in Anglo-Catholicism and was well known as a small but glorious prize of the Movement. Over the years, as a visitor to London, I have heard prayers there for Pius XII, "our Pope," and his successors as well as, of course, the successive Anglican diocesan bishops. Its tract case would be full of literature explaining for the lay-man the catholicity of the Anglican Church and the steps taken for its full realization in such a parish as this. If Eliot as an enquirer looked at some of them, he would be sure to find an explanation of the six points of ritual for which, not many years before, five priests had been sent to prison and many parishes plagued by hoodlums of the "Protestant underworld," to use the eloquent phrase coined by Eliot's old sparring partner, Bishop Hensley Henson. These six points were: the eastward position of the celebrant, "facing God"; eucharistic vestments, especially the chasuble; altar lights (i.e., candles "in broad daylight!"); the mixed chalice (water with wine, to recall the wound in Christ's side); unleavened bread; and incense.[8] All these pertain to the celebration of Holy Communion, or as they boldly came out and called it, the Mass. All imply, indeed proclaim, the Real Presence in the Sacrifice of the Altar. Near the door the visitor could see the announcements for the week and the month and become acquainted with the marks of a D.S.C.R. parish. Let me explain. Mow-brays, the bookshop and High Church publisher, brought out annually a *Church Guide to Britain*, listing churches, county by county and city by city, that offer daily mass (D), sung mass as main observance on Sunday (S), regular posted times for confession (C), and the Reserved Sacrament (R). A great boon for the tourist. As a tourist who resolved many years ago to visit every historic cathedral in England, and achieved that goal, I found only one without a chapel where the footsore pilgrim may visit the Sacrament. Unthinkable in Samuel Johnson's time, or Jane Austen's time, or the long lifetime of John Henry Newman. Do not call it progress, call it "advance."

In all probability Eliot was aware of St. Magnus and what it stood for by the time he wrote *The Waste Land*, but parish life he could hardly have glimpsed there. Being in the heart of the financial district, it had hardly any resident parishioners, the weekday masses being for people drop-ping in and the Sunday high mass mainly attended by a cohort from across the river in Lewisham. We may surmise, however, if only from "A Dialogue on Dramatic Poetry," that he had some continuing familiarity with highly developed ritual, as anthropologically interesting and as comparable with ballet, a familiarity probably begun in Paris along with other non-Unitarian adventures, but just as probably continued in Eng-lish churches, especially after his meeting William Force Stead in 1923. There was a great Anglo-Catholic Congress that year with all sorts of high liturgical celebrations. The next Congress, equally triumphant, was to be held in 1927, the year of Eliot's baptism. It will be interesting to note, in the third volume of Eliot's letters, whether these events involving thousands, even tens of thousands of enthusiasts, registered with him at a time of great personal stress.[9]

And so, piecemeal, Eliot would come to be familiar with catholicity as a quiet place for meditation, as a coherent set of principles and practices, and perhaps even as a force in the world of events, all of which, in the context of his immensely complex personal and intellectual life, led to his baptism and subsequent lifelong loyalty to the Church. As a layman, of course, he was not required to assent to the "Thirty-Nine Articles of the Christian Faith," as attached to *The Book of Common Prayer*, but by the crucial time he would know that priests and ordinands of his persuasion were swearing to them "in the sense of *Tract Ninety*." The last of the *Tracts for the Times* of the Oxford Movement argues that the Thirty-Nine Articles, being an act of Parliament, are subject to close legal scrutiny and wide interpretation and that their wording, ostensibly Calvinist, is patient of a Catholic sense, especially since they had been promulgated before the clarifying doctrines of the Council of Trent were proclaimed. For this, its author, John Henry Newman, was condemned by the University of Oxford, an action that gave force to his Romeward movement. Many continuing Anglicans thought the condemnation wrong, and by the end of the century the Tractarian position was widely regarded as allowable. Eliot must have known Newman's *Apologia* and the subsequent history of the Oxford and Ritualist Movements. The head of his publishing house, Geoffrey Faber, is to dedicate his study of *The Oxford Apostles* (1934) to Eliot as an authority in the field.

In that field, which is a field of battle, there were many casualties. The vocabulary of anger, euphemism, forgiveness, is rich: to turn papist, to pope, to pervert to Rome, to which may be added the distinctively Canadian, to turn Mick. So much for anger. Now, mildly: to submit to St. Peter, to go over to Rome. The inevitable question arises: if Anglo, why not Roman? Why did Eliot not follow Newman and many others? How well he could understand Newman's longing for a nation "vastly more superstitious, more bigoted, more gloomy, more fierce in its religion." The Eliot of *After Strange Gods* belongs in this vicinity, the Eliot drawn to Villon and St. John of the Cross, to Pascal and Baudelaire. But the movement of Newman's mind, so minutely documented, does not resemble Eliot's. One great climax of the *Apologia* that every reader will remember comes when the close student of Christian antiquity exclaims, "I saw myself in that mirror and I was a Monophysite!" Given the fact that Newman himself had never entertained a monophysite thought, that none of his friends in the Oxford Movement and none of his opponents in the Establishment was a monophysite, that the only monophysites any of them might have encountered were Egyptian Copts, the analogy with the Anglican and Roman Churches vanishes unless one has already intuited that all truth in all controversies must reside in Rome and that anyone outside might just as well be a monophysite. For Eliot such a mirror must seem a distorting mirror. He appears to have been untroubled in his acceptance of the claims of Canterbury and subsequently troubled only by the scandal and confusion that are an undertone if not a note of the Church in any age.[10]

Consider in this connection three major influences on Eliot's thought in the 1920s—Dante, Pascal, Maurras. Dante was a White Guelph, an outspoken partisan of the imperial against the papal power. Gabriele Rossetti, father of Dante Gabriel and Christina, worked hard on an anti-papal interpretation of Dante in his years of exile from the papal states; and in 1932 Faber was to publish *The Passing of Beatrice*, by Gertrude Leigh: its subtitle, *A Study of Heterodoxy in Dante*. One must presume that Eliot, as a director and an informed reader of Dante, approved its publication if not necessarily its argument. Dante contributed to making Eliot a Catholic, but he could never have directed him to ultramontane papalism.[11]

Eliot's essay on Pascal is concerned with the *Pensées*, wrestling with the spirit of belief and the demon of doubt, and so we cannot be sure that he entered into the combative arena of the *Provincial Letters*, where the supremely witty and adroit Jansenist Pascal routs the indulgent probabilism of the Jesuits so completely that the reader quite forgets that he and the author are consigning vast numbers of souls to hell with a sternness hardly matched except in Puritan New England. For the Jansenists were extreme rigorists, "Puritan Papists," and were condemned by Rome.[12]

Charles Maurras must have his paragraph here, as he has had in countless other considerations of Eliot. One of these, Kenneth Asher's *Eliot and Ideology*, presents a mass of evidence and is so well argued that I think it argued into the ground. It is both true and significant that Eliot's famous or notorious phrase "classicist in literature, royalist in politics, anglo-catholic in religion" (later raised to *Anglo-Catholic*, as *jew* as raised to *Jew*), a phrase he grew very tired of, was a direct echo of Maurras. Maurras he lists as a direct influence on his thought, along with T. E. Hulme, Julien Benda, and Jacques Maritain, though only Maritain is to survive into his later sociological thinking. The condemnation of the *Action Française* by the Vatican in 1926 was an event that profoundly shook Eliot, to judge by the attention given it in the *Criterion*. The condemnation, proclamation of which had been long delayed, can be explained and justified as an objection to the whole cast of mind lying behind the slogan "Catholicism without faith." The condition could be lived with but not the slogan. Maurras was what Matthew Arnold, thinking of Carlyle, called a "moral desperado." In the 1920s and 1930s he was the Mediterranean desperado, Oswald Spengler the Teutonic. Spengler was a heathen, Maurras a pagan—not a particularly philosophical high-minded pagan on the model of Marcus Aurelius, but a cut-and-thrust wrangler in the Forum. In this he is "classical" enough, in direct descent from the Roman forensic orator who sets out to wipe the floor with his opponent and to convict him not of one crime but of every conceivable crime. If, as the poet Verlaine, speaking for the whole Symbolist movement, prescribed, we must take rhetoric and wring its neck, the first neck to be wrung should be that of Charles Maurras. To this Eliot could not assent, and it is a measure of his detachment from Symbolism. Eliot, who recognized in Elizabethan drama rhetoric as the language of conflict, recognized in rhetoric in general the art of persuasion, everything in the use of language that makes it interesting, arresting, effective. He could enjoy Chesterton's reply to the charge that he was "arguing for effect": how do you expect me to argue, to no effect?

Many readers and students of Eliot are surprised, even aghast, at the prolonged hold that Maurras exercised over him. I surmise a twofold explanation. Maurras and his cause drew him back to Paris and his friendship with Jean Verdenal, perhaps the last time he was happy before his second marriage. There he discovered French rightist journalism and politics and street demonstrations—so alluring, so transgressive, especially to one brought up among the better elements of St. Louis and Boston. It was, in its way, young Tom Eliot's Woodstock. The other explanation is that it took him closer to the genius of the French language. By all competent accounts, Maurras is a writer of high distinction, a stylist, and the proper response to style is prolonged, repeated appreciation. His influence on Eliot's thought, at its height in 1928, began to wane, and it is difficult to think of there being much occasion to show it at Church discussion groups, or at the Moot, or in the company of his fellow signatories of *Catholicity*. Maurras as a collaborator ended his days in disgrace, though at the very end he made a good end. Eliot stood up for him as he stood up for his old friend and benefactor Ezra Pound, expressing the very sensible regret that Maurras had entered practical politics instead of acting as the conscience of royalism.[13]

Eliot's occasional references to "Liberalism"—most notoriously, "worm-eaten with liberalism"—fit well into the continental context of the liberal as libertine—anti-clerical, anti-Catholic, anti-Christian—as denounced in Pius IX's *Syllabus of Errors*, and into the Maurrasian attack on romanticism, sentimentalism, and the enemies of order in Europe and the realm of France. A similar mind-set was to be found at the outset of the Oxford Movement, which Newman characterized as counter to a liberalism that was skeptical and careless in religion, hostile to the Church, and destructive of moral and social order. Somehow or other, a second term, "humanitarianism," gets mixed up with this, a word handled with acute distaste by Eliot, by Irving Babbitt and T. E. Hulme before him, and even by the usually genial Russell Kirk. Certainly, the humanitarian voice, from the Abolitionists to the Animal Rights people, can be most irritating, but we cannot help wondering which humanitarian achievements their critics would like to undo: the emancipation of slaves, the end of child labor, the prevention of cruelty to animals, women's rights, public health measures, the Red Cross?[14]

As one becomes better acquainted with the Oxford Movement and its successors, one finds them by no means illiberal, concerned as they were with the needs of the embodied soul, with freedom, and with hope. They may have been, most of them in the beginning, church-and-state, crown-and-altar Tories, but they were not the sort of Whig whose rule of life is "make yourselves rich" —in money, land, culture, and power. As the nineteenth century progresses (a good verb for the nineteenth century, not applicable to the twentieth), it is significant that the leader of the Liberal Party, Gladstone, should have been a devout High Churchman, whereas the rival Conservative leader, Disraeli, was of a churchmanship so low as to be undercut only by Queen Victoria's. Disraeli sponsored the Public Worship Regulation Act of 1874, the measure that sent five ritual-ist priests to prison and harried the saintly Bishop King, of Lincoln before it was found to be unenforceable. Eliot, in the address on "The Literature of Politics," published by the Conservative Party, confesses a partiality for Gladstone over Disraeli in this single regard. Increasingly, the young-er High-Church clergy, lacking the local squire's preferment to safe and prosperous old parishes and excluded from parishes tied up in the Evan-gelical interest, found themselves in newer parishes in the great expand-ing cities, often slum parishes, found themselves also caught up in urgent social concerns, sometimes in positions of leadership. Recall the magnetic and effective clergyman who is married to Bernard Shaw's Candida. Eng-land is to produce a socialism different from the continental in not being anti-clerical but rather suffused with a genuine though often nebulous Christian hope. Maurras could not have prepared Eliot for this last phase of his catching up with the living development of Catholic thought and action in the Anglican Church. As he moves into the world of active debate, of committees and discussion groups and summer schools, he will be finding that many who are committed to his way of thinking in matters of belief and church order are well on the left or very moderately right in politics. I wonder if he knew anyone at all who stood for a plutocratic imperialistic Establishment. A signatory of *Catholicity*, Am-brose Reeves, Bishop of Johannesburg, was a lifelong socialist; for his public protest at the Sharpville massacre he was banished from South Africa by the apartheid government. In the course of this development the tone of Eliot's writing moderates into something unrecognizable to Maurras: he becomes, in a good sense, an elder statesman. That is why he could be proposed for the highest civilian honor at the King's bestowal, the Order of Merit, by a Labour Government.[15]

FITTING IN

The foregoing discussion has been concerned with Eliot catching up with the catholicity of the Church of England. We have just begun to observe him fitting in with the Anglican communion as a whole.

On 29 June 1927 Thomas Stearns Eliot was baptized in a small rural Oxfordshire church by the Rev. William Force Stead, an American friend of four years standing, an Oxonian in Anglican orders, very much in continuity with the Oxford Movement. He had already introduced Eliot to the venerable patriarch of Anglo-Catholicism, Lord Halifax (father of the statesman), and to Evelyn Underhill, the authority on mysticism, but they were not in attendance at the very private event. Its privacy, which would be most unusual now except in emergency conditions, was much less so then, when baptisms were seldom part of a regular church service but were semi-private family affairs: no one could be turned away, of course, but an outsider would feel himself uninvited. The locking of the church door, however, was uncanonical, then as now. Adult baptisms were rare; Eliot was an intensely private man with a growing public reputation; most of his friends were unchurched or even anti-religious. It should be noted that though he had of course received religious instruction in childhood and youth, he had not been baptized with water in the name of the Trinity; the Anglican Church accepts as valid all such baptisms but nothing short of that.

The two sponsors were friends of Fr. Stead, one well known, the other obscure, both Oxford dons. Canon B. H. Streeter was a theologian of note. In the previous year he had published *Reality: A New Correlation of Science and Religion* (Stead is thanked in the preface), and in the present year *Adventure: The Faith of Science and the Science of Faith*. He may be discerned as something of a liberal catholic, in the spectrum of the time, certainly not "extreme" (which is the dark side of "advanced"). Later he is to emerge as a champion of the Buchmanites, or Moral Rearmament, about which Eliot will have some sharp words to say. The second sponsor, Vere Somerset, a historian and fellow of Stead's college, will bring out in 1928 *Half a Hundred Epigrams* and later a collection of Edmund Burke's early writings. The duties of the sponsors were not prolonged: Eliot was confirmed by the Bishop of Oxford, again privately, within the week.

The very protestant and individualist notion of being a church to oneself ("John Milton Englishman to all the Churches") was not to last. It was Eliot's old mentor, Irving Babbitt, who induced him to come out in public. The modernist world was amazed at the lost leader, the renegade from modernity; Virginia Woolf in her *Diaries* is shocked; and years later a Left Book Club writer wonders indignantly how anyone can be "an Anglo-Catholic, in 1937!" A collector's item of dated progressivism at its most provincial.

Before settling into parish life, Eliot had a brief encounter with a curious sort of private churchmanship at close quarters when, on returning from America and *After Strange Gods* in 1933, he boarded in an establishment (chosen for him by Robert Sencourt) presided over by the Right Reverend William Edward Scott-Hall, Bishop of Winchester, who had been consecrated in 1911 by A. H. Mathew, Archbishop of London. (The Archbishops of London were "bishops at large" in a communion that boasted seven bishops and perhaps a hundred laity all told.) Conversation at the boardinghouse table must have turned on strictly but obscurely valid orders and details of church furnishings and church millinary and private and coterie devotions of rococo complication.[16]

He soon took up lasting residence in the vicarage of St. Stephen's, Gloucester Road, and his life as an Anglican layman took settled form. Now it is not just a matter of quietly "slipping out" for early mass on weekdays before work; now he presents himself Sunday by Sunday at the main parish mass, takes collection and counts it, serves many terms as vicar's warden (was he ever elected people's warden?), attends vestry meetings, deals with parish finances and diocesan assessment, for he always had a good business head. Eliot was later to smile ruefully when he recalled the lines in his "Hippopotamus" — "While the True Church need never stir/ To gather in its dividends."

The Rev. Martin Jarrett-Kerr has recorded some "retrospective reflections on Eliot's churchmanship" in a deft and informative essay, "Of Clerical Cut." Particularly interesting is an episode in the Parish House of St. Thomas's, Washington, D.C., in 1948. Eliot had been invited to address the Episcopal Fellowship and had prepared some observations on parochial concerns. Hundreds of people had turned up to see the celebrity, who, not to disappoint the parish people, went ahead and talked as a church warden about repairing bomb damage in a shortage of building material and a mass of bureaucratic red tape. Dry rot was a special problem—in church buildings and in the Church as an institution. Members of the audience tried to provoke him into attacking Clement Attlee's Labour Government, but he was not to be drawn. He described his recent membership in the committee on *Catholicity*. A rather breathless contemporary account is quoted. "Mr Eliot, growing visibly warmer, was deeply stirred while recalling a long list of 'young, brilliant Anglican theologians' who had rendered 'brilliant' services. . . . Mr Eliot lingered long and affectionately over every one of them." How one wishes we had the particulars! Austin Farrer was the only member who could be called young, and he was certainly brilliant; Gregory Dix was a very witty monk who provoked wit in others. It is good to know that service on at least this one committee was in Eliot's recollection brilliant.

It goes without saying, or without elaborating, that Eliot's intellectual life, from his college days, concerned itself with the philosophy of religion and the anthropology of religion, that he made serious incursions into oriental religious thought as well as the mind of Christendom in its many manifestations. His lifelong devotion to Dante must have brought with it a sense of Thomism as a system experienced from within, and we have good evidence of his coming to know the English and Spanish mystics, Lancelot Andrewes and the Caroline divines, the religious thought of Coleridge and the Oxford Movement, and a wide spectrum of French opinion. At the end of the evening "a young student from a local university rose . . . and asked impatiently: 'Mr. Eliot, why are you opposed to a secular, rationalist society?' Recovering quickly from the unexpected protest, Mr. Eliot replied briefly, with an undertone of irony: 'I proceed on the assumption that the Christian idea is a true idea; and that it is better to embrace a true idea than any other. Of course, we might push the enquiry further back and question these assumptions; but I daresay this is neither the place nor the time for such an enquiry.'" The chairman ended the meeting and benediction was pronounced.[17] It is difficult to imagine Babbitt or Hulme or Maurras or the earlier Eliot or the earlier Maritain responding with such simplicity, gravity — and effectiveness.

For Lancelot Andrewes and "Thoughts After Lambeth" prove that Eliot was making an effort to enter the mind of the Church of England, past and present. What is in its nature less apparent is the intense life of devotion concurrent with the ordering of ideas. *Ash-Wednesday* and *Four Quartets* point the way for a reader similarly inclined, but for present purposes what concerns us is the imaginative and discursive work that can be related to a discussion of churchmanship — *The Rock, Journey of the Magi, Murder in the Cathedral,* and the essays bearing on church and society.

On the Feast of the Epiphany, after the children in procession have sung "We Three Kings of Orient Are," a student or teacher might well read *The Journey of the Magi*: it might even be the springboard for a sermon. Likewise, a thoughtful and arresting sermon might well explore, from *Murder in the Cathedral,* the implications of "the greatest treason/ to do the right deed for the wrong reason," or "If I am worthy, there is no danger," or even (in expiation for the slight irregularity at the poet's baptism), "Unbar the door!"

The Rock is ecclesiastical in origin and nature, being "a pageant play written for performance at Sadler's Wells Theatre — 28 May–9 June 1934 on behalf of the forty-five churches fund of the diocese of London." While Eliot never listed it among his plays, the choruses he regularly included among his poems. As a dramatic entertainment it is a very simple organism, a procession of events with morals drawn, in this case the building and maintenance of church structures and parish life over the centuries from the founding of London to the present. However "advanced" Eliot's catholicity, *The Rock* is rooted in England, and the catholicity implied in it is gothic and eclectic, not the currently fashionable Tridentine baroque. Its strong sense of the parish as rooted in the parish communion is altogether congruent with the arguments of *The Parish Communion*, published the year before, under the editorship of A. G. Hebert, who will later, with Eliot, sign *Catholicity*. Bishop Blomfield, a mid-Victorian Bishop of London, appears in a good light in the grand panorama, as a builder of churches who stirred himself to get the teeming new populations to church and communion on Sundays. He was an opponent though not an enemy of the Ritualist movement, but that is not held against him here. He is the sort of clergyman, an excellent sort, who can tell a story against himself. Once, after preaching on the text, "The fool hath said in his heart, there is no God," he was approached by one of his hearers (I like to think of him as a warden): "Strong sermon, sir. Almost convinced me. But I still rather think there is a God." [13]

The Rock is a pageant for amateur actors, written for a special occasion. The action is episodic and the characterization is—no, not "one-dimensional," whatever that is—two-dimensional, lacking depth. Though the choruses have precedent in Seneca and the Greeks, it is hardly an exercise in "classicism." Eliot the royalist remembers that "our King did well at Acre," recalling the Lion-Heart as Crusader, but one could hardly call this a "royalist" play, or even "anglo-catholic" in any partisan sense. It is noteworthy that in the context of its contemporary social scene false diagnoses are rejected, the communists with some respect, the anti-semitic fascists with scorn. *The Rock* had all the success it deserved, so much that within the decade two pageants came in its wake, both with a vision of England over the centuries, both quite secular—E. M. Forster's *England's Pleasant Land*, written in 1938, published in 1940, and Virginia Woolf's *Between the Acts,* complete but not revised at her death in 1941. It is as if both these secular modernists said, if Eliot can do it, I can do it. [19]

Eliot's keen dramatic sense, shown both in the excellence of his essays on the Elizabethan dramatists and in the dramatic character of many of his poems from "Prufrock" on, was given new stimulus by the success of *The Rock* as it must have been dampened shortly before that by his failure to finish *Sweeney Agonistes*. Here the ecclesiastical hierarchy was a decisive influence. George Bell, Dean of Canterbury, soon to be Bishop of Chichester (and, like Eliot, to fly to Stockholm in 1942), was impressed by *The Rock* and resolved to encourage the revival of liturgical drama such as had flourished, especially in England, in the Middle Ages. The story of the commissioning of *Murder in the Cathedral* and its successful achievement has been told by the original Becket, Robert Speaight, and by E. Martin Browne, the director of this and all Eliot's plays. Its early and continued success Eliot took as a challenge: can he write a play, not explicitly Christian but suffused with Christian feeling and ethos, that could stand its chances in the commercial theater? He gave four answers: *The Family Reunion* explores sin and the hope of redemption; *The Cocktail Party* the affirmative and negative Ways; *The Confidential Clerk* the question of vocation; and *The Elder Statesman* resignation and a good death.

The late 1930s found Eliot, like many another, preoccupied with international events leading to the Munich Agreement, which so depressed him that he brought the *Criterion*, with its vision of a European Mind, to an end. At the same time that he was writing *The Family Reunion*, treating privileged people in a remote country house, with only the ghost of a mission at the end—a sort of tractarian slum-parish of half a century before—Eliot brought out *The Idea of a Christian Society*, the two works being as startlingly different as *Ash-Wednesday* and its contemporary, *Sweeney Agonistes*.

In one of his earlier *Criterion* Commentaries (Jan. 1927) Eliot had referred to "Sociology," in quotation marks, as a new, somewhat American pursuit carried on by people "who often write badly," forgetful of Auguste Comte, a major, if disapproved figure in French thought, of Herbert Spencer, a somewhat smaller figure in English, not to mention such luminaries as Max Weber, R. H. Tawney, and Thorstein Veblen. His association, which became quite close, with Canon V. A. Demant, a prolific writer on social questions—and a signatory of *Catholicity*, and with Maurice Reckitt, the editor of *Christendom*, accustomed him to a field of study and discussion that came right out and called itself Christian Sociology. Of Eliot's often-cited endorsement of the ideas of T. E. Hulme, Julien Benda, Charles Maurras, and Jacques Maritain, only Maritain enters the new context with his widely circulated and admired *True Humanism* (1938), whose title might just as well have been *The Idea of a Christian Society*.

Eliot's title recalls that of W. G. Ward's *The Ideal of a Christian Church* (1844), a vigorous, boisterous brick of a book that propelled its author over to Rome (he was the first to "Pope") and provoked the University of Oxford to deprive him of his degrees. It stands out among all serious, ambitious, and independent treatments of an important subject as perhaps the worst written. No two books could be more unlike. Ward, who began writing a pamphlet and ended with six hundred pages, writes like a fox with its tail on fire, Eliot like a hedgehog. In *Idea* he finds the greatest difficulty in beginning and is at pains to explain everything that he does not mean and will not discuss; he is no less guarded in his conclusion. His earlier criticism is memorable to a high degree, not only for its superbly appropriate quotations but for casual remarks and magisterial or mischievous dicta. Few sentences from the two books of social criticism or the uncollected articles stand out so as to lodge in the memory, though they all show care in writing and are adequate to their occasion. Canon, later Archbishop Michael Ramsey (the Chairman of the *Catholicity* committee) once warned of the danger of "conference mentality," with its tendency to neutralize one's style, talking not the common language of men but the common language of committeemen.[20]

As Eliot worked hard to grasp the real nature of his own society and culture, he fell out of love with gallic polemical journalism and its concomitant street rowdyism. Canon Demant could introduce him to the social thinking of John Neville Figgis and R. H. Tawney and of course his own books, many of them Faber books. Maurice Reckitt and Alex Vidler maintained in renewed life the social gospel, from the mid-Victorian Frederick Denison Maurice to Scott Holland, Charles Gore, and William Temple—Englishmen all, Anglicans all.

Maurice Reckitt edited a periodical called *Christendom: A Journal of Christian Sociology* (1930–1950), in which Eliot appeared several times as contributor or in lists of speakers. It sponsored a Summer School of Sociology, and associated with it was a loosely defined "Christendom Group," which Eliot attended, as he did another, not specifically Christian, discussion group, the Moot, which flourished as best it could in wartime until the death of its leading figure, the exiled German-Jewish philosopher of sociology, Karl Mannheim. All these are well discussed by Roger Kojecký in his study of *T. S. Eliot's Social Criticism.*[21] I have had something to subtract from Kenneth Asher's *T. S. Eliot and Ideology*, with its crushing emphasis on Maurras. I have little to add to Kojecký, except one lighthearted note. The term "Christian Conspiracy" was bandied about for a time in these circles, to apply something like Coleridge's "clerisy" or Eliot's nucleus of educated, reflective, and devout church-people. It relies on the Latin for drawing breath together and alludes to a passage in a well-known hymn, "Bright the Vision":

> Thus conspire we to adore Him. . . .
> Holy, Holy, Holy, Lord.

This was rejected as smacking too much of conspiratorial politics (you do not find Shakespeare or the English Bible making giggly puns on "conspiracy"), and the *New English Hymnal* now has "thus unite we."

One thing I missed in reading the files of *Christendom* was any attempt to define its title, any "notes toward the definition of Christendom." This I have been tempted to undertake, but must resist the temptation here. Suffice it to say that Islam from its beginning was a polity, and "Christendom," the idea and the word, emerges as a polity in answer to Islam, as the Crusade answers the Jihad, the bell-tower the minaret. The Crescent as challenge to the Cross was just about invisible in Eliot's lifetime.[22]

In preparing this essay about Eliot and Catholicity—how he caught up with the Anglo-Catholic Movement, fitted into parochial life, and emerged as a figure of weight in the councils of the Anglican communion—I came upon a field of investigation that has not, to my knowledge, been much explored by anyone. Everybody knows that Eliot as a director of Faber and Faber, had prime responsibility for its very distinguished poetry list, and that the immensely influential *Faber Book of Modern Verse* (first edition, 1936) reflected his taste and judgment. It was edited by Michael Roberts, the one person Eliot thought might be entrusted with editing the *Criterion* if it had been continued.[23] But Mr. Eliot's Other List, for the discussion of which he would, even in his later years, remain at editorial meetings, was of books on religion and a wide range of subjects related to religion. Eliot was a man of conscience, and he must have had a publisher's conscience, asking himself such questions as these, always in the context of the book business as a paying proposition: Which books will I champion, come what may? Which will I recommend for publication? Which will I recommend conditionally? Which am I inclined to reject? Which do I reject out of hand?

I have compiled and hope to publish with brief comments a list of about fifty Faber books that Eliot is very likely to have seen, read, reported, and voted on. All I need say here is that the reader will be struck by their (lower-case) catholicity, and by how few take notice, positively or negatively, of Eliot's own religious views. The question of "influence" inevitably arises.

T. S. Eliot was for seventeen years the editor of a major journal of the humanities and, concurrently and for the rest of his life, an active director of a publishing house; he was much in demand as a speaker at conferences or on special occasions. How did such a pattern of life mark him? What is influence? An influence is an encounter that adds to knowledge and experience and thereby modifies taste, opinion, and action, lightly or heavily. To put it in the present context, Eliot's singing or reciting of the Creed, if only once a week, from his baptism to his death, a total of over two thousand acts of assent most of them not involving deliberate reexamination, argues for imprint at a very deep level: it is possessed as part of oneself. Again, the acceptance of nomination to the *Catholicity* committee, the discussion, drafting, and signing of the Report—all these constitute a serious commitment, not to be lightly undertaken. During the Spanish Civil War, Eliot declined to "take sides" on the ground that he did not know enough. Ten years later he knew enough theology and had experienced enough church life to take sides on the question of catholicity. Writing discursively on ecclesiastical and social matters is likewise serious but involves less of a commitment. Close reading for purposes of reviewing or editing will focus the attention sharply for a limited time and a limited purpose but leaves much less of a mark. And ordinary reading and informal discussion and conversation may produce windfalls of insight, but such should not be expected, still less required of them.

NOTES

1. Together with a short précis of its argument, I have appended the list of signatories to *Catholicity: A Study in the Conflict of Christian Traditions in the West* (Westminster: Dacre Press, 1947).

2. The early Victorian Tractarians and the late Victorian Ritualists were notable for their replacing Matins by Holy Communion as the main parish celebration of the

week; the more "advanced" Anglo-Catholics moved to the Roman practice of low masses with communion followed by a high celebration, the priest only communicating. The Liturgical Movement began on the Continent late in the nineteenth century and gained force in the twentieth, with some impact in English Roman Catholic circles, especially those in which Eric Gill moved. Fr. Hebert's collection, *The Parish Communion* (London, S.P.C.K., 1939 and 1961), with articles by himself, Dix, and Farrer, made the case in the Anglican context. The field was won at Vatican II.

3. Eliot would be almost certain to know at least two books of Dom Gregory Dix: *The Shape of the Liturgy* (Westminster: Dacre Press, 1946) and *The Question of Anglican Orders* (Westminster: Dacre Press, 1945). For his character and thought, see also Simon Bailey, *A Tactful God: Gregory Dix, Priest, Monk, and Scholar* (Leominster: Gracewing, 1995), esp. 136–8; W. T. Levy and Victor Scherle, *Affectionately, T. S. Eliot* (New York: Lippincott, 1968), 69; E. L. Mascall, *Saraband: The Memoirs* (Leominster: Gracewing, 1992), 151–63; Kenneth Hylson-Smith, *High Churchmanship* (Edinburgh: T and T Clark, 1993), 291–7.

4. Eliot was born in 1888, Heidegger and Wittgenstein in 1889, but by the time of the appearance of the *Tractatus* in 1921, Eliot had ceased to write for philosophical journals, and by the time of *Sein und Zeit* (1927) he was out of the professional world altogether, though his last quasi-philosophical meditation (in *Burnt Norton*) was on the question of time.

5. Of Eliot's biographers, the most useful in regard to his churchmanship is Peter Ackroyd, *T. S. Eliot* (London: Hamish Hamilton, 1964), 160–2 and notes 350, 186–7, 210–11, 242–3, 257, 277; Levy and Scherle, passim; Robert Sencourt, *T. S. Eliot: A Memoir* (New York: Dodd, Mead, 1971), 123–39, 166–7; E. W. F. Tomlin, *T. S. Eliot: A Friendship* (London: Routledge, 1988) 34, 82, 96, 166–9, 182, recalling an anachronistic "no Popery" disturbance at Eliot's parish church as late as 1955.

6. Eliot's emphatic rejection of Protestantism needs no documentation. As late as *Notes towards the Definition of Culture* (1948) he could write: ". . . the tendency in some quarters to reduce theology to such principles as a child can understand or a Socinian accept, is itself indicative of cultural debility" (80). But the polemical note is dropped by 1953, when he recalls the Unitarian Church of the Messiah, the City of St. Louis and Washington University, and comments: "These were the symbols of Religion, the Community and Education, and I think it a very good beginning for any child to be brought up to reverence such institutions and to be taught that personal and selfish aims should be subordinated to the general good which they represent" (*To Criticise the Critic*, 44). Writing on "Goethe as the Sage" (1955), he surprised his readers with another of his triads, speaking of himself as combining "a Catholic cast of mind, a Calvinistic heritage, and a Puritanical temperament" (*On Poetry and Poets*, 209). The middle term is puzzling. The founder of Unitarianism, Michael Servetus, was burnt at the stake in 1553 by Calvin, and Unitarians reject the specifically Calvinist "TULIP" doctrines (Total depravity, Unconditional predestination, Limited atonement, Irresistible grace, Perseverance of the elect). Eliot was no closer to New England Calvinism than were the New Yorkers, William and Henry James, who were brought up as dissident Swedenborgians.

7. Commentary, *Criterion* 4 (October 1926): 628–9. St. Magnus Martyr is named on the page before the passage quoted.

8. The Six Points were of course not themselves *de fide*, but their denial was clearly intended to deny Catholic essentials. Widespread acceptance of Reservation in Anglican churches took place almost entirely in Eliot's lifetime.

9. Handsome and substantial Reports of the Anglo-Catholic Congresses of 1923 and 1927 were published, with elaborate baroque title-pages, by the Society of St. Peter and St. Paul, the first concluding with the ringing address of Bishop Frank Weston, of Zanzibar, quoted for decades thereafter, saying that the ritual battle is won but the need to unite the church, Christianize the world, and serve the poor is a great challenge. Like the *avant-garde* in the arts, like the vanguard of the proletariat, the advanced Anglo-Catholics had a vision of victory without tarrying for any.

10. John Henry Newman, *Apologia Pro Vita Sua*, ed. A. Dwight Culler (Cambridge: Riverside Press, 1956), 64, 121.

11. A second Faber book on Dante, Charles Williams's *The Figure of Beatrice* (1943), has a chapter on *De Monarchia* and many observations on the images of the emperor and the pope, but Eliot in his two essays on Dante (in *The Sacred Wood*, 1920, and *Selected Essays*, 1929) severely concerns himself with bringing his readers to the poems first, before any questions of philosophy and theology, of commentary and controversy arise. See concluding paragraphs (*SE*, 276–7).

12. Without raising questions of orthodoxy, I think it can be agreed that Eliot and Pascal shared a "Puritanical temperament."

13. The thesis of Kenneth Asher in *T. S. Eliot and Ideology* (Cambridge: Cambridge University Press, 1995) is stated at the outset: "From beginning to end, Eliot's work, including both the poetry and the prose, was shaped by a political vision inherited from French reactionary thinkers, especially from Charles Maurras" (2–3). Others assign Maurras a much less central place: Roger Kojecký, *T. S. Eliot's Social Criticism* (New York: Farrar, Straus and Giroux, 1971), 58–69; John D. Margolis, *T. S. Eliot's Intellectual Development 1922–1939* (Chicago: University of Chicago Press, 1972), 87–98; Tomlin, 46–7. It may be noted that Philip Spencer in *Politics of Belief in Nineteenth-Century France*, published in 1954 by Faber and therefore likely to have received some scrutiny by Eliot, observes how the influence of Veuillot's journalism reverberated "down to the distorting caverns of *La Libre Parole* and *L'Action Française*" (217). Again, "Veuillot represents the good anti-humanist, and perhaps for this reason he has never had a true successor. Maurras, who possessed a comparable talent, had none of his faith" (264).

14. In reading the attacks on sentimental progressive liberalism in the wake of Rousseau early in the twentieth century, it is hard for us to reconstruct its maddening complacency before the Great War and before the advent of Hitler and Stalin. How strong must have been the appeal to the intelligent young of the hard, dry, dogmatic, even (under control) the violent. And what a stroke of luck it would have been for Eliot in the Paris of 1910, perhaps after a lecture by Bergson, to have met T. E. Hulme and introduced him to Irving Babbitt. Babbitt and Hulme, both aggressive talkers, would have hit it off splendidly until (perhaps after) one had stood armed as the champion, the other as the enemy, of Humanism. A classic opportunity for Eliot to play possum—and a superb scenario for a story by Guy Davenport.

15. Eliot's Toryism, or Conservatism (he called it "Royalism" only once), is best to be understood in the context of his approval of Russell Kirk's *The Conservative Mind*, the rights for which he secured for Faber, and Kirk's own study of *Eliot and His Age* (1971; second ed., Wilmington, DE: ISI Books, 2008).

16. The full story of such *Bishops at Large* is told with mild sympathy and dead-pan humor by Peter F. Anson (London: Faber, 1964), esp. 148, 182.

17. Martin Jarrett-Kerr, "Of Clerical Cut," in *Eliot in Perspective*, ed. Graham Martin (New York: Humanities Press, 1970), 239–42, 250–1.

18. Malcolm Johnson, *Bustling Intermeddler? The Life and Work of Charles James Blomfield* (Leominster: Gracewine, 2001), 153. (I give a more definitive wording of the anecdote.)

19. *The Rock* assumes the continuity of Western Christendom as not broken in England by the Reformation, but the only bigoted or "spiky" characters in it are some twentieth-century churchgoers who reject anything later than 1484, the last "Gothic" year before the "Tudor" infestation in church furnishings.

20. Michael De-la-Noy, *Michael Ramsey* (London: Collins, 1990), 149.

21. See Kojecký, passim, including his bibliography and attendance lists at discussion groups. Of V. A. Demant's books, the following are published by Faber: *Christian Polity* (1936), *Religion and the Decline of Capitalism* (1952), *Theology of Society* (1947); by Maurice Reckitt, also Faber books: *Prospect for Christendom* (1945), *Maurice to Temple* (1947), to which should be added his autobiography, *As It Happened* (London: Dent, 1941).

22. Geoffrey Parrinder, professor of comparative studies of religions in the University of London, a Faber writer, published in 1965 *Jesus in the Qur'an*.

23. Michael Roberts, who moved from the Marxism of the 1930s to a religious position similar to Eliot's, in his pioneering book on *T. E. Hulme* (London: Faber, 1938) was perceptive enough to see that a doctrine of original sin implies and requires a doctrine of redemption (134); he also sees that laissez-faire is a utopian ideology (186).

TWO

Catholicity: A Précis

William Blissett

CATHOLICITY: A STUDY IN THE CONFLICT OF CHRISTIAN TRADITIONS IN THE WEST BEING A REPORT PRESENTED TO HIS GRACE THE ARCHBISHOP OF CANTERBURY

List of Signatories

The Revd E. S. Abbott, Dean of King's College, London, and Canon of Lincoln.

The Revd H. J. Carpenter, Warden of Keble College, Oxford, and Canon Theologian of Leicester.

The Revd Dr. V. A. Demant, Canon and Chancellor of S. Paul's Cathedral.

The Revd Dom Gregory Dix, Monk of Nashdom Abbey.

T. S. Eliot, Esq.

The Revd Dr. A. M. Farrer, Fellow of Trinity College, Oxford.

The Revd F. W. Green, Canon and Vice-Dean of Norwich Cathedral.

The Revd Fr A. G. Hebert, of the Society of the Sacred Mission.

The Rt. Revd E. R. Morgan, Bishop of Southampton.

The Revd R. C. Mortimer, Regius Professor of Pastoral Theology in the University of Oxford, and Canon of Christ Church.

The Revd A. M. Ramsey, Van Mildert Professor of Divinity in the University of Durham, and Canon of Durham.

The Revd A. Reeves, Rector of Liverpool, and Canon Diocesan of Liverpool.

The Revd C. H. Smyth, Canon of Westminster and Rector of S. Margaret's; Fellow of Corpus Christi College, Cambridge.

The Revd Dr. L. S. Thornton, of the Community of the Resurrection.

CATHOLICITY: A PRÉCIS

The Primitive Unity

The Lord's prayer for the unity of His disciples is linked with the prayer for their sanctification in truth. They do not constitute this unity themselves but are brought into a unity already there. The wholeness is apparent in the Old Testament as in the New and continues to manifest itself in a visible church in its outward order—in baptism, its single rite of initiation, and in its central act of worship, the eucharist. Out of this context of Christian life, embodied in teaching, worship, and institutions, proceeded the New Testament. To oppose "Scripture" and "tradition" is wholly artificial and arbitrary. Within this wholeness there were inevitable tensions—between the eternal and the temporal, between the Church's apartness from the world and its mission to ensoul the world, between the divine nature of the Church and the sinfulness of its members.

The Background of the Western Schisms

The Early Church was threatened many times with loss of wholeness, but the most grievous harm was done by the breach of East and West. In the West it resulted in excesses of legalism and clericalism, theological rationalism, individual piety, which the East might have corrected. The East became too dependent on the civil power; it failed to translate its spiritual principles into moral practice; and it missed both Renaissance and Reformation. The Reformation broke down a wholeness already severely impaired and produced the three main types of Western Christianity—strict Protestantism, liberal modernism, and post-Tridentine Catholicism—all represented in Anglicanism.

Orthodox Protestantism

Its great positive truths include, first and chief, its emphasis on the Gospel of the Living God and His direct and personal action in the salvation of mankind; its appeal to the authority of the Bible; its insistence on the necessity of faith on man's part; the active participation of the laity; and the importance of preaching. It makes two radical errors: the dissociation of Justification from the doctrine of Creation and from Sanctification. The first, springing from a catastrophic pessimism concerning the results of the Fall, wipes out the image of God in man and makes God's judgment irrational and tyrannous. The second, rejecting the possibility of growing in grace through sacramental life, leads to subjectivism: "Multitudes today go to Church in the hope of recovering some glimpse of their conversion experience, and if they do not get such a glimpse they are sadly cast down." From these two faults spring Protestantism's distrust of reason, rejection of natural law, and a cult of inwardness whereby the soul is confronted directly with Calvary as the one significant moment in history. It is grievously misleading to appeal to the Bible without appealing also to the apostolic Church as witness and keeper.

Renaissance and Liberalism

While the Reformation was proclaiming the helplessness of man, the bondage of the will, and the doctrine of Justification by Faith alone, the Renaissance was asserting its own idea of the dignity of man, and pointing toward the ideal of human freedom, and the idea of history as a steady progress toward happiness and enlightenment. Possessing roots both in ancient classical humanism and in the culture of the Western Church, the Renaissance had among its fruits many that could be authentically Christian. The devotion to truth for its own sake—whether in the study of the Bible or in the discoveries of natural science—the reverence for man as created in the image of God, the insistence that all that is true and good and beautiful is of God: these insights are as necessary as is the Reformation insistence upon the priority of God's grace, or the Catholic insistence on the visible Church. Liberalism, however, is fiercely intolerant. It cannot tolerate the Evangelical's emphasis on Atonement, because it disallows the situation between God and man in which Atonement is needed. It cannot tolerate the Catholic's conviction that Church order is vital, because it disallows the place of the visible Church in relation to the Incarnation of God. It is one thing to recover the positive insights of Liberalism within a Catholic and Evangelical faith: it is another thing to take the common and popular sentiments of Liberalism as a kind of norm of Christian broadmindedness wherein we can all "get together."

The Post-Tridentine Papal Communion

The Church of the Counter-Reformation was in important respects the successor, rather than the mere continuation, of the unreformed Church of the fifteenth century. In liturgy and administration its practical reforms were far-reaching. It consolidated the Western theological tradition, maintained the many-sidedness of medieval church life, and revivified the missionary impulse in the Orient and the New World. Why has it not in four hundred years reabsorbed Protestantism? Partly because of its long identification with Bourbon and Habsburg and *ancien-régime* politics, partly because of rigidity in scholastic philosophy and canon law and what is called "papal absolutism." Yet whenever it can forget sectarianism and give a deliberate lead to Christendom, the Papacy can still command the attention and to a large extent secure the following of all Christians, and it is the only Christian institution that can do so. It is at once the strongest single bulwark of the historic tradition of Christian civilization in Europe, and a pioneer of the modern Christian social teaching by which it is sought to remedy the desperate sickness from which that tradition now universally suffers.

Fragmentation and Synthesis

After tabulating a dozen sharp contrasts between Orthodox and liberal Protestantism, the authors observe that modern Catholicism has not succeeded in the task of reintegration of the truth, for it is itself the product of a long process of dissociation. Questions remain concerning the doctrine of sacrifice in the Eucharist, the Atonement, the authority of Scripture. In discussing these there is danger of drifting into false methods of theological synthesis that contain seeds of fresh disunity: we do not arrive at truth by fitting errors together. Nevertheless, the movements toward visible unity, springing from a sense of defeat and need, represent a penitence of a thoroughly practical kind.

The Anglican Communion

The comprehensiveness of the Church of England opens the way for it to become a school of synthesis over a wider field than any other church in Christendom. It reaches toward Eastern Orthodoxy and Western Catholicism and Protestantism, traditional and modern. But the forces of disintegration too are strong: English nationalism, pietistic ecclesiasticism, "progressivism." It is idle to be content that the Church of England includes a "rich variety" if that variety represents a distortion and fragmentation of the truth. The report reaffirms the Lambeth Quadrilateral of 1930 as a symbol of the fullness of Tradition: the appeal to Holy Scripture and the Creeds will mean the recovery of the pattern of the biblical faith in God, Creator, Redeemer, and Judge; the appeal to the sacraments of the Gospel will mean the recovery of the primitive fullness of Christian initiation by baptism into Christ and the sealing of the Holy Spirit in Confirmation, and the primitive fullness of the Eucharistic life. The appeal to the historic Episcopate will mean the recovery of the true place of the Bishop in the Church, not as the organiser of a vast administrative machine but as the guardian and exponent of the faith, as the bond of sacramental unity, and as the organ of the Body of Christ in true constitutional relationship to the presbyters and people.

II

French Catholic Influences

THREE

T. S. Eliot and the French Catholic Revival: 1910–1911 Paris

John Morgenstern

In early 1910, while Eliot was imbibing Aristotle in Irving Babbitt's Harvard lecture hall and Dante in W. H. Schofield's, Jules Laforgue's blend of philosophical skepticism and spiritual dread began to work on his mind. Determined in "Autobiographical Preludes" to "bring a little order to this drawer," to sort out the antithetical Catholic and Schopenhauerian philosophies cluttering his view of the Absolute, Laforgue looks for a sign of divinity, of "the dear Whole" across the star-filled Parisian sky.[1] "[D]ead drunk on doubt" and hesitant "to elixerate in [himself] the Absolute," when he gazes "across the infinite" from the quays of the Seine behind Notre Dame, he sees only the mechanical operation of the universe. Likening himself to a diver searching for life on the floor of the Seine, Laforgue recalls "scuttling through the books" that informed his doubt, like a Prufrockian crab, cut off from spiritual insight by the reasoning of his own mind. "With books, beneath heaven's Eternullity," he imagines himself drifting "past corals, eggs, green feelers, tresses that shift/ In the eternal whirling of the dying throes," before drowning "dead drunk" in "[l]akes of aesthetic swoons." Laforgue's "torments of sensibility, of body and soul" pulled at Eliot from the inside out, and pushed him to contemplate his spiritual course.[2]

Whereas Laforgue saw a universe without heaven circling above Paris, when Eliot confronts his religious skepticism in a derelict Cambridge square in "First Debate between the Body and Soul" (January 1910) and along the city streets of "Silence" (June 1910), he glimpses hell's circles. Taken together, these poems foresee a visionary progress that leads inevi-

59

tably from doubt to damnation.[3] At least as palpably as he feels the "emphatic mud of physical sense," in "First Debate," he senses the hand of an angry God marking him for purgatory, the "cosmic smudge of an enormous thumb/ Posting bills/ On the soul." Harnessing a declarative power drawn more from within himself than from Laforgue, in "Silence," Eliot acknowledges the fear that wells up in him at the thought of divine judgment:

> Along the city streets
> It is still high tide,
> Yet the garrulous waves of life
> Shrink and divide
> With a thousand incidents
> Vexed and debated: —
> This is the hour for which we waited —
> This is the ultimate hour
> When life is justified.
> The seas of experience
> That were so broad and deep
> So immediate and steep,
> Are suddenly still.
> You may say what you will,
> At such peace I am terrified.
> There is nothing else beside.

As much as the first verse paragraph of "Silence" resonates with the more mature voice of *Four Quartets*, the still point in its second paragraph induces terror, not beatitude. At twenty-one, Eliot was still too bound by the "practical desire" of his flesh to give himself wholly over to the ecstatic silence of "Burnt Norton." Nevertheless, he was stung into revelation by his first contact with the still point: as skeptical as he may have remained, in June 1910, he was convinced that doubt had consequences, and the thought scared the hell out of him.

Eliot's earliest spiritual insight coincided with his decision in the spring of 1910 to spend the following academic year in Paris. Despite recognizing that Eliot's mind edges "beyond 'Silence' and 'The First Debate' towards a religious, even Christian, point of view," in France, Lyndall Gordon has nevertheless maintained that "Paris did not change Eliot very much."[4] To the contrary, this essay argues, Paris was central to Eliot's adoption of a more explicitly Christian idiom. Moreover, the prevailing critical view of Eliot's French engagement looks only to the Symbolist writers he encountered at Harvard, whose loose spirituality was more shadow than substance. The generation of writers and critics that he encountered in the city of light, however, had already by 1910 rejected Symbolism's vague spirituality for Catholicism. The religious passions of Eliot's French contemporaries, I contend, shifted his spiritual footing from the Symbolist shadow toward the more solid ground of Christianity.

Reflecting on his formative year in France, Eliot opined in his April 1934 *Criterion* editorial that an "atmosphere of diverse opinions," like that to which he was exposed in 1910–1911, "seems to me on the whole favorable to the maturing of the individual; because when he does come to a conviction, he does so not by 'taking a ticket,' but by making up his own mind." Eliot's period of Parisian receptivity, he concludes, eventually delivered him to Christianity: "What ultimately matters," he resolved, "is the salvation of the individual soul. You may not like this principle, but if you abjure it, you will probably in the end get something that you like less. The world tends now to scramble for its salvation by taking a ticket."[5] As a twenty-two-year-old student, Eliot turned to the *Nouvelle Revue Française* (henceforth *NRF*) to guide him through this diverse milieu, and its manifestly Christian character, the following pages suggest, changed the terms of the debate between his body and soul. Together with his tutor Henri Fournier, and with his confidant Jean Verdenal, Eliot analyzed contemporary French literature to determine its value for his inner life. In particular, Charles-Louis Philippe's pimps and prostitutes showed Eliot the transformative power of suffering to turn bodily sin into spiritual salvation.

When Eliot arrived in Paris in late September or early October 1910, he discovered that France was in the midst of its own religious awakening and that events of the two decades since Laforgue's "Preludes" had steered a succeeding generation of French writers away from skepticism toward belief. In the wake of the Dreyfus Affair, to isolate the pivotal controversy of this generational shift, a polarized religious right found middle ground with the French youth on the basis that a return to Catholicism could unify the county and provide a foundation for moral reconstruction.[6] Henri Massis and Alfred de Tarde's 1912 survey of university students, published as *Les jeunes gens d'aujourd'hui* the following year, claimed that one-third of students in the École Normale had embraced the Church.[7] "Catholicism seems to them," Massis and Tarde reported, "to be less a system of speculative philosophy and more of a rule, a doctrine for moral and social action."[8] Reviewing this survey in the *NRF*, Jacques Copeau hailed Massis and Tarde as observers of a "revolution of temperament, which is, finally, a national renaissance," both religious and political.[9]

More specifically revealing of a poet's path to the Church, *Les jeunes gens d'aujourd'hui* showed the extent to which this rebirth of religious sentiment colored the literary imagination of Eliot's contemporaries. Speaking for their generation, Massis and Tarde deplored the kind of lyrical mysticism associated with Symbolism. "Nothing was more foreign," their findings revealed, "to the new generation than the 'Godless mysticism,' the 'atheistic devotion,' of a Maeterlinck, unless it is the aesthetic dilettantism of [the skeptical, nineteenth-century critic Ernest] Renan for whom Christianity should cease to be a dogma in order to become a 'poetic.'"[10] "Religion as an artistic theme, Christianity as a mythology," Massis and Tarde reported, "inspires a profound repugnance in the realist mind of these young men. . . ."[11] In line with Eliot's condemnation of d'Aurevilly's, Huysmans's, and Oscar Wilde's "imitation[s] of spiritual life" in his eighth Clark lecture in 1926, Massis and Tarde accused the previous generation of emptying Catholicism of its essential spirit:

> The previous generation . . . asked this question: "Is there no way to be Catholic, without believing in Catholicism?" They dreamed of a religion without dogma, drama without a stage, heat without a flame. And it is exactly this kind of cult for nonbelievers Oscar Wilde had in mind when he wrote [in *De Profundis*]: "the Confraternity of the Fatherless one might call it, where on an altar, on which no taper burned, a priest, in whose heart peace had no dwelling, might celebrate with unblessed bread and a chalice empty of wine."[12]

While the previous generation filled the pages of Remy de Gourmont's Symbolist monthly, the *Mercure de France*, with spiritually vacant poetry worthy of recitation before this Confraternity of the Fatherless, Massis and Tarde contended, the religious spirit of the new generation overflowed in the monthly magazine that guided Eliot through literary Paris: the *NRF*.[13]

Massis and Tarde's association of the *NRF* with the religious youth came in the wake of a controversy that erupted in April 1910, and continued throughout Eliot's Parisian residence, when André Gide published a harsh critique of Remy de Gourmont's "Dialogue des Amateurs" in the *Revue*. Gourmont's "Dialogue," serialized by the *Mercure de France*, dramatized his skeptical worldview through the mouthpieces of fictional characters Messieurs Desmaisons and Delarue. Gide judged Gourmont's "Dialogue" of 15 June 1909 mocking religious art to be particularly antiquated, and countered that "[s]kepticism may sometimes be the beginning of wisdom; but, it is just as often the end of art."[14] Much like the diver in Laforgue's "Preludes," Gourmont's characters, Gide charged, were cut off from eternal truths by their cold devotion to verifiable fact:

> Delarue, Desmaisons, these are souls *sans paysages*. Their horizon halts at the booksellers' crates that line the Seine. At times I doubt if perhaps they have ever taken hold of life except that which they have grasped from books, ever known foreign lands except from maps, ever at all felt the passions that speed and slow the heart—so much so that they stand out against everyone who has. [In Gourmont's dialogues], nothing trembles, nothing suffers.[15]

Gourmont's detached skepticism, his inability to suffer, Gide emphasized, set him against the Catholic youth in 1910. "When Nietzsche amputates," Gide further stressed this point, he at least "bloodies his fingers; we could say that Gourmont," as dispassionate as the characters he invents, "only operates on anatomical charts."[16]

In suggesting that the editor of the *Mercure de France* had lost touch with the aesthetic preferences of the new generation, Gide effectively positioned the review he edited, the *NRF*, against the most fashionable literary magazine of Symbolist France. In the aftermath of Gide's coup, Claudel advised him to sanctify the review's affiliation with the Church.[17] Their doctrinal stance, the Catholic poet contended, was "the most current and urgent issue on which they must take a side."[18] Although the *Revue* officially maintained its policy of neutrality, it assumed an ostensible religious character under Gide's editorship and attracted many recent converts to its pages.[19] According to popular opinion, Jean Royère reported in the *Phalange*, "the entire new generation was behind M. André Gide, whereas only M. Remy de Gourmont's admirers were behind M. Remy de Gourmont."[20] In the eyes of the Catholic youth, who swiftly anointed Gide the pope of literary Paris, the *NRF* emerged from the affair rechristened as the twentieth century's most *au courant* literary magazine.

Although Eliot had not yet arrived in Paris when Gide launched his campaign against Gourmont, the controversy it precipitated was instrumental in creating the "diverse atmosphere of opinions" that he recalled experiencing in 1910 Paris. "Anatole France and Remy de Gourmont," he remarked in his April 1934 *Criterion* editorial, "still exhibited their learning [in 1910], and provided types of scepticism for younger men to be attracted by and to repudiate."[21] It also seems likely that Eliot acquired a copy of Gide's article from one of these young men, perhaps from Fournier, upon his arrival in Paris. When Gide asked Eliot to contribute to the *Revue* in 1921, he sent along a copy of his recent prose collection, *Morceaux choisis*, which included his 1910 attack on Gourmont. Eliot thanked Gide for sending the volume, adding that he had been familiar with some of the essays in it since 1910.[22] Most strikingly, the poetry Eliot wrote in his spiky Paris hand offers evidence to indicate that he read, or heard about, Gide's attack on Gourmont in 1910. Moving beyond Laforgue's and Gourmont's detached spiritual contemplations, and in line with Gide's dicta that poetry ought to tremble, to exhibit spiritual anguish, Eliot began to use suffering to animate the movements of his inner life during his student year in France. One Paris fragment, "The Little Passion, From 'An Agony in the Garret,'" takes pains to illustrate Passion in the Christian sense:

> Upon those stifling August nights
>   I know he used to walk the streets
> Now following the lines of lights
>   Or diving into dark retreats

Or following the lines of lights
And knowing well to what they lead:
To one inevitable cross
Whereon our souls are pinned, and bleed.[23]

The first stanza of "The Little Passion" follows the nocturnal wanderings of an unidentified man as he walks along the same path of streetlights and shadows that runs through "Rhapsody on a Windy Night." Unlike "Rhapsody," however, this poem has beams of light that intersect in the second stanza, casting "one inevitable cross" along the pavement. Through the lens of his own agony, the man sees his soul among many, crucified in a public square. This inevitable transfiguration of private experience into universal pain is effected in the movement from the personal "I" in the first stanza to the more inclusive "our" in the second. Having dismissed Paris as the turning point in Eliot's spiritual quest, it strikes Gordon as "curious that the path, which in other poems of this period is so tortuous, should lead, in [the] one case [of "The Little Passion"], directly to the Christian terminus."[24] The primacy that Gide accorded to suffering in the expression of the new religious tendency provides a missing context for Eliot's earliest, explicitly Christian poem.

Furthermore, the theme of spiritual communion by way of bodily pain provides a thematic bridge between Eliot's Paris fragments and his martyr poems of 1914–1915. Eliot's "The Burnt Dancer" (June 1914), for instance, turns pain into an art form. In the eyes of the voyeur-narrator, a moth dances around a ring of flame, reveling in its pain. Looking on, as Gordon has suggested, as if witnessing the expiation of a martyr, the narrator commands in French refrain: "O danse mon papillon noir!" before "[t]he patient acolyte of pain" extinguishes its desire, and its life, in the flame.[25] In "The Love Song of St. Sebastian" (July 1914), Eliot's saint imagines himself in the delight of self-torture, circling a lamp with blood in movements mirroring those of the singed moth in "The Burnt Dancer":

I would come with a lamp in the night
And sit at the foot of your stair;
I would flog myself until I bled,
And after hour on hour of prayer
And torture and delight
Until my blood should ring the lamp
And glisten in the light.

In addition to Mantegna's Ca d'Oro *St. Sebastian*, which Eliot saw during his tour of Italy in the summer of 1911 and later associated with this poem, Harvey Gross and Nancy Hargrove have both sourced Eliot's Sebastian to Gabriele d'Annunzio's mystery play, *Le Martyre de Saint Sébastien*, which debuted on 29 May 1911, in Paris's Théâtre du Châtelet.[26] D'Annunzio's *Saint Sébastian* brought together the collective talents of composer Claude Debussy, set and costume designer Léon Bakst, and the scantily clad dancer Ida Rubenstein in an unorthodox portrayal of the saint as a masochist, erotically aroused by the flow of his own blood. The diverse cultural atmosphere of 1910–1911, it seems, momentarily coalesced in Eliot's mind three years after his *annus mirabilis* in Europe to form "The Love Song of St. Sebastian." If, as Gordon has suggested, Eliot's martyr poems of 1914–1915 mark the beginning of his protracted and painstaking conversion to Anglo-Catholicism, this transformation began in 1910 Paris, with "The Little Passion," his first attempt to transcend private pain through its sublimation in Christianity's universal symbolism.

While the *NRF* put Eliot in contact with Catholic literature hot off the press, his tutorials with Fournier primed him in the literature that had put his generation in communion with their souls. Most notably, at Fournier's instigation, Eliot read Paul Claudel's early religious plays as well as Charles Péguy's *Le mystère et la charité de Jeanne d'Arc*, a verse play dramatizing the early spiritual life of France's patron saint. More than the combined weight of Claudel and Péguy, Fyodor Dostoevsky made a lasting impression on Eliot's moral imagination. Under Fournier's tutelage in Paris, Eliot read Victor Derély's translation of *Crime and Punishment*, as well as French translations of *The Idiot* and *The Brothers Karamazov*.[27] It was also likely at Fournier's suggestion that Eliot attended a performance of Jacques Copeau and Jean Croué's stage adaptation of this last novel, which debuted at the Théâtre des Arts on 6 April 1911.[28] Essential to his earliest reception of these novels, Eliot's French contemporaries, Gide recalled in 1922, conceived of Dostoevsky's Christianity in terms given to them by the late-nineteenth-century critic Melchior de Vogüé, as "*the religion of suffering.*"[29] In their own sins, Eliot's French contemporaries saw reflections of Rodion Raskolnikov's; they addressed their inner demons with the voice of Ivan Karamazov speaking to the devil. As John Pope first observed, Raskolnikov's comparison of his own spiritual ascendance to Jesus's raising of Lazarus likely inspired Eliot to contrast the spiritually fraught tragic hero of his 1911 "The Love Song of J. Alfred Prufrock" with the same Biblical figure.[30]

Although Dostoevsky's mark on Eliot became more and more pronounced as he moved toward religious conviction in the 1920s and 1930s, the novelist who most impressed him in 1910–1911 was the Russian's French disciple Charles-Louis Philippe. In December 1909, at the age of thirty-five, Philippe succumbed to typhoid fever at the Velpeau hospital in Paris,[31] and was swiftly sainted in Dostoevsky's religion of suffering by the French literary elite. "Charles-Louis Philippe," Marcel Ray eulogized in a memorial number of the *NRF* issued in February 1910, "knew very young the law of poverty, which is to suffer. [H]e quickly learned to live far away from others, and to suffer more than they did. . . ." Philippe, Ray continued, "always had in view the portrait of Dostoevsky, whom he had chosen as master of suffering; and under the portrait, on a white banner, which he remade each time he moved house, he had written this thought of his master: 'To whom it hath been given to suffer, he it is who deserveth greater suffering.'"[32] Philippe himself affirmed his faith in Dostoevsky's religion of suffering in a letter to his childhood friend Henri Vandeputte, published in the *NRF* in April 1911, and added, "I also look at a portrait of Dante, with sunken lips and lines full of bitterness, and [feel] that he has also suffered. He is an old friend of misery. He was much greater than I, but he is my brother."[33] After establishing his place in a confraternity of suffering that included Dostoevsky and Dante, Philippe told his friend, "I am working on my novel about prostitution, about which I have already spoken to you. My chap is walking along the Boulevard Sébastapol, in the wee hours of the morning, and misfortune is about to come upon him."[34] Philippe's novel about prostitution appeared in 1901 as *Bubu de Montparnasse,* the book that made the single deepest impression on Eliot in Paris. "It was a good many years ago," he recalled in his 1932 preface to the English translation, "it was in the year 1910, that I first read *Bubu de Montparnasse,* when I first came to Paris. Read at an impressionable age, and under the impressive conditions, the book has always been for me, not merely the best of Charles-Louis Philippe's books, but a symbol of the Paris of that time."[35]

Although Eliot also read Philippe's *Marie Donadieu,*[36] *La Mère et L'Enfant,* and his *Lettres de Jeunesse* as they appeared serially in the *NRF* during his Parisian sojourn, none of these activated his moral imagination as much as *Bubu.* As well as pointing out numerous verbal echoes and intertextual references between Philippe's novels and "Preludes," "Rhapsody on a Windy Night," and "Prufrock," Grover Smith has suggested that *Bubu*'s broader presence in Eliot's imagination extends to "the atmosphere of loneliness, demimondaine sterility, and cultural desolation. . . . The memories, the sights of street-lamps in iron rows, the glimpse of a woman in a doorway, the awareness of smells—all came from the novel. . . ."[37] Hargrove has most recently reaffirmed Smith's now standard view that Philippe showed Eliot "new possibilities for using materials from the urban metropolis, for portraying characters from the lower spectrum of the human race, and for the creation of atmosphere, mood, and color from the underside of the urban world."[38] Indeed, the prepared faces, faint odor of stale beer, indifferent passersby, cheap hotels, rancid butter, and innumerable other sordid images undoubtedly flowed from Philippe's world to color the gray atmosphere of Eliot's Paris poetry. Critical focus on Philippe's decadent imagery, however, has eclipsed the novel's more substantive moral intent, which Eliot himself emphasized in his preface: "[E]ven the most virtuous," he affirmed, "in reading it, may feel: I have sinned exceedingly in thought, word and deed."[39]

More than a portrait of metropolitan decadence, *Bubu* tells the redemptive tale of a prostitute's spiritual salvation. The novel opens on the

Boulevard Sébastapol, the evening of Bastille Day. As the celebrations die with the setting sun, they leave behind the dingy residue of the holiday as the night comes to life and street-walkers ply their trade.[40] Twenty-year-old Pierre Hardy, on his way home from the office, meets the lust and din of the boulevard's "Babel-like confusion."[41] The following day, Pierre returns to the boulevard, where he meets the "weak" and "gentle" Berthe Méténier.[42] The story then follows Berthe to her rented room on the rue Malebranche, where her husband and pimp, Maurice Bélu, known on the streets as Bubu, awaits Pierre's five francs. As day attempts to enter Berthe and Maurice's hotel room the following morning, the soiled décor of their rented home brings to light the corruption of their shady souls, from their dirty windowpanes and furnishings "corroded by vice" to the impress of brownish sweat on their bed, indicating that their "bodies are dirty and the souls are as well."[43] With the world around them in decay, Berthe tells her husband that she has contracted syphilis. An enraged Maurice takes the previous night's five francs to a sidewalk café on the Avenue du Maine, where he encounters his syphilitic friend, Grand Jules. Believing themselves superior to all other beings, Grand Jules and Maurice sip absinth and judge passersby. Here, and throughout, Philippe attributes a dual significance to his characters, who play out the stories of their lives unaware that their creator has cast them in Biblical roles, in a modern-day retelling of man's Fall and salvation. "It was like the day of the Creation," Philippe explains, allegorically transplanting Maurice and Grand Jules from Paris into the Garden of Eden, "when Adam, the king of the world, sat at the foot of an oak and watched the animals pass, and scrutinized them and gave them names."[44] As Maurice and Grand Jules consume rounds of absinthe, the knowledge of good and evil seeps into their minds just as it did into Adam's after the Fall:

> Walking beside Grand Jules down the Avenue du Maine, Maurice had recovered his virile faith, and he walked, relishing in his consciousness all good and all evil. The knowledge of evil is as good as a good fruit on the dusty road, and helps us to walk between the pox and prison, like great travellers without hypocrisy and without fear. The absinthe stirred this knowledge, shook it, with fever and happiness, in the brain.[45]

With these biblical parallels established, Maurice's mind wanders to a common song he had heard many years before, the lyrics of which Philippe borrowed from Dostoevsky: "To whom it hath been given to suffer, he it is who deserveth greater suffering."[46]

Even as the knowledge of good and evil sets into Maurice's consciousness, events are in motion to bring about Berthe's salvation. While Maurice stumbles homeward, Pierre visits his "somewhat dogmatic" friend Louis Buisson in his fifth-floor room on the Quai du Louvre, which, by contrast to Maurice and Berthe's, he keeps clean and simply furnished "in the image of his own soul."[47] Pierre tells his friend that Berthe has been hospitalized, and Louis urges him to save her. Pierre sees Berthe through convalescence and, at least temporarily, frees her of Maurice's servitude. Several nights later, at another sidewalk café, Louis convinces Pierre that to rescue Berthe, he must save her soul:

> I am reading the Gospels. One night, Jesus went up to the Garden of Olives with His disciples. It was a night like these Paris nights when we know that pleasure is evil because men put into it no love. He looked over Jerusalem where harlots and debauchery clashed like evil weapons which slay you so that you may forget. . . . He mounted to the Garden of Olives to say to His apostles: "I am Love. Let us meditate up there and keep watch, on the eve of my death. . . . And to-morrow, when I shall be dead upon the tree, you will set forth into the world and you will say: 'Love is born and we have come to bear the glad tidings.'" Then He went and prayed for a long while. . . . [In the course of prayer, He asks His Father,] "If the best succumb, if the good are too frail for the Good Word, why then did You send me? There is not enough human warmth. I have preached burning love and my poor love is about to die."
>
> And I thought of Berthe, Pierre, because of what Jesus said in the Garden of Olives. Christ, on His last day, may have wept, but the Good Word is still alive. . . . [T]he Spirit is strong if the Flesh is weak. . . . And we, my friend, we have been found by a prostitute. . . . I do not know if we can save her, but I know that there are no limits to the Good Word. If we fail, my brother, let us console ourselves with the thought that we will have cast a little light into her soul and, for all we know, we may have been the beginning of her salvation.[48]

Over the course of months, Pierre shepherds Berthe toward God, addressing her in several passages as if from upon a pulpit. One of these sermons, about sin and resurrection, extends so far beyond Pierre's grasp of language that Philippe interjects to clarify: "This is not how Pierre spoke, this is not how Berthe heard him speak, but these words dominated the atmosphere around their heads and passed over them like a breath higher than their human words."[49] The good words that communicate before Berthe or Pierre understands them emphasize the necessity of their suffering to the course of resurrection:

> If your pain be great, act so that your pain be beautiful, bow your head like a good angel beneath the Justice of God, then raise your head and smile at your brother Satan. . . . And I say to you: you must forget [Maurice] because he has poured the abominations of the males upon your head, but I kneel at your feet and I beseech you, if that man be wounded, go and staunch his blood. Say to him: "I think of you who are in the pit of hell, and I send you my breath to cool the flames." And because there will be a day of resurrection, because the torments are not everlasting, on that day you will raise your brow, and you will answer: "I was a sister of charity, and I dressed your wounds. I am a

woman whom you wounded, and who wishes to live. If you are healed, I am a woman who wishes to live, and to be healed, and who knows you no more."[50]

Over Berthe and Pierre looms the understanding of desire as a residual manifestation of Satan's temptation embodied in their flesh. The body suffers the burden of original sin as the soul labors to transcend physical desire. Those who seek salvation, Philippe's sermon suggests, submit themselves to their afflictions because "there will be a day of resurrection, because torments are not everlasting."

Berthe finally finds her salvation through tragedy. When her father dies, the shame of her profession overwhelms her, and the pain of it guides her to the divine light. Berthe feels her father's eternal reproach, Philippe explains, setting her spiritual revelation against the fabric of Dostoevsky's *Crime and Punishment*, "as one is frightened in sleep by nightmares, by remorse, when the obscurity is thick and heavy, after the *crime*, like a *punishment*. . . . That night was her salvation."[51] Berthe's suffering transforms her: through it she "was illuminated, Mary Magdalen, and when she stood up to dry her wet face, it seemed to her that her heart was lit with the primal light. . . . She perceived all this without fully grasping it, but her soul was refreshed as after eating fruit. Alleluiah, the angels sang!"[52] While Maurice ultimately comes in the middle of the night to return Berthe to prostitution, Pierre manages to put some light into her soul.

In large measure as a result of *Bubu*'s Christian implications, the Catholic youth took Philippe as one of their masters. In the January 1910 *Phalange*, Valéry Larbaud remarked that the new generation had already cast Philippe in a Christian light before he was laid to rest:

> I know that Philippe was fairly indifferent to religious practices and dogma, and that he was only a Christian by temperament. And yet, listening to the august Latin words pronounced [during the oration of his funeral] by the young men of France and in looking back on my friend's life, I could not stop myself from thinking about this fundamental and terrible division: The *Enfants du Siècle* and the *Enfants de la Lumière*.[53]

In its memorial issue the following month, and repeatedly throughout 1910, the *NRF* promoted Philippe as a pillar of Catholic virtue. "[T]here was a place in [Philippe's] heart," Maurice Beaubourg assured readers of the review, "for more than a paragon of evangelical virtue. . . . There are, in his work," he pointed out, "admirable sermons."[54] Above the gray streets of *Bubu*'s world, Beaubourg continued, loomed "the evangelical soul, the soul of profound charity and comprehension of Charles-Louis Philippe."[55] Philippe's "sense of justice" in *Bubu*, Michel Arnault affirmed, "convinces us that these brutes are our brothers, and that their acts are made of the substance of our desires."[56] Paul Souday reminded readers of *Le Temps* in June 1911 that Philippe had "Catholic impulses," adding that "the soul was always the essential matter" to Philippe.[57] At the *Salon d'Automne*, on 5 November 1910, Gide gave a memorial lecture in which he announced the serial publication of Philippe's letters to Vandeputte in the *NRF*. Gide told his Grand-Palais audience that in these letters, he heard the voice of Dostoevsky echoing behind Philippe's.[58] Drawing on this correspondence, Gide solidified martyrdom within the Catholic movement for the author of *Bubu*:

> Anatole France is delightful, [Gide quoted Philippe from December 1897] he knows everything, he expresses everything, he is erudite even: it is because of this that he belongs to a race of writers nearing its end, it is in this way that he is the conclusion of nineteenth-century literature. Now, we need barbarians. We need writers who have lived close to God without having studied him in books. . . . The time of gentle dilettantism is over. Today begins the time of passion. . . . I do not know who among us will be a great writer, but I do know that we belong to the race being born, that we will each be minor prophets who foresee Christ's coming just before he arrives, and already preach his doctrine.[59]

Philippe's discovery of Dostoevsky, Gide further suggested, led him to this revelation. "I read Dostoevsky's *The Idiot*," Gide quoted Philippe, "and there was the work of a barbarian." With this philosophy as his inspiration, Gide concluded, Philippe wrote *Bubu de Montparnasse*.[60]

While *Bubu*'s Christian undertones were drawn to the surface in the Parisian little reviews and dailies, and by Gide's public lecture, conversations Eliot had with Verdenal gave them particular poignancy for him. At the time of his death, Verdenal's library contained numerous tomes illustrating the generational shift from skepticism to Catholicism in French literature, including, among others, Renan's *La Vie de Jésus*, ten volumes of Anatole France's writings, various volumes by Baudelaire, Laforgue's *Poésies*, Gide's *La Porte Étroite* and *Isabelle*, Claudel's *L'Annonce Faite à Marie*, and Charles-Louis Philippe's *La Mère et l'Enfant*.[61] Verdenal's extant letters to Eliot suggest that he navigated Eliot's spiritual course through French literature just as Louis Buisson led Pierre Hardy to the Gospels. In early July 1911, Verdenal declared in his first epistle to Eliot, who was then in Munich, that "[t]he will to live is evil, a source of desires and suffering," and then immediately turned to Philippe: "I have just read—only last evening—*Mother and Child* by Philippe," Verdenal told Eliot, "what a good and beautiful book; as wholesome as bread and milk, without artifice or rhetoric."[62] As soon as Eliot returned to Paris, in September 1911, he acquired his own copy of *La Mère et l'Enfant*.[63] The next letter Verdenal sent to Eliot in Munich, around Bastille Day 1911, suggests that Philippe's correlation of sexual desire and the Fall of man in *Bubu*, his association between Berthe's suffering and her salvation, featured centrally in discussions of their own spirituality. With emotional waltzes still ringing in his ears and patriotic rosettes still lining the streets, Verdenal described Paris on the evening of 14 July 1911 in terms redolent of Philippe's boulevard Sébastapol, in the wake of Bastille Day 1902:

> [T]he evening is filled with an ever-mounting sensual excitement; sweat makes the girls' hair stick to their temples; lottery wheels spin; a merry-go-round, attractively lit and alluring, also revolves, and with every jerk of the wooden horses, the whores brace their supple busts and a shapely leg can be glimpsed through the slit of a "fashionably split skirt"; a heavy, sensuous gust flows warmly by. [64]

"All of this outward demonstration corresponds, without doubt" Verdenal went on, "to the present dominant tendency among the Parisian populace." While positivism had spread through society, Verdenal observed, an elite aspired toward a higher ideal, which, he explained, "frequently takes the form of a return to Christianity, whether Catholic or Galilean and evangelical." Verlaine, Huysmans, Barrès, Francis Jammes, Péguy, Bourget, Claudel, Le Cardonnel, and many others, Verdenal told Eliot, exhibit innumerable manifestations of this tendency. "The main thing is to say, in the case of each," he specified emphatically, *"how far he can influence our inner life towards the knowledge of the supreme good."* Pierre Hardy's path from the dark, desire-laden boulevard Sébastapol to the Church continued to inform Verdenal and Eliot's correspondence, right up to their final exchange. Eliot's somewhat dogmatic friend ended his final surviving letter in prayer: "I wish you," Verdenal told him, "for the coming year, an oft-renewed ardour—ardour, flame—but its source is in the heart, and here it is that our wishes must be prudent. 'Bring good upon me, O Lord, whether I ask for it or not, and remove evil from me, even though I ask for it.'" [65]

Eliot left evidence littered throughout his poetry notebook to suggest that the sins of Philippe's characters weighed heavily on his mind in Paris. The original notebook draft of "Rhapsody on a Windy Night," dated March 1911, for instance, describes the moon's craters as "hideous scars of a washed out pox," "pox" being the colloquialism Maurice and Grand Jules use to discuss syphilis at the street café. Another draft fragment, dated the same month, portrays the Absolute sitting inside the geometric net of a "syphilitic spider." Yet more plainly, Philippe's moral signature appears in Eliot's notebook draft of "Preludes." An epigraph to section III, added in July 1911, establishes a spiritual correspondence between the poem he was writing and *Bubu de Montparnasse:* "'Son âme de petite putain': Bubu." As Christopher Ricks has pointed out, rather than direct quotation, Eliot's epigraph compresses numerous lines, paraphrased from Philippe's novel, including perhaps *"un sourire de pauvre petite putain"* and *"ses histoires de pauvre petite putain."* [66] That Eliot interjected *"son âme"* into these phrases suggests that he recognized, along with his French contemporaries, that the soul was always the essential matter for Philippe. In taking this modified expression as an epigraph, Eliot ascribes an obvious, yet rarely emphasized, religious connotation to "Preludes." Whereas Laforgue's "Prelude" failed to transcend skepticism, Eliot's "Preludes" take the disorder and mystery of life and suffering to illustrate the corrosion of souls. This spiritual dimension is best illustrated in the fourth prelude, where a man's soul suffers public crucifixion in a manner redolent of "The Little Passion." As evening falls, "His soul [is] stretched tight across the skies." Testing the prophetic role with momentary confidence, as Gordon has suggested,[67] a lone conscience rises omnisciently above the passersby to declare at the poem's end,

> I am wrought by various fancies, curled
> Around these images, which cling—
> The notion of some infinitely gentle
> Infinitely suffering thing.

"Thing," as Gordon observes, "is not a casual word for an articulate poet. Whatever it is," she rightly concludes, "transcends the limitations of language in the same manner as 'Silence'. . . ."[68]

While the cancelled epigraph to "Preludes" provides the clearest evidence that *Bubu* left its moral impress on Eliot's creative mind, Philippe's correlations between Maurice and Adam, between Berthe and Mary Magdalene, between the temptation of his characters and original sin, all intensify J. Alfred Prufrock's tortured negotiations between what he believes and what he desires. More than any other persona Eliot imagined before or after, Prufrock has a mind to conceive, and the sensibilities to feel, the mystery of life and suffering. As Prufrock listens to the women converse in an adjacent room, he hears "voices dying with a dying *fall*"[69] and then imagines himself "pinned and wriggling on the wall" like the crucified souls in "The Little Passion" and the fourth "Prelude." "Prufrock's Pervigilium" has Eliot's tragic hero wander out into the narrow streets, where he sees women of Berthe's trade, "spilling out of corsets" as they stand in the doorways of "evil houses leaning all together." Prufrock feels these brothels point "a ribald finger at [him] in the darkness." While characteristic inaction prevents him from crossing the threshold, into Berthe and Maurice's world, the streets nevertheless "follow" him, as Robert Crawford has pointed out, so that he "carries his streets with him."[70] The desire Prufrock cannot outrun makes him a part of Philippe's demimonde; Philippe's streets are in part made of Prufrock's desires. While Prufrock was as spiritually conflicted as Eliot in 1911, both began to conceive of their inner life in Christian terms.

The Catholic poetry, plays, and novels Eliot discovered in the *NRF*, and in discussion with Fournier and Verdenal, led him away from Symbolism's vague spirituality in the direction of the Church. Although Eliot was decades away from resolving his debate between body and soul in Christianity, Catholic Paris in general, and Philippe in particular, taught him that "ultimately [what] matters is the salvation of the individual soul." Eliot's allusions to the Catholic literature he read in France, especially to *Bubu de Montparnasse*, necessarily import some of a hitherto underemphasized religious context into his Paris poetry. Their presence adds a substantial, though often dismissed, layer of subtext to his early, more spiritually conflicted verse, and helps to substantiate the literary foundation of his later, more religious meditations.

NOTES

1. All translations are my own, unless otherwise indicated. Here, I have relied heavily on Peter Dale's translation, *Poems of Jules Laforgue* (London: Anvil, 2001).
2. Eliot, *The Varieties of Metaphysical Poetry*, ed. Ronald Schuchard (New York: Harcourt, 1993), 283. Cited hereafter as *VMP*.
3. Lyndall Gordon, *T. S. Eliot: An Imperfect Life* (New York: Norton, 2000), 49, and Ronald Schuchard, *Eliot's Dark Angel* (Oxford: Oxford University Press, 1999), 121, have both observed the religious significance of "Silence."
4. Gordon, *T. S. Eliot*, 49, 61, and 54.
5. Eliot, "A Commentary," *The Criterion* 13 (April 1934): 453.
6. R. C. Grogin, *Bergsonian Controversy in France* (Calgary: University of Calgary Press, 1988), 139.
7. Henri Massis and Alfred de Tarde, *Les jeunes gens d'aujourd'hui*, ed. Jean-Jacques Becker (Paris: Imprimerie Nationale, 1995), 105.
8. Massis and Tarde, *Les jeunes*, 107.
9. Jacques Copeau, "L'Enquête d'Agathon sur 'Les jeunes gens d'aujourd'hui,'" *NRF* (November 1912): 929–35.
10. Massis and Tarde, *Les jeunes*, 122.
11. Massis and Tarde, *Les jeunes*, 122.
12. Massis and Tarde, *Les jeunes*, 122.
13. Massis and Tarde, *Les jeunes*, 254.
14. André Gide, "L'Amateur de M. Remy de Gourmont," *NRF* (April 1910): 430.
15. Gide, "L'Amateur," 431.
16. Gide, "L'Amateur," 431.
17. Maaike Koffeman, *Entre Classicisme et Modernité* (Amsterdam and New York: Rodopi, 2003), 158.
18. Claudel to Gide, *Correspondance 1899–1926*, ed. R. Mallet. (Paris: Gallimard, 1949), 192; quoted in Koffeman, *Entre Classicisme et Modernité*, 158.
19. Koffeman, *Entre Classicisme et Modernité*, 157–59.
20. Jean Royère, "Remy de Gourmont et André Gide," *Phalange* (20 October 1910): 372.
21. Eliot, "A Commentary," 451.
22. Eliot to Gide, *The Letters of T. S. Eliot*, vol. 1, second ed., ed. Valerie Eliot and Hugh Haughton (New York: Harcourt, 2009), 615. Cited hereafter as *L1*.
23. There are two extant versions of "The Little Passion." Observing that the loose draft is written in Eliot's spiky Paris hand, Gordon concludes, rightly, I believe, that he drafted the version quoted above in Paris and copied the revision into his notebook in 1914 or 1915 (*T. S. Eliot*, 60 and 539).
24. Gordon, *T. S. Eliot*, 61.
25. Gordon, *T. S. Eliot*, 88.
26. Harvey Gross, "The Figure of St. Sebastian," in *T. S. Eliot: Essays from the Southern Review*, ed. James Olney (Oxford: Clarendon Press, 1988) and Chapter 5 of Nancy

Hargrove, *T. S. Eliot's Parisian Year* (Tallahassee: University Press of Florida, 2009), 114–24.

27. John Pope, "Prufrock and Roskolnikov Again: A Letter from Eliot," *American Literature* 18 (January 1947): 320.

28. See Eliot, *The Letters of T. S. Eliot: Vol. 1, 1898–1922*, ed. Valerie Eliot (San Diego: Harcourt Brace Jovanovich, 1988), 25. Cited hereafter as *L1*, 26. For a more detailed account of Copeau and Croué's *The Brothers Karamazov*, and its 1911 reception, see Hargrove, *T. S. Eliot's Parisian Year*, 111–14.

29. André Gide, *Dostoevsky* (London: J. M. Dent and Sons, 1925), 40.

30. For a detailed comparison of Prufrock's and Raskolnikov's Lazarus, see Peter Lowe, "Prufrock in St. Petersburg: The Presence of Dostoevsky's *Crime and Punishment* in T. S. Eliot's 'The Love Song of J. Alfred Prufrock,'" *Journal of Modern Literature* 28 (2005): 16–22.

31. André Gide, *Journals: 1889–1913*, trans. Justin O'Brien (New York: Alfred A. Knopf, 2000), 242.

32. Marcel Ray, "L'Enfance et la Jeunesse de Charles-Louis Philippe," *NRF* (February 1910): 169–70.

33. Charles-Louis Philippe to Henri Vandeputte, "Lettres de Jeunesse de Charles-Louis Philippe," *NRF* (April 1911): 604.

34. Philippe to Vandeputte, 27 November 1899, "Lettres de Jeunesse."

35. T. S. Eliot, Preface to *Bubu of Montparnasse*, by Charles-Louis Philippe (New York: Avon, 1948), 3.

36. "It will be a very interesting experience to read this book again, because I have not read it since 1911, at a period when the works of Philippe made a very deep impression upon me." Eliot, *Inventions of the March Hare: Poems 1909–1917*, ed. Christopher Ricks (New York: Harcourt, 1996), 407.

37. Quoted in Hargrove, *T. S. Eliot's Parisian Year*, 16.

38. Hargrove, *T. S. Eliot's Parisian Year*, 16.

39. Eliot, Preface to *Bubu of Montparnasse*, 6–7.

40. Philippe, *Bubu*, 14 and 92. All excerpts from *Bubu* are from the 1948 English edition that included Eliot's preface. The translator is unknown.

41. Philippe, *Bubu*, 20–22.

42. Philippe, *Bubu*, 28.

43. Philippe, *Bubu*, 49–51.

44. Philippe, *Bubu*, 55.

45. Philippe, *Bubu*, 59.

46. Philippe, *Bubu*, 61.

47. Philippe, *Bubu*, 65, 64.

48. Philippe, *Bubu*, 99–101.

49. Philippe, *Bubu*, 114.

50. Philippe, *Bubu*, 113–14.

51. Philippe, *Bubu*, 116. My emphasis.

52. Philippe, *Bubu*, 119.

53. Valéry Larbaud, "Charles-Louis Philippe: In Memoriam," *Phalange* (January 1910): 13.

54. Maurice Beaubourg, "Notes," *NRF* (February 1910): 293.

55. Beaubourg, "Notes," 293.

56. Michel Arnault, "L'Oeuvre de Charles-Louis Philippe," *NRF* (February 1910): 146.

57. Paul Souday, "Charles-Louis Philippe: *La Mère et l'Enfant*," *Le Temps*, 29 June 1911.

58. Gide, *Charles-Louis Philippe* (Paris: Éditions Athéna, 1922), 10.

59. Quoted in Gide, *Charles-Louis Philippe*, 13.

60. Gide, *Charles-Louis Philippe*, 14.

61. Claudio Perinot, "Jean Verdenal: T. S. Eliot's French Friend," *Annali di Cà Foscari* 35 (1996): 265–75.

62. Verdenal to Eliot, July 1911, *L1*, 22. Mrs. Eliot's translation.

63. An inscription on the title page of his copy of Philippe's *La Mère et l'Enfant*, held in the T. S. Eliot Bequest at Harvard's Houghton Library, reads "T. S. Eliot Paris September 1911."

64. Jean Verdenal to T. S. Eliot, mid-July 1911, *L1*, 24. Mrs. Eliot's translation.

65. Jean Verdenal to T. S. Eliot, 26 December 1912, *L1*, 34.

66. Eliot, *Inventions of the March Hare*, 336.

67. Lyndall Gordon, *T. S. Eliot*, 70

68. Lyndall Gordon, *T. S. Eliot*, 70.

69. My emphasis.

70. Robert Crawford, *The Savage and the City* (Oxford: Oxford University Press, 1987), 30.

FOUR

Eliot and Maurras on Classicism

William Marx

If we want to understand how and why classicism could become such a key concept for T. S. Eliot's criticism, we must absolutely go back to the origins of this concept, that is to French literature and especially to one of the main defenders of classicism in the twentieth century, Charles Maurras. Then we shall see that there was at least as much difference between Eliot's and Maurras's classicisms as between Anglo-Catholicism and Roman Catholicism.

CLASSICISM AND AVANT-GARDES:
FIGHTING FOR THE SAME THING

From the end of the nineteenth century right up until the 1930s, classicism was pervasive in French literature: Symbolism had at last buried in its ruins the romantic ideal of poetry, an event that effectively ushered in a forty-year stretch during which the palpable and pressing need to re-found literature was felt with particular intensity by writers. The term *re-found* implies obviously an act of *foundation*, but the *re* is no less essential. On the side of *foundation*, of *tabula rasa*, of the opening onto unexplored possibilities, we can find all the avant-garde movements: *Dada* and the *surrealists* of course, but also those who went before them, like the *naturalists* and the *unanimists*. On the side of the *re-founding*, or of returns, that is to say of the meter's reset to zero, we find classicism or neoclassicism, or even (as they preferred their movement to be called) the classical renaissance (*renaissance classique*). So despite appearances, the avant-garde and the militants for the cause of classicism were waging the same battle

77

against the normal course of literary history, which, it was assumed, had ended in failure. In other words, both demonstrated a will to turn the tide of history and to move it in unexpected directions.

In order to do this, two methods presented themselves as the most plausible. The first, which was apparently the simplest and the most direct, consisted of promoting radical novelty, which the avant-garde readily and constantly did. It is worth noting here that surrealism dominated other progressive movements by advocating the non-sequitur or incongruity as a figure of reference, both of which became the very basis of the history avant-gardists wanted and even attempted to provoke. In other words this type of history would advance by breaks and ruptures, and in so doing would connect instant t and instant $t + 1$ with about as little harmony as that which exists between an umbrella and a sewing machine lying on a dissection table (to take a famous surrealist simile). The surrealist had to "break up the derisory sequence of facts" (*La Révolution d'abord et toujours!*). So the surrealist praise for chance and for non-premeditation implied in and of itself a vision of literary history as an anarchic and disordered succession of coincidences.

The second method of circumventing the normal course of literary history was perhaps no less efficient: it consisted of simply inverting the direction of history and having it make a U-turn. Because the future is always suspected of having sprung from the present that precedes it, it does not replace the present so much as it completes it or is the product of it. The future is not newness. Only that which could never, in any situation, arise from the present is truly, radically *new.* So what could be less susceptible to having sprung from the present than that which long ago produced the present, that is to say, the past, and especially the distant past? Only the past possesses integral alterity and only the past is guaranteed to have no common ground with the present and only the past supposes a complete rupture with the expected march of history. Radical newness is inherent to the past and only to the past. Obviously, this implies a departure from history, and of the game, and it requires a denial of the succession of time in the name of a lost paradise to be regained.

THE ANTISYMBOLIST CLASSICISM OF MAURRAS

It is upon this paradox that the classical renaissance movement was founded at the dawn of the twentieth century. This movement's conception of history had as small a dialectical element as possible. They saw in historical processes no system, no hidden logic, no constrained development at all: as with the avant-gardes, it was the triumph of chance, which was in itself the defining condition of a resurrection of the past. "All of history," writes Charles Maurras in his *Enquête sur la monarchie*, "is a succession of accidents, all of it uncoordinated if you only look to the next instant: only the whole has any rigor, but it can only be seen from afar. For future events, expected or unexpected, we can only predict the unpredictable."[1] This last sentence strikes a resoundingly surrealist note: rigor from afar, anarchy up close. But even the rigor of the whole had moments of weakness, when everything could be overturned. It is in these moments that anything and everything becomes possible and that unexpected developments, apparently inexorable progressions, hopes, and fears that are formed according to the best evidence invert to become their exact opposite.[2] The only philosophy of history that was openly supported by the classical renaissance was the system of nudging, of an impulse that, no matter how slight, could at the right moment change the course of history (or even reverse its direction) in a way that was entirely unpredictable.

That was the only lesson to be gained from history: the disproportion of cause and effect and the importance of *kairos*, in Greek, or, in Latin, of "*junctura rerum*, the joint where the bone structure, which is rigid in every other part, bends, the place where the driving force behind action will engage."[3]

The classical renaissance, which rigorously applied these principles, arrived in the nick of time in a history that was in the process of being toppled: the transformation of symbolism into something that had not yet been defined and for which it was so well timed to fashion the new traits. Two troubling facts show how much the period under consideration was unstable from an aesthetic point of view. First, the ease with which writers changed camps: it was thus the case with the author of the first manifesto of symbolism, Jean Moréas, who, in a few short years, became the primary model of neoclassicism by founding the *École romane*. Such a rapid shift, between 1886 and 1891, illustrates the remarkable mobility of the actors of literary history. This mobility is largely due to the fact that positions were not yet fixed *ad æternitatem*: there was still room for movement.

Nearly twenty years later, history was destined to repeat itself in an even more dramatic fashion: two diverging opinions, this time not within the same person at a few years' interval, but within the same review at the same time. I am referring to the famous anecdote of the bungled start of *La Nouvelle Revue française* in 1908, whose inaugural issue contained an attack against Mallarmé. Beyond the question of Mallarmé himself, the debate was in reality about the place that should be reserved for Symbolism within the *NRF*: was the review going to assume its symbolist heritage or was it to take up the banner of newness, so clearly advertised in its title, through the refusal of symbolism, which had become rather cumbersome? In 1909, when the review started again, the question had been resolved: the complex and ambiguous classicism defended by the *NRF* saw in Symbolism a useful experiment, one which had been worth trying and from which much could be learned. This was to be Albert Thibaudet's position as well as Paul Valéry's.

On the other side, there was ultra-classicism, defended by the neoclassicists, a movement that entered a golden age between 1908 and 1914.[4] This classicism was founded on a single hypothesis, namely that Symbolism had failed. But regardless of whether Symbolism had failed for some or, for others, had left a viable heritage, it did not keep the *NRF* and the neoclassicists from coming together to form a demanding principle: go beyond the symbolist moment and profit from the historical opportunity afforded by *junctura rerum*, in order to propose another way of making literature, a way that, at the *NRF* as well as for the neoclassicists, allied intellectual reforms with formal constraints. Both ways clearly departed from the aspirations of Symbolism.

On the other hand, what distinguished neoclassicism from the *NRF* was the former's steadfast refusal to progress and take part in the period's advances in literature: all things classical are located outside of history and represent a kind of Eden beyond ages and places. As Maurras put it, "there are works written for all cultivated men from all countries and all times. There are works that pass above the differences between nations and civilizations, go straight to the heart of our hearts and to the heart of human reason."[5] These were classical works, existing beyond all "local color" and beyond all "historical traits."[6]

THE PARADOXES OF MAURRASSIAN CLASSICISM

Classicism thus introduced the question of uchronia and of utopia. But how can you be of no specific time nor of any specific place? One can easily grasp the desperate nature of such a goal, especially for the French neoclassicist, the member of *Action Française*, for example, who wanted to be French and who wanted to be so purely and unequivocally, but who also wanted to be universal and recognized everywhere, tasted and loved in all climates. Both entrenched and universal, the neoclassicism of the twentieth century had thus all the defining characteristics of a chimera and of a specifically French chimera, one whose roots lay in the Revolutionary spirit and in the providential identity of nation and reason: from the wars of the Revolution right up to contemporary debates about secularism—passing along the way through the challenges posed by colonization—the successive incarnations of the French Republic are perpetually imprisoned by this dilemma, pulled between national singularity on the one side and the universality of their mission on the other. It might seem paradoxical that royalists would transpose this republican debate onto an aesthetic terrain, but it is only paradoxical on the surface of things. This paradox was founded upon the two camps' common (and wanton) admiration for Greece and for classical Greece in particular, with just one subtle but major difference: that Maurras returned from Athens convinced of the failure of the democratic model. That particular classical Greece was sadly no more, but the *translatio studii et imperii* gave cause for a certain kind of hope, namely that it could be reborn *hic et nunc* in France, in the middle of the twentieth century.

Along with the promotion of classicism came another development: mourning the past molted into a desire that was by definition unsatisfied. Because how could a love of the past create the future? How could one revive the lost object? Neoclassical literary criticism became at this point a kind of fiction and even a kind of compensatory fiction. Classicism is a novel, but it is a family novel in the way that Marthe Robert means, when the child imagines fabulous parents and substitutes for his real antecedents imaginary ones. Maurras' voyage to Greece thus became an occasion for a mythical reunion: a moment of exaltation on the Acropolis, an ode to Minerva, an embrace of columns, etc.[7] On the whole, these displays showed far too much disproportion for an adept of classicism.[8] As if this were not enough, this exaggerated love for Greece was as selective as it was incoherent: if Maurras only retained of ancient Greece the century of Pericles illustrated by Phidias, and if the least little archaism excited his disgust, that did not keep him from simultaneously praising Homeric poems, which were nonetheless far older.[9] Already a form of historical fiction, classicism also presented itself as an aesthetic fiction. Was it not aesthetic fiction for instance to blindly trust that seventeenth-century French tragedies were faithful in every way to the principles of Sophocles and Horace?[10] Of course Maurras could not have read the work of Jean-Pierre Vernant or of Pierre Vidal-Naquet, but Nietzsche at least could have helped him identify the Dionysian thread in Greek art and literature, a thread which was foreign, to the say the least, to Apollonian neoclassicism from the century of Louis XIV. It is precisely around this denial of differences that the image of classical permanence, existing above centuries and civilizations, was built. In the end, whether it be historical or aesthetic fiction, the ultraclassicism of the classical renaissance was above all a critical combat fiction, whose aim was essentially utilitarian, destined to reverse the course of a derailed literary history. The by-word was to *re-found*, whatever the cost.

ELIOT'S ANTI-NEOCLASSIC CLASSICISM

In these conditions, it is easy to see how an Anglo-American author like T. S. Eliot could adopt the slogans of the classical renaissance without a moment's hesitation despite the fact that they made little sense outside a French context or, at the very most, a Latin one: the claims to classicism should be considered more as the symptom of a crisis than as a literal vindication. By 1911, Eliot had read Maurras's *L'Avenir de l'intelligence*.[11]

And in 1916, during his course of evening classes on modern French literature, he expounded in great detail upon the ideas of Pierre Lasserre, whose work he recommended.[12] So Eliot's knowledge of the movement was both direct, because he spent the academic year 1910–1911 in France when the anti-romantic polemic was in full swing,[13] and indirect, through the works of Irving Babbitt and T. E. Hulme, who both imported the French debate into Anglophone countries. The concept of classicism nevertheless only found its true place in Eliot's work when he founded *The Criterion*, and especially from 1923 onward, when he entered into a debate on romanticism with John Middleton Murry and his review *The Adelphi*.[14] Whether in France or in England, classicism was born out of adversity. It was an ideal weapon or a perfect target for any review editor or party head. But very quickly, Eliot tried to work his way out of the trap he could well have fallen into with classicism, by explicitly and clearly distancing himself from the French classical renaissance movement. In 1924, he wrote in *The Criterion*,

> The weakness from which the classical movement in France has suf-
> fered is that it has been a critique rather than a creation; the movement
> may claim Paul Valéry, but that elusive genius will hardly allow itself
> to be placed. It would be as tenable, and as dubious, to claim James
> Joyce in England. Of both of these writers it may as cogently be said
> that they belong to a new age chiefly by representing, and perhaps
> precipitating, consummately in their different ways, the close of the
> previous epoch. Classicism is in a sense reactionary, but it must be in a
> profounder sense revolutionary.[15]

It would be difficult to demonstrate any greater opposition to the French neoclassicists, even allowing for the fact that Eliot placed Valéry within the classical renaissance: in France as well, critics like André Thérive were of a like mind.[16] But Joyce? It is difficult to see how Maurras could have accepted the Irish writer. Thus, unlike the French neoclassical devotees like Maurras, Eliot bestowed upon the term *classicism* a definition that was more abstract than properly historic:

> A new classical age will be reached when the dogma, or *ideology*, of the
> critics is so modified by contact with creative writing, and when the
> creative writers are so permeated by the new dogma, that a state of
> equilibrium is reached.
>   For what is meant by a classical movement in literature is surely a
> moment of *stasis*, when the creative impulse finds a form which satis-
> fies the best intellect of the time, a moment when a type is produced.[17]

Classicism was thus for Eliot a moment of equilibrium between the forces of negation and of return on the one hand, and the forces of creation ever pushing forward on the other: the *re* on one side, the *foundation* on the other. It had nothing to do with the simple resurrection of an aesthetic model or with the departure from history, as was the case in France.

The reason Eliot rejected Maurras's literal references to the Greek model and progressively cultivated a more "analogical" vision of classicism had certainly something to do with the fact that in England attacks against neoclassicism were becoming more pointed and precise.[18] In April of 1927, the shortlived review *The Calendar* had defined the movement as "the literary version of a reactionary Latin philosophy which is being adapted, in one or two English reviews, into a repressive instrument of literary criticism."[19] The allusions here to *Action Française* and to *The Criterion* are transparent. Of course Eliot responded immediately, first by denying (as he always did) any ties to neoclassicism:

> We have used, and shall continue to use the word "classicism", unsatisfactory as it is—to most people it connotes little more than alexandrine couplets, the painting of David, and the architecture of the Madeleine or possibly the British Museum. The term "neo-classicism" is not ours, and is not particularly commendable; for all "neos" indicate some fad or fashion of the moment, and it is not our concern to be fashionable.

Then the poet adopted a more defensive and personal tone:

> Those persons who find even a little stay and comfort in the word "classicism" are always at a disadvantage. If they confine themselves to criticism, they are reproached for their lack of creative power; if they do "create", and if (as is sure to happen) what they create bears little resemblance in form to the work of Racine, or Dr. Johnson or Landor, then it is immediately said that their precept and practice are utterly in divorce: for if you cannot deny that their creative work has merit you can always deny that it has any of the characteristics of "classicism."[20]

Almost imperceptibly Eliot changed interlocutors here: he was not so much talking to the progressive critics who reproached him for his reference to classicism, as to the neoclassical partisans themselves, who were forced to acknowledge an incomprehensible antinomy between Eliot's critical discourse, which raised high the banner of classicism, and his work, which was clearly of a modernist bent. Later on, Paul Elmer More would describe a "cleft Eliot," who surprised and disappointed all observers whatever their stripe.[21] Was it not true that, on the whole, the kaleidoscopic instants from *The Waste Land* made the poem more like a cubist painting than a landscape by Poussin? To defend himself (and in so doing to defend his poetry against his own critical principles) Eliot was obliged to elaborate on the concept of analogical classicism, which allowed him to save his works as a creative author.

He had to defuse, at all costs, the neoclassical time bomb which could at any moment ruin, not only his critical system but his poetical work as well. Since English literature, unlike French literature, left but a small, barely visible place for classicism, it was necessary to envisage it in a perspective that went well beyond simple aesthetics. In September of 1927, Eliot wrote:

"Neo-classicism" cannot have a definite meaning until "classicism" has a definite meaning. But there was never any age or group of people who professed "classicism" in the sense in which St. Thomas and his followers professed "Thomism". One of the points to be cleared up is this: whether the term "classicism" can be used in England as it can be used in France; and whether, in either country, it can be applied strictly to *literary* or *art* criticism; or whether it has meaning only in relation to a view of life as a whole.[22]

To the first question (can we use the term *classicism* in England as in France?) the response could only be affirmative if Eliot answered no to the second question (can it be restricted to a purely literary domain?) and yes to the last question (does it imply a generalized vision of existence?): if classicism was ever to be defended in England, a country that never really had a classical literature, there was no other choice but to make it imply a global perception of the world.

MAURRAS, THIBAUDET, ELIOT:
TOWARD A GENERALIZED CLASSICISM

The scene was thus set for Eliot's famous declaration in 1928, included as a preface to his collection of essays *For Lancelot Andrewes*, whose perspective he described in the following manner:

The general point of view may be described as classicist in literature, royalist in politics, and anglo-catholic in religion. I am quite aware that the first term is completely vague, and easily lends itself to clap-trap; I am aware that the second term is at present without definition, and easily lends itself to what is almost worse than clap-trap, I mean temperate conservatism; the third term does not rest with me to define. The uncommon reader who is interested by these scattered papers may possibly be interested by the small volumes which I have in preparation: *The School of Donne*; *The Outline of Royalism*; and *The Principles of Modern Heresy*.[23]

Critics glossed over this radical profession of faith for a long time. Preferring to associate it with Eliot's British naturalization and with his recent baptism into the Anglican Church, they saw it as the zealous expression of the newly converted. But just what kind of conversion to classicism could it possibly have been? On the contrary, writing in the same vein as his aforementioned critical comments, in this passage Eliot aimed above all to apply the *coup de grâce* to a term that had been a source of relentless embarrassment to him. Indeed, he was seeking here to drown classicism in political and religious categories which extended far beyond it. So, through a kind of conceptual dynamite, in an expansive description that conferred upon classicism all the traits of a *Weltanschauung*, Eliot effectively discarded a tool that had become too cumbersome, but which had nonetheless once allowed the critic to reshape his poetics along the lines of the French model.

What is even more fundamental (and striking) is the impertinence of the concepts put into play by this text, as it was already emphasized by the auto-deprecating commentary that immediately followed this abrupt profession of faith. And by impertinence, I do not mean the provocative value of the terms Eliot used, but rather the question itself of how these terms acquired, in their enunciative context (England of 1928), any value at all, whether it be provocative or not. The secret of this impertinence is of course that Eliot was dealing here with the pure and simple transposition of words which were proper to the *Action Française*: classicism, royalism, Catholicism were all slogans which could be taken up word for word by any French royalist supporter. But their trip across the Channel had erased their meaning: on British soil, classicism and royalism meant next to nothing; and as for Anglo-Catholicism, the point, of course, is that it was not Roman Catholicism.

It is thus no accident that Eliot found this triad not in Maurras's work, since Maurras never tried to systematize his doctrinal corpus,[24] but in Thibaudet's, either in a long article in the *NRF* from 1913 ("L'esthétique des trois traditions"), or in his monograph from 1920 on *The Ideas of Charles Maurras*.[25] For even though Thibaudet's analysis of Maurrassian classicism was somehow a benevolent one, there were many signs of a critical tone: he attacked radical neoclassicism, preferring instead a far more flexible definition of classicism, one that was more tendency than movement, such as the one proposed by Sainte-Beuve. He also finally refuted the hypothesis that a classical literature could "be born from another within the same language" in order to introduce the possibility — the only truly valid one in his eyes — of a "foreign classicism inspired by French classicism."[26] So what emerged from these crucial pages was the foundations of a program that Eliot would begin to develop in *The Criterion* from 1923 onward.

There are a number of points that Thibaudet's text and Eliot's thought had in common. When the former defined classicism less as an "integral accepted tradition" than as "a discernment, a choice, a deliberate consent,"[27] it is not hard to see a direct tie with an idea the latter would take up in 1919 in his article "Tradition and the Individual Talent." When Thibaudet defined classicism, in a falsely naïve fashion, as "the doctrine that allows us to class and that invites to class,"[28] one can only think of the manner in which Eliot spoke of tradition as "an ideal order" existing between works. Still more concretely, when Thibaudet announced that he would devote an essay to each term of the triad, Eliot for his part promised an entire book on each of them.[29]

However, tradition according to Eliot was not a mere copy of classicism according to Thibaudet. There was a fundamental difference that separated them: Eliot's classicism was always perceived more from the point of view of the creator than of the critic. So when Thibaudet wondered aloud if classical works are determined by the classical tradition that precedes them or if it is the other way around ("Is the line determined by the points or the points by the line?"), he was content to provide an ambiguous response: "One and the other, one like the other, obviously," which was hardly satisfying.[30]

The particular point of view Eliot enjoyed as a poet allowed him to resolve the contradiction of the hermeneutical circle more efficiently. For Eliot the problem posed by work and tradition, by the line and the point, was a false problem. It was necessary to go back further: it is the writer himself, an entity who exists before the work, who through his knowledge of the past and his creative conscience, creates order between works. Mind and writer thus become the crucible of order: it is not hard to see here the influence of Bradley's philosophy upon Eliot, a corpus that was in turn derived from Hegelian idealism. Classicism thus became in this context an ideal fiction with a utilitarian function. It was a field in perpetual redefinition and outside of which nothing valid could be formed and where not only the vision of the work was determined, but also its very being:

> The existing monuments form an ideal order among themselves, which is modified by the introduction of the new (the really new) work of art among them. The existing order is complete before the new work arrives; for order to persist after the supervention of novelty, the *whole* existing order must be, if ever so slightly, altered; and so the relations, proportions, values of each work of art toward the whole are readjusted; and this is conformity between the old and the new.[31]

What had emerged as a simple line in Thibaudet's theory thus became a three-dimensional space of an ideal nature in Eliot's. Within this space one can measure the breadth that separated the binary thought of someone like Maurras, which was based on oppositions as simple as *classicism* and *romanticism*, *acceptable* and *unacceptable*, and, across the divide, the complex architecture of literature as Eliot conceived of it, one that was endowed with a structure far more spatial than historical. It is this complexity that allowed him to consider as classical in their own way such unexpected authors as the metaphysical English poets, Baudelaire and Laforgue—or even Joyce and Lawrence.

From a historical classicism to a spatial one: that is how the mutation of the concept can be summed up, after its voyage across the Channel, a mutation parallel in many ways to the transformation of Roman Catholicism into Anglo-Catholicism. Maurras would most certainly not have recognized his own possession, because Eliot's classicism was fundamentally an anti-neoclassicism. Yet in Eliot's work, as in Maurras's, classicism was never anything more than a fiction: a historical fiction, a geographical fiction, an aesthetic fiction and a conceptual fiction. In a word, it was a critical fiction. But it was also a useful fiction and perhaps even a necessary one. In general, what is history itself but a mental object? In a moment of crisis or in an impasse—and what a crisis it was, that of modernity and postsymbolism—to make or to remake the history of literature was also to provide the means to make and to remake, yet again and always, literature itself.

—*Translation by Jane Blevins*

NOTES

1. Maurras, *Enquête sur la monarchie,* "édition définitive" (Paris: Nouvelle Librairie nationale, 1925), 398.
2. Maurras, *Dictionnaire politique et critique,* vol. 2, edited by Pierre Chardon (Paris: À la cité des livres, 1932), 227–28.
3. Maurras, "Mademoiselle Monk ou la génération des événements," in *L'Avenir de l'intelligence* (Paris: Albert Fontemoing, 1905), 285.
4. This was a time of proliferation for some reviews (notably for the *Revue critique des idées et des livres* and for *Les Guêpes*).
5. Maurras, *Le Soleil* (11 January 1897), quoted in *Dictionnaire,* vol. 1, 264.
6. See also *Prologue d'un essai sur la critique* (1896), cited in *Dictionnaire politique et critique,* vol. 1, 264; and a slight variant in *Œuvres capitales,* vol. 3 (Paris: Flammarion), 31.
7. Maurras, *Anthinéa: d'Athènes à Florence* (Paris: Champion, 1920), 24–25.
8. This is the reproach formulated by Julien Benda in a note of *Belphégor* on the "romanticism of reason." "*Anthinéa, L'Avenir de l'Intelligence,* is the love of the classical mind which has been taken as the substance of a kind of romantic exaltation . . ." (206). Following Benda's lead, Eliot described Maurras as a "French Romantic." "A French Romantic," *Times Literary Supplement* 980 (28 October 1920): 703.
9. Maurras, *Anthinéa* V.
10. Maurras, *Prologue d'un essai sur la critique* (Paris: La Porte étroite, 1932), 36–37.
11. Edward J. H. Greene, *T. S. Eliot et la France* (Paris: Boivin, 1951), 173.
12. Ronald Schuchard, "T. S. Eliot as an Extension Lecturer, 1916–1919," *Review of English Studies* 25, no. 98 (May 1974): 165–68.
13. The allusions contained in the letters addressed to Eliot by his friend Jean Verdenal in 1911 and 1912 show that Eliot was well versed in every aspect of Maurras's inspired criticism, and that he was particularly well informed about the debate between the "Sorbonnards" and the "scientific critics." See, for instance, *Letters* I, 21.
14. See David Goldie, *A Critical Difference: T. S. Eliot and John Middleton Murry in English Literary Criticism, 1919–1928* (Oxford: Clarendon Press, 1998), 96–115.
15. Eliot, "Hulme and Classicism," *The Criterion* 2, no. 7 (April 1924): 231.
16. André Thérive, "Poètes: F. P. Alibert," *L'Opinion,* 15, no. 41 (13 October 1922): 200–208. See also Thérive, "Poètes: Paul Valéry," *L'Opinion,* 15, no. 39 (29 September 1922): 1095–1108.
17. Eliot, "Hulme and Classicism," 231.
18. Eliot, "The Idea of a Literary Review," *The Criterion* 4, no. 1 (January 1926): 5.
19. Bertram Higgins, "Art and Knowledge," *The Calendar of Modern Letters* 4 (April 1927): 58. Quoted by Eliot, "A Commentary," *The Criterion* 5, no. 3 (June 1927): 284.
20. Eliot, "A Commentary," *The Criterion* 5, no. 3 (June 1927): 284–85.
21. Paul Elmer More, "The Cleft Eliot," *Saturday Review* 9 (12 November 1932): 233–35. Quoted by Graham Clarke, *T. S. Eliot: Critical Assessments, IV: The Criticism and General Essays* (London: Christopher Helm, 1990), 9–13. See Ronald Bush, "But Is It Modern? T. S. Eliot in 1988." *The Yale Review* 77, no. 2 (March 1988): 195–96. See also

Kenneth Asher, *T. S. Eliot and Ideology* (Cambridge: Cambridge University Press, 1995), 160, 188.

22. Eliot, "Neo-Classicism Again," *The Criterion* 6, no. 3 (September 1927): 193–94.

23. Eliot, *For Lancelot Andrewes: Essays on Style and Order* (London: Faber, 1929): ix–x.

24. The three concepts were effectively linked in Maurras's work, but never in an explicit way. See Antoine Compagnon, "Maurras critique," *Revue d'histoire littéraire de la France* 105 (3 July 2005): 521. For example, they were united in a single sentence as early as 1896, in *Prologue d'un essai sur la critique* (82): ". . . if our France holds together, it is because the pieces were put in place by classical architects. One can see the traces of their dynamic and delicate hand: I call them, among other things, the Catholic church and the Roman Administration, the ancient counseling body to the Kings of France."

25. Albert Thibaudet, "L'esthétique des trois traditions" (second part) *La Nouvelle Revue française* 9, no. 51 (March 1913): 355: "classical, catholic and monarchic traditions"; *Trente ans de vie française, I: Les Idées de Charles Maurras* (Paris: Éditions de La Nouvelle Revue française, 1920), 101: "[. . .] Reform, Revolution, Romanticism. Mr Maurras is far from placing the three Rs in opposition to the three Cs, Catholicism, Counter-Revolution, Classicism, but it is within this triple perspective that the whole of his doctrine is revealed to his reader." Back at Harvard in 1911, after his stay in France, Eliot subscribed to the *NRF*, where Thibaudet's article appeared. Thibaudet cited his article in *Les Idées de Charles Maurras*, the anonymous review of which we know Eliot read in *The Times Literary Supplement* ("A French Romantic," 30 September 1920), since he responded to it (same title, 28 October 1920).

26. Thibaudet, "L'esthétique des trois traditions," 374, 377. Maurras also evoked, though with some hesitation, the possibility of a foreign classicism or even a "cosmopolitan" one (*Prologue d'un essai sur la critique,* 89).

27. Thibaudet, "L'esthétique des trois traditions" (first part), 35.

28. Ibid., 37.

29. See above. Eliot would only finish one of the promised books. *The Principles of Modern Heresy* seemed to announce the 1934 essay *After Strange Gods*, whose subtitle read *A Primer of Modern Heresy. The School of Donne* evoked the Clark lectures of 1926, which were published posthumously in *The Varieties of Metaphysical Poetry.* Only the project entitled *The Outline of Royalism* seems not to have produced any concrete results.

30. Thibaudet, "L'esthétique des trois traditions" (first part), 33.

31. Eliot, "Tradition and the Individual Talent," in *Selected Essays* (London: Faber, 1999), 15.

FIVE

T. S. Eliot, the *Action Française*, and Neo-Scholasticism

Shun'ichi Takayanagi, S.J.

Though most studies of Eliot advert to his classicism, which took in the earlier part of his literary career a somewhat polemical tone, few discuss seriously his sympathetic attitude toward a controversial intellectual movement, the *Action Française*, which was condemned by Pope Pius XI and is in general regarded as right-wing and reactionary.[1] The *Action Française* had many followers, supporters, and sympathizers in the first half of the century, but its reputation plummeted in post-war France when Charles Maurras was imprisoned for his apparent collaboration with the Vichy regime under Marshal Petain and the Nazis. This development was heavily ironic given Maurras's hatred of all things Teutonic. He came to be regarded as a *collaborateur* by committing the naive but fundamental *faux pas* of moving to Vichy instead of choosing the way of the *Resistance*.[2] In an emotion-charged, accusatorial intellectual atmosphere the case of the *Action Française* was closed with the imprisonment of its leader.

The movement had had its genesis in late nineteenth-century France, an era of strained Church-State relations and increasing anti-clericalism. It was gaining popularity at the time of its condemnation by the Vatican. Even at its most influential, however, it never grew into an organized movement with the momentum of fascism; it was essentially an intellectual movement. Its central idea was a reaction to the French Revolution and its political and spiritual aftermath. The controversies raised by the *Action Française* now seem dated, and since it is an uncomfortable memory, people now prefer to forget.

In the early twentieth century, many French Catholic intellectuals were sympathetic to the movement, but the Vatican condemnation of 1926 was a turning point. Afterwards, the *Action Française* lost many of its supporters, while Maurras, feeling himself betrayed and isolated, began to attack the Vatican in the most bitter terms. He took a more extreme position, one which led him on the catastrophic path he took after the war began. Jacques Maritain was originally sympathetic towards Maurras and his followers, and at the time of the condemnation he received a visit from Maurras, accompanied by Henri Massis, at Meudon. He endeavored to mediate between the Vatican and the *Action Française*. He even published an article he had written, "Une Opinion sur Charles Maurras et le Devoir des Catholiques."[3] But no mediation was finally possible, and Maritain became a critic of Maurras.

In the contemporary French Catholic milieu, the whole intellectual horizon was taken up by the problem of allegiance, and it was a crisis of conscience. In his article, Maritain tried to reconcile the factions within the Church created by this crisis. But the condemnation came on December 29, 1926: the Sacred Office published the hitherto withheld condemnation of Maurras's works by Pius X (January 29, 1914). After the condemnation, Maritain immediately ceased supporting Maurras. In 1927, Maritain published *Primauté du Spirituel*, in which he defended the Church's authority to lead even the mundane domain and argued that the Church's authority required obedience. In this book, he maintains that the intellectual life is to be the starting point for the effort to restore the material world to its pristine purity and redeem the time: "Menacée par une civilisation dégradée qui livre l'homme à l'indéfini de la matière, il est nécessaire que l'intelligence se défende, revendique son droit et son essentielle supériorité," he writes in his introduction and continues, "Il n'y a d'ordre et de paix dans l'être humain que si le sens est soumis à la raison, et si la raison elle-même est soumise à Dieu, ce qui ne se fait que par la foi et par l'amour surnaturel." ["Menaced by a degraded civilization which hands Man over to the undefined nature of matter, intelligence must defend itself, assert its right and its essential superiority. . . . There is only order and peace in the human being if the senses are submitted to reason, and if reason itself is submitted to God, which is not done except through faith and through supernatural love."][4] It is within this general framework that Maritain takes up the *Action Française* in the second chapter, "Une Crise de l'Esprit Catholique" [A Crisis in the Catholic Spirit].[5] We can still feel, in reading this book, the urgency Maritain felt in the 20s. It appears that he shared many of the tendencies of Maurras: both of them had an intellectual and hierarchical view of cultural values. But Maurras wished to subordinate all to the royalist cause, while Maritain demanded the supremacy of the spiritual and obedience to the claims of the spiritual, even in the temporal realm: "La condamnation de l'Action Française, qui est un groupement politique, non religieux, retentit de fait sur l'ordre temporel: mais elle a pour motif et pour objet formel de parer aux dangers d'ordre spirituel que l'Église, par la voix du Pape déclare apercevoir dans ce groupement." ["The condemnation of the *Action Française*, which is a political group, not a religious one, affects indeed the temporal order: but it has as its purpose and formal aim to fend off dangers of the spiritual order that the Church, through the voice of the pope, declares it perceives in this group."][6]

For Maritain, the supernatural order is always supreme, but Maurras ultimately falls into naturalism. In December of 1927 a pamphlet appeared entitled *Pourquoi Rome a parlé* [*Why Rome Has Spoken*], and it contained a contribution by Maritain, "Le sens de la condamnation de l'Action Française" ["The Meaning of the Condemnation of the *Action Française*"].[7] Maurras responded to his critics, carrying on his increasingly lonely literary fight. Maritain, however, receded from the controversy. In the context of Maritain's long philosophical career, his connection with the *Action Française* came to be seen as a minor episode with little lasting influence.

My interest in the present essay does not lie primarily in the *Action Française* as such or in neo-scholasticism as such but in the degree of knowledge of this movement and interest in it on the part of T. S. Eliot. It seems to me that in his works of cultural criticism (especially his "Commentaries" in *The Criterion*) his thinking closely resembles neo-scholasticism. Of course, in assessing Eliot's social and political criticism we have to keep in mind complex layers, including the influence of Lancelot Andrewes, F. H. Bradley, and contemporary Anglo-American thinkers. Even Matthew Arnold, whom Eliot often criticizes, is someone in whose steps he follows rather closely.

Certainly Maurras, too, was an important influence for a time. It is well known that Eliot's statement "classicist in literature, royalist in politics, and anglo-catholic in religion" must have been formulated in imitation of Charles Maurras's position.[8] In his 1926 essay "The Idea of a Literary Review," Eliot mentions several books as representing the contemporary tendency which he calls classicism. Maurras's *L'Avenir de l'intelligence* is mentioned, along with Maritain's *Réflexions sur l'intelligence* (1924) and works by Georges Sorel, Julien Benda, T. E. Hulme, and Irving Babbitt. These are divergent in their points of view, Eliot grants, but he sets this group up in contrast to H. G. Wells and Bertrand Russell. Herbert Howarth summarizes the main ideas in *L'Avenir de l'intelligence*: Western civilization "had originated in Greece, emigrated to Rome, marched with the legions into France, ramified with the Roman colonists alike into Spain and up the Rhine; it was best preserved in France, and the health of Europe lay in its development around the French massif." The French Revolution and the nineteenth century had crippled this traditional civilization, but Maurras hoped for a counterrevolution that might bring about a fourth great age of European

culture.[9] As Maurras puts it, "Au nom de la raison et de la nature, confor-
mément aux vieilles lois de l'univers, pour le salut de l'ordre . . . toutes
espérances flottent sur le navire d'une Contre-Révolution" ["In the name
of reason and of nature, in conformity with the old laws of the universe,
for the preservation of order . . . all hope rides on a Counter-Revolution"].[10]

Maurras considers that the classical man creates a superior domain
among humankind. However, one may notice in his emphasis on pagan
Greece as an ideal civilization a strange incongruity—to be seen in the
invocation of Minerva in Appendix I, which makes even the Church
sacrifice at her altar. When he speaks of the Counter-revolution, he
idealizes the *ancien régime*: "Le sacrifice de Louis XVI représente à la
perfection le genre de chute que firent alors toutes les têtes du troupeau"
["The sacrifice of Louis XVI represents to perfection the type of downfall
that all the leaders of the pack experienced"].[11] For Maurras, the French
Revolution is the source of all evil, which consolidates its hold on Europe
in the nineteenth century, through bourgeois plutocracy and romanticism
(imported from Germany), which incites man's emotion: "Non seulement
l'Intelligence ne fit pas son métier d'éclairer et d'orienter les masses ob-
scures: elle fit le contraire de son métier, elle les trompa."[12] He further
writes, "Mais le romanticisme se connut pour ce qu'il est. Il aima en lui
ses qualités de barbare. Étranger, il aima l'étrange. Non seulement il
l'accueillit, mais il l'afficha en s'efforçant de déterminer dans le goût
public une révolution qui assignât à l'art d'écrire, comme au plaisir de
lire, des objets tout à fait nouveaux" ["Not only did the intelligentsia not
do its work of enlightening and directing the lowly masses: it did the
opposite, it misled them. . . . But romanticism knew itself for what it was.
It loved in itself its own barbaric qualities. A foreigner, it loved the
foreign. Not only did it (romanticism) welcome it (the foreign), but it
paraded it in endeavoring to cause a revolution in public taste that assigned to the art of writing, as to the pleasure of reading, completely new
aims"].[13] This way of thinking is reflected in Hulme's condemnation of
romanticism as heresy, which in turn influences Eliot's use of the term
"heresy" in *After Strange Gods*. Hulme acknowledges that his use of the
word "romanticism" derives from Maurras.[14] However, Hulme refuses
to make his thought into a political slogan, as Maurras did. Similarly,
Julien Benda, who shared the same classical temperament, points out that
Maurras's extreme position betrays his desire to make his ideas into a
political cause, and here lies Benda's critique of Maurras—a critique of
which Eliot was well aware.[15]

Though Maurras was brought up by an ardent royalist Catholic mother and sent to receive a Catholic secondary education in Aix-en-Provence,
he claimed that from early youth he was an atheist. Intellectually he was
heavily dependent on French Ultramonanists like Joseph de Maistre and
the Viscount of Bonald, but at the same time he gave perhaps greater

weight to Comte's positivism and Darwin's theory of natural selection, which Maurras turned into an anti-egalitarian doctrine. French Catholics had been hesitant in their allegiance to the Republic since the radically anti-clerical Revolution. Pope Leo XIII's policy made it possible for the faithful to participate in the Republican form of government, but his successor, Pius X, took a different course. Catholics were caught in a dilemma, being forced to choose between faith and nation. The upper classes traditionally backing the Church were royalist, and since the Dreyfus affair was increasingly made by the socialists an effective means of propaganda against the military (traditional stronghold of the aristo-crats), Catholic intellectuals were attracted to the anti-Dreyfus position. In this intellectual climate, a Christian democratic position was practic-ally impossible, and Maurras ridiculed those who attempted to take such a compromise position. Nevertheless, his Catholicism was a strictly cul-tural concept. The *Action Française* had influential supporters as well as strong enemies in Rome. Pius X was understandably in favor of it by temperament, and when the negative dossier was presented to him, he did not make his decision public, saying "damnabiles, non damnandi" ["damnable, but not condemned"].

Although Eliot in his early cultural essays shows signs of Maurras's influence, he adopted as a central idea the belief in a conjunction of the temporal and the eternal, which could not have come from Maurras. Rather, it must have been from Maritain (as well as Andrewes) that Eliot derived his idea of the realization of the eternal in the corporeal. In *Réflex-ions sur l'intelligence* (1924), Maritain argues that the scientific mode of thought from Descartes to Einstein did violence to intelligence, which belongs to the spiritual dimension and has redoubled importance in a world that refuses it:

> Il convient encore et surtout de remarquer l'immense besoin de spiritu-alité qui travaille en ce moment le monde. De ce besoin je vois un signe ténébreux dans le pullulement horrible de tant de maladives expéri-mentations de l'au-delà et de tant de contrefaçons à bon marché de la mystique, mais je vois un signe lumineux dans l'humble redressement d'une multitude d'âmes, auxquelles l'Ésprit qui crie: *Abba, Pater!* en-seigne à prier dans le secret.
> [It is appropriate to note once again and above all the immerse need for spirituality which obsesses the world at this moment. Of this need I see a shadowy sign in the horrible proliferation of so many unhealthy experiments with the other world and so many cheap counterfeits of the mystical, but I see a luminous sign in the humble reformation of a multitude of souls, whom the Spirit that cries "Abba, Father" teaches to pray in secret.][16]

Maritain considers contemplation the highest act of intelligence — an idea that resonates with Eliot's interest in mysticism. This passage is also echoed in *The Dry Salvages*, where Eliot lists counterfeits of the mystical:

"To communicate with Mars, converse with spirits, / To report the beha-
viour of the sea monster, / Describe the horoscope, haruspicate or
scry. . . ."

In 1927, the year of his baptism, Eliot published an article by Maritain
on "Poetry and Religion" in *The Criterion*. In his Commentary for that
issue, Eliot says, "We present a new and unpublished essay by M.
Jacques Maritain, the most conspicuous figure, and probably the most
powerful force, in contemporary French philosophy."[17] Neo-scholasticism was not usually associated with aesthetics, but Maritain was an
exception. Largely under his wife's influence, he had from the start of his
career manifested interest in poetry and aesthetics. The essay Eliot published is somewhat an application of *Primauté du spirituel* to literary
theory, mingled with Maritain's assessment of the modern world and
culture. With what may be called Christian classicism, he distinguishes
poetry as the vision of the corporeal world, high though its activity may
be, from metaphysics and religious contemplation. He writes, "The spiritual virtue of human art, when it has arrived at a certain height in its own
heaven, perceives that it is translating into analogy and figure the movement of a higher inaccessible sphere."[18] This point of view is similar to
Eliot's when he disagrees with Matthew Arnold and others who think
poetry can take the place of religion.

In 1928, Eliot was preoccupied with Maurras and the *Action Française*.
The Criterion in that year ran Eliot's translation of Maurras's "Prologue to
an Essay on Criticism" in two installments, January and March. Just before the second part of the essay, Eliot placed his own piece on "The
Action Française, M. Maurras and Mr. Ward," a response to Leo Ward's
critique of Maurras. Ward answered in the June issue, followed by Eliot's
response and a final rejoinder from Ward. At the end of this debate, Eliot
puts a postscript announcing that "This controversy must now be
closed," and the matter is simply dropped from further consideration in
The Criterion—nor does Eliot mention Maurras again in print until years
later. Eliot then proceeds to distance himself and his journal from discussion of issues of the day: "In the theory of politics, in the largest sense,
The Criterion is interested, so far as politics can be dissociated from party
politics, from the passions or fantasies of the moment, and from problems
of local and temporary importance."[19] Though Eliot at this point defends
Maurras, it is clear that he is categorizing the controversy over his views
as an instance, not of the "theory of politics, in the largest sense" but
rather as one of "the passions or fantasies of the moment." He is moving
on.

From this time on, Eliot's concept of Christian society and culture
cannot simply be explained in terms of Maurras's influence: there are
other stronger influences, such as Bradley, Coleridge, and Christopher
Dawson's historical perspective. After 1928, Maurras's influence on the
majority of French Catholic intellectuals also declined. Eliot's desire to

distance himself from Maurras is visible in an unpublished letter to the editor of the New York *Bookman* in which Eliot emphasizes that he did not have any personal acquaintance with Maurras.[20] During the 1930s, Eliot continues to be interested in Maritain's work and to treat it with respect. He writes in 1938, "If the intellectual is a person of philosophical mind philosophically trained, who thinks things out for himself, then there are very few intellectuals about, and indeed the position of M. Maritain is as 'intellectual' a position (as well as being Christian) as anyone could adopt."[21] Evidently he considered the political ideas of Maritain to be of the larger theoretical type worthy of discussion in *The Criterion*.

The *Action Française* was in a sense rehabilitated in the summer of 1939, when Pope Pius XII lifted the ban on Catholics who followed the movement. But by this time Eliot's ideas were quite different from those of Maurras. Writing for the *Christian-Newsletter*, he mentions the "considerable contributions" Maurras made as a political thinker, and admires his literary abilities. However, he now supports the decision of Pius XI, who "was condemning a heresy which asserted that only one form of government, the monarchical, was compatible with Catholicism. Perhaps also condemning a dangerous intolerance which classified Jews, Protestants, and Freemasons in one comprehensive condemnation."[22] At about the same time, Eliot writes in *The Idea of a Christian Society*, "To identify any particular form of government with Christianity is a dangerous error: for it confounds the permanent with the transitory, the absolute with the contingent."[23] He is evidently retreating from his earlier Maurrasian commitment to royalism. He notes that Maurras was "a disciple of Comte" and points out that "it was precisely his support of The Church solely on political and social grounds that exposed him to ecclesiastical censure and led to the condemnation of the *Action Française* in 1926."[24]

Years later, in 1955, Eliot mentioned Maurras again in a lecture he gave to the London Conservative Union, "The Literature of Politics." He concludes that writers' influence on politics should not go beyond what he calls the "pre-political area," by which he means broad political theory rather than engagement in the issues of the day. And he gives Maurras as an example of a writer who did not observe that limitation:

> I think of a man whom I held in respect and admiration, although some of his views were exasperating and some deplorable. . . . I have sometimes thought that if Charles Maurras had confined himself to literature, and to the literature of political theory, and had never attempted to found a political party, a *movement* — engaging in and increasing the acrimony of political struggle — if he had not given his support to the restoration of the Monarchy in such a way as to strengthen instead of reducing animosities — then those of his ideas which were sound and strong might have spread more widely, and penetrated more deeply, and affected more sensibly the contemporary mind.[25]

It was not only Maurras's imprudent involvement in political struggles but his decision to put politics above faith that caused Eliot to distance himself from Maurras from 1928 onward. He came to a fuller appreciation of the element of faith in what his friend Fr. Martin D'Arcy called the Thomistic synthesis. Eliot's mature political theory reflects the profound influence of that Thomistic synthesis—especially as it was expressed by Maritain.

NOTES

1. This essay is a revision of an article published in *English Literature and Language* 16 (1980): 47–75. It is reprinted by permission of the publisher, Department of English Literature, Sophia University, Tokyo.

2. See H. Howarth, *Notes on Some Figures behind T. S. Eliot* (London: Houghton Mifflin, 1965), 175–7; A. Cunningham, "Continutiy and Coherence in Eliot's Religious Thought," in *Eliot in Perspective*, ed. G. Martin (London: Macmillan, 1970), 217–25; R. Kojecký, *T. S. Eliot's Social Criticism* (London: Faber and Faber, 1971), 58–69; J. D. Margolis, *T. S. Eliot's Intellectual Development, 1922-1939* (Chicago: University of Chicago Press, 1972), 87–98; W. M. Chace, *The Political Identities of Ezra Pound and T. S. Eliot* (Palo Alto, CA: Stanford University Press, 1973), 140–2; G. Watson, *Politics and Literature in Modern Britain* (London: Macmillan, 1977), 71–84. Studies of the *Action Française* include E. Nolte, *Der Faschismus in seiner Epoche* (Munich: R. Piper, 1971), 61–190; M. Mourre, *Charles Maurras* (Paris: Éd. universitaires, 1953); E. Weber *The Action Française* (Palo Alto, CA: Stanford University Press, 1962); J. de Fabrègues, *Charles Maurras et son Action Française* (Paris: Perrin, 1966); J. McCearney, *Maurras et son temps* (Paris: A. Miche, 1977); H. Massis, *Maurras et notre temps* (Paris: La Palatine, 1961). Jeo-Yong Noh, *"Action Française Condemnation" and Other Essays* (Seoul, Korea: Brain House, 2003). Gaetano DeLeontibus, *Charles Maurras's Classicising Aesthetics and Politics: Aestheticization of Politics* (New York: Peter Lang, 2000).

3. H. Bars, *Maritain en notre temps* (Paris: La politique selon, 1959), 376.

4. Jacques Maritain, *Primauté du Spirituel* (Paris: Plon, 1927), 7. All translations are by Micheline Lockerd.

5. Ibid., 73–112.

6. Ibid., 77–8.

7. Jacques Maritain, *Pourquoi Rome a parler* (Paris: Spcs, 1927).

8. T. S. Eliot, *For Lancelot Andrewes* (New York: Doubleday, Doran, 1929), 7. Maurras identified his ideals as *"classique, catholique, monarchique."*

9. Howarth, 175–6.

10. Maurras, *L'Avenir de l'intelligence* (Paris: A. Fontemoing, 1909), 99.

11. Ibid., 31.

12. Ibid., 222. Maurras says Romanticism means "un arrêt des traditions" (an arrest of traditions).

13. Ibid., 225.

14. T. E. Hulme, *Speculations* (London: Routledge 1924), 114.

15. Julien Benda, *The Betrayal of the Intellectuals*, trans. Richard Aldington (Boston: Beacon Press, 1955), 60–74.

16. Jacques Maritain, *Réflexions sur l'intelligence* (Paris: Desclée, de Brouwer et cie, 1924).

17. "A Commentary," *Criterion* 5 (1927): 3.

18. Maritain, "Poetry and Religion," *Criterion* 5 (1927): 20.

19. *The Criterion* 7 (June, 1928): 291–2.

20. Kojecký, 62.

21. *The Criterion* 18 (October, 1938): 58–9.

22. Quoted by Kojecký, 67.

23. Eliot, *Christianity and Culture* (New York, 1949), 45.

24. Quoted by Kojecký, 67–8.

25. Eliot, "The Literature of Politics," in *To Criticize the Critic* (Lincoln, NE: University of Nebraska Press, 1965), 142–3.

SIX

An "Organ for a Frenchified Doctrine": Jacques Maritain and *The Criterion*'s Neo-Thomism

James Matthew Wilson

By 1936, T. S. Eliot's literary review, *The Criterion*, had been so frequently associated with the fashionable French neo-Thomism of Jacques Maritain that the young W. H. Auden could cheekily remark on the connection with justice. In his *Letter to Lord Byron*, he describes his avant-garde undergraduate affinities in light of Eliot and Aquinas thus:

> All youth's intolerant certainty was mine as
>   I faced life in a double-breasted suit;
> I bought and praised but did not read Aquinas,
>   At the *Criterion*'s verdict I was mute,
>   Though Arnold's I was ready to refute;
> And through the quads dogmatic words rang clear,
> "Good poetry is classic and austere."[1]

As Eliot had observed some years previous, the Victorian liberal humanist defense of culture voiced by Matthew Arnold, with its vaguely Platonic appeals to the true, the good, and the beautiful had "not worn at all well."[2] Undergraduates of the post-War decades, such as Auden, may no longer fall into reverent silence before the sometime Oxford Professor of Poetry's exhortative "purple passages" celebrating culture and decrying Philistinism, but they would indeed stand "mute" before the verdicts of the austere classicism of which Eliot's magazine was vicar.[3] The generation that emerged under the tutelage of Eliot had little trouble discerning that, where the Victorians had been romantic, they must be classical;

if the Victorians paid overwrought lip-service to Plato, young moderns must speak plain praise of Aristotle. Although it was less than clear to Auden and many others precisely what *The Criterion*'s pronouncements owed to St. Thomas Aquinas, they sensed that the often unread volumes of that "baptized" Aristotle provided them a rational and metaphysical foundation all the more attractive for appearing intellectualist, technical, and arcane.

In a 1928 review of Maritain's *Three Reformers*, Eliot would advise his readers that Maritain "is becoming known in England as" contemporary France's "most popular and influential exponent of neo-Thomism," and that the present book indicates that serious study of the man and his movement is warranted by English intellectuals.[4] But Eliot could have been speaking of his own role as editor of *The Criterion*, when he wryly observed of Maritain's work that the "influence of neo-Thomism has reached many persons who have probably never read a word of St. Thomas."[5] As Jason Harding has documented, Herbert Read proposed in 1926 that Aquinas and neo-Thomism informed the review's editorial position, because it was "consonant with our deepest instincts" and offered to Englishmen of a classicizing persuasion a "fruitful" attitude and "method."[6] And, in the years that followed, writers antagonistic to *The Criterion* took the influence of Aquinas on the journal as absolute, responding to it "with incomprehension, or with irritation."[7] Eliot would paraphrase one such attack, which appeared in *The Calendar* in April 1927, by noting "Neo-Classicism, we are told, is 'the literary version of a reactionary Latin philosophy which is being adapted, in one or two English reviews, into a repressive instrument of literary criticism.'"[8] A year later, he would make an ambiguous nod to certain critics who called "*THE CRITERION* . . . an organ for a 'Frenchified' doctrine called neo-Thomism."[9]

If all parties acknowledged the charge as true, again, what it entailed remained obscure. Was the association between neo-Thomism and classicism anything more than a medievalizing nostalgia on the part of its advocates? Were its critics reacting with objections more substantial than traditional English anti-Catholic bigotry? In hopes of illuminating the role of an Aquinas who has been bought but left unread in the pages of *The Criterion*, I shall seek to establish two points. First, I shall show the role Maritain played in helping Eliot to define the "classical tendency" of his age and his review. This will also entail indicating the limit of that influence. Second, I shall consider the uneven but prolonged engagement of Eliot's review in scrutinizing not only Maritain's work but also the many books published by prominent neo-Thomists between 1926, when Eliot first mentioned Maritain in print, and 1939, when *The Criterion* ceased publication. Such a survey hardly exhausts the myriad historical connections and intellectual affinities between Maritain and Eliot. However much Maritain's Thomist metaphysics and aesthetics tempered *The*

Criterion, only at the time of that review's cessation did Eliot come under the profound influence of Maritain's volumes of political philosophy.[10] Moreover, Eliot became a major authority in Maritain's writings on art and poetry in subsequent decades. But this tight focus will give us a surer view of the oft-mentioned but little-explained Thomist contribution to that *Criterion* classicism which so awed Auden.

IN SEARCH OF METAPHYSICAL FOUNDATIONS FOR CLASSICISM

In Eliot's Clark lectures of 1926, he celebrated the intellectualism found in Dante, and in the medieval scholasticism and monasticism of Aquinas and the Victorines. There, he saw reason fused to and guiding emotion, drawing mind and heart to their proper ends. And so, while Eliot's sensibility and critical position might have come to be called scholastic rationalism, ontological realism or, less felicitously, "Aristotelian-Victorine-Dantesque mysticism," he allowed it to be identified with a broad post-Victorian tendency toward "classicism."[11] What he would describe to the students of Cambridge, later that winter, in terms of medieval theology and poetry, he outlines in the January 1926 number of *The Criterion* as a contemporary trend:

> I believe that the modern tendency is toward something which, for want of a better name, we may call classicism. I use the term with hesitation, for it is hardly more than analogical. . . . Yet there is a tendency—discernable even in art—toward a higher and clearer conception of Reason, and a more severe and serene control of the emotions by Reason. If this approaches or even suggests the Greek ideal, so much the better: but it must inevitably be very different.[12]

Eliot's inspiration for the term "classicism" in the context of modern art and intellectual life derives, of course, initially from Charles Maurras, who used it, in 1904, to announce a new anti-romantic movement in French literature, and secondarily from T. E. Hulme's posthumous *Speculations*, which appeared twenty years later and translated Maurras's anti-romanticism to English soil, aligning it in the process with advanced art. Because of this easily traced origin, scholars have under valued the substantial contribution Maritain made in suggesting how modern "classicism" might build itself upon the same cornerstone as the works of Aquinas and Dante: the "severe and serene" doctrines of scholastic metaphysics.

Following his outline of the classical tendency, Eliot offers a list of authors and works that exemplify that tendency; he includes the names of Maurras and Hulme (among others), but also makes reference to "*Réflexions sur l'intelligence*, by Jacques Maritain." First published the same year as Hulme's *Speculations*, *Réflexions* gathers together some of Maritain's essays from various French reviews that address Thomist theories of knowledge to specific modern conundrums and confusions. The particular antagonists engaged, and the mode of engagement, could scarcely have been better crafted for an audience suspicious of Victorian idealism and romanticism. Furthermore, the chapters on Pascal as an apologist, on "metaphysical pluralism" and the emergence of national philosophies, and, above all, the closing chapter on the return to Thomist realism among the post-War generation, read more as essays in cultural and literary criticism than as philosophical treatises. As such, they define a perspective, tendency, or aesthetic as much as they argue for a logical conclusion.

In the early chapters, Maritain furnishes extended and rigorous (not to say exhaustive) explanations of Thomist intellectualism; he contends that the screen between subject and object that constituted the chief epistemological problem of Cartesian and Kantian idealism is one grounded in a poor understanding of the ontological nature of ideas as merely "formal" signs of real objects. Only Thomist psychology adequately shows that human beings have real knowledge of extra-mental beings.[13] He makes frequent reference to recent and contemporary thinkers (including to Harvard's William James and the novels of his brother) in his effort to show that all post-Kantian epistemologies have failed because they treat thought and knowledge as rarified subjective abstractions (*O*, 3:309). They fail to recognize that the human mind is ordered to being and, therefore, one cannot have pure thought or knowledge, but only the idea of such-and-such or the knowledge of this-or-that (*O*, 3:50–53). Theories of the intelligence that begin in the subject can never finally reach extra-mental being, because they fail to appreciate this *a priori* dependence of the mind on the encounter with actual beings for knowledge.[14] Therefore, modern epistemologies ineluctably conclude in severing the knower and the idea of a thing from the thing known. No matter how ingenious the effort of different idealists to secure the mind's knowledge of objects, they are all equally untenable, because their epistemologies begin with the knower rather than the thing known (*O*, 3:51).

Maritain's version of Thomist epistemology depends upon the concept of intentional being. By this term he expresses the manner in which an extra-mental thing can exist substantially (on its own), as *esse entitativum*, while it also comes to exist, once perceived and then known by the agent intellect, as *esse intentionale*, as an intentional being, an accident in the mind of a knower. Elaborating on these concepts, Maritain explains why a thing known is *really* present to the knower, and why, therefore, the idea of said thing is the thing itself under another mode of being, rather than a mere image or distorted impression *of* that thing. Intriguingly, Maritain's manner of explaining this point suggests a continuity between knower and known, subject, idea, and object that reassures the reader that reality constitutes an intelligible whole. Reason takes its measure, but reason must also be "measured" or disciplined by objective realities (*O*, 3:66).[15] Contrary to the preaching of Arnold and other Victorians, all things, including art, must be understood in terms of intellect and being, rather than emotion and imagination. Not incidentally, Maritain's account of intellect and being also stands athwart the materialism and subjectivism that was obscured by and drove the Platonizing rhetoric of the Victorian age. Maritain refers substances, including material ones, and intentions alike to being. What has being is real, but things have being, are real, under different modes. Maritain thus chastens romantic rhetoric without encouraging one to embrace a rationalistic materialism. Rather, Aquinas, like Aristotle before him, provided modern man a compelling account of metaphysical realism that was at once austerely scientific and rich in its view of the intelligibility or meaningfulness of the world.

In subsequent chapters, Maritain critiques thinkers who, directly or by association, at one time influenced Eliot, whether by positive or negative example. Maritain's chapter on Blondel would not at first glance seem relevant to Eliot's own intellectual interests. However, Maritain argues against Blondel's theories of notional and real knowledge (*O*, 3:102), a theory Blondel develops out of John Henry Newman's *Essay in Aid of a Grammar of Assent* (1870).[16] In the Clark lectures, Eliot would denigrate Newman alongside F. H. Bradley as part of the modern tradition of "intellectual psychologism" that signaled the loss of the "severe and serene control of reason."[17] Eliot opposed the pychologistic or "immanentist" spirit of theological modernism with which Blondel was associated, and which Hulme had condemned in his first manifesto proclaiming a new classicism, as much as he did the rhetoric of Arnold.[18] Similarly, the penultimate chapter of *Réflexions* examines modern Anglo-American philosophy, critiquing the pluralism of Bradley and William James. Both are condemned because their philosophies are subjective expressions of defensiveness against the peculiar absolutisms of Hegelian monism and materialist positivism. Contemporary pluralist philosophers practice their discipline with the sentiment and will rather than with reason (*O*, 3:309). Maritain thus dismantles the authority of the leading lights of Harvard and Oxford, where Eliot was educated, and contrasts their pluralist voluntarism with the *classical* discipline of the ancient and medieval philosophers, who grounded their thought on an intellectual asceticism, a "severe disinterestedness" that aided them in working upon the material of their inquiry with the intelligence alone:

> The high, classical discipline of the ancients and medievals joined a sort of intellectual asceticism with a particular kind of purification that demanded the pure contemplation of the object in its otherness, in abstraction from all the particular ways it affects us—without thought of the good or of our appetite—, touching the things themselves with the intelligence alone (of which the proper function is to become the other as such, with the unique power to assimilate things in a non-material

mode of being). The philosopher, in his function as philosopher, practices a severe disinterestedness, giving up, disengaging from, his ego
and his concupiscent inclinations, extinguishing what is in him of the
flesh and blood: in brief, he spiritualizes himself as much as possible.
(*O,* 3:309)

The scholastic philosopher anticipates the austere sensibility of the "classical" artist. The moderate realist metaphysics of Aquinas therefore provide in coherent and fully articulated form method (restraint), theory
(intellect over emotion), and substance (being) for the unofficial position
of *The Criterion.*

The care Maritain took in his arguments clearly impressed Eliot, convincing him that here was a thinker capable of re-founding an ontologically informed philosophy and objective or exact theology upon the rub-
ble of modern idealism and materialism. E. W. F. Tomlin, in his memoir
of Eliot, observes that he often "spoke about the need for an 'exact' theology, and Maritain, with his handbooks on logic, gave the impression of
exactitude which most English theologians, brought up in the Hegelian
tradition, failed to do."[19] Appropriately, when Eliot wrote a letter of
introduction to Maritain for the young Tomlin in 1938, he referred to the
latter as a "cadet of *The Criterion*" who was interested in aesthetics, sociology, political philosophy, and "*qui comprend l'importance fondamentale,
pour notre époque, d'une théologie exacte.*"[20] Maritain promised what the
circle surrounding Eliot's *Criterion* required; as we shall see below, that
circle did not stint in allying with or relying on Maritain and other neo-
Thomists within limits.

In the last chapter of *Réflexions,* Maritain turns from the presentation
of Thomist philosophy by way of critique of the moderns. Abandoning
the categories of philosophical argument, he seeks to sketch a vision of
the present age as abandoning romantic emotionalism and returning to
the (ontologically) Real. Two years before Eliot would recommend Maritain's book as exemplary of the "classical tendency" with its return to
austere reason, Maritain would outline that tendency and insist that it
would find its entelechy, its fulfillment, only in Thomist metaphysics. As
would Eliot in the Clark lectures and elsewhere, Maritain felt justified in
summarizing the self-image of historical periods and suggesting that
they operated as *Zeitgeists,* partially determining the intellectual possibilities available to a given time (*O,* 3:337–38). The recent past had been lost
to idealism on the one hand and positivist materialism on the other, and
both had offered inadequate accounts of reality because of their alter-
nately purblind or narrow grasp of being. But the present moment witnessed tendencies toward "*réalisme, intellectualisme, spiritualisme. Retour
au réel et à l'absolu, par les voies de l'intelligence, pour la primauté de l'esprit*"
(*O,* 3:363).

Maritain here offers as a platform what Stephen Schloesser has defined as the Catholic species of "dialetical realism" that came to prominence in Maritain's post-War Paris. What Schloesser calls "hylomorphic realism" proposed that Catholic theology, ritual, and sacrament allowed one to penetrate at last to the real within, but often concealed by, mere appearances.[21] Rejecting the positivism and rationalism of an earlier generation, Maritain, Eliot, and other classicists or "dialectical realists" sought to recover the union of intellect and emotion, faith and reason, that modernity had seemed to rend asunder. For Maritain as for Eliot, this tendency particularly entails a rejection of romantic theories of the artist as mage or god (*O*, 3:363). Convinced of the need for an exact theology grounded on a convincing metaphysics as a guard against romantic obscurantism about the origin and purpose of art, Eliot would to a large extent find that need answered in Maritain's work. Maritain bequeathed to Eliot a reason that was not rationalistic, a realism that was not reductive.

In return, Maritain would soon acknowledge his own appreciation for the work of Eliot as exemplary of the classical tendency. The last edition of Maritain's *Art and Scholasticism* would cite Eliot three times in defense of its positions on aesthetics.[22] More impressively, in 1939, Maritain revised the text of the last chapter of *Réflexions* in preparation for an English edition (which, in fact, never appeared). In the revised text, Maritain mentions Paul Cézanne and Ernest Psichari (his close friend, the Catholic convert and novelist, who died in the Great War) as anticipating the return to the real that Maritain's book announced. He then added a citation of Eliot as its most distinguished representative, despite the fact that, by that late date, Maritain had led many artists and writers, English and French, to embrace his Thomist philosophy of art. Eliot unites a poetic gift with a well-developed critical intelligence and an admirable, rational lucidity that penetrates the deepest religious realities, Maritain writes (*O*, 3:365). In the mid-1920s, then, Maritain promised Eliot an exact metaphysics and theology upon which could be founded an entire culture and a modern "ontological" art. Conversely, Maritain subsequently came to see in Eliot the highest realization in poetry of what he had prescribed in theory. Only their key terms differed: Eliot recommended "classicism," while Maritain proclaimed "the Real."

A year after Eliot first cited Maritain in *The Criterion*, he praised the French neo-Thomist again in those pages as "the most conspicuous figure, and probably the most powerful force, in contemporary French philosophy."[23] In the same issue, Eliot printed the first part of his own (pseudonymous) translation of Maritain's *Frontières de la poesie* as "Poetry and Religion."[24] It would seem he had found that exact theology had extended via philosophy to an exact aesthetics, and Maritain made it possible to calibrate and respect the distinction and relation of these several fields of human knowledge. With the many books of the French neo-

Thomist held up as evidence, Eliot could translate and, later, echo Maritain's Christian intellectualist equipoise. In *Frontières*, Maritain explains,

> Religion alone can help the art of our epoch to keep the best of its promises . . . by putting it in a position to respect its own nature and to take its true place. For it is only in the light of theology that art today can achieve self-knowledge and cure itself of the false systems of metaphysics which plague it. By showing us where moral truth and the genuine supernatural are situate, religion saves poetry from the absurdity of believing itself destined to transform ethics and life, saves it from overweening arrogance.[25]

A sound doctrine of being could integrate all aspects of reality without subordinating them to scientific materialism. In the light of such Thomist metaphysics, and the religion for which it served as ballast, Eliot would reinterpret his own literary career. While still a graduate student, he had claimed to have lost belief in philosophical claims, and so gave up philosophy for art in the spirit of George Santayana.[26] But in the 1920s, he came to conceive his first literary critical efforts—the most important of which were collected in *The Sacred Wood* (1920)—in less despairing terms and as part of a less reductive endeavor to discern what poetry was in its own right. As he put it in the preface to the second edition of that volume, poetry "is not the inculcation of morals, or the direction of politics; and no more is it religion or an equivalent of religion, except by some monstrous abuse of words."[27] By 1926, he had expanded his interests so that determining what poetry was in isolation came to appear as merely a preface to a more integrative project. In 1928, he would observe that he had moved on to the exploration of "the relation of poetry to the spiritual and social life of its times and of other times."[28] Art need not stand as an alternative to the reality of physical science or the ghost of philosophy; all of these now stood in organic relation under the patronage of "exact" metaphysics and theology. Although Eliot's attentions would return to the study of this relation for the rest of his life, his most systematic reflections would come in his 1932–1933 Charles Eliot Norton lectures at Harvard, and there he would quote other comments of Maritain to the same effect as those above in seeking to define the "use" of poetry and criticism.[29] By that time, Eliot's reputation was well established as a poet, cultural critic, and political and religious thinker, and we may rightly insist that Maritain's writings helped show Eliot the way to this expansive and integrated Christian vision.

However, the 1926 translation marks the closest to unity Eliot's classicism and Maritain's Thomist realism would achieve. While Eliot's engagement with Maritain and neo-Thomism was extended indeed, its documentary evidence is somewhat ambiguous. Almost immediately after his conversion in June 1927, Eliot wrote Maritain in thanks for the gift of two brief books, one on aesthetics, *Art et Scholastique* (1920), and the other on political theology, *La Primauté du Spirituel* (1927). Responding to an invitation Maritain had made for him to collaborate on a new publication series, called Correspondence, Eliot questions his own suitability, noting that he is Anglo-Catholic, not Roman Catholic, and that, therefore, on some points they do not see eye-to-eye.[30] Maritain's Thomism had made plausible on metaphysical grounds the classicist tendency Eliot approved and wished to promote; in doing so it may have abetted Eliot's conversion to Christianity.[31] But Eliot did not join what was, in his words of a decade earlier, "the only Church which can even pretend to maintain a philosophy of its own."[32]

Eliot's conversion to the self-described *via media* of Anglicanism is, in some sense, bound up with a reservation about Maritain's Thomism. The year before his baptism, Eliot made comments to this effect in *The Criterion*. In a review of new books by Herbert Read and Ramon Fernandez, Eliot compares Read's budding, non-Christian interest in Aquinas favorably with Maritain's in at least one respect:

> Mr. Read is a seeker after truth, whose researches we, as Anglo-Saxons, can follow understandingly; whereas M. Massis and M. Maritain are for us, as Anglo-Saxons, less cognate, because they have, for themselves and in a way which is not exactly ours, found truth.[33]

This observation would suggest that Eliot doubted the usefulness of Maritain's writing not on account of any intrinsic limitation, but because of national differences less easily accounted for. There is more to the case, however. In Tomlin's memoir of Eliot, he twice notes the interest Eliot took in Maritain's work and the admiration he felt for Maritain himself. But Eliot did not think Maritain's style was a proper modernization of Aquinas's method. It was too streaked with traces of Bergson and modern French intellectual culture. Tomlin recalls that

> although [Eliot] much liked Maritain as a person (as who could not?), he felt that the French post-Bergsonian intellectual approach, even if called "Neo-scholastique," differed markedly from that of St Thomas himself: it was the difference between a hovering darting kestrel and a "dumb ox" pawing at the ground.[34]

Eliot's prose largely corroborates such recollections. As we noted at the start, a year and a half after his conversion, Eliot reviewed the English translation of Maritain's *Three Reformers* in the *Times Literary Supplement*. Recapitulating and expanding the classicist tendency that, now, Eliot absorbed within French neo-Thomism, he equivocates on the meaning of the latter. Neo-Thomism can

> be applied to the philosophic work of Dominicans and members of other Orders which has gone on at least since the pronouncement of Leo XIII in favour of Aquinas. . . . Or it can be applied to the popularization of intellectual Catholicism in the life of contemporary Paris.[35]

This distinction cuts two ways in the review. At first sight, it divides formal academic philosophy in the seminary from the mode of neo-Thomism that seemed to be transforming Parisian, and potentially London, intellectual life. But as the review continues, one senses an uncertainty on Eliot's part that the Parisian neo-Thomism of Maritain is quite authentic.

Eliot proceeds to observe that, though Maritain is "a brilliant and accomplished scholar, [he] is more important as a popularizer of ideas than as an original thinker. He owes his place partly to a charm of personality and beauty of character, to great enthusiasm, and to a vigourous and vivacious style." [36] There is a "poetic quality" in his prose that makes him "the lyrist of Thomism. The champion of intellectualism, he found his own way to Christianity by a different route; he is an emotional rather than an intellectual Catholic." Finally, Eliot acknowledges, his work "always stimulates the intellectual appetite, even though it does not always give intellectual satisfaction." [37] Only a dumb ox, methodically answering every question put to his claims, could satisfy; Maritain, in contrast, asserted more than he answered.

Eliot is careful to insist these observations are not intended as criticism or dismissal, and yet, one can hardly miss the tempering of enthusiasm for a man he had only recently called the most powerful force in French philosophy. One source of these qualifications may be the genre of *Three Reformers* itself. It is a work of destructive criticism, intended to show the role Martin Luther, René Descartes, and Jean-Jacques Rousseau played in the advent of modern individualism, skepticism, and romantic solipsism. While engaging these figures with the technical equipment of Aquinas, and thereby providing both substantial arguments against them as well as detailed outlines of what we might call the true Thomist anthropology, the book remains principally a polemic. According to Schloesser, it was greeted as partisan and parochial when first published in Paris, hindering Maritain's burgeoning reputation among the cultured elite. In contrast, Eliot's review welcomes the book as an opportunity for the English reading public to orient itself to the more extensively developed French "classicist" or neo-Thomist culture. Through it, the metaphysical, aesthetic, and political synthesis in which Maritain had proven instrumental, could be easily encountered.

Even so, the work did not give entire "intellectual satisfaction," Eliot indicates. In so doing, he muffles a more severe criticism he had rendered months earlier in an essay on another representative of the classical tendency, Julien Benda. In *The Cambridge Quarterly*, Eliot reflected on Benda's criticisms of the French Catholic writer Léon Bloy, and in the process makes a severe observation about Bloy's unhappy influence; it "begat Maritain, who begat the emotional and popular vulgarised neo-Thomism of our time." [38] Maritain and Bloy alike are prey to "a romantic excess of feeling over thought."[39] Eliot diagnoses this excess by attributing it to

> The influence of Bergson again, as well as that of Péguy and the ecstatic Léon Bloy . . . upon the leader of the Catholic rationalists, M. Jacques Maritain. I have a warm personal admiration for M. Maritain, though it is as much for his saintly character as for his intelligence; but I have never seen a more romantic classicist, or a Thomist whose methods of thought were less like those of Aquinas.[40]

Indeed, few of Maritain's works during the nineteen-twenties, with the possible exception of *Art et Scholastique*, are as closely thought out, as "exact," as Eliot may have hoped. And even this work was criticized in *The Criterion* for being "foggy" in places.[41] Besides his well-received textbook introductions to Philosophy and Logic, most of Maritain's early books were compilations of periodical essays. Collected essays seldom make for unified, careful argumentation. Indeed, Maritain tended to elaborate rather than plod through the premises needed to demonstrate his claims, so that an initial assertion appearing in one essay is repeated in greater detail in another, and so on, like so many concentric rings radiating from a point. The account of reason sketched in the opening chapters of *Antimoderne* (1922), for instance, receives fuller treatment in the first two chapters of *Réflexions*, but only achieves something approaching full demonstration a decade later in *Les Degrés du Savoir [The Degrees of Knowledge]* (1932).

Eliot was disappointed by this partial mode of presentation, writing to Herbert Read as early as December 1925 that Maritain's *Réflexions sur l'intelligence* was "valuable and significant" but revealed Maritain as "in too great a hurry to arrive" at his final position. Maritain may defeat his present opponent in a debate, but he does not establish his own position decisively. Only a "thorough historical defense of thomism or of the Church," careful and gradual of argument could do so.[42] There was much enthusiasm, charm, and lyricism in the prose style, and a confidence that Aquinas can best any modern in close debate—all of which promised to draw attractive ideas into real, substantial being. But Eliot hoped to find in neo-Thomism the same thoroughness of argument one found in the pages of St. Thomas himself, but applied to modern conditions. He needed to be convinced, not persuaded. And yet, however incomplete Maritain's argumentation, he evidently increased Eliot's interest in and openness to neo-Thomism in the period just before and after Christian conversion.

THOMISM IN *THE CRITERION*

Eliot's repeated criticisms of Maritain make for an unfavorable, but illuminating, comparison with the simple confidence he expressed at this time in the scholarly authority of another major French neo-Thomist, Étienne Gilson.[43] Maritain presented himself chiefly as an apostle and apologist, Gilson as a historian and medievalist. Tellingly, while John Gould Fletcher complained in *The Criterion* of Maritain's "fogginess" of argument, the glowing *Criterion* reviews Algar Thorold and Evelyn Underhill would give Gilson's books in the nineteen-thirties especially praised his simple elegance of prose style, "lucidity," and above all thoroughness of argument.[44] We should note the evident development here, however: Eliot's criticisms of Maritain are made in implicit comparison with other neo-Thomists, and the importance of Thomism for *Criterion* classicism seemed to be a given. The only questions remaining were, to what extent Aquinas could be appropriated for this modern classical project, and on which exponents of Aquinas one might best rely.

In consequence of such praises, Eliot's *Criterion* soon came to be associated in the minds of its writers, readers, and critics with French neo-Thomism, prompting Eliot's June 1927 remarks that neither endorsed nor denied the identification of classicism with the "reactionary Latin philosophy" of neo-Thomism.[45] Although Eliot refused, here and elsewhere, to insist upon a strict platform for his journal, its acceptance of neo-Thomism for a sort of intellectual standard and object of study became unmistakable. Aside from frequent references to Aquinas in the journal, Eliot's 1926 review of books by Read and Fernandez (mentioned above) would set off a debate in its pages on the notion of "intelligence" and "intuition," which would serve to strengthen the alliance between *Criterion* classicism and Thomist realism.

John Middleton Murry, a frequent sparring partner of Eliot's, published "Towards a Synthesis" in *The Criterion*'s June 1927 issue. There, he suggested that Eliot and Read's "classicism" was either cherry-picking from, or bowdlerizing, the *Summa Theologica* of Thomas Aquinas. This was a futile project because the *Summa* stands or falls as an integral metaphysical system, and that system no longer corresponds to the experience of modern man.[46] Murry agreed with Eliot that some sort of classical synthesis was necessary, but it must be of a very different sort from the Christian theological synthesis of Aquinas, precisely because modern man's experience no longer corresponded to the Thomist system of metaphysics, which had been itself only a projection of the subjective experience of medieval man. For, while the scholastics had reconciled faith and reason, modern man had only reason and intuition.[47]

Eliot had two responses prepared for the September issue, the most important of which was by M. C. D'Arcy, S.J., whose entire essay sought to defend the Thomistic theory of intellection, and the distinction of faith and reason, from what he saw as Murry's confused and relativistic assault. According to D'Arcy, Aquinas distinguishes sufficiently between the objects of faith and reason that one need not be a Christian theologian to accept the cogency of Aquinas's philosophical arguments: "The question therefore between Thomism and modern philosophy . . . can be argued without reference to Faith."[48] D'Arcy then proceeds to defend the Thomistic conception of reason. He first defends reason from its modern usage, which "reduces the rational to that science which deals with quantity."[49] This account of reason cannot satisfy and so tempts human beings to abdicate and go in search of "other loves," such as "sentimentalism, voluntarism, intuition, ineffable experience, art, history and emotional religion."[50] Thomists, in contrast, view reason as "the eye which alone makes us cognizant of the world," as "the activity whereby we are enabled to be or become another according to the manner of being or nature of that order."[51] Such descriptions could have been lifted directly from the opening chapters of Maritain's *Réflexions*. So could D'Arcy's insistence that one must neither reduce nor abdicate, but maintain a clear sense of, human reason as occupying an inferior rung on the great ladder of intellect that rises up to the divine.

The bulk of D'Arcy's essay is dedicated to elaborating this last point by laying out the Thomist theory of reason (*ratio*) as a discursive and composite mode of thought that nonetheless participates in intellect (*intellectus*), the supreme vision of truth singularly, eminently realized in God's knowing all things at once simply by knowing His own essence.[52] While our plodding reason pales in comparison with the divine mind, it nonetheless reaches toward it as an ideal limit. The scholastics were well aware of the inferiority of human reason; *contra* Murry, nothing significant has changed between Aquinas's day and ours regarding our confidence in or doubts about its sufficiency. Human reason is by nature a rickety instrument in comparison with the eternal and instantaneous knowledge of the divine mind; further, it is pale with abstraction in comparison with the vision of truth the angels enjoy or the fullness of God's knowledge by simply knowing Himself. These remarks, as D'Arcy acknowledges, derive from another French neo-Thomist, the late Pierre Rousselot, whose writings on the participation of *ratio* in *intellectus* and their analogous, hierarchical relationship would be reviewed in *The Criterion* nearly a decade later.[53] Although Rousselot's thought was informed by modern philosophy and revealed the absorption of Platonic theories of participation in Aquinas's writings, D'Arcy's account of it also hews closely—but less obviously—to Maritain's published reflections on intelligence (Maritain was more reserved than was Rousselot regarding the centrality of Platonic "participation" metaphysics in Aquinas's thought).[54]

Curiously, Murry's claim that a new classical synthesis was required for modern culture repeats an observation Eliot had made on several occasions in the past.[55] But Eliot's response to Murry's essay was uniformly negative. That said, he would not decisively assent to D'Arcy and the neo-Thomist position either. Perhaps Eliot recognized traces of his early disillusionment with philosophy and temptation by scientific mate-

rialism and relativism in Murry's argument, and perhaps D'Arcy's refu-
tation of such crude rationalism provoked Eliot to confess his status as an
ignorant amateur regarding Aquinas:

> I am not yet certain to what point I should wish to champion the 'sys-
> tem' of St. Thomas; I am quite certain that I am not at present qualified
> to do so. . . . My knowledge of Aquinas is slight: it is limited to the
> accounts of Gilson and de Wulf, to two volumes of extracts, one pre-
> pared by Professor Gilson and the other of M. Truc, to two or three
> books by M. Maritain and modern Dominicans, and to the new edition
> of the *Summa* published by Desclée. Only nine volumes of this edition
> have yet appeared, and in these nine volumes I have only read here
> and there. I am in every way unfitted to pose as an authority on 'non-
> Christian neo-Thomism'; and it may be that my slight and piecemeal
> knowledge of the texts is the reason why I do not think of St. Thomas's
> work primarily and panoramically as a 'system', in Mr. Murry's
> sense.[56]

Even this list of books betrays more than a "slight" acquaintance with
Aquinas, but more interesting perhaps is that we know it to be incomplete. Aside from the modern French edition of the *Summa*, Eliot here
cites no books published before the 1920s; but in the years after abandoning academic philosophy, he had reviewed the entire curriculum of neo-
scholastic philosophy in Cardinal Mercier's *Manual of Scholastic Philosophy* and Fr. Peter Coffey's *Epistemology*, and he read other works by Thomists, at least as early as 1917. Perhaps Eliot had come to identify Aquinas chiefly with the French neo-Thomism of Maritain, despite his criticisms of Maritain's "romanticism." Perhaps he had simply forgotten the
extent of his early philosophical reading.

Whatever his uncertainty, Eliot admitted that the modern classical
tendency should not merely be analogical to what Murry had called the
"classicism" of Aquinas and Dante.[57] Rather, it should absorb any
"crumbs of truth" it might find in the *Summa* and it may, as D'Arcy drily
proposed, draw its entire philosophy from Aquinas.[58] The considerable
number of reviews of neo-Thomistic works—particularly those of Regi-
nald Garrigou-Lagrange, Étienne Gilson, and Maritain—*The Criterion*
printed during the remaining decade of its existence testifies to Eliot's
efforts to draw intellectual nourishment from Aquinas. But, unsurpris-
ingly, most of the texts we have cited have focused on questions of epistemology and metaphysics, of being and reason.

The Criterion's reviews of and essays by neo-Thomists would stray
from these foundational elements of "classicism" as time went on. It is
true that new lines of convergence and departure would emerge between
Eliot and Maritain themselves in the thirties, as both authors turned to
political questions, and as both continued to meditate on the nature of art
and poetry in light of theology. But more striking than this is the subtle
shift, in Eliot's writing and in *The Criterion*, away from intellectualist

metaphysics and toward a wider, less obviously "classical," appreciation of Christian thought. Having rejected the rhetorical Platonism of Arnold and other Victorians, Eliot seemed open to a more substantial Christian Platonism. The most intriguing clue to such a shift may be found in a 1938 *Criterion* review of Gilson's book on St. Bonaventure, written by the young philosopher Arthur N. Prior. The review begins with a sardonic comment on the triumph of Thomist intellectualism as a "popular creed" and "propaganda."[59] It then proceeds to hold up St. Bonaventure as an alternative to the Thomist and Cartesian rationalism of modern Catholicism, concluding,

> it is not easy to resist the conclusion that the spirit of the Seraphic Doctor has largely departed from the Thomas-and-Ignatius-ridden Church of Rome and is finding a different resting-place in these latter days. At all events, it is neither in Barth nor in Maritain but in [F. D.] Maurice and those who have learned from him that we now find St. Bonaventure's clear refusal to co-ordinate Christianity with a completed philosophy such as Aristotle's and his attempt instead to take up the essentially fragmentary philosophy of Plato into one that is Christian through and through.[60]

While I would not ascribe these positions to Eliot—especially the reference to the suspect nineteenth-century "broad churchman," F. D. Maurice—he clearly was open to them, as is evident from his attraction, during this period, to certain ideas of the German philosopher Joseph Pieper, who was a Thomist imbued with a Platonic sensibility, and his nod of approval regarding the thought of the moderate Anglican bishop and Christian Platonist, William Temple.[61] Further, Eliot had years earlier already found a connection between the "fragmentary philosophy of Plato," the discontinuities of Pascal, and the classicism of T. E. Hulme, manifest in the writings of his close friend and fellow Anglican convert, Paul Elmer More.[62] Eliot repeatedly expressed his admiration for More's critical achievement, and especially for his "Anglican Platonism," which sought by means of dense and solitary scholarship to recover the Christian Platonist tradition for modern men. But he strongly disagreed with More's individualistic ecclesiology and disregard for the Sacrament of the Eucharist.[63] Further, he saw that More's Christian-Platonic conception of God as the Good and the One had caused him to lapse "into Humanitarianism" regarding the existence of Hell as the product of God's love and justice.[64]

Once again, I mention these details not to indicate Eliot's identification with either More or Prior, but to suggest that his increasing devotion to the study of theology after his conversion came, not only at the expense of an interest in mere literary criticism, but at the expense of his need for a rigorously intellectualist philosophy.[65] It must, therefore, also have lessened his need to adhere closely to the Thomist realist line espoused by Maritain, though he would continue to draw upon it to good effect in his post-conversion intellectual life, particularly in his social and political criticism. He would also take Maritain for a model of how to live out one's vocation as a modern Christian intellectual.[66]

As for *The Criterion*, its writers would replicate Eliot's admiration and ambivalence regarding Maritain and neo-Thomism. Maritain's books received courteous but aloof notices, among them Tomlin's review of *Freedom in the Modern World* (October 1935) and Philip S. Richards's of *True Humanism* in the journal's final issue (January 1939).[67] Richards there notes with trepidation that Maritain believes modern civilization will collapse—a prediction that would largely be validated as the world descended into total war. And thus, we may rightly conclude that Maritain's neo-Thomism helped *The Criterion* establish a critical position that contrasted with the liberal humanist Platonism of the Victorian age; that the journal's engagement with Thomist philosophers helped it develop and nuance that position during the years of its flourishing; and that the prophetic voice of Maritain was in a profound sense present at the moment when the era of *The Criterion*'s awe-inspiring authority came to a close.

NOTES

1. W. H. Auden, *The Complete Works. Prose and Travel Books in Prose and Verse Volume 1: 1926–1938,* ed. Edward Mendelson (Princeton: Princeton University Press, 1996), 333.

2. T. S. Eliot, *Selected Essays 1917–1932* (New York: Harcourt, Brace and Co., 1932), 361.

3. Eliot, *Selected Essays*, 360.

4. T. S. Eliot, Review of *Three Reformers* by Jacques Maritain, *Times Literary Supplement* (8 November 1928): 818.

5. Eliot, Review of *Three Reformers*.

6. Jason Harding, "'The Just Impartiality of a Christian Philosopher': Jacques Maritain and T. S. Eliot" in *The Maritain Factor*, ed. Rajesh Heynickx and Jan De Maeyer (Leuven: Leuven University Press, 2010), 183. Herbert Read, "Books of the Quarter," *Criterion* 4, no. 1 (January 1926): 191–92.

7. Harding, 185.

8. T. S. Eliot, "A Commentary," *Criterion* 5, no. 3 (June 1927): 284.

9. T. S. Eliot, "A Reply to Mr. Ward," *Criterion* 7, no. 4 (June 1928): 376.

10. Roger Kojecký, *T. S. Eliot's Social Criticism* (London: Faber and Faber, 1971), 131.

11. T. S. Eliot, *Varieties of Metaphysical Poetry*, ed. Ronald Schuchard (San Diego: Harcourt Brace and Company, 1996), 104.

12. T. S. Eliot, "The Idea of a Literary Review," *Criterion* 4, no. 1 (January 1926): 4.

13. Jacques and Raïssa Maritain, *Oeuvres Complètes* 17 vols. (Fribourg: Éditions Universitaires, 1984), 3:41–42. Cited hereafter in the text as *O*.

14. Cf. Jacques Maritain, *Degrees of Knowledge* (Notre Dame: University of Notre Dame Press, 1995), 78; and Thomas Aquinas, *Summa Contra Gentiles*, 4 vols., trans. A.C. Pegis, et al. (Notre Dame: University of Notre Dame Press, 2001), 3:26.

15. Cf. Maritain, *Degrees of Knowledge*, 120.

16. John Henry Newman, *An Essay in Aid of a Grammar of Assent* (Notre Dame, IN: University of Notre Dame Press, 1979).

17. Eliot, *Varieties of Metaphysical Poetry*, 93.

18. T. E. Hulme, *Speculations* (New York: Routledge and Kegan Paul, 1987), 10.

19. E. W. F. Tomlin, *T. S. Eliot: A Friendship* (London: Routledge, 1988), 73.

20. T. S. Eliot, letter to Jacques Maritain, 24 July 1938 (Jacques and Raïssa Maritain Archive, Kolbsheim, France).

21. Stephen Schloesser, *Jazz Age Catholicism: Mystic Modernism in Postwar Paris, 1919–1933* (Toronto: University of Toronto Press, 2005), 7–8.

22. Jacques Maritain, *Art and Scholasticism and the Frontiers of Poetry*, trans. Joseph W. Evans (Notre Dame, IN: University of Notre Dame Press, 1974), 115, 227, 228.

23. T. S. Eliot, "A Commentary," *Criterion* 5, no. 1 (January 1927), 3.

24. Jacques Maritain, "Poetry and Religion," Part 1, trans. F.S. Flint, *New Criterion* 5, no. 1 (January 1927): 7–22 and "Poetry and Religion," Part 2, trans. F.S. Flint, *New Criterion* 5, no. 2 (May 1927): 214–230.

25. Maritain, *Art and Scholasticism*, 139.

26. T. S. Eliot, *The Letters of T. S. Eliot. Volume 1: 1898–1922 Revised Edition*, ed. Valerie Eliot and Hugh Haughton (London: Faber and Faber, 2009), 87.

27. T. S. Eliot, *The Sacred Wood* (London: Methuen, 1953), ix.

28. Eliot, *Sacred Wood*, ix.

29. T. S. Eliot, *The Use of Poetry and the Use of Criticism* (Cambridge: Harvard University Press, 1933), 116–17.

30. T. S. Eliot, letter to Jacques Maritain, 10 August 1927 (Jacques and Raïssa Maritain Archive, Kolbsheim).

31. Shun'ichi Takayanagi, S.J., "T. S. Eliot, Jacques Maritain, and Neo-Thomism," *The Modern Schoolman* 73, no. 1 (November 1995): 74.

32. T. S. Eliot, "A Contemporary Thomist" *The New Statesman* (29 December 1917): 312.

33. T. S. Eliot, Review of *Reason and Romanticism*, by Herbert Read, and *Messages*, by Ramon Fernandez, *Criterion* 4, no. 4 (October 1926): 754.

34. Tomlin, *T. S. Eliot*, 73.

35. Eliot, Review of *Three Reformers*, 818.

36. Eliot, Review of *Three Reformers*, 818.

37. Eliot, Review of *Three Reformers*, 818.

38. T. S. Eliot, "The Idealism of Julien Benda," *The Cambridge Review* 49, no. 1218 (6 June 1928): 486.

39. Eliot, "The Idealism of Julien Benda," 486.

40. Eliot, "The Idealism of Julien Benda," 488.

41. John Gould Fletcher, Review of *Art et Scolastique* and *The Philosophy of Art*, *Criterion* 11, no. 36 (1929): 347.

42. T. S. Eliot, *The Letters of T. S. Eliot: Volume 2: 1923–1925*, ed. Valerie Eliot and Hugh Haughton (London: Faber and Faber, 2009), 796.

43. Eliot, "The Twelfth Century," *Times Literary Supplement* (11 August 1927): 542.

44. Evelyn Underhill, review of *La Théologie Mystique de Saint Bernard*, by Étienne Gilson, *Criterion* 14, no. 55 (January 1935): 341. Algar Thorold, review of *L'Esprit de la Philosophie Médiévale*, by Étienne Gilson, *Criterion* 13, no. 50 (October 1933): 170.

45. T. S. Eliot, "A Commentary," *Criterion* 5, no. 3 (June 1927): 284.

46. John Middleton Murry, "Towards a Synthesis," *Criterion* 5, no. 3 (June 1927): 298, 309.

47. Ibid., 300.

48. M. C. D'Arcy, S.J., "The Thomistic Synthesis and Intelligence," *Criterion* 6, no. 3 (September 1927): 216.

49. D'Arcy, 219.

50. D'Arcy, 224.

51. D'Arcy, 220, 222.

52. D'Arcy, 222.

53. D'Arcy, 223.

54. Richard O'Sullivan, review of *The Intellectualism of St. Thomas*, by Pierre Rousselot *Criterion* 15, no. 60 (April 1936): 563–65. O'Sullivan summarizes Aquinas's position that created beings have their own goodness, and thus the human person can pass on his good through procreation and the human intellect knows in its own right, not merely by participation in the intellect of God. And yet that "proper autonomy of the human intellect" stands in analogous and hierarchical relation to the divine intellect (564). Thus, we think discursively (by reasoning, *ratio*), and in so doing stand in a particular analogous relation to God who sees all truth by seeing His own essence (as D'Arcy expresses it, this is the "ideal" or archetype of intelligence from which our own derives).

55. See, for example, Eliot, "The Idea of a Literary Review," 5.

56. T. S. Eliot, "Mr. Middleton Murry's Synthesis," *Criterion* 6, no. 4 (October 1927): 340–41.

57. Murry, 304.

58. Eliot, "Mr. Middleton Murry's Synthesis," 346.

59. Arthur N. Prior, review of *The Philosophy of St. Bonaventure*, by Étienne Gilson, *Criterion* 18, no. 70 (October 1938): 141.

60. Ibid., 143.

61. T. S. Eliot, Introduction to *Leisure: The Basis of Culture*, by Joseph Pieper, trans. Alexander Dru (London: Faber and Faber, 1952), 14–15; T. S. Eliot, untitled essay in *Revelation*, ed. John Baillie and Hugh Martin (London: Faber and Faber, 1937), 35.

62. T. S. Eliot, "Mr. P.E. More's Essays," *The Times Literary Supplement*, 21 February 1929, 136.

63. T. S. Eliot, "An Anglican Platonist: The Conversion of Paul Elmer More," *The Times Literary Supplement*, 30 October 1937, 792.

64. Manju Jain, *T. S. Eliot and American Philosophy* (New York: Cambridge University Press, 1992), 227–28.

65. Kojecký, 78.

66. Kojecký, 74.

67. E. W. F. Tomlin, review of *Religion and the Modern State*, by Christopher Dawson; *Freedom in the Modern World*, by Jacques Maritain; and *Preface to a Christian Sociology*, by Cyril E. Hudson, *Criterion* 15, no. 58 (October 1935): 130–37; Philip S. Richards, review of *True Humanism*, by Jacques Martin, *Criterion* 18, no. 71 (Janauary 1939): 329–33.

III

Christian Tradition

SEVEN

The Mind That Suffers, the Mind That Creates, and the Mind of Europe: T. S. Eliot's Use of Aristotle's *De Anima*

William Charron

In 1919, T. S. Eliot watched with horror the imposition of what he called a "bad peace" by the winning powers of the First World War—bad because it would economically destroy Germany and because it was an arbitrary reorganization of nations without any historical sense of the cultures involved.[1] That same year, Eliot was moved to write a poem and an essay that expressed his alarm and that called for a new way of thinking about European culture. The poem is "Gerontion" and the essay is "Tradition and Individual Talent." The seminal character of these two works for Eliot's philosophy of culture and tradition is widely appreciated. But I think those who read these pieces as expressions of a Bradleyan, Hegelian, or even Buddhistic philosophy, go wrong.[2] The philosophy most directly informing his thoughts on this subject is that of Aristotle, especially as Aristotle's thought is set out in the *De Anima*.

The point of this paper is to demonstrate the connection between Eliot's account of mind and culture—including what he calls the mind of the man who suffers, the mind of the poet who creates, and the impersonal mind of Europe—with the equally complex account of mind presented by Aristotle, and developed over the centuries by Arabian philosophers and Dante.

It is well to note that while Eliot studied a year at Oxford (the academic year 1914–1915), with the intent of meeting and working with Bradley, on whom he was writing a dissertation, he, in fact, spent most of his effort in making an in-depth study of ancient Greek philosophers,

119

especially Aristotle. In this study, he was advised by his tutors to make use of Zabarella's commentary on Aristotle's *De Anima*.[3] From this Renaissance commentator (1532–1589), Eliot would acquaint himself with the history of the centuries-old controversy over the correct interpretation of Aristotle's theory of the mind. This controversy immediately began among Aristotle's disciples; it continued through the Middle Ages among Arabian commentators in Persia and in Spain; it then worked its way into European thinking during the high Middle Ages, and ultimately affected the work of the Italian poets Cavalcanti and Dante, and ultimately the Enlightenment and Romantic philosophers Kant and Hegel. This controversy is known as *the problem of the substantial unity of the soul*. The issue is this: Is the mind, as Aristotle understands it, but one of the several faculties of a unified soul, or is the mind a "thing apart" from the individual soul? I think it is clear that Aristotle treats the mind as a "thing apart." Allow me to provide what I consider to be one of the proof texts demonstrating Aristotle's rejection of the doctrine of the substantive unity of the soul. As you read this quotation from Aristotle, I would ask you to keep in mind Eliot's poem "Gerontion"—in which a dying old man is losing his sensory powers of sight, smell, hearing, taste, and touch.

> . . . mind [*nous*] is different; it seems to be an independent substance implanted within the soul and to be incapable of being destroyed. If it could be destroyed at all, it would be under the blunt influence of old age. What really happens in respect of mind in old age is, however, exactly parallel to what happens in the case of the sense organs; if the old man [*geron*] could recover the proper kind of eye, he would see just as well as the young man. The incapacity of old age is due to an affection not of the soul but of its vehicle, as occurs in drunkenness or disease. Thus it is that in old age the activity of mind or intellectual apprehension declines only through the decay of some other inward part; mind itself is impassible. Thinking, loving, and hating are affections not of mind, but of that which has mind, so far as it has it. That is why, when this vehicle decays, memory and love cease; they were activities not of mind but of the composite which has perished; *mind [nous] is, no doubt, something more divine and impassible*.[4]

When Eliot explains to his reader what he is attempting to do in his difficult essay "Tradition and Individual Talent," he says this: "The point of view which I am struggling to attack is perhaps related to *the metaphysical theory of the substantial unity of the soul*: for my meaning is, that the poet has, not a 'personality' to express, but a particular medium, which is only a medium and not a personality."[5] As I read it, Eliot in referencing the ancient problem of the metaphysical relation of the mind (*nous*) to the individual soul (*psychē*), wants us to consider, as did Aristotle, that the individual human being is an instrument or the medium through which a mind, a superior mind, works and develops itself. To cement this connection with the Aristotelian theory of the mind, Eliot employs the italicized last line of the text just given as the epigraph of the third section of his essay: he provides only the Greek text without referencing the *De Anima*: "ὁ δὲ νοῦς ἴσως θειότερόν τι καὶ ἀπαθές ἐστιν": "The mind is certainly a thing more divine and cannot be affected or suffer."[6]

The case for the Aristotelian theory of mind behind Eliot's work becomes stronger when one considers the details of each man's account of the mind. In "Tradition and Individual Talent," Eliot speaks of three sorts of mind:

1. "the private mind" of the man who "suffers"—the mind that functions as a "receptacle" or "chamber" in which "personal impressions and experiences combine";
2. the mind that "creates"—the mind that functions as a "transforming catalyst," or "transmuter" of the impressions and experiences of the mind that suffers; and, finally
3. "the mind of Europe," "a mind which [one] learns in time to be much more important than his own private mind"—a mind that changes, but whose change "is a development which abandons nothing *en route.*" In mere physical matter the acquisition of one form is the exclusion of another. But in the mind, the acquisition of a form or a new idea excludes no other. Mind is, in short, a place of forms "having a simultaneous existence and composing a simultaneous order."

In the third book of the *De Anima*, Aristotle identifies three sorts of mind that closely parallel in function the three identified by Eliot.

1. The passive or suffering mind (*nous pathetikos*): which perishes with the death of the individual.[7] Some commentators, including Thomas Aquinas, identify the passive or suffering mind with the imagination, which is the seat of memory and dreams.[8] The passive or suffering mind, as the imagination, is the place of the images or phantasms without which there is no thinking. "The soul never thinks without an image (*phantasma*)." In fact, for a human, nothing is intelligible to the mind unless "it thinks the universal forms (*eidē*) *in* the images (*phantasmata*)."[9]
2. The active or maker mind (*nous poiētikos*) renders all things intelligible. Aristotle compares it to light which makes the potentially visible actually so: "It is a sort of positive state like light, for in a sense light makes potential colours into actual colours" and the active mind makes what is potentially known actually so.[10]
3. The potential or possible intellect (*nous dunamei*), which is what it is by virtue of its ability to come to know the forms or essences of all things. It is a sort of "place of forms" (*topon eidōn*) in which ideas come to reside accumulatively and interactively, without dispossessing or destroying those already acquired.[11]

As already noted, the interpretation of Aristotle's theory of mind has a long history which takes us through the Arabian philosophers, Thomas Aquinas, Dante, and up through Kant and Hegel. Eliot's version is not Thomistic, at least at this early point in his career. His version is, I contend, substantially that which Dante advanced in his work *De Monarchia*, and which Dante claimed to derive from the Arabian philosopher Averroes.

AVERROES/IBN ROSCHD (1126–1198)

A devoted scholar of Aristotle's corpus, Averroes, a Muslim, was born in Cordova, Spain. When the bulk of Aristotle's writings first entered Christian Western Europe in Latin translation, they came together with Averroes's commentaries. Among Western scholars, Aristotle became known as "The Philosopher" and Averroes as "The Commentator." Latin translations of Aristotle and Averroes were made in the thirteenth century in the courts of Frederick II of Sicily and of Archbishop Raymond of Toledo, Spain.[12] In all his commentaries, Averroes intended to stay as close as possible to what he took to be the meaning and argument of Aristotle's works. Of his three commentaries on the *De Anima* of Aristotle—the "short," the "middle," and the "long"—the last[13] became the standard text for scholars through the Renaissance and the Enlightenment.

In his long commentary on Aristotle's *De Anima*, Averroes interprets Aristotle as recognizing three minds or intellects: (1) the passible intellect (*intellectus passibilis*), which is the intellect of the individual human, (2) the agent intellect (*intellectus agens*), which is a single entity and distinct from individual humans whom it enlightens, and (3) the possible intellect (*intellectus possibilis*), which is also one for all humankind and distinct from that of any individual. Consider them in turn.

1. The passible intellect (*intellectus passibilis*) is the mind that "suffers," undergoing changes through experiential encounters with material nature. This intellect is reducible to the individual's faculty of imagination, the faculty that receives and stores the personal impressions and phantasms that make possible personal memory and desire. The abilities of the passible intellect in humans differ, determining individual talents for cognition and contribution to the common knowledge of humankind.[14]

2. The agent intellect (*intellectus agens*) is one and the same in all human beings. As such it preexists any individual, being the efficient cause or source of abstract thinking in humans. As Aristotle had said, the agent intellect functions like a light that works upon the store of impressions and phantasms in the imagination of the individual, transforming them into something intelligible and universally meaningful.[15]

3. The third sort of mind is the possible intellect (*intellectus possibilis*). Like the agent intellect, it is also independent of the individual who suffers in his imagination or passible intellect. It is "one in number in all individuals" and is "neither generable nor corruptible," as is the passible intellect of the individual. Once the possible intellect has been activated by the agent intellect, the possible intellect is, in the proper sense of the term, *that-which-knows*, that which in its detachment from the personal experience and feeling serves as traditional wisdom, that is, the *universal meaning* of countless impressions and emotions of the individuals who suffered them. Upon the annihilation of the individual in death, the knowledge of the universal and eternal is not lost; rather it continues to exist as habitual knowledge in the impersonal possible intellect; it is the sharable inheritance of humankind, thanks to the institution of teaching. To paraphrase Averroes—although what is known by the teacher and the student is different in respect of the imaginative forms in which it is known, it is one in respect of the knower, which is the one existing and abiding possible intellect common to all individuals. For the individual, knowing is somehow a participation to some degree or other in the knowledge built up in this one, universal mind.[16]

Since Averroes's interpretation of mind excluded the possibility of personal immortality, the Christian Thomas Aquinas found it necessary to argue against the idea that the active and possible minds, which are immortal, are universal and distinct from the individual soul. To the contrary, Thomas argues, in his treatise *De Unitate Intellectus Contra Averroistas*, that Aristotle, when correctly read, does not treat either the active or the possible intellect as separate from the individual or as one for all individuals. Rather there is a substantial unity of the individual soul such that the active, the possible, and the passive intellects are three *faculties* of the one individual soul and the individual soul is immortal.[17]

Jumping to Eliot's day, it is provoking to note that Ezra Pound, aware of this controversy between Thomists and the Latin Averroists on the nature of the intellect, chides Aquinas for his attack on Averroes.[18]

DANTE (1256–1321)

In his work *De Monarchia* (1308), Dante develops his theory of mind as an extension of the theory of Averroes.[19] What Dante adds to Averroes's reading of Aristotle is that the one possible intellect of mankind has reality not as a single being or substance, but, rather, as the *collective intelligence* of humankind taken as a whole. The possible intellect is a broad and universal community of generations of individuals existing through time. As Gilson explains it, "Dante has transposed the thesis of Averroes by taking the human race, in other words, the individuals existing at all times on earth regarded collectively, as the equivalent of the single possible intellect of Averroes."[20] (We are here close to the heart of Eliot's concept of *tradition*.) In Dante's words,

> [T]he ultimate capacity is that which constitutes a species. . . . [For humans] it consists in the capacity to apprehend by the possible intellect. . . . [T]he potentiality [for complete knowledge and wisdom] cannot wholly and at once be actualized by any one man, or by any particular community. Mankind has to be composed of a multitude of communities and generations through which this entire potentiality can be actualized. . . . Averroes agrees with this opinion in the commentary on the *De Anima*.[21]

The task proper to mankind then is to fulfill the total capacity of the possible intellect raising it to the state of knowledge or wisdom which then becomes the "common inheritance" of individuals who in turn have a duty to perpetuate, as well as to contribute to the same.

The basis of Dante's interest in elaborating this Averroist interpretation of the mind of humanity—or what for Dante reduces to the *mind of Europe*, since the world *is* Europe—is the part it plays in his overall reformist program for Universal Monarchy in politics, Roman Catholicism in religion, and Classical Philosophy in culture.[22] We again meet this trinity of aims in Charles Maurras, and his followers, and then in Eliot himself. Each in his own way works toward some variant of royalism, catholicism, and classicism. Dante's Averroist understanding of the mind of humanity figures directly into his argument for the restoration of the European monarchy which was the Roman Empire of Augustus and its reincarnation in the Holy Roman Empire of Charlemagne. Dante's argument for the restoration of monarchical world government is this:

1. The task of humanity as a species is to actualize the capacity of the possible intellect of humanity (*intellectus possibilis*)—that is, the mind of Europe.

2. The necessary condition of that achievement is a universal (that is, European) peace, for as Aristotle recognizes, the mind actualizes its potential for truth as such only when it is free from the utilitarian and animal demands of survival and has the leisure (*skolē*) to pursue knowledge (*epistēmē*) and beauty or nobility (*kalon*) for its own sake.

3. Only a single monarchical world empire can secure a universal peace among the cities and peoples, since wherever there is a possibility of dispute there has to be a superior judge to settle it; otherwise the only remedy is war, and a multiplicity of sovereign states would be without a remedy for dispute other than war.

THEREFORE
4. To fulfill the task of actualizing the capacity of the possible intellect of (European) humanity, it is necessary to (re)institute world government.[23]

On Dante's reading of history, the only time when the world enjoyed perfect universal peace was during the reign of the Roman Emperor Augustus:

> At no time do we see universal peace throughout the world, except during the perfect monarchy of the immortal Caesar Augustus. The fact that mankind at the time was resting happily in universal peace is attested by all the historians and the illustrious poets. Even St. Luke, the recorder of Christ's gentleness [Gospel of Luke, 2:1], has deigned to bear witness to it. St. Paul, also, described that blissful state [of the Empire] as "the fullness of time.". . . But what a terrible state the world has been in since that seamless garment was rent on the nail of cupidity [of the princes of Europe and the Church].[24]

Reading this lament of Dante brings to mind Eliot's "Gerontion," written at the same time Eliot was working on "Tradition and the Individual Talent." "Gerontion" is a poem defining the state of European humanity and the state of its collective mind. As a piece which Eliot considered incorporating in *The Waste Land*, "Gerontion" moves within the perspective of the twentieth-century European mind, whose most recent memory is the wasting of its finest young men in the "rats alley" trenches of the First World War. Looking back in regret through the cunning passages of history, the poem recalls the birth time of a Europe unified and organized under the Roman monarchy in the service of classical ideals. It was also the moment in history when "Christ the Tiger" sprang in the new year. It was the moment which defined for Europe an ideal of politics, religion, and culture; it was the beginning that defined the end for the collective mind of Europe.[25]

> In the juvescence of the year
> Came Christ the tiger. . . .
> History has many cunning passages, contrived corridors
> And issues, deceives with whispering ambitions,
> Guides us by vanities.
> . . . Think
> Neither fear nor courage saves us. Unnatural vices
> Are fathered by our heroism. Virtues
> Are forced upon us by our impudent crimes.
> These tears are shaken from the wrath-bearing tree.[26]

Eliot, like Dante, is intent upon the idea of the collective mind just because he senses and suffers the cultural fragmentation of Europe. Thinking this cultural collapse is not unconnected with the political and religious situation, he talks of royalism as a counter to democratic levelling and Catholicism as a counter to Protestant pluralism. And like Dante he casts his reformist program in terms of restoring the religious and political conditions that would enable the resumption of the task of humanity: the task of the actualization of the total capacity of the possible intellect of humanity, the collective mind of Europe.

With Averroes's and Dante's accounts in mind, consider Eliot's account of the mental dynamics of creating poetry, metaphysical poetry: The *agent intellect* (what Eliot calls "the mind which creates") works on the emotional or affective materials of the *passive intellect* (what he calls "the mind of the man who suffers"), from which is created a new being that may embody a new emotion, an "artistic emotion" distinct from and irreducible to any personal emotion previously felt by anyone. The new being is a creation of art, together with the significant emotion it can evoke in an appreciative spectator, may then become part of the tradition, part of the *habitual knowledge* of the *possible intellect* that is the shared, the collective mind (what Eliot calls "the mind of Europe"). The mind that creates, the creative poet as agent intellect, will succeed in its task of creating significant art from the chaos of materials of the individual who suffers only if the poet works with a deep sense and understanding of the tradition. The creative poet incorporates the perfections of the tradition in order to generate new and significant art from the experiential materials of the private imagination; in short, *the truly creative artist must also be traditional.* Here is the heart of Eliot's classical stand against romantic expressionism. Aristotle himself was the first to set down this first principle of classicism: he wrote, "the poet should be inventive, but he in doing so must make good use of traditional stories." Aristotle demands, as does Eliot, both tradition and individual talent. [27]

It is a notable fact that when Eliot says that the collective mind of Europe is "a mind that changes and that this change is a development which abandons nothing *en route*," he pinpoints precisely that feature of the potentiality of the mind or intellect which distinguishes it from the potentiality of matter. [28] Matter in changing takes on a new form or perfection only as it loses its current form or perfection. Change in matter is then a sort of *destruction*: in Aristotle's words, the generation of one thing is necessarily the destruction of another. By contrast, the change characteristic of mind—the possible intellect—implies a certain *preservation* and perfecting of a thing in potency, rather than a destruction or replacement of one quality by its excluding contrary. [29] The mind, says Aristotle, is like a blank tablet or sheet of paper of indefinite magnitude. [30] On this tablet or sheet new words can always be written, without any words that have already been written being destroyed, replaced, or lost. Such is the character of the potentiality for change characteristic of mind as distinct from matter. Stepping into the world of mind, we can escape the cycle of generative and destructive changes of matter; we enter into an order in which there is preservation of acquired perfection and a sort of participation in eternity in escaping time's destructions in matter.[31]

The question that now suggests itself is this: What is to be achieved in actualizing the total capacity of the possible intellect? Put another way, what is the proper aim of the culturation of the mind of humanity? Eliot and Dante both repeat Aristotle's answer to the question. In essence, the proper aim of humanity is the achievement of a social and cultural order that assigns a significant place to a life of contemplation (*theoria*) and a subordinate place to mere work, that is, to practical business and service occupations. The key texts in Aristotle to which Eliot points us are Book 12 of the *Metaphysics* (1072b) and Book 10 of the *Nicomachean Ethics* (1177a13–1178a9).[32] In these texts, Aristotle argues that the most complete happiness to which any human may aspire is that which is achieved, even if only for brief periods of time, in the practice of contemplation. That achievement is a steady and intellectual comprehension and appreciation of all things in their order and worth. It is a sublime vision and understanding in which the mortal individual escapes time and enters eternity, if only for a time. In these moments of simple vision, one achieves, as Aristotle says, a vicarious immortality, a divine life.

Coming to this vision and understanding is possible only for the educated individual who has made the effort to obtain the discipline of the classical intellectual tradition to which many generations of agent minds have contributed. If the felicitous vision of this classical contemplative life is to be called "mysticism," it is, Eliot insists, "classical mysticism" — the mysticism of the intellect — and not "romantic mysticism" — the mysticism of a thoughtless state of feeling. As a mysticism of the intellect, it requires "the development and subsumption of emotion and feeling through intellect into . . . vision."[33] Rather than being an escape from reality into mental oblivion, it is a steady and alert contemplation of all things in their ordered worth, a contemplation that makes bearable the horrors that human life can present and the suffering it frequently exacts.[34]

Although classical contemplation is an act of the intellect, it is not without involvement of the imagination. As noted above, Aristotle insists that the mind never thinks without an image or phantasm. The mind attains to the contemplation of universal meanings only in conjunction with the imagination which provides a phantasm in which the meanings are incarnated, as it were.[35] The artist or poet who provides an image adequate to the steady and saving contemplation of things in their order and worth is in that respect *a philosophical poet*. On Eliot's estimation, the imagination of Dante provides the most adequate image in which to contemplate the value and relation of things as that is understood in the classical tradition commencing with Aristotle. *The Divine Comedy*, then, is the supreme phantasm of classical, intellectual mysticism.

What was revealed to Aristotle, to Dante, and to Eliot in each of their own moments of comprehensive contemplation—and I am assuming that each experienced such supreme moments—is an order of things that is both terrifying and supernal.

Terrifying and horrifying is the vision of the essential evil and ugliness of human beings acting without the constraints of some higher discipline, some higher culture—a culture that prizes acquired excellence (*aretē*) in action and the noble (*to kalon*) in motive. As Aristotle saw, when man is not disciplined in virtue, he is naturally the most unscrupulous and savage of animals, and the most consumed in lust and most gorged by gluttony - man undisciplined in virtue is a veritable monster.[36] Dante's *Inferno* is the perfect imitation of the Aristotelian vision of man without virtue: the ugliness of undisciplined action is given visible expression in the array of horrifying punishments that each sort of evil brings to its perpetrator. "Gerontion" and *The Waste Land* are together Eliot's *Inferno* of the lustful and the vulgar crowd undone by their dissipation and moral indifference. Eliot's *Inferno* provides the objective correlative for the emotions of terror and pity in the contemplation of the actions of flawed and wounded characters: rape, abortion, abandonment, and sexual coupling that is little more than evacuation; all these are brought within a single apprehension, the vision of Gerontion and the vision of Tiresias. The first emotions provoked are horror and pity; but then a distance is obtained, a sort of metaphysical peace is achieved. As Aristotle, Dante, and Eliot all recognize, the steady and objective contemplation of evil in a horrific vision has the power to free the soul from inner turmoil and to move it to inner peace, as the soul is pulled in opposing directions by pity and by fear. An impartial and comprehensive vision of terror can purge the contemplative of a confusion of personal emotion and secure for one a point of view on life which moves one to the sublime emotion of *metaphysical detachment*:

Shantih shantih shantih

But metaphysical peace is only the first felicity of the contemplative life, as that life is understood by Aristotle, Dante, and Eliot. The achievement of a steady and comprehensive understanding and appreciation of all things in their ideal order and worth can also be felicitous. Achieving any such understanding or vision is possible only to an individual initiated in a tradition of learning enforcing habits of comprehensive contemplation. In this apprehension in which a totality of things is grasped in ordered vision, the contemplative is made ready to respond with an appreciation in which one loses oneself in an object greater than oneself; the contemplative responds to the object of understanding with another metaphysical emotion, the emotion of acceptance, free from any practical desire to be other than one is.

NOTES

1. *The Letters of T. S. Eliot, Vol. I, 1889–1922*, ed. Valerie Eliot (New York: Harcourt, 1988), 337, 353.

2. See, for example, Sanford Schwartz, *The Matrix of Modernism: Pound, Eliot, and Early 20th Century Thought* (Princeton, NJ: Princeton University Press, 1985), 170–71; Cleo McNelly Kearns, *T. S. Eliot and Indic Traditions: A Study in Poetry and Belief* (Cambridge: Cambridge University Press, 1987), 62; Tatsuo Murata, "Buddhism in T. S. Eliot," *The Modern Schoolman* 73, no. 1 (1995): 40–46.

3. Jacobi Zabarella, *De Rebus Naturalibus in Aristotelis Libros "De Anima"* (Venice, 1605). In his letter of 28 January 1915 to Professor J. H. Woods, Eliot remarks "my notes on *Post-Anal.* and Zabarella on *de An.* are brief and marginal, but I will put them in order for you." *Letters*, 84; see also pages 67 and 117.

4. Aristotle, *De Anima* I.4, 408b11–29, trans. J. A. Smith , vol. 3 of *The Works of Aristotle*, 12 vols., edited by W. D. Ross (Oxford: Clarendon, 1930). The term "*nous*" has several meanings for Aristotle. First, it is the name of the entity or power by which the soul thinks: "by mind (*nous*) I mean that by which the soul thinks or judges" (*De Anima*, III.4, 429a23). Second, the term "*nous*" is the name of the intellectual virtue by which the soul grasps first principles of theoretical sciences; used in this sense, "*nous*" is sometimes translated as "intuitive reason" or "the power of intuition" (*Nicomachean Ethics*, VI.6, 1140b30–41a7, trans. W. D. Ross, vol. 9 of *The Works of Aristotle*). Our concern is with *nous* in the first sense, *nous* as mind or intellect.

5. T. S. Eliot, *The Sacred Wood: Essays on Poetry and Criticism* (London and New York: Methuen, 1920), 56. Emphasis added.

6. *The Sacred Wood*, 59. For quotation, see Aristotle, *De Anima* I.4, 408b29–30.

7. *De Anima* III.5, 430a29.

8. Thomas Aquinas, *Commentary on Aristotle's "De Anima,"* trans. Kenelm Foster and Silvester Humphries (New Haven: Yale University Press, 1951), §745, p. 432.

9. Aristotle, *De Anima* III.7, 431a14–431b5.

10. Aristotle, *De Anima* III.5, 408a12.

11. Aristotle, *De Anima* III.5, 429a27.

12. F. Van Steenbergen, *Aristotle in the West* (Louvain: Nauwelaerts, 1955).

13. Averroes, *Cordubensis Commentarium Magnum in Aristotelis De Anima Libros*, ed. F. Stuart Crawford (Cambridge, MA: The Medieval Academy of America, 1953). For an accessible English translation, see *Averroes's Great Commentary on the Third Book of Aristotle's "De Anima,"* trans. James C. Doig.

14. *Averroes's Great Commentary*, Comm. 20, 56.

15. *Averroes's Great Commentary*, Comm. 18, 43–46.

16. *Averroes's Great Commentary*, Comm. 5, 17–19.

17. Thomas Aquinas, *On the Unity of the Intellect Against the Averroists*, trans. Beatrice H. Zedler (Milwaukee, WI: Marquette University Press, 1968).

18. Ezra Pound, "Cavalcanti" in *Literary Essays of Ezra Pound*, ed. T. S. Eliot (New York: New Directions, 1968), 149–200. In a footnote, Eliot remarks that the essay on Cavalcanti was written over a twenty-one-year period, 1910–1931. "We may trace [Guido Cavalcanti's] ideas to Averroes and Avicenna. . . . I do not think he swallowed Aquinas" (149). "Renan has a note *(Averroès et l' Averroïsm* [1866] . . . combating Averroes regarding 'intellect passif'. 'L'intellect passif n'est alors que la faculté de revoir les PHANTASMATA.' This is exactly what I think is NOT in Guido Cavalcanti. The terms *intellectus possibilis*, POSSIBLE, and *Passive* intellect belong to two different schools, two different sets of terminology. In dealing with Guido Cavalcanti, we should stick to such authors as use 'possible intellecto'" (184–85). And later, Pound affirms "the reality of the *nous*, of mind, apart from man's individual mind, of the sea crystalline and enduring, of the bright as it were molten glass that envelops us, full of light." *Guide to Kulchur* (New York: New Directions, 1960), 44. See also Pound, *The Cantos* (New York: New Directions, 1970), LXXIV, 463.

19. Dante, *De Monarchia*, trans. Donald Nicholl (New York: Noonday Press, 1947).

20. Étienne Gilson, *Dante and Philosophy*, trans. David Moore (Gloucester, MA: Peter Smith, 1968), 166–71.

21. Dante, *De Monarchia*, I.iii, 7.

22. Gilson, *Dante and Philosophy*, 161.

23. Dante, *De Monarchia*, I.iv, 5, 8–11.

24. Dante, *De Monarchia*, I.xvi, 26.

25. For a notable treatment of "Gerontion" and the Mind of Europe, see Jewel Spears Brooker, *Mastery and Escape: T. S. Eliot and the Dialectic of Modernism* (Amherst: University of Massachusetts Press, 1994): "Gerontion's mind is quite simply the Mind of Europe on the edge of doom" (15). See also A. D. Moody, "The Mind of Europe," in *T. S. Eliot at the Turn of the Century*, ed. M. Thormählen (Lund, Sweden: Lund University Press, 1994), 24.

26. T. S. Eliot, "Gerontion," in *The Complete Poems and Plays* (New York: Harcourt, 1950), 21–23. The "wrath-bearing tree" might well be taken as a reference to "original sin."

27. Aristotle, *De Poetica*, trans. Ingram Bywater, vol. 10 of *The Works of Aristotle*, ed. W. D. Ross (Oxford: Clarendon, 1946), XIV, 1453b21–26. "The traditional stories must be kept as they are. . . . At the same time even with these there is something left to the poet himself."

28. The Greek word for agent or maker and word for the poet are the same word: ποιήτης, *poiētēs*. In respect of the Greek language, then, Aristotle's agent mind and Eliot's poetic mind point to the same thing. When Eliot talks of "the mind that suffers," the Greek term for to suffer is πάσχω, *paschō*, and, as has been noted, νους παθετικὸς, *nous pathetikos*, is the name given by Aristotle to the imagination in its function as a receptacle for storing impressions and affective materials for the transformative work of the agent intellect.

29. Aristotle, *De Anima*, II.5, 417b1–20.

30. Aristotle, *De Anima*, III.4, 430a1–10.

31. Or to change the metaphor, the mind, as Aristotle says, is a "place of forms" (*topon eidōn*), specifically the place of meanings or the forms of objects which as residents in the intellect are just those objects made intelligible (*De Anima* III.4, 429a). Indeed, the intellect is an old house occupied by generations of (thought) tenants, none of which need be evicted if new ones are to enter. "I have said before," says Eliot, "the past experience revived in the meaning / Is not the experience of one life only / But of many generations" ("Dry Salvages," II).

32. T. S. Eliot, *The Varieties of Metaphysical Poetry*, ed. Ronald Schuchard (New York: Harcourt, 1993), 99.

33. Eliot, *The Varieties of Metaphysical Poetry*, 103–04.

34. A 1948 interview of Eliot by Françoise de Castro finds Eliot still holding to the intellectualist understanding of mysticism, the classical mysticism of Aristotle, Aquinas, Richard of St. Victor and Dante: "Eliot then said what seemed to be the centre and luminous point of the entire interview: 'But intellect pushed to its depths leads to mysticism.' 'Do you not believe,' I asked him . . . 'that intellect and mysticism are two faculties opposed in human nature?' A sign of denial was his only response, and this affirmation: 'All human faculties pushed to their limits end in mysticism.'" The interview was located by Donald Childs in the Hayward Bequest, King's College Library, Cambridge and quoted in his *T. S. Eliot: Mystic, Son and Lover* (New York: St. Martin's, 1997), 191.

35. Aristole, *De Anima*, III.7, 431a15–431b5.

36. Aristotle, *Politica*, trans. Benjamin Jowett, vol. 10 of *The Works of Aristotle*, ed. W. D. Ross (Oxford: Clarendon Press, 1921), I.1, 1253a35–37.

EIGHT

T. S. Eliot and John Henry Newman

Lee Oser

The unexpected obstacle to our juxtaposition of these two authors is that Newman does not answer that illustrious roll call, the index of Donald Gallup's *T. S. Eliot: A Bibliography*. Eliot never devoted a single essay to him. What could be the cause of so protracted a silence? Certainly, it was not lack of familiarity. For three straight years, fall and winter, beginning in the fall of 1916, Eliot's University of London Extension class on "Modern English Literature" spent a week on Newman. The printed syllabus gives only a tantalizing glimpse of the proceedings: "His temperament, with regard to his change in religious attachment. Reasons for joining the Church of Rome. His thought. Style. Read: *Apologia, Idea of a University*."[1] Eliot's concern with Newman's "temperament" possibly reflects the pragmatism of William James, whose celebrated distinction between the "tough-minded" and the "tender-minded" rests expressly on the personal basis of temperament.[2] We should also note that Eliot assigned neither Newman's poetry nor his sermons. The supplementary reading for the course included Wilfrid Ward's *Life of John Henry Cardinal Newman*.[3] Ward was the son of Newman's devoted follower, W. G. Ward, a fellow at Balliol College, Oxford, from 1834 to 1845. Eliot would soon cross paths with a similarly prominent son of the Oxford movement.

Let us begin with Newman's profile and legacy, as they might have struck Eliot in 1916. Newman wrote a superb narrative of conversion; he wrote a major treatise on education; and he influenced Matthew Arnold's cultural writings. With one possible exception, Newman's poetry did not affect Eliot deeply. Likewise, Newman's prose did not matter to Eliot, in the way that it mattered to James Joyce. Eliot appreciated Newman's prose, but it never taught him the possibilities of his own idiom.

If Newman's impact on Eliot was not exactly literary, how, then, do we describe it? Newman, I will argue, marks an important terminus for Eliot. He is antipodal to Emerson, whom Oliver Wendell Holmes, in a poem admired by Arnold, called "the Buddha of the West."[4] Eliot would explore that role in *The Waste Land*, a poem where faith and poetry converge. Newman stands at the opposite pole, where dogma repels literary modernism.

Published in 1920, "Gerontion" is an unusual case, because it owes a debt to Newman's poetry. The upper classes knew *The Dream of Gerontius* through Elgar's musical setting, which appeared in 1900.[5] With haunting delicacy and Wagnerian craft, Elgar brought to life the high European culture that Eliot saw dying. Eliot, I suspect, was riffing as much on Elgar as on Newman. Several critics, most notably Northrop Frye, have construed "Gerontion" as a "parody" of *The Dream of Gerontius*.[6] Not only does Eliot vacate Newman's celestial machinery, but there is a minor level of allusion and verbal echo that lends support to Frye's view.[7] But whether or not we choose to employ the literary term "parody" (and I remind you that Northrop Frye had the *Anatomy of Criticism* on his mental shelf), we should notice the serious, theological tension between the two poems. Religious thinkers do not parody one another. Calvinism is not a "parody" of Roman Catholicism. Atheism is not a "parody" of theism. The skeptical and possibly atheistic sensibility at work in "Gerontion" holds aloof from all consolations. Its angle of attack against human vanity, with a hint of the revenge play, arouses feelings of terror and isolation that are alien to *The Dream of Gerontius*.

In 1922 Eliot founded the *Criterion*. After publishing *The Waste Land* in its inaugural issue, he used the new journal as a vessel for his spiritual odyssey. In an illuminating letter to Herbert Read, who later dated it "apparently of October, 1924," Eliot allows for differences between himself and his contributors, while advancing his own agenda:

> I do *not* expect everyone to subscribe to all the articles of my own faith, or to read Arnold, Newman, Bradley, or Maurras with my own eyes. It seems to me at the present time we need more dogma, and that one ought to have as precise and clear a creed as possible.[8]

From Oxford, where he did graduate work for the academic year 1914–15, Eliot yokes the liberal Arnold, the conservative Bradley, and the dogmatic Newman, before reaching over the Channel for the reactionary founder of the *Action Française* (condemned by Pius XI in 1927), Maurras the atheist. When Eliot insists, "I do *not* expect everyone to subscribe to all the articles of my own faith," he seizes on a medieval figure of speech, which precedes the Thirty-Nine Articles of the Anglican faith. But the phrase ("articles of faith") is especially germane to Newman, who put a notoriously Catholic construction upon the Thirty-Nine Articles in his *Tract 90*, which shook the dreaming spires of Oxford in 1841. By reading

Newman with his "own eyes," Eliot insists on putting his own construction upon the author of the *Apologia pro Vita Sua*. And this construction stands on a paradox, because Newman upheld Rome in reaction against Protestant interpretations of faith.

1926 was a year of adjustment and conversion. Eliot had gone to work for Geoffrey Faber at Faber and Gwyer in the autumn of 1925. In November 1926, he asked the American-born priest William Force Stead to receive him into the Anglican Church. The name of Newman weaves in and out of Eliot's texts at this time. One reference shows Eliot adopting an Anglo-Catholic outlook well in advance of his formal conversion on June 29, 1927. He wrote in his editorial "Commentary" for April 1926: "The old Roman Empire is . . . an idea which comprehends Hooker and Laud as much as (or to some of us more than) it implies St Ignatius or Cardinal Newman. It is in fact the European idea—the idea of a common culture of western Europe."[9] We can hear in this comment the subtle negotiating power that Anglo-Catholicism afforded Eliot. Culturally, Anglicanism was a means of wielding the authority of Rome, without becoming Roman Catholic. It enabled Eliot to push Newman from the front of Europe's "common culture" into a secondary position.

Other references show a similar ambivalence. Eliot's essay "Lancelot Andrewes" first appeared anonymously in the *Times Literary Supplement* in September 1926. The reader may feel that he has been dropped, headfirst, into one of the underworld currents in Eliot's mind:

> When Andrewes begins his sermon, from beginning to end you are sure that he is wholly in his subject, unaware of anything else, that his emotion grows as he penetrates more deeply into his subject, that he is finally "alone with the Alone," with the mystery which he is seeking to grasp more and more firmly. One is reminded of the words of Arnold about the preaching of Newman.[10]

Eliot refers to Arnold's 1883 American lecture on Ralph Waldo Emerson, where Arnold says about Newman: "Who could resist the charm of that spiritual apparition, gliding in the dim afternoon light through the aisles of St. Mary's, rising into the pulpit, and then, in the most entrancing of voices, breaking the silence with words and thoughts which were a religious music, subtle, sweet, mournful?"[11] It hardly matters that Arnold's lecture sheds no light on the preaching of Andrewes. What strikes us is that Arnold has led Eliot, or Newman has led Arnold, to a place where the rival spirits of literature and dogma stare at each other in disbelief. For Arnold, "The name of Newman is a great name to the imagination still; his genius and his style are still things of power."[12] Having said so, Arnold informed his Boston audience, in the wake of Emerson's death, that Emerson "was your Newman."[13] This poetic license—the metaphorical exchanging of Emerson and Newman—leaves its mark on Eliot, insofar as he, like Arnold, shuffles Newman around. It may be recalled that

Newman described himself as being "alone with the Alone" in Chapter IV of the *Apologia*, the chapter of conversion: "the soul was 'sola cum solo'; there was no cloud interposed between the creature and the Object of his faith and Love."[14] Did Eliot have Newman in mind, "alone with the Alone?" We may notice that the creature alone with "the mystery" differs from the creature alone with "the Object of his faith and Love." In any case, Newman is summoned in the next sentence—there he is, by God—not for any purpose of critical analysis, but as it were to witness and to sanctify Eliot's own conversion, in all its heterogeneous urgency.

As Eliot steered toward the Church of England, he continued to read Newman with his "own eyes." In other words, he continued to *interpret* Newman's faith. The following passage comes from the October, 1926 number of the *Criterion*. Eliot is reviewing books by Herbert Read and Ramon Fernandez:

> Fernandez is, from a certain point of view, in closer sympathy with Newman than are many of Newman's Christian and literary apologists; he is in much closer sympathy with Newman in his place and *time*; with Newman, in fact—and it is a large part—in so far as Newman was *not* Christian or Catholic. He does not understand, perhaps, that in which Newman believed or tried to believe, but he understands, better than almost anyone, the *way* in *which* Newman believed or tried to believe.[15]

This line of argument draws conflicting responses from two of Eliot's best critics: one conservative and one liberal. To Russell Kirk, Eliot is "always a partisan of right reason," who allows that "insights of faith—the 'leap of being' of the man of vision, the sudden direct experience of reality—are essential. . . ."[16] To Jeffrey Perl, Eliot is looking at things in a more formal and aesthetic way, such that "the key to a belief is not so much its content as its context, kind, and quality."[17] Kirk is right that dogma is essential to Eliot. Perl is justified in observing that Eliot, "from a certain point of view," could imagine a non-Christian Newman as a template for the Christian Newman. The gap between the two critics, between the dogmatist and the skeptic, might be closed if Kirk could accommodate Perl, without sapping the vitality of dogma. But is that possible? How can dogma maintain its vitality under the skeptical conditions to which Perl draws our attention? First, with Newman, as with Coleridge before him,[18] we can admit a psychological consideration, namely, that the need for revelation is not diminished by an apparent shortage of signs and miracles.[19] Recollecting Eliot's 1924 remarks to Read ("we need more dogma"), we can place them in a decade of theological searching that runs from "Gerontion" to *The Waste Land* to *The Hollow Men* to *Ash-Wednesday*. What occurred in Eliot's case was poetry and conversion. And what Kirk saw, through Eliot's achievement, is that imagination and dogma can strike new harmonies. Firmly and wisely, Kirk aligned what he called "the moral imagination" with Newman's "illative sense."[20] The illative sense is "the power of judging and concluding, when in its perfection."[21] In the area of religion, it serves our personal capacity for believing in dogma sufficiently to act on it. It works, as Kirk suggests, by way of experience, inference, and imagination.

But there are strong reasons why neither Kirk nor Perl can have the last word. Near the very end of the *Grammar of Assent*, a phrase occurs that Eliot quotes at least twice, where Newman speaks of reasons for belief that are "powerful and concurrent."[22] This phrase, in its original context, bears the whole weight of Newman's vast book. The "proof of its divine origin," Newman says of Christianity,

> is addressed . . . to minds which are in the normal condition of human nature, as believing in God and in a future judgment. Such minds it addresses both through the intellect and through the imagination; creating a certitude of its truth by arguments too various for direct enumeration, too personal and deep for words, too powerful and concurrent for refutation.[23]

Newman trusted a "normal," healthy imagination to serve the purposes of salvation. Eliot, by contrast, distrusted his own imagination. He feared that his poetry was fostering religious and moral decline.[24] He was self-conscious to a degree that Western culture has found intolerable, and the sword he wielded against romantic self-infatuation has been beaten into the plowshare of postmodern bourgeois liberalism. From Newman's point of view, literary modernism confirms the sad lesson that moral self-consciousness is not the same as assent to dogma. Even if we strongly agree with Newman and Kirk, that imagination and dogma can pull in the same direction, yet Eliot's imagination does not fix his skeptical bias. The modern imagination is a means of living with doubts and ambiguities; the illative sense is a means of overcoming them. Eliot may be "a *partisan* of right reason," but that does not make the party of right reason the possessor of right reason. In the end, it must be the reader's private response to Eliot that tilts the balance in favor of Kirk or Perl.

The Newman who encounters Eliot is not a "familiar compound ghost." He may be "familiar," but he resists being compounded. A further case in point is Eliot's 1931 essay "The *Pensées* of Pascal," where the *Pensées*, in one of several references to Newman, are referred to as "a kind of Grammar of Assent (*sic*), setting forth the reasons which will convince the intellect."[25] Granted, Newman could appreciate Pascal, and quotes him sympathetically in the *Apologia*. But he is always armed against the heresy of Jansenism. In his lecture entitled "English Catholic Literature," he makes the terse comment: "Pascal . . . does not approve himself to a Catholic judgment."[26] Most important, in the *Grammar of Assent*, he acknowledges that Pascal's case for Christianity is "powerfully stated," but he finds that it leaves too much "to the respective dispositions, opinions, and experiences, of those to whom the argument is addressed. Thus its value is a personal question."[27]

Eliot smooths the theological wrinkles in his highly sympathetic portrait of Pascal. By writing with hypnotic brilliance, and by laying stress on Pascal's literary stature, he tends to shift and blur the boundary between literature and religion. Newman, trained in the history of the Church, enforced that boundary with superb vigilance. Here we must tread the subtler reaches of doctrine, where, as Eliot remarks, "a slight excess or deviation to one side or the other will precipitate a heresy."[28] To a person of Newman's persuasion, Pascal overemphasizes "the corruption of human nature after the Fall and the powerlessness of man to become or do anything pleasing to God without divine grace. . . ."[29] As we have seen, Newman had real hopes for the imagination; by contrast, Pascal called it a "mistress of error and falsehood" and a "proud, powerful enemy of reason."[30] And yet others find a foreshadowing of Newman in Pascal's famous remarks about "the submission and use of reason in which Christianity consists."[31] More, Pascal's distinction, which Eliot quotes in its classically precise French, "between the mathematical mind and the intuitive mind,"[32] bears a rough-and-ready likeness to Newman's distinction between notional assent and real assent. Certainly, the misguided charge, exploded by Eliot, that Pascal was a pure fideist can be placed alongside the misguided charge that Newman was a pure fideist.

But there are limits. It would be a false comparison to liken the *Pensées* to the *Apologia* on the basis of Pascal's facing "unflinchingly the demon of doubt which is inseparable from the spirit of belief."[33] Unlike Eliot or Pascal, Newman was never impressed by what he called "Montaigne's sceptical bias and great indifference of temperament."[34] Newman admitted doubts occasionally and conditionally: they did not inspire his theology. It follows that there is no correlation in Eliot or Pascal to Newman's crucial doctrine of conscience, which "teaches us, not only that God is, but what He is."[35] I would also underscore the point that Eliot connects Pascal to T. E. Hulme.[36] Between Newman and Hulme there is an abyss. Eliot ends his essay by elevating Pascal over Newman: "I can think of no Christian writer, not Newman even, more to be commended than Pascal to those who doubt, but who have the mind to conceive, and the sensibility to feel, the disorder, the futility, the meaninglessness, the mystery of life and suffering, and who can only find peace through a satisfaction of the whole being."[37] This piercing conclusion opens us with poetic intensity to the mystery of our being. It does so by converting the very grounds for Newman's judgment against Pascal into grounds for high praise. What to Newman was a "powerfully stated" but thoroughly subjective argument, is to Eliot a revelation. Yet, after all this, I would add that Eliot's brief observation, in *The Use of Poetry and the Use of Criticism* (1933), of Wordsworth's influence on Newman,[38] goes to the real heart of the matter: there is a romantic, lyrical, individualizing quality in Newman's approach to reason that links Newman to Eliot in ways that Eliotic modernism, almost by definition, could not give adequate expression to.

In the cultural sphere, Eliot grew concerned about the relation of Church and State. It was a relation that absorbed Newman's attention. The Oxford movement, for example, made use of the term "Erastianism" to mean "the union . . . of Church and State."[39] Newman saw Erastianism as a religious expression of liberalism, which he blasted in the *Apologia*. In *The Idea of a Christian Society*, Eliot aimed at the same target: "A permanent danger of an established Church is Erastianism: we do not need to refer to the eighteenth century . . . to remind ourselves of that."[40] By "the eighteenth century," Eliot alludes to that memorable Whig, Bishop Benjamin Hoadley.[41] But where is the nineteenth century? It is relegated to an elaborate note, where Eliot avouches by the seven sacred mysteries: "I have no first-hand acquaintance with the doctrines of Dr. Arnold. . . ."[42] Delayed on his way to the nineteenth century by the untimely intervention of Bishop Benjamin Hoadley, Eliot never came to study "first-hand" the Erastian policies of Matthew Arnold's father, the influential Thomas Arnold, earnest, liberal Head of Rugby School and Newman's major antagonist in the 1830s and 1840s.

Of all the cats who inhabit the field of Eliot's cultural writings, it is Newman who most resembles Macavity: the evidence is overwhelming — but *Macavity's not there!* Before there was Eliot championing Hooker, Andrewes, and Bramhall as examples of the Anglican *via media* or compromise between "Popery" and "Dissent," there was Newman championing the same men for the same reason. Even on the most delicate ground of all, adjusting the right relation of Canterbury and Rome, there is Newman traversing every step of the problem. I pass over Eliot's writings on education, except to make the commonplace observation that the author of *Notes towards the Definition of Culture* and *The Aims of Education* is a close student of *The Idea of a University*.

Why couldn't Eliot express his ambivalence toward Newman, as he expressed his ambivalence toward Matthew Arnold? One possible explanation is that Newman was a turncoat. Newman writes in Chapter IV of the *Apologia*: "I was angry with the Anglican divines. I thought they had taken me in." He continues, "There are but two alternatives, the way to Rome, and the way to Atheism; Anglicanism is the halfway house on the one side, and Liberalism is the halfway house on the other."[43] Strong stuff, but the Anglo-Catholic Revival, which flourished in the 1920s and 1930s, did not really see Newman as a threat.[44] As for Eliot, the editor of the *Criterion* sought to protect the life of the mind from partisan politics, though he could acknowledge his own prejudice, as we noted in his April, 1926 "Commentary." And if we follow Eliot's principles without prejudice, we are led irresistibly to Newman's greatness as a European thinker, a man who brought England closer to the continent.

To get at the real reason behind Eliot's silence, we need to do more digging. I mentioned that Eliot the Extension Lecturer would soon cross paths with a prominent son (I should have said "grandson") of the Oxford movement. I also mentioned that he went to work for Geoffrey Faber in the fall of 1925. It happens that Faber was intensely devoted to Oxford. He had taken a double first in classics from Christ Church shortly before Eliot went up to Merton. His engrossing, opinionated, and loquacious book *Oxford Apostles: A Character Study of the Oxford Movement* was first published in 1933 and dedicated to T. S. Eliot "with affection and respect." A staunch if witty defender of the *via media*, Faber showed himself to be a formidable authority on Anglo-Catholicism. His family history, including a wealth of correspondence, afforded him a superb vantage point for studying and judging the Oxford of Newman. His original Preface underscores the family connections:

> In 1834, the second year of the Oxford Movement, my grandfather, the Rev. Francis Atkinson Faber, then a man of thirty, was elected a Fellow of Magdalen. His younger brother, Frederic, became a Fellow of University three or four years later. Both brothers were well known figures in the Oxford of the late thirties and early forties. Fred was a fascinating, romantic, ardently religious young man, a poet before he became a hymn-maker, and a brilliant or showy talker, according to the taste of the listener. Like Newman, he was brought up an Evangelical. At Oxford he fell under Newman's spell. He followed his leader to Rome in 1845, became the head of the Brompton Oratory (an offshoot of Newman's Birmingham Oratory), and is still remembered, by Anglicans as well as Romans, as the author of many popular hymns.
>
> Frank Faber was a different type, a scholar rather than a poet, more cautious but more independent. His contemporaries respected his judgment as that of a moderate and sensible man, and enjoyed his company as that of an amusing and pointed controversialist. A saving sense of humor prevented him going all the way with the Tractarians; but, though he was not an out-and-out Newmanite or Puseyite, he was strongly attracted by Newman and the revival of Catholic ideas. . . . For Newman, his admiration was profound.[45]

Beyond the grandfather, F. A. Faber, and the granduncle, the well-known F. W. Faber, there was the grandfather's uncle, the Rev. George Stanley Faber, "a learned and redoubtable antagonist of Popery in the North of England."[46] To the grandson of Reverend William Greenleaf Eliot, Geoffrey Faber's past must have looked familiar. A genealogy of clerics cast its long shadow on Eliot's own inheritance. We can see why Faber, in 1929, when he parted ways with Maurice Gwyer, called the new house Faber and Faber. There was only one Geoffrey, but those other Fabers were very lively ghosts.

In his book, Faber shows flashes of sympathy for Newman's genius, but he wants to debunk Newman's character. Faber reserves his real sympathy for Edward Pusey, co-leader of the Oxford movement and loyal Anglican:

> Where Newman was weak, Pusey was tough. His mind was not of the order which is shaken by sudden impressions. He had his teeth in the *Via Media*, and he was never going to let go his hold. Far more than Newman he knew what sorrow and responsibility could be. He had experienced the essential human passions. He was, in fact, what Newman never was—a man. Let Newman, with his little band of hermaphrodites succumb to these alien, imperious fascinations.[47]

It is doubtless ironic, given Faber's dedicating his book to Eliot, that the hero of *The Waste Land* is a hermaphrodite. More important is Faber's caustic comparison. It suggests the presence not so much of an axe as an atmosphere.

Our first answer to the question facing us—the question of why Eliot said so little about Newman—seemed to fall short: Eliot kept silent because Newman was a traitor who abandoned the Church of England and embraced her ancient enemy. A further possibility, if we may here regather the impetus of our earlier discussion, is that Eliot's response to Newman threatened to expose the flank of his own inconsistences. If Newman wasn't right in his "Reasons for joining the Church of Rome," Eliot needed to say why not. He needed to say it against the grain of his sympathy (think of his falling to his knees before the Pietà in the spring of 1926). He needed to pit Anglican against Roman, and that he was not willing to do. To venture further down the blind road of speculation, I would suggest that an adequate realization of Newman's achievement, for example, Newman's superior revision of Aristotle, was not yet available to Eliot, if only because it was not yet available to anyone.[48]

We arrive at our final explanation for Eliot's silence. It is more personal, as are most explanations regarding a poet who claimed above all to be "impersonal." In this case, however, the main personality was not Eliot's. I am suggesting that Geoffrey Faber, in his authority as grandson and grandnephew and owner of Fabers, effectively made Newman taboo. Faber's manly Church of England dominated over Eliot's sympathy for Newman the man. We may recall that, soon after beginning work at Faber and Gwyer, Eliot delivered his 1926 Clark Lectures at Cambridge University. I think Geoffrey Faber would have approved: "In much English prose, even the finest, of the nineteenth century, I find just the faintest, indefinable perfume of femininity. I find it in Newman."[49] Eliot was not at Faber and Gwyer for more than a year before he chose the path to conversion. He became part of the Faber family: "Uncle Tom" to Geoffrey's son Thomas. To my knowledge, no one has perceived the influence of the Fabers on Eliot's life as an Anglican. We can be certain, at least, that the boss had strong feelings about Newman. Did Eliot notice? Tactful and observant, he would have understood that interest in Newman sent the wrong signal, or could not send the right signal, with the result that Eliot, to galvanize a cliché, chose to keep Newman buried in the closet.

That would be my last word on the subject, except that I am haunted by a peculiar parallel, by one of those twilight allusions or distant echoes that may or may not be a figment of the reader's imagination.

By way of preliminaries, I would observe that the ideal of saintliness arises fleetingly, with respect to Newman, in that elaborate note about Erastianism in *The Idea of a Christian Society*.[50] It also comes up, more generally, in the essay on Pascal. Saintliness is, of course, a leitmotif throughout Eliot's writings, from Saint Narcissus to Celia Coplestone.[51] It finds its intensest expression in *Murder in the Cathedral*, which appeared in 1935.

The echo I have in mind is not a strict verbal parallel. It concerns words and context: repetition of the verb *to wait*, a duration of time involving seven years, the destiny of the English Church, and an anxious mood of impending sacrifice. First I will quote the pertinent passage from the *Apologia pro Vita Sua*. Newman has reached the turning point of his life:

> so I have *waited*, hoping for light . . . I am *waiting* because friends are most considerately bearing me in mind . . . And then this *waiting* serves the purpose of preparing men's minds. *I dread shocking, unsettling people.* Any how, I can't avoid giving incalculable pain. So, if I had my will, I should like to *wait* . . . a full *seven years.* . . .[52]

Here are Eliot's Women of Canterbury, as they wait, in effect, for the future saint to return and assert the authority of Rome against its usurpation by an English monarch:

> *Seven years* and summer is over
> *Seven years* since the Archbishop left us . . .
> Now *I fear disturbance of the quiet seasons* . . .
> And the poor shall *wait* for another decaying October. . . .
> What shall we do in the heat of summer
> But *wait* in barren orchards for another October?
> Some malady is coming upon us. We *wait*, we *wait*,
> And the saints and martyrs *wait*, for those who shall be martyrs and
>   saints.
> Destiny *waits* in the hand of God. . . .[53]

It is curious, after our discussion of Newman and manliness, that the Women of Canterbury sound like him. But surely the point to be gained is that these suffering women are the tragic chorus, which Eliot modeled on Attic tragedy. The chorus is the conservative soul of the drama, the stubborn ambassador of the old ways, faithful to the rites from which it originates. Unlike the little old man of "Gerontion", the chorus would have stirred Newman's admiration. If we hear Newman in *Murder in the Cathedral*, we may remember that he concluded his lecture "Christianity and Letters" by placing the poets at the feet of the saints, including "St. Thomas of Canterbury." Eliot would have found this subordination just, but he did not possess Newman's clear-eyed conviction and commanding logic. It was the mystery of suffering, conversion, and saintliness that compelled his imagination.

NOTES

1. Ronald Schuchard, *Eliot's Dark Angel: Intersections of Life and Art* (New York: Oxford University Press, 1999), 33.

2. See William James, *Writings 1902–1910* (New York: Library of America, 1987), 488–91.

3. Schuchard, *Eliot's Dark Angel*, 36.

4. See Matthew Arnold, *Prose Works*, ed. R. H. Super, 11 vols. (Ann Arbor: University of Michigan Press, 1961–1977), 10:185.

5. "The fame of *The Dream of Gerontius* derives, of course, from the oratorio which Edward Elgar completed in 1900, while the verses which form the hymn 'Praise to the Holiest in the Height' are familiar to countless people who never read a word of Newman." Ian Ker, *John Henry Newman: A Biography* (Clarendon Press: Oxford, 1988), 575.

6. Northrop Frye, *T. S. Eliot: An Introduction* (Chicago: University of Chicago Press, 1981), 58. I am indebted to B. C. Southam, *A Student's Guide to the Selected Poems of T. S. Eliot*, fifth ed. (London: Faber and Faber, 1990), 54.

7. For Newman, it is the Demons who say "Virtue and vice, / A knave's pretence, / 'Tis all the same." John Henry Cardinal Newman, *Works*, 39 vols. (London: Longmans, 1897), 33:348. For Eliot, the confusion of virtue and vice is part of our fallen state. Lyndall Gordon, who is cited in Southam (*Student's Guide*, 60), asserts the following: "'I have lost my passion . . . I have lost my sight, smell, hearing, taste, and touch' is an allusion to Newman's sermon on Divine Calls, quoted in *Apologia pro Vita Sua*: 'Let us beg and pray Him day by day to reveal himself to our souls more fully, to quicken our senses, to give us sight and hearing, taste and touch of the world to come.'" Lyndall Gordon, *Eliot's Early Years* (New York: Farrar, 1977), 103n. I am not sure why Eliot would not be alluding to a passage in *The Dream of Gerontius* itself: "Nor touch, nor taste, nor hearing hast thou now / Thou livest in a world of signs and types, / The presentations of most holy truth / Living and strong, which now encompass thee." Newman, *Works*, 33:349.

8. T. S. Eliot to Herbert Read [October 1924?], in *T. S. Eliot: The Man and His Work*, ed. Allen Tate (New York: Dell, 1966), 21.

9. T. S. Eliot, "A Commentary," *Criterion* 4 (April 1926): 222.

10. T. S. Eliot, *For Lancelot Andrewes* (New York: Doubleday, 1929), 21.

11. Arnold, *Prose Works*, 10:165.

12. Ibid.

13. Ibid., 167.

14. John Henry Cardinal Newman, *Apologia pro Vita Sua: Being a History of His Religious Opinions* (New York: Sheed and Ward, 1946), 130.

15. Eliot, "Books of the Quarter," *Criterion* 4 (October 1926): 753. Quoted in Jeffrey Perl, *Skepticism and Modern Enmity* (Baltimore, MD: Johns Hopkins University Press, 1989), 109.

16. Russell Kirk, *Eliot and His Age: T. S. Eliot's Moral Imagination in the Twentieth Century* (New York: Random House, 1971), 141.

17. Perl, *Skepticism and Modern Enmity*, 109.

18. "Evidences *of Christianity! I am weary of the word. Make a man feel the* want *of it; rouse him, if you can, to the self-knowledge of his* need *of it; and you may safely trust it to its own Evidence.*" Samuel Taylor Coleridge, *Aids to Reflection,* quoted in Basil Willey, *Nineteenth-Century Studies: Coleridge to Matthew Arnold* (Harmondsworth, England: Penguin Books, 1964), 49.

19. See John Henry Cardinal Newman, *An Essay in Aid of a Grammar of Assent* (Notre Dame, IN: University of Notre Dame Press, 1979), 328–31.

20. Kirk, *Eliot and His Age,* 47.

21. Newman, *An Essay in Aid of a Grammar of Assent,* 276.

22. Ibid., 379. Quoted in T. S. Eliot, *Essays Ancient and Modern* (New York: Harcourt, 1936), 153, and T. S. Eliot, "The Modern Dilemma: Christianity and Communism," *Listener* 7, no. 166 (March 16, 1932): 383.

23. Newman, *An Essay in Aid of a Grammar of Assent,* 379.

24. See, for example, Eliot, *Essays Ancient and Modern,* 107, and T. S. Eliot, *After Strange Gods* (New York: Harcourt, 1934), 10.

25. Eliot, *Essays Ancient and Modern,* 151.

26. John Henry Newman, *The Idea of a University,* ed. Frank M. Turner (New Haven: Yale University Press), 190.

27. Newman, *An Essay in Aid of a Grammar of Assent,* 245.

28. Eliot, *Essays Ancient and Modern,* 161.

29. Frederick Copleston, S.J., *A History of Philosophy,* 9 vols. (New York: Doubleday, 1985), 4:156.

30. Blaise Pascal, *Pensées and Other Writings,* trans. Honor Levi (Oxford: Oxford University Press, 1995), 16–17.

31. Ibid., 60.

32. Ibid., 150.

33. Eliot, *Essays Ancient and Modern,* 158.

34. Newman, *Idea of a University,* 190.

35. Newman, *An Essay in Aid of a Grammar of Assent,* 304.

36. Eliot, *Essays Ancient and Modern,* 167 n. 1.

37. Ibid., 168.

38. T. S. Eliot, *The Use of Poetry and the Use of Criticism* (Cambridge: Harvard University Press, 1964), 72.

39. Newman, *Apologia,* 25 and see 27.

40. T. S. Eliot, *Christianity and Culture* (San Diego: Harcourt, 1977), 41.

41. For more Hoadley, see T. S. Eliot, *Selected Essays 1917–1932* (New York: Harcourt, 1932), 327.

42. "I have no first-hand acquaintance with the doctrines of Dr. Arnold, and must rely on Mr. [Middleton] Murry's exposition of them." Eliot, *Christianity and Culture,* 62.

43. Newman, *Apologia,* 135–36.

44. See, for example, W. J. Sparrow-Simpson, *The History of the Anglo-Catholic Revival from 1845* (London: George Allen and Unwin, 1932).

45. Geoffrey Faber, *Oxford Apostles: A Character Study of the Oxford Movement* (Harmondsworth, England: Penguin Books, 1954), 12–13.

46. Ibid., 13.

47. Ibid., 328.

48. For the interested reader, the following quotations may prove fascinating. Here is Eliot: "Aristotle had what is called the scientific mind—a mind which, as it is rarely found among scientists except in fragments, might better be called the intelligent mind. For there is no other intelligence than this, and so far as artists and men of letters are intelligent (we may doubt whether the intelligence of men of letters is as high as among men of science) their intelligence is of this kind." *The Sacred Wood: Essays on Poetry and Criticism* (London: Methuen, 1960), 13.

Here is Newman: "And now I come to a further peculiarity of this natural and spontaneous ratiocination. This faculty, as it is actually found in us, proceeding from concrete to concrete, is attached to a definite subject-matter, according to the individual. In spite of Aristotle, I will not allow that genuine reasoning is an instrumental art. . . . The ratiocinative faculty, then, as found in individuals, is not a general instrument of knowledge, but has its province, or is what may be called departmental. . . .

It is natural, then, to ask the question, why ratiocination should be an exception to a general law which attaches to the intellectual exercises of the mind; why it is held to be commensurate with logical science; and why logic is made an instrumental art sufficient for determining every sort of truth, while no one would dream of making any one formula, however generalized, a working rule for poetry, the art of medicine, and political warfare?" *An Essay in Aid of a Grammar of Assent,* 266–67, 280.

At every turn, Newman's modernization of Aristotle is superior to Eliot's. The one is an organic growth or development, a correction that leaves the roots unhurt (and even reinvigorated); the other is a brilliant misreading.

49. T. S. Eliot, *The Varieties of Metaphysical Poetry,* ed. Ronald Schuchard (New York: Harcourt, 1993), 92.

50. I duly quote the most relevant part of the note:

> Mr. Murry appears . . . to follow Dr. Arnold in attaching little importance to the apostolical succession. With regard to the position of Matthew Arnold, he says . . . "in this situation no mere revival of Christian piety could possibly avail: not even a rebirth of Christian saintliness (such as he admired in Newman) could be efficacious against it." It is only a short step from employing the adjective *mere* to ignoring Christian piety. He continues, "What was required was a renovation of Christian understanding, an enlarged conception of the spiritual life itself."
>
> How such an enlargement of the conception of the spiritual life is to take place without spiritual masters, without the rebirth of saintliness, I cannot conceive. (Eliot, *Christianity and Culture,* 64.)

51. There is just the slightest reference to Newman in the Notes to *The Idea of a Christian Society.* It is very much a case of someone slipping in the back door. Quoting Middleton Murry on Matthew Arnold's admiration of Newman's "Christian saintliness," Eliot doesn't say himself that Newman was a saint, but Arnold's idea is tacitly approved. Ibid.

52. Newman, *Apologia,* 154.

53. T. S. Eliot, *The Complete Poems and Plays: 1909–1950* (San Diego: Harcourt, 1950), 176.

NINE

T. S. Eliot, Charles Williams, and Dante's Way of Love

Dominic Manganiello

T. S. Eliot and Charles Williams held each other in high esteem, not least for the writings that bore the unmistakable imprint of their neo-Dantism.[1] The gifted poet, novelist and theologian who hailed from London had long considered Eliot as "[il] *poeta nostra*" ("our poet"), the English heir to the Italian genius.[2] Eliot in turn admired his compatriot's extensive knowledge of the *Commedia*, commissioning Williams in 1942 to write *The Figure of Beatrice*. Although the cross-fertilisation of their work has been well documented,[3] significant areas of their reliance on Dante overlap and require further exploration. Of particular significance is the role Williams played in inspiring Eliot's rediscovery of Dante as the master of the affirmative way of love.

For some critics such fruitful interaction between the writers seems impossible due to Eliot's acceptance of the negative way as a spiritual ideal for most of his career. Humphrey Carpenter, for instance, argues that "they might, in fact, have achieved a real exchange of thought, for as Christian poets their work was largely a matter of related opposites. Williams wrote about such 'affirmative' aspects of Christianity as the Dantean approach to romantic love, while Eliot was concerned largely with the 'negative' or ascetic rejection of the world. . . . Their differences far exceeded any . . . slight similarities."[4] Readings that stress the incompatibility of these literary approaches, however, tend to overlook how they are organically linked. Williams's main contribution to theological poetics, as Anne Ridler noted, lies in "his perception of the relation between the two Ways."[5] He often illustrated their correlation through the geometrical symbol of the asymptote, which shows a straight line that does not meet a given curve within a finite distance, but continually draws near to it by moving in the same direction. There is therefore, by analogy, no contradiction between the divergent traditions of Christian mysticism. Williams maintained that they serve, in fact, as complementary routes to eternal life:

> Neither of these two ways is, or can be, exclusive. . . .
>
> Our sacred Lord, in his earthly existence, deigned to use both methods. . . . The Crucifixion and the Death are rejection and affirmation at once, for they affirm death only to reject death; the intensity of that death is the opportunity of its own dissolution; and beyond that physical rejection of earth lies the re-affirmation of earth which is called the Resurrection.
>
> As above, so below; as in him, so in us. The tangle of affirmation and rejection which is in each of us has to be drawn into some kind of pattern, and has so been drawn by all men who have lived.[6]

The great exponents of either the "sacramental" or the "mystical" way to God[7] all agreed that both patterns converge in the person of Jesus, whose life provides the sole model for their characteristic mimesis, or *imitatio*. Dante's integral vision of man as a composite being made up of a body and soul follows this venerable Christian tradition.[8] Eliot corroborates Williams's Dantesque insight in *The Cocktail Party* when he has Reilly tell Celia, "Neither way is better. / Both ways are necessary."[9] So, too, we must set Eliot's declaration in 1930 that "ordinary human affections" are incapable of leading one to divine love next to his mature reflection on the subject as he expressed it in 1958:

> One has to be otherworldly and yet deeply responsible for the affairs of this world. One must preserve a capacity for enjoying the things of this world such as love and affection.[10]

Eliot's use of the way of negation, as Brother George Every observed, ultimately leads to an affirmative culmination, for the process of rejecting the void leaves "the ear open for 'hidden laughter.'"[11] In the period that stretches from the writing of *The Family Reunion* through to the *Four Quartets* and *The Cocktail Party*, Eliot dramatized the paradox of "affirmative attainment through negative withdrawal"[12] by juxtaposing St. John of the Cross's descent into the dark night with Dante's ascent toward the heart of light. The romantic element, which is present in Eliot's verse since at least "La Figlia che Piange," becomes more pronounced at the end of his career, culminating with the publication of *The Elder Statesman*. Eliot's aim in sparking a Dante revival, Brother George Every also noted, was precisely to facilitate a new understanding of "the religious significance of romance and the romantic significance of all religion."[13] This later conviction grew out of personal experience, for Eliot once confessed to a friend that he had known in his own life the way Dante had trans-muted love for Beatrice into love of God in the *Vita Nuova*.[14]

Eliot's gradual change of perspective owes something, I think, to Williams's reading of Dante. In *The Figure of Beatrice* much is made of Dante's habit of starting from "the common thing"—a girl in the street, the people he knew, his native tongue. From these natural images "the great diagrams are perceived; from them the great myths open; by them he understands the final end" (*Figure*, 44). According to Eliot, a similar pattern operates in the novels of Williams: "he is as much concerned with quite ordinary human beings, with their struggle among the shadows, their weaknesses and self-deceptions, their occasional moments of under-standing, as with [Dante's] vision of Love."[15] Another Dante-inspired modern writer extended the connection farther still. Mindful of Williams's comments on Dante, Allen Tate proceeded to apply them to Eliot himself: "he was the uncommon man committed to the common reality of the human condition."[16] In his middle age, Eliot began to focus on the struggle for sanctity of ordinary people engaged in their everyday activities.[17] Whether during their moments in the rose-garden or even in "sordid particulars," the "eternal design" always appears.[18] Eliot's char-acters, no less than Williams's, affirm the holiness of the common thing.[19]

For Williams sanctifying the ordinary means in the first place the ability to distinguish between illusion and reality, or dream and fact. The distinction becomes especially crucial when placed in its philosophical context. Nietzsche's denial of extra-human facts, couched in the sweep-ing statement, "truths are illusions," had provided the rationale for adopting the modern (and post-modern) attitude of "absolute skepticism toward all inherited concepts."[20] In Williams's Dantesque revision of Nietzsche's proposition, a genuine spirit of inquiry is seen as a natural process, spurring the mind on to truth to greater truth and then to ulti-mate Truth.[21] For Williams salvation depends on the acceptance of things as they are.

Lawrence Wentworth's descent into hell illustrates well this key prin-ciple. Gripped by envy, Williams's academically concupiscent historian distorts evidence in a vain effort to discredit the research of his colleague, Aston Moffatt, "a pure scholar . . . who would have sacrificed reputation, income, and life, if necessary, for the discovery of one fact."[22] Went-worth's rejection of one "insignificant" fact concerning a negligible mili-tary skirmish leads to another—lying about the historical accuracy of uniforms being used for a play rehearsal—and then to another until, at last, he professes "then and for ever, for ever, for ever, that he would hate the fact, and therefore facts" (*Descent*, 81). Piling illusion on illusion, Wentworth the new historicist seals his fate, for as Williams formulates it, "hell is always inaccurate" while "heaven is always exact."[23]

In a parallel move, Wentworth also fails to acknowledge that human love exists. Hell for him as for Sartre is other people since "he had never had a friend or a lover, he had never, in any possible sense of the word, been 'in love'" (*Descent*, 36). When Williams defined romantic love as "a state of facts,"[24] he recalled how the beloved flourished in Dante's imagination:

> The image of Beatrice existed in his thought; it remained there and was deliberately renewed . . . the subjective recollection within him was of something objectively outside him; it was an image of an exterior fact and not of an interior desire. (*Figure*, 7)

The reference here is to a crucial point in Virgil's great discourse on love in the *Purgatorio*:

> Vostra apprensiva da esser verace
> tragge intenzione, e dentro a voi la spiega,
> sì che l'animo ad essa volger face;
> e se, rivolto, inver' di lei si piega,
> quell piegare è amor.[25]
> (Your faculty of apprehension draws an image from a real object that it internalizes and brings to the mind's attention; if, when so enticed, the mind turns towards the image, then that inclination is love.)

The true lover beholds an actual person, not a phantasm generated by his perception and by his libido. But Dante succumbs to this very type of "pseudo-romantic mirage" (*Figure*, 166) in a dream that plagues him just before dawn in the next canto. The object of his sexual fantasy is, in fact, a homely creature that becomes increasingly beautiful as the beholder gazes upon her (*Purg.* XIX.7–15). Dorothy L. Sayers interprets the appearance of the siren in this scene as

> the projection upon the outer world of something in the mind: the soul, falling in love with itself, perceives other people and things, not as they are, but as wish-fulfillments of its own: i.e. its love for them is not love for a "true other". . . but a devouring egotistical fantasy, by absorption in which the personality rots away into illusion. (*Purg.*, 220)

For Williams the siren functions as a false image of Beatrice (*Figure*, 165–66), and, Sayers notes, he expands Dante's theme in *Descent into Hell*. Particularly brilliant is the defining moment during which Wentworth runs down "the path that coiled round the edge of Eden" (*Descent*, 89), the objective correlative to his own circular reasoning about Adela, the woman he is infatuated with. Resentful of the fact she is dating a rival named Hugh instead of him, Wentworth compensates for the snub by manufacturing a simulacrum of Adela to gratify his lust. Responding to the suggestion made by the demon-lover, Lily Sammile, that he should think more about himself in order to find the elusive "it," Wentworth becomes the dupe of her semantic incoherence and withdraws into the inner recesses of his secret fantasy:

He didn't understand the first phrase [of Lily] . . . Much difficulty in finding what? in finding it? the it that could be found if he thought of himself more; that was what he had said, or she had said, whichever had said that the thing was to be found, as if Adela had said it, Adela in her real self, by no means the self that went with Hugh; no, but the true, the true Adela who was apart and his; for that was the difficulty all the while, that she was truly his, and wouldn't be, but if he thought more of her truly being, and not of her being untruly away, on whatever way, for the way that went away was not the way she truly went, but if they did away with the way she went away, then Hugh could be untrue and she true, then he would know themselves, two, true and two, on the way he was going, and the peace in himself, and the scent of her in him and the her, meant for him, in him; that was the she he knew, and he must think the more of himself. (83)

Like the inhabitants of Dante's hell,[26] Wentworth has lost the good of the intellect, the capacity to seek truth, and he hopelessly entangles himself in the convoluted logic of unending self-reflection that produces an infernal, "meaningless gabble" (*Descent*, 207). The "it" in the above passage has no referential locus antecedent in his self-enclosed world. The hermeneutic impasse Wentworth reaches here becomes emblematic of his later inability to understand the repeated warnings about his impending doom contained in his recurring dream of a rope, as the cords of his sins drag him in a continuous downward slide.[27] The muddle-headed narcissist resists "the creation of fact . . . the making of things other than the self" (*Descent*, 89) and consequently misses the opportunity to experience the Beatrician vision, "the glory of truth that broke out of the very air itself upon the agonized Florentine in the Paradise of Eden: 'ben sem, ben sem, Beatrice'" (88).[28] Hell awaits Wentworth because he dares to "look, in [the] Dantean phrase, on the head of the Gorgon in Dis" (*Descent*, 216), that is, on the sensual yet terrifying face of the Medusa whose gaze petrifies the beholder in *Inferno* IX and fills him with despair. Wentworth fails, in other words, to translate the "singular" of his private erotic dream, the "I am" of the Siren, into the "plural" of a common love story, the "we are" of Beatrice. For him love is a supreme fiction, not the supreme Fact.

Eliot also examines the anamorphoses of love produced by the narcissistic individual in *The Cocktail Party*. Edward pinpoints the quandary everyone faces with a memorable dictum: "Hell is oneself, / Hell is alone, the other figures in it / Merely projections" (*CPP*, 397). In terms reminiscent of Virgil's account of the nature of love, each set of paired lovers at the play's opening find themselves in Dante's underworld, suffering the isolation resulting from seeing others exclusively from their private optic. Celia, for example, admits that she has subconsciously transferred an intense personal desire to an external object of choice, in effect loving an image of Edward she invented on first meeting him (*CPP*, 382). Peter, another figure in the intersecting love triangles, agrees in retrospect with Lavinia's assessment of his own egoistic impulse: "you've been living on . . . an image of Celia / Which you made for yourself, to meet your own needs" (435). Unsure about whether she can love only someone she has fabricated in her own imagination, Celia in turn is troubled, like Edward and Peter, by the frightening possibility that if one is alone, "Then lover and beloved are equally unreal / And the dreamer is no more real than his dreams" (416). The disturbing implications of Dante's dream of the siren resurface here. Sayers's gloss on this episode of the *Purgatorio*, drawn from a spiritual writer, illuminates Celia's predicament as well as Dante's: "If you exalt the objects of your love until your picture is a false one; if you idealize them; *if you project upon them your own ideal self;* then you are loving not a real person but a dream" (*Purg.*, 221). This is the "old dream" of being separated from true love that Harry in *The Family Reunion* identifies as being one type of hell. The second hell, which follows from the first, consists of being parted from the "real self" (*CPP*, 330, 308).

Eliot dramatizes two ways of finding the road back to real personhood (cf. *CPP,* 396). One involves a human agent, the other a divine. To break out of his perceptual prison Edward must change his point of view and learn to see himself through the eyes of his beloved (395). This is the lesson Dante profits from in the earthly paradise, as Giuseppe Mazzotta explains: "Beatrice's love is for Dante that viewpoint, the look which allows him to overcome the temptation to reduce the world to the measure of his own narcissistic subjectivity and of his own imaginary delusions, as if the world were a mere tangle of objectified entities there for him, for his mastery and purview."[29] Similarly, in *The Family Reunion,* Mary opens the eyes of Harry, her childhood friend, to the possibility of starting a new life beyond geographical boundaries. Harry cannot regain his innocent self simply by returning to his first home in Wishwood, she points out, but by clearing up a moral space in his psychological hinterland: "What you need is to alter something inside you / Which you can change anywhere---here, as well as elsewhere" (*CPP*, 308). This encounter with Mary in the sunlit rose-garden that stirs Harry's natural love gives rise to another Beatrician "moment of clarity" (337), this time mediated by Agatha, who sets him on a purgatorial pilgrimage through the desert (333) of his disordered desires toward a supernal love. In *The Cocktail Party*, Celia follows Dante's footsteps, too, on "the way of illumination" towards a "transhumanised" love (*CPP*, 421), the expansive, centripetal movement towards the light that makes the face of God visible to his creatures who find peace only in looking at Him (*Par.* XXX.100–02).[30]

Before attaining this final peace, Celia passes through the crucible of suffering. To chart this stage of her spiritual progress Eliot relies once again on *Descent into Hell* as a reference point. In Williams's novel, Pauline Anstruther recoils at first from confronting an image of her double she has seen in a vision. The whole world appears to her as a canvas painted with "unreal figures," its curtain ready to roll up at any time on "one real figure" (22). Pauline's consternation grows on hearing an account of the martyrdom of her ancestor, John Struther, which took place in the sixteenth century. In the ensuing discussion, Margaret, her grandmother, gently insists that "salvation . . . is quite often a terrible thing—a frightening good" (56). The consoling truth of this paradoxical saying slowly dawns on Pauline. The more she perceives that her flight from fact, or self-knowledge, is really a flight from love (69), the more her fear dissipates. Peter Stanhope lifts her dread of encountering her true "other self" and bears it for her. Pauline for her part reaches back in time to endure vicariously the suffering of her ancestor (169–70) in accordance with the pattern laid down in Christ's Passion, that act of "just vengeance," as Dante puts it (*Par.* VII.20), carried out in atonement for humanity's sins. Reilly imparts the same wisdom to the partygoers at the Chamberlaynes's flat at the end of Eliot's play. Unlike Pauline, Celia never sees her double; only Reilly does. He reveals this fact by quoting most of the same lines from Shelley's *Prometheus Unbound* Pauline has in mind when she is first introduced. Reilly intuits from the outset that Celia will meet a violent death, but he is not certain what form it will take. In his consulting room Celia had faced the unusual symptoms of her condition courageously. Like Harry in *The Family Reunion*, she demonstrates an awareness of the burden of sin, of a failure towards "someone, or something, outside of [herself]" (416) that engendered a desire to atone for her past. Her crucifixion at the hands of some natives in Kinkanja fulfills that hope. Despite this terrifying ordeal, Reilly reminds his audience that Celia voluntarily chose "a way of life" which prepared her for what he calls a "happy death" (437). Crucifixion, in other words, affirms the Resurrection as "part of the design" so that human tragedy can always become a divine comedy.

The reconciliation of Edward and Lavinia complements Celia's entry into a new life. Just as Beatrice welcomes back Dante as her "prodigal lover," as Dorothy L. Sayers puts it (*Purg.,* 28), so, too, the Chamberlaynes patch up their differences to save their marriage. By making both husband and wife culpable for their brief separation, Eliot privileges an idea only hinted at in the *Commedia*. Williams elaborates the point: "Beatrice as a sinner does not come into the poem for the reason that the Way of Affirmation is much the same for all—for her, in her turn, as for him. Dante's spiritual movement is the pattern of hers; reverse the names, and it holds" (*Figure,* 182). The principles of Dante's way can apply to any human love, whether in family or in friendship, but marriage, according to Williams, affords a unique opportunity of seeking holiness (*Outlines,* 92, 111). Accordingly, Edward and Lavinia undertake the affirmative way together, determined to renew contact with their estranged partner, and to revive their mutual love, each playing the role of Beatrice to the other's Dante. So when Lavinia finally notices that Edward is like a child lost in a forest, as Celia pictured him (416), she proposes that he spend some time recuperating in a hotel located in a symbolically charged area called the New Forest (406). With this image Eliot evokes not only the dark wood Dante finds himself in at the start of his journey but also the moment he stands at the edge of the world's first forest before two streams, Lethe and Eunoe: the former removes the memory of sin, while the latter restores the memory of good (*Purg.* XXVIII.127). Like Dante, the Chamberlaynes resolve to live with the memories of their failings and "make them / Into something new." Only by accepting the past will they alter its meaning (*CPP*, 439) and look forward to the future. Their commitment to sanctifying the "common routine" of family life (417) marks a new beginning; the child Lavinia is expecting constitutes its visible proof. Through an act of exchanged marital love new life (literally) exists.[31]

Pauline's act of substituted love also bears fruit. In the figure of Peter Stanhope she saw "the vision of the glory incarnate"[32] because he drew her gaze up toward the divine light, just as Beatrice lifted Dante to the same celestial height with cords of love (cf. *Par.* XXVIII.127–129). By following the lead of her guide and relieving her ancestor of his mental anguish, Pauline is again brought face to face with her glorified self. This time she is not afraid, rather she marvels at it:

> She opened her eyes . . . there, as a thousand times in her looking-glass—there! The ruffled brown hair, the long nose, the firm compressed mouth, the tall body, the long arms, her dress, her gesture. It wore no super-natural splendour of aureole, but its rich nature burned and glowed before her, bright as if mortal flesh had indeed become what all lovers know it to be. (170–71)

Pauline's response to her specular image reverses the tragic fate of Narcissus once he looked into his vanity mirror. The epiphanic scene corresponds to the one in which Dante beholds the transfigured body of Beatrice in the *Vita Nuova*.[33] Intended by God to be "cosa nova" ("a new thing"), a miracle rooted in the very Love of the Trinity itself,[34] this marvellous creature who suddenly appears to her lover is someone real. She is not "realer," as Williams says, than the actual Beatrice, who doubtless had many serious faults, but she is just as real: "Both Beatrices are aspects of one Beatrice" (*Figure*, 27). It can likewise be said that both Paulines are mirror images of one Pauline. The action of grace elevates her fallen nature, making it a new creation, a union of the spirit with the "holy and glorious flesh" (*Par.* XIV.43) of the risen body. The recurring biblical phrase (*Descent*, 151, 173) taken from the book of Revelation (21:5), *Ecce, omnia nova facio* ("Behold, I will make all things new") unfolds a "new vision of the world" (*Descent*, 188) for Pauline as she, like Dante, delights in the miracle of newness, a reflection of the transcendent Beauty that is, in St. Augustine's phrase, "at once so ancient and so new"[35] : "*tam antiqua, tam nova, vita nova, nova creatura*, a new creature, no more in any sense but new, not opposed to the old, but in union with the old, new without any trick of undermeaning, new always, and now new" (*Descent,* 205).

Spiritual renovation does not require eros to be forever on its knees to agape, Williams maintains (*Outlines,* 111), but they need not be separated either. The Incarnation ensured their compatibility once and for all (*Image,* 161). Divine love came down to meet human love, to heal it, to redirect it, and to raise it to a higher plane (*Par.* VII.30–33); since then, Williams adds, it is beheld "through and in a carnality of joy" (*He Came Down,* 113). In his view, two opposing philosophical tendencies, one ancient, the other modern, undermine the significance of the body as it is known in love. The early gnostic docetists "had refined the body into an unreal phantom of dim light and called it the Resurrection," while D. H. Lawrence degraded cerebralism in order to extol what he called the "phallic consciousness" (*Image,* 72). The example of Dante, "the spring of all modern love literature" (*Outlines,* 55), contradicts the extremes of both spiritualism and sensualism. When he first sees Beatrice, the spirits of his entire being, his sensations, emotions, and intellect, are all stirred at once (*Image,* 72). There is no dissociation of sensibility. Dante praises Beatrice's physical beauty, but a greater affirmation lies ahead. His "passionate intellect"[36] impels him to know what exactly the revelation of her beatitude means (*Image,* 72). And later, Beatrice imparadises the mind in love (*Par.* XXVIII.3). Sexual attraction, like every natural desire, finds its issue in love of God (*Par.* VII.142–144).

Eliot's Dante is also the great poet of Love. Some of the figures in Eliot's early poems, such as St. Narcissus and St. Sebastian, are "tormented by unresolved religious and sexual yearnings."[37] These unhappy souls counterpoint Dante's brave attempt to make "something permanent and holy" out of his "personal animal feelings."[38] They resemble instead the characters in Lawrence's fiction who transgress the boundaries of individual privacy and seek the Absolute in the wrong place by deifying eros. "Human intimacy can be wonderful and life-giving," Eliot remarked, but it cannot possibly be an end in itself. Echoing Dante, he believed that human love is only "made perfect in the love of God."[39] *The Cocktail Party,* as we have seen, dramatizes this belief. Freud thought the desire for God was a substitute for sex; the experience of Celia, as well as that of Edward and Lavinia, shows that, in Eliot's view, sexual desire can often act as a substitute for God.

Before Lester Furnival makes the same discovery in *All Hallows' Eve,* she must relinquish "the common vague idea of her age that if your sexual life was all right you were all right."[40] Thrown unexpectedly into the "new life" of the recently dead six months after her marriage, Lester is given ample chance to find out why her old life had been "disordered in love" (*AHE,* 192). No relationship makes her faults as plain as the one with her husband: "it was her willingness to commit herself with Richard

that made her believe she (as she called it) loved Richard" (10). The
parenthetical comment of the narrator casts doubt on whether she genuinely understands the meaning of love.[41] In fact, she retains traces of her
former selfishness and pride in her personality. In her previous life she
had been a material girl interested only in "gadgets" rather than in people (9). She unwittingly treated Richard as an object, too. When he appears to her on Westminster Bridge, she pushes him away in a fit of
peevishness and demands to know why he had kept her waiting (4–5). In
their quarrels, the Furnivals, like most couples, had been "fools and
quick-tempered, high egotists and bitter of tongue" (6). This realization
leaves Lester with two options: either her love for Richard must be
"transhumanized to heaven" or it will be "dehumanized in hell" (cf.
Figure, 124). At first thoughts of selfish love abound: "Richard . . . should
be there with her, prisoner with her, prisoner to her. If only he too would
die, and come!" (89). But then the "good sense native to her," expressed
with "a new and holy shyness" (90), prevails. Lester calls out Richard's
name with the same love that Beatrice, after her death, called Dante in the
earthly paradise. Lester's positive response to the voice of her conscience
indicates her readiness to participate in the fullest expression of Love as
Williams, recalling Dante, defines it: "To love is to die and live again; to
live from a new root" (*He Came Down*, 120).[42]

As the old self embarks on the new way (cf. *He Came Down,* 119),
Lester gradually purges her imperfections. Purgation is part of what
Williams refers to as Dante's great law of exchange: "[It] involves no folly
of denial of the girl's faults or sins. The vision of the perfection arises
independently of the imperfection; it shines through her body whatever
she makes of her body" (*Figure,* 63–64). Thus charity is exhibited in the
selfish, and humility in the proud. The first touch of repentance Lester
feels on hearing an inner voice inviting her to be more generous (*AHE,*
90) prepares the way for a second meeting with her husband. On this
occasion she greets him with joy:

> [Richard] added, across the room to Lester, without surprise, but with a
> rush of apology, and only he knew to whom he spoke, "Darling, have I
> kept you waiting? I'm so sorry." Lester saw him. She felt, as he came,
> all of her old self lifting in her; bodiless, she seemed to recall her body
> in the joy they exchanged. He saw her smile, and in the smile heaven
> was frank and she was shy. . . . She said, "I'll wait for you a million
> years." She felt a stir within her, as if life quickened. (169)

A number of Dantesque echoes resonate in this passage. Just as "the
embers of the ancient flame" are rekindled when Dante first sees Beatrice
in Eden (*Purg.* XXX.48), so too Lester's passion for Richard is sparked by
memories of their conjugal love. Earlier, while a friend spoke to her,
Lester could think of nothing but her husband's eyes, remembering how
he had come "to meet her once and again, and how her heart had swelled

for the glory and vigor of his coming" (135; cf. 88). Williams thereby connects the poignancy of their reunion with Lester's vision of Richard's glorified body: "She almost did see Richard so, in his whole miraculous pattern, all the particles of him. . . . She loved him the more passionately for the seeing" (239). Lester affirms the eidetic image of her husband's DNA with a distinctive smile, the "signature gesture" of Dante's theology of joy,[43] since, as Williams explains, this normal form of greeting between the young lovers in Florence became their passport to eternity (*Outlines*, 110).

Lester's Beatrician moment helps her, moreover, to appreciate her spouse's redeeming qualities. She remembers in particular how one night he brought her a glass of water to quench her thirst:

> In her drowsiness a kind of vista of innumerable someones stretched before her, but it was not as if they were being kind, for it was not water they were bringing but their own joy . . . and everything was altered, for no one had to be unselfish any more. . . . She thought, all the same, "Darling, darling Richard!"—because the fact that he was bringing her his own joy to drink . . . was a deed of such excelling merit on his part that all the choirs of heaven and birds of earth could never properly sing its praise. (163)

The recollection of Richard's simple gesture inspires Lester to be charitable in the same way towards her dead and gloomy friend: "There rose in her the vague idea of giving Evelyn a drink, a cup of tea or a sherry or a glass of water—something of that material and liquid joy" (183). Each small act of courtesy, no less than Christ-like gestures of "substituted love" shown to others (*AHE*, 183–4), recapitulates the affirmative way that leads to eternal life (*Figure*, 10).[44]

In spite of her defects, then, Lester exerts a salutary influence on Richard. Williams sets the two on the affirmative way together, as Eliot would later do with Edward and Lavinia, to underwrite their interchange of function (cf. *Figure*, 182). It occurs to Richard in retrospect that he had habitually thought of Lester only in relation to himself, never as an individual in her own right. He acknowledges his neglect of her as well as the fact that

> she knew more of him in himself than he had ever troubled to know in herself. It was why her comments on him, in gaiety or rage, always had such a tang of truth. . . . The infinite accuracy of a wife's intelligence stared out at him. . . . He thought how many chances he had missed of delighting in her entire veracity, instead of excusing, protesting, denying. (46–47)

Richard later makes amends on this front when he heeds Lester's gentle advice to rebuke Simon simply and graciously, and not to engage him in a self-righteous, imperious manner (255).

Purification for Richard, as for Dante, entails "the real recovery of the exterior image" (*Figure*, 167). But he occasionally falters, lured by the temptation to falsify the way things were in his marriage:

> He was surprised . . . to remember how much he had considered Lester. . . . he had been, in that sense, a very good husband. He almost wondered if he had been too indulgent, too kind. No; if it were to do again, he would do it. . . . But . . . now she was gone, he could attend to himself. (98–99)

Richard yields to the deceit of the "Francescan moment" (*Figure*, 118–119), "the quiet distilled *luxuria* of his wishes, the delicate sweet lechery of idleness, the tasting of unhallowed peace" (*AHE*, 99). The pseudo-romantic reverie lurks behind his dismissal of Lester's image during the hypnotic "relaxation" of Simon the magician: "He thought of Lester, but not of her glory or her passion, he thought of her in a moment of irritation" (115). Once the spell is broken, however, Richard looks back on the whole episode with shame and regret:

> Rash, violent, angry, as [Lester] might have been, egotistic in her nature as he, yet her love had been sealed always, to another and not to herself. She was never the slave of false *luxuria*. When she had served him—how often!—she had not done it from kindness or unselfishness; it had been because she wished what he wished and was his servant to what he desired. Kindness, patience, forbearance, were not enough; he had had them; but she had had love. (214–15)

This honest revaluation is made possible by a previous insight: "he had tasted the new life in Jonathan's flat; he had drunk of it in his wife's eyes" (170). Her eyes are not paradise, but they do reflect that heavenly abode (cf. *Par.* XVIII.21). Lester's "immortal greeting" (170), like the one heard on a young girl's lips in Florence many centuries before, rescues Richard from irreparable spiritual harm.

The Beatrician state is not everlasting, however (*He Came Down*, 109). The quest has yet to reach its peak in the region of pure light that fills love with a joy that transcends all earthly delectation. After realizing that Beatrice has become the beloved of the "First Lover" (*Par.* IV. 118–20), Dante is so moved himself by the desire for God that for the first time in the whole saga he forgets his childhood sweetheart altogether: "sì tutto 'l mio amore in lui si mise, / che Beatrice eclissò" ("yes, my love was so totally committed to God that it eclipsed Beatrice") (*Par.* X.59–60). What is the response of Beatrice to this dramatic turn of events? "Ma sì se ne rise"—she is so delighted at the prospect, in Williams's gloss, that "she laughs at the heavenly infidelity." This splendid give and take presents an accurate image of what actually happens to most ordinary people in love (*Outlines*, 109).

The transition from an earthbound love to its highest latitude is not an easy one, though, for the ordinary couple in *All Hallows' Eve*. When Lester phones Richard to arrange for one last rendezvous, her voice of "serene grief" disconcerts him enough to reply, "Nothing shall make me give you up. I've only just begun to find you." Lester tries to reassure him, "But you will, even if nothing makes you. . . . It'll have to be like that. . . . Don't be too distressed about anything. . . . I do love you, Richard" (228). Understandably, Richard still clings to her, especially now that she has temporarily reappeared. Their reconciliation scene produces no change of attitude on his part:

> Lester . . . said, "Have I been very long? I'm so sorry."
> "I've been tiresome so often, darling. I've been beastly to you. I—"
> He said, "You've never been tiresome," and she,
> "No; speak true now, my own. I—"
> He said, "Very well, you have. And what in all the heavens and hells, and here too, does it matter? Do we keep accounts about each other? If it's the last word I speak I shall still say that you were too good for me." (233)

Truth, of course, does matter, and it is incumbent upon Richard to "find what she had—another kind of life" (215). Williams does not show us his full development along the way; he focuses instead on the advancement of Lester. She is not immune to the sharp pain of separation either. Her heart sinks as she wonders, "without him, what was immortality worth?" This Francescan moment soon fades for she realizes that "yet only without him could she even be that which she now was" (256). The consolation might initially be bittersweet, but once she comes to believe, like Pauline Anstruther, that "all facts are joyous" (*Descent,* 205), then even parting from her beloved fills the pilgrim soul with hope. She knows that love reaches beyond the limits of death and into the afterlife.

Lester's touching departure has paradisal overtones. She is granted a new vision of herself "no longer bodily understood, but a point...a spark of the light floating in the air" (256–57). The imagery calls to mind the moment Dante enters the Empyrean and a flash of light enwraps him (*Par.* XXX.52–55). Lester's soul is rendered fit to do so as well. Other allusions to the *Paradiso* surface as Lester bids Richard a fond farewell:

> She looked across at Richard. She said, "Dearest, I did love you. Forgive me. And thank you—Oh, Richard, *thank you!* Goodbye, my blessing!" She stood, quiet and very real, before them; almost she shone on them; then . . . the tremor of brightness received her. (269)

Lester pays tribute to Richard, her "blessing," just as Dante expresses his deepest gratitude to Beatrice, the instrument of his salvation, once she departs from him to take her seat among the blessed (*Par.* XXXI.64–93). The hallows proceed to take Lester up into the same celestial rose, formed by the circle of light resplendent of God's glory, from where Beatrice smiles at Dante for the last time. In her transfiguration, Lester, like the souls of all the blessed, becomes a dazzling point of divine light. She *did* love Richard in her earthly life; now, in the eternal present, even though his figure loses its "immediate urgency," something "infinitely precious, which had belonged to it" (257) remains, and, on account of this fact, Lester's new self loves and lives again from a new root.

Eliot replays the Beatrician moment in his final work too. To say that *All Hallows' Eve* simmered in his mind while writing *The Elder Statesman* would perhaps be overstating the case. Other factors—biographical not least—contributed to the fermentation of the Dantesque theme. The dedicatory poem to his wife stands as Eliot's most explicit testimony to the affirmative way and to the sanctity of the body. To her he owes "the leaping delight" of the conjugal love that unites newlyweds. The consummation of his second marriage in 1957, Eliot agreed, made him feel the way Dante did after he had passed into paradise.[45] The rebirth of human love in Eliot occurs as a natural consequence of his incarnational theology. One must not "deny the body," the chorus exhorts the audience in *The Rock*, because the human form divine acts as "The visible reminder of Invisible Light" (*CPP*, 165). Over the next several years Eliot's imaginative exposure to *Descent into Hell* and *All Hallows' Eve* made a profound impression. Through the lens of Williams's theology of romantic love Eliot considered anew the manifestation of the divine in ordinary life from a Dantesque perspective. The possibility of loving someone for who she is, even with her frailties, the idea that it is never too late to change and be reconciled to God's will, and the meaning of the death of a loved one: these elements, and more, are present in Williams's novels. Eliot engages them fully in *The Cocktail Party* and with fresh energy in *The Elder Statesman*. Lord Claverton, for example, discovers in his twilight years that it is enough to confess the truth about himself to one person to keep his soul "safe." Then "he loves that person, and his love will save him" (*CPP*, 568). A young couple ratifies the salvific power of love as the curtain falls. Claverton's death, Charles says, gives birth to a "new person" who is both lovers together. And death itself no longer dismays Monica since she is firmly rooted in "the certainty of love unchanging" (583). As a contemporary reviewer of the play concluded, "This late touching vision of youthful love in an aging author is an endearing thing. The world of the 'hollow men,' terminating with a whimper, now regenerates itself with a kiss."[46] In this climactic epiphany eros and agape achieve a Dantesque balance. The experience of both a moment and a lifetime confirms that what is true of Eliot is also true of Williams: "Love reciprocated is always rejuvenating."[47]

NOTES

1. Following Eliot, Williams stated that "Dante is generally accepted as a great Christian poet, and there will be few doubts as to his orthodoxy." See *Outlines of*

Romantic Theology, ed. Alice Mary Hadfield (Grand Rapids, MI: Eerdmans, 1990), 91. Hereafter cited in the text as *Outlines*.

2. Charles Williams, "A Dialogue on Mr. Eliot's Poem," *The Dublin Review* 212 (April 1943): 114–22.

3. See Carol Smith, *T. S. Eliot's Dramatic Theory and Practice* (Princeton: Princeton University Press, 1963), 156ff.; Sebastian D.G. Knowles, *A Purgatorial Flame: Seven British Writers in the Second World War* (Philadelphia: University of Pennsylvania Press, 1990), 153–72; and Suzanne Bray, "Disseminating Glory: Echoes of Charles Williams in the Works of T. S. Eliot," *Seven: An Anglo-American Literary Review* 14 (1997): 59–73.

4. Humphrey Carpenter, *The Inklings: C. S. Lewis, J. R. R. Tolkien, Charles Williams, and Their Friends* (New York: Ballantine, 1978), 106–7. More recently, Alison Milbank maintains that Eliot's reading of Dante is in "total disagreement with that of his later correspondent Charles Williams" since Eliot supposedly eschews the medieval poet's "incarnational theology." See *Dante and the Victorians* (Manchester: Manchester University Press, 1998), 229.

5. Anne Ridler, Introduction to *The Image of the City and Other Essays*, by Charles Williams (Oxford: Oxford University Press, 1970), xl.

6. Charles Williams, *The Figure of Beatrice: A Study in Dante* (London: Faber and Faber, 1943), 9–10. Hereafter cited in the text as *Figure*.

7. Cf. Ridler, ix.

8. Vittorio Montemaggi reiterates the point in a recent article: "for Dante—and in this he is at one with most of the medieval theological tradition—negative and affirmative theological discourses are *not* mutually exclusive, neither discourse being properly meaningful if not somehow understood in conjunction with the other." See "'La Rosa in che il verbo divino si fece': Human Bodies and Truth in the Poetic Narrative of the *Commedia*," in *Dante and the Human Body: Eight Essays*, ed. John C. Barnes and Jennifer Petrie (Dublin: Four Courts Press, 2007), 192n. In *The Image of the City and Other Essays* (Oxford: Oxford University Press, 1970), Williams deplored attempts to falsify the "central energy" animating the *Comedy*: "Thus Dante, in whose vision flesh and spirit were so greatly one, has been turned into a spiritual teacher and even into something like a refined preacher of spirituality as separate from the body" (142). Hereafter cited in the text as *Image*.

9. T. S. Eliot, *The Complete Poems and Plays of T. S. Eliot* (London: Faber and Faber, 1969), 419. Hereafter cited in the text as *CPP*.

10. See Bonamy Dobrée, "T. S. Eliot: A Personal Reminiscence," in *T. S. Eliot: The Man and His Work*, ed. Allen Tate (London: Chatto and Windus, 1967), 81; see also Henry Hewes, "T. S. Eliot at Seventy," in *T. S. Eliot: The Contemporary Reviews*, ed. Jewel Spears Brooker (Cambridge: Cambridge University Press, 2004), 32.

11. Brother George Every, "The Way of Rejections," in *T. S. Eliot: A Symposium*, ed. Richard March and Tambimuttu (London: Editions Poetry, 1948), 188.

12. Grover Smith, *T. S. Eliot's Poetry and Plays: A Study in Sources and Meaning* (Chicago: University of Chicago Press, 1974), 212.

13. Every, 188.

14. Lyndall Gordon, *Eliot's New Life* (New York: Farrar, Straus and Giroux, 1988), 12.

15. T. S. Eliot, introduction to *All Hallows' Eve*, by Charles Williams (Grand Rapids, MI: Eerdmans, 1982), xvii. First published in 1948.

16. Allen Tate put it the following way: "Poetry begins with the common reality, and ends with it, as our friend's friend, Charles Williams, said of Dante. It could be equally said of Tom Eliot." See "Postscript by the Guest Editor" in *T. S. Eliot: The Man and His Work*, ed. Allen Tate (New York: Dell, 1966), 390. G. K. Chesterton identified the "common mind" as the quality "all the artists and heroes" possessed, including Dante. See *Charles Dickens*, vol. 15 in *The Collected Works of G.K. Chesterton* (San Francisco: Ignatius Press, 1989), 99.

17. Lyndall Gordon remarks, "The heroes Eliot created after his conversion—the martyred Thomas, the missionary Harry, his own reminiscent self in *Four Quartets*—

work out their salvation at home, among mostly predictable people and familiar English scenes." See *Eliot's Early Years* (London: Oxford University Press, 1977), 121.

18. The rose garden is, of course, a recurring image in Eliot's poetry. The words in quotation marks are taken from the third priest's speech in *Murder in the Cathedral* (*CPP*, 265).

19. Walker Percy explains that a Christian sacramental vision confers "the highest significance upon the ordinary things of this world, bread, wine, water, touch, breath, words, talking, listening." What is the result? "You have a man in a predicament and on the move in a real world of real things, a world which is a sacrament and a mystery; a pilgrim whose life is a searching and a finding." In short, you have "a recipe for the best novel-writing from Dante to Dostoevsky." See "The Holiness of the Ordinary" in *Signposts in a Strange Land* (New York: Farrar, Straus and Giroux, 1991), 369. Consider also, for example, the final chorus in *Murder in the Cathedral* in which all things and all creatures in the air, on the earth, and in the soil "affirm Thee [God] in living" (*CPP*, 281).

20. Friedrich Nietzsche, "On Truth and Lies in a Nonmoral Sense," trans. Daniele Brazeale, in *Philosophy and Truth: Selections from Nietzsche's Notebooks of the Early 1870's* (Atlantic Highlands, NJ: Humanities Press, 1979), 84; *The Will to Power*, trans. Walter Kaufmann and R. J. Hollingdale (London: Weidenfeld and Nicolson, 1968), par. 409.

21. See Dante Alighieri, *The Divine Comedy III: Paradise (Il Paradiso)*, trans. Dorothy L. Sayers and Barbara Reynolds (Harmondsworth, England: Penguin, 1969), *Par.* IV.129–32. Hereafter cited in the text as *Par.*, followed by canto number (in Roman numeral) and verse numbers. In this connection, Nietzsche's statement, "there are no facts, only interpretations" (*The Will to Power*, par. 481) needs to be considered along with Dante's verses in *Paradiso* IV. Williams aligned himself with Kierkegaard, whose "life of skepticism was rooted in God." See *The Descent of the Dove: A Short History of the Holy Spirit in the Church* (London: Longmans, 1939), 213.

22. Charles Williams, *Descent into Hell* (Grand Rapids, MI: Eerdmans, 1980), 38. Hereafter cited in the text as *Descent.*

23. *Image*, 30; Charles Williams, *Collected Plays* (London: Oxford University Press, 1963), 298.

24. Cited in Ridler, xliii.

25. Direct quotations of Dante are taken from *Dante Alighieri: La Commedia secondo l'antica vulgate*, ed. Giorgio Petrocchi (Florence: Le Lettere, 1994). English translations are my own. I have consulted Dante Alighieri, *The Divine Comedy II: Purgatory (Il Purgatorio)*, trans. Dorothy L. Sayers (Harmondsworth, England: Penguin, 1988), *Purg.* XVIII.22–26. Hereafter cited in the text as *Purg.* Glosses on the text provided by Sayers will be cited simply as *Purg.*, followed by the page number of the volume from which the gloss is taken.

26. Dante Alighieri, *The Divine Comedy I: Hell (L'Inferno)*, trans. Dorothy L. Sayers (Harmondsworth: Penguin, 1971), *Inf.* III.18. Hereafter cited in the text as *Inf.*

27. For Williams's use of the rope imagery cf. the biblical passages in Psalms 119:61; Psalms 18:5–7; 2 Peter 2:4–5.

28. Williams translates what he calls "almost the greatest line in Dante and therefore in all poetry" as follows: "Look well: we are, indeed we are, Beatrice" (*Purg.* XXX.73). See *He Came Down from Heaven* (London: Heineman, 1938), 104. Hereafter cited in the text as *He Came Down*. Williams also points out how the appearance of the siren and the words of her opening song, "Io son . . . io son dolce Sirena—I am, I am the sweet Siren" (*Purg.* XIX.19) are a deliberate echo and contrast to the words of Beatrice when she first appears in *Purgatorio* XXX (*Figure*, 165).

29. Giuseppe Mazzotta, *Dante's Vision and the Circle of Knowledge* (Princeton: Princeton University Press, 1993), 150.

30. Evelyn Underhill, from whose book Eliot took copious notes in his student days at Harvard (Gordon, *Eliot's Early Years*, 60), cites this passage from the *Paradiso* to illustrate the illuminated state of the individual who discerns the "cosmic vision of Infinity, exterior to the subject"; see *Mysticism: A Study in the Nature and Development of*

Man's Spiritual Consciousness (London: Methuen, 1967), 250. Williams wrote an introduction to an edition of Underhill's letters published in 1943.

31. The fact that Lavinia is expecting a child is not indicated in the stage directions as such but by Eliot himself, Nevil Coghill pointed out in "An Essay on the Structure and Meaning of the Play" in T. S. Eliot, *The Cocktail Party,* ed. Nevil Coghill (London: Faber and Faber, 1974), 281. For Williams childbirth is the "one great natural fact." The child exists because of the love of man and woman, and that "operation involves something of the nature of substitution" (*Image,* 150). That is why Lester Furnival, even while she is dead, contemplates "the name of the child Richard and she would one day have for they never meant to wait too long" in *All Hallows' Eve* (Grand Rapids: Eerdmans, 1982), 164. In Eliot's poetry, from "Marina" to *Burnt Norton,* the laughter of unborn children is an image of new promise, of hope, as it is in Forster's *Howards End* (Harmondsworth: Penguin, 1985): "And all the time their salvation was lying round them---the past sanctifying the present; the present, with wild heart-throb, declaring that there would after all be a future, with laughter and the voices of children" (292). In *The Cocktail Party,* to sanctify the common routine means not only to beget and bear a child. The next step, Eliot explained, is for parents to try to "understand what they have created." See "The Aims of Poetic Drama," *Adam International Review,* no. 200 (November 1949): 16.

32. Dorothy L. Sayers, *Further Papers on Dante* (London: Methuen, 1957), 195.

33. Sayers, *Further Papers,* 196.

34. *Dante's 'Vita Nuova': A Translation and an Essay,* trans. Mark Musa (Bloomington: Indiana University Press, 1973), 35, 62.

35. St. Augustine, *Confessions,* trans. R. S. Pine-Coffin (Harmondsworth: Penguin, 1984), 231.

36. Sayers, *Further Papers,* 35.

37. Harvey Gross, "The Figure of St. Sebastian," *The Southern Review* 21 (Autumn 1985): 975.

38. T. S. Eliot, *Selected Essays* (Faber and Faber, 1972), 137.

39. T. S. Eliot, review of *Son of Woman: The Story of D.H. Lawrence,* by John Middleton Murry, *The Criterion* 10 (July 1931): 773. D. H. Lawrence lamented the split between body and soul he detected in Dante's writings: "Why do we slur over the actual fact that Dante had a cozy bifurcated wife in his bed, and a family of lusty little Dantinos?" See *Phoenix II: Uncollected, Unpublished, and Other Prose Works by D.H. Lawrence,* ed. Warren Roberts and Harry T. Moore (New York: Viking, 1968), 422. E. M. Forster lodged a similar complaint. He remarked that the sexual relation should be "cheerful," with "none of the solemnity which Christianity has thought essential to Romance,—and which e.g. so puts me off the Vita Nuova." *Selected Letters of E.M. Forster,* ed. Mary Lago and P. N. Furbank, vol. 1 (Cambridge, Mass.: Belknap Press, 1985), 258.

In contrast, Eliot maintained that even in the work of "a deformed Dante" such as Baudelaire (see "The Lesson of Baudelaire," *Tyro* [Spring 1921]: 4), his depiction of "the sexual act as evil is more dignified, less boring, than as the natural, 'life-giving', cheery automatism of the modern world" (*Selected Essays,* 429). Eliot admired Christopher Dawson's defense of the Christian ideal of marriage in response to Lawrence's critique of it: "[Marriage] is the physical expression or incarnation of a spiritual union in which the sexual act has become the vehicle of a higher creative purpose. It is for this reason that marriage is regarded by the Church as a type and a sacramental participation of the central mystery of the Faith—the marriage of God and man in the Incarnation" (see "Christianity and Sex," in *Enquiries into Religion and Culture* (Freeport, N.Y.: Books for the Libraries Press, 1968), 289–90; see also 285ff.) That is why the penitents on the circle of lust in the *Purgatorio* praise the married couples (unnamed because countless) who lived the virtue of chastity (*Purg.* XXV.133–5).

40. Charles Williams, *All Hallows' Eve* (Grand Rapids, MI: Eerdmans, 1982). Hereafter cited in the text as *AHE*.

41. Marlene Marie McKinley, "'To Live from a New Root': The Uneasy Consolation of *All Hallows' Eve*," *Mythlore* 59 (Autumn 1989): 13.

42. Williams goes on to say that "part of the experience of romantic love has been precisely that; the experience of being made new, the 'renovation' of nature, as Dante defined it in a particular experience of love" (*He Came Down,* 120; see also 96). In her fine article, Marlene Marie McKinley notes the relevance of Williams's definition of love for Lester's situation, but she does not connect it to Dante as Williams does in *He Came Down from Heaven* and as I do here.

43. Peter Hawkins, *Dante: A Brief History* (Oxford: Blackwell, 2006), 129.

44. Cf. the Gospel teaching on this subject contained in Matthew 10:42, 25:40.

45. Lyndall Gordon, *Eliot's New Life*, 248.

46. Derek Stanford, "Mr. Eliot's New Play," in *T. S. Eliot: The Contemporary Reviews*, ed. Jewel Spears Brooker (Cambridge: Cambridge University Press, 2004), 575.

47. Henry Hewes, "T. S. Eliot at Seventy," 569.

TEN

T. S. Eliot, W. R. Lethaby, and Sacred Architecture

Hazel Atkins

Details of architecture, if "architecture" is defined most simply and broadly as a structure or building, are everywhere in T. S. Eliot's poetry. Eliot uses vivid images of church edifices, gardens, houses, bridges, ships, pubs, staircases, windowsills, doorways, streets, walls to lend memorable visual clarity to his poems. These details are so prolific and various that they raise the question of whether this quintessentially urban poet incorporated features of his built surroundings into his work simply because they were useful as widely recognizable images and tropes, or whether architecture in fact held some magnetism for him, whether it was important to him and was therefore used by him to some other, symbolic end.

The symbolic importance of setting and landscape in Eliot's work has long been of interest to critics, including Helen Gardner (1968), Nancy Duvall Hargrove (1978), and John D. Boyd (1998). The city, as a specific architectural setting in Eliot's work, has been studied in detail by critics such as Robert A. Day (1965), Marianne Thormählen (1978), Robert Crawford (1987), Bernard Bergonzi (1994), Jean Bessière (2003), and Hee-Sung Kim (2004). Very focused studies of the architectural elements of Eliot's poems include Steve Ellis's *The English Eliot: Design, Language and Landscape in "Four Quartets"* (1991) and Jesse T. Airaudi's "Finding the Stairs Lit: Contemporary Architecture's Return to Tradition and the Relevance of *The Waste Land* at the Fin de Millénaire" (1999). All of these readings specifically devoted to architecture reveal its importance and symbolic potential in Eliot's oeuvre, and consequently it seems that a more detailed study of this recurring image and of its relationship to Eliot's thought may be long overdue. On the other hand, these readings also indicate the complexities and difficulties inherent in such a study, as Eliot's textual representations of details of architecture are so prolific and so various that the ways in which these images can be understood seem inexhaustible.

The question, then, of what exactly the poet intends to convey by his use of plentiful images of buildings and structures is still unanswered and perhaps even ultimately unanswerable. That the details of architecture are interesting within the broad symbolic significance of landscape or setting within the poet's oeuvre seems, to the critics named above, largely acceptable, but how these details are to be grouped, read, or understood, or what conclusions can be drawn about them, is still unresolved. Perhaps the best way to approach the question is to narrow the focus. Studies of landscape or setting are too broad to do justice to the abundance of architectural images within the poems. In addition, the images of structures and buildings are so various, appearing in so many different guises, that it will be helpful to limit the focus still further and ask whether there is a particular style or type of building on which the poet's mind seems to dwell.

An answer to this question can be reached in part by looking closely at what Eliot has to say in his personal letters and in his writings for *The Dial* and *The Criterion* in the 1920s and 1930s. These reveal not only an acute sensitivity to the built environment in which he found himself, but an interest in and concern for ecclesiastical architecture in particular. The majority of his London Letters and Commentaries regarding architecture make up what might be called a campaign for the preservation of City churches. His personal letters also demonstrate a more than cursory interest in church buildings. Viewing Eliot's poetic oeuvre, it is noticeable that vivid images of ecclesiastical architecture recur in works as various as *The Waste Land, The Rock, Murder in the Cathedral,* and *Four Quartets.* It is important to note that the interest in church architecture in his pieces in the reviews, his letters, and his poems and plays spans the years before and after he joined the Church of England. It is possible to conclude, therefore, that not just architecture in general, but church architecture in particular preoccupied T. S. Eliot enough to become a recurring trope in his poetry. Indeed, Eliot's representations of ecclesiastical architecture in his poems and plays reveal much about the nature and purpose of his intellectual and spiritual journey.

Perhaps one of the best ways of discovering why Eliot was especially interested in church buildings, and how this interest can be understood as running parallel to his broader ideas about the nature and role of art in society, is to look closely at his engagement with the work of architect and historian W. R. Lethaby. In January 1928, at the end of a Commentary for the *Criterion* subtitled "The Stones of London" in which Eliot argues for the preservation of Westminster Abbey, he adds a postscript acknowledging the work of Lethaby (1857–1931): "As we go to press we learn with regret that Professor W. R. Lethaby has resigned his charge of the Abbey structure, which he had held for twenty-two years. Our greatest living authority on architecture, he will be difficult to replace."[1] Coming from Eliot, this is strong praise. This public avowal of respect for Lethaby was not Eliot's only expression of interest in the work of this architect. In September 1923, Eliot had written to Lethaby on behalf of the *Criterion*:

> Dear Professor Lethaby,
> I think that it is over a year ago that I wrote to you about the *Criterion*, so that you cannot complain that I have plagued you. You will see from this circular that your name represents a defect in what seems to me an otherwise brilliant list. I am sending you the essay on architecture which I enclose, in the hope that it may stimulate you to write at least a little paper for us. But remember that any subject in connexion with art or architecture that you choose would be welcome to us; and if this essay does not interest you, or if you are too busy, or for any other reason, do not bother to return it. There is no one else whom we should ask to write about these subjects.[2]

As the second volume of Eliot's collected letters reveals, he was in 1923 avidly seeking papers from a variety of scholars for the *Criterion*. In a compliment to Lethaby, he indicates that the fact that Lethaby's name is so far missing on the circular is a "defect." Moreover, he elicits Lethaby's response to an article on architecture, concluding with the remark that Lethaby's would be accepted as the last word on the subject. Though it is unknown which article on architecture Eliot sent to Lethaby, and though Lethaby never did write for the *Criterion*, he evidently answered Eliot's letter, and in October 1923 Eliot wrote to him again:

> Dear Mr Lethaby,
> I think that I have not thanked you for your letter. Certainly it is right that you should not notice such an essay, and as you have that opinion of it I certainly would not let anyone else do so. But we do indeed want something from you very badly; it is appalling that there should be no one else in England who can write sense about architecture, but it is the truth.
> I have just seen your book on Roman London: I congratulate you on an important and extremely interesting book: important I think as much by reason of the point of view toward architecture in general and the subject in particular, as by the erudition itself. (*Letters*, 2:253)

Here, again, is a very strongly worded expression of praise and respect. This third letter from Eliot to Lethaby reveals two important points. First, in saying that Lethaby is the only person in England who can "write sense about architecture," Eliot seems to indicate that he knows about other published works on architecture and that he admires Lethaby's above all. In other words, Eliot's interest in Lethaby does not exist in a vacuum but appears to be part of a wider awareness of scholarship on the subject of architecture. Second, he reveals that he is keeping up to date with Lethaby's work. Lethaby's book (*Londinium: Architecture and the Crafts*), mentioned here, was published earlier in 1923, so it appears that Eliot lost no time in getting hold of it. On the basis of his remarks in these letters, it is possible to assume that Eliot had read not only Lethaby's most recently published book but also other works by him. This speculation is possible because Eliot's September 1923 letter, which was apparently written before Eliot had seen *Londinium*, reveals a respect for Lethaby's opinion about architecture that suggests that he was familiar, at least in part, with Lethaby's earlier works.

Lethaby was a follower of John Ruskin and William Morris and was also deeply influenced by the English school of anthropology led by Sir James George Frazer. This same anthropological school was, of course, very important to T. S. Eliot's development of a theory of tradition in art and of "the mythical method." Given Eliot's enthusiasm for Lethaby, and given the similarity between their understandings of the cultural importance of myth and tradition, I argue that there is an affinity between the ways in which Eliot and Lethaby viewed the role of art and architecture in society, and I speculate that Eliot's knowledge of Lethaby's work adds an important layer of complexity to Eliot's views on ecclesiastical architecture.

It is easy to see how followers of Ruskin would be drawn to the study of anthropology. In connecting the age of machinery with slavery and discussing the forms of the Gothic as symbolic of freedom in design, Ruskin's works encourage his followers to look to a pre-industrial society for inspiration. Additionally, Ruskin writes,

> A picture or a poem is often little more than a feeble utterance of man's admiration of something out of himself; but architecture approaches more to a creation of his own, born of his necessities, and expressive of his nature. It is also, in some sort, the work of the whole race, while the picture or statue are the work of one only, in most cases more highly gifted than his fellows. And therefore we may expect that the first two elements of good architecture should be expressive of some great truths commonly belonging to the whole race, and necessary to be understood or felt by them in all their work that they do under the sun.[3]

Without agreeing necessarily with what Ruskin says here about the picture or poem, it is important to note that he associates architecture with "the work of the whole race." The importance and meaning of architecture belongs, he says, not to any one civilization, but to humanity universally. This raises the question of precisely which "truths" in architecture inspired humans through the ages. It should not be surprising, therefore, that an architecture historian and disciple of Ruskin such as Lethaby should be interested in and influenced by the work of the English anthropologists who sought "truths" of the human mind across the ages and should undertake his own investigation into "some great truths commonly belonging to the whole race." Eliot would certainly have known of Lethaby's connection with the Arts and Crafts Movement and of Lethaby's association with Ruskin's ideas. It is highly probable, also, that Eliot would have recognized in Lethaby's works the influence of the English school of anthropology, and it is perhaps most helpful for this study to explore in some detail the anthropological influence, given that Lethaby's knowledge of Ruskin's famous work, "The Nature of Gothic" in *The Stones of Venice* was probably instrumental in leading him to a study of the work of the anthropologists, and these anthropologists were similarly influential on the development of Eliot's thought.

ELIOT AND ANTHROPOLOGY: RETURN TO THE SOURCES

In 1913, at Harvard, Eliot attended Josiah Royce's seminar for which he wrote a paper, "The Interpretation of Primitive Ritual." Eliot's study of anthropology at this time marked the beginning of an interest that would last over twenty years. His reading in anthropology was extensive, and his knowledge of the subject was synthesized in his work in a number of interesting ways.

Eliot's extensive reading in anthropology, from Frazer and Harrison to Durkheim and Lévy-Bruhl, led him to the view that the origins of art were in ritual, and that art had not, in ancient and primitive cultures, been created solely for aesthetic pleasure. In his review of Durkheim's *Elementary Forms of Religion*, Eliot accepts Durkheim's thesis that ritual was not created to explain a myth; rather myths were "invented to make sense of inherited rituals."[4] He also accepts from Durkheim that a ritual is a collective experience that stems from "group consciousness"; individual members of a tribe "partake in a common nature which it is the function of the religious festival to arouse" (quoted in *Cultural Divide*, 74). Art, therefore, emerges from ritual which is tied to this group consciousness.

Eliot is acutely interested in the communal role art had, through ritual, in primitive society. In his review of W. J. Perry's *The Growth of Civilization* and *The Origin of Magic and Religion* in 1924, he finds himself asking, "At what point . . . does the attempt to design and create an object for the sake of beauty become conscious? at what point in civilisation does any conscious distinction between practical or magical utility and aesthetic beauty arise? . . . [S]urely the distinction must mark a change in the human mind which is of fundamental importance."[5] And additionally, Eliot writes, "a further question we should be impelled to ask is this: Is it possible and justifiable for art, the creation of beautiful objects and of literature, to persist indefinitely without its primitive purposes: is it possible for the aesthetic object to be a *direct* object of attention?" (490–1). He asks whether, in the present, art has become too separated from its ritual roots to survive.

Eliot is interested not only in the distance separating the primitive from the civilized man, but also in the ways in which this distance is illusory. While admiring the work of Lucien Lévy-Bruhl, Eliot criticizes him for differentiating too sharply between the civilized mind and the "pre-logical" primitive mind: "he appears to me to draw the distinction between primitive and civilized mental process altogether too clearly."[6] Eliot does accept from Lévy-Bruhl the notion that in the primitive consciousness there is an intimate connection between the human mind and the environment.[7] Lévy-Bruhl theorizes that the primitive mind imbues objects or phenomena with mystical properties that are intrinsic and unified (he calls this "collective representation"), while the civilized mind separates past from present, thought from object, being from non-being (this is translated by Eliot into the post-Cartesian "dissociation of sensibility"). Eliot does not accept, however, that there are pre-logical ways of thinking that are now extinct. The connection between primitive and civilized man can, he says, be rediscovered through art. If art is understood as developing out of ritual, then it can go some way toward repairing the modern dissociation of sensibility because this understanding places art in a communal role closely linked to a culture's way of life.

Eliot's study of primitive ritual, and his statement that "The maxim, Return to the sources, is a good one," was not an endorsement of a nostalgic program of reaching into the past. Rather, anthropology shows that art (recalling what he says about ritual in the Introduction to *Savonarola*) can alter "so completely in social function as to become a different object altogether" (quoted in *Cultural Divide*, 77). The meaning of ritual, the meaning of art, is not static over time. Therefore, as Chinitz says, "Anthropological thinking makes it possible to reimagine the possibilities of one's own culture" (77). When Eliot says famously in his essay "*Ulysses*, Order and Myth" (1923) that the mythical method is "a step toward making the modern world possible for art,"[8] he means that the mythical method proposes a renovation of the role of art in society in which art becomes central to the experience of the world, as it was in primitive cultures (*Cultural Divide*, 80). A return to the sources would enable art to be revivified in the present.

LETHABY THE HISTORIAN: "IF YOU WOULD KNOW THE NEW, YOU MUST SEARCH THE OLD"

The starting place for Lethaby's theory of architectural history was his conviction that art means something more than the mere aesthetic style of any given era. This idea was fueled by his reading of Ruskin's "The Nature of Gothic" in 1888. Because he believed that the meaning of art was essentially symbolic, Lethaby sought in his own work as architect a modern style that would be more meaningful than a mere pattern of rearranging or recombining aesthetic styles of the past. Lethaby was unimpressed by much contemporary art, believing it to be a hollow recopying and recombining of elements of past artistic styles without any deeper meaning.[9] He therefore set out to examine the myths, legends, and forms of ancient architecture to determine what meaning architecture might have had in the past. In this enterprise he was greatly aided and influenced by the work of the English anthropological school. In his first book, *Architecture, Mysticism and Myth* (1891), which is arguably as much a work of anthropology as it is one of history, Lethaby argues that there is more to be learned from ancient architecture than the history and development of man's use of materials and tools; that ancient architecture in fact symbolizes human philosophy and psychology: "It is of this . . . that I propose to write; the influence of the known and imagined facts of the universe on architecture, the connection between the world as a structure, and the building, not of the mere details of nature and the ornaments of architecture, but of the whole—the Heavenly Temple and the Earthly Tabernacle."[10] He begins by distinguishing between "building" and "architecture," writing that the study of "utilitarian origins" of structures, and "the adjustment of forms to the conditions of local circumstance" is the history of *building*, whereas a study of the thought that was behind the form is the history of *architecture*: "Architecture, then, interpenetrates building, not for satisfaction of the simple needs of the body, but the complex ones of the intellect" (*Mysticism*, 1). He therefore makes the distinction between architecture and building as one between soul and body, and continues,

> Of the modes of this thought we must again distinguish; some were unconscious and instinctive, as the desire for symmetry, smoothness, sublimity, and the like merely aesthetic qualities, which properly enough belong to true architecture; and others were direct and didactic, speaking by a more or less perfect realisation, or through a code of symbols, accompanied by traditions which explained them. The main purpose and burthen of sacred architecture—and all architecture, temple, tomb, or palace, was sacred in the early days—is thus inextricably bound up with a people's thoughts about God and the universe. (2)

Importantly in Lethaby's theory, the form is given meaning from the philosophy or religion; similarly, in the anthropological argument about art (such as is revealed in Jane Harrison's book, *Art and Ritual*), the art-form develops out of the ritual.

In 1928 Lethaby rewrote *Architecture, Mysticism and Myth* for publication in *The Builder*. He retitled the work *Architecture, Nature and Magic*. He opens this rewriting with a recapitulation of his debt to the anthropologists: "I would specially mention Sir James Frazer's *The Golden Bough*; Dr. Solomon Reinach's *Cults, Myths and Religions*; Dr. Farnell's *Cults of the Greek States*; A. Della Seta's *Religion and Art*; and Dr. A. B. Cook's immense work entitled *Zeus*."[11] On the whole, *Architecture, Nature and Magic* is a much clearer presentation of the ideas in *Architecture, Mysticism and Myth*, and in it Lethaby reveals one of the most important points of his theory of architecture. Because ancient architecture was built in connection with the development of the human mind, architecture, and the meaning of architecture, is always changing as the human mind changes. Architecture reveals the "enlarging" of the human mind across history. Paradoxically, it is because the developments of human philosophy and psychology direct the changing forms of architecture that the meaning of architecture through the ages remains the same; in other words, universally architecture symbolized the changes and growth of human understandings of the world:

> Behind every style of architecture there is an earlier style, in which the germ of every form is to be found; except such alteration as may be traced to new conditions, or directly innovating thought in religion, all is the slow change of growth, and it is almost impossible to point to the time of invention of any custom or feature. . . . It has, rightly, been the habit of historians of architecture to lay stress on the differences of the several styles and schools of successive ages, but, in the far larger sense, all architecture is one, when traced back through the stream of civilisations, as they followed or influenced one another. (*Mysticism*, 2–3)

This point, that the symbolic meaning of architecture is always the same (architectural form is always developed out of human reaction to the universe) and always changing (human understanding of the world is always growing and this growth is reflected in the forms of architecture) is one Lethaby returns to again and again in his historical writing. A study of the history of architecture is necessary, says Lethaby, not merely to see alterations across time in aesthetic style or to be able to hearken to a specific historical style in a contemporary building, but to understand deeply the growth and development of human philosophy and psychology, symbolized by architecture's changing forms, and thereby to comprehend how contemporary society has grown out of the past.

Integral to Lethaby's understanding of the history of architecture is the notion that, for the architecture of any given age to "live" or to have meaning and symbolic value, it must not reach back nostalgically to the past but must leap forward, adventurously, into the future. Architecture must change as human society changes. His study of ancient architecture concludes not that contemporary forms should look to the past for aesthetic styles, but that a study of the past reveals the importance of revivifying contemporary building for contemporary life.

ELIOT AND LETHABY: MAKING THE MODERN WORLD POSSIBLE FOR ART

It is striking that their different studies of the work of the anthropologists led Eliot and Lethaby to similar conclusions about art. They were each interested in the ways in which, in primitive societies, art developed as part of ritual, thus making art an integral part of the primitive human's understanding and celebration of the universe. Eliot and Lethaby were both convinced that modern society had lost this sense of ritual and connectedness in art, and that for art to be meaningful in the present moment a return to the sources was necessary. This return did not engender a nostalgic attempt to "get back" the old meanings of art—both Eliot and Lethaby were acutely aware of the separation between the modern post-Enlightenment scientific mind and the primitive religious or mystical mind, and they did not wish to create a false bridge between them— rather, they saw that a renewed understanding of the ways that art used to function in primitive society could lead to exciting potentialities for what art could become in the present. Broadly speaking, Eliot's and Lethaby's reading in anthropology led them to believe that a return to the sources was a necessary step in the process of modernizing art.

For Eliot, a study of the art of the past gives the artist a better understanding of his own task in the present, not to hearken unnecessarily to the past, but to move art forward. These ideas concerning the relationship between the past and the present in the creation of art are expressed in Eliot's famous essay "Tradition and the Individual Talent," where he explains his theory of tradition in art. Firstly, a knowledge cr respect for tradition should not prompt the contemporary artist merely to imitate his predecessors: "if the only form of tradition, of handing down, consisted in following the ways of the immediate generation before us in a blind or timid adherence to its successes, 'tradition' should positively be discouraged. We have seen many such simple currents soon lost in the sand; and novelty is better than repetition" (*SP*, 38). Tradition, as he sees it,

> is a matter of much wider significance. . . . It involves, in the first place, the historical sense, which we may call nearly indispensable . . . and the historical sense involves a perception, not only of the pastness of the

past, but of its presence. . . . This historical sense, which is a sense of the
timeless as well as of the temporal and of the timeless and of the temporal together, is what makes a writer traditional. And it is at the same
time what makes a writer most acutely conscious of his place in time, of
his own contemporaneity. (*SP*, 38)

A sense of the pastness of the past involves an understanding of the ways
in which there is always a distinction between the past and the present.
However, Eliot also says that the historical sense perceives the presence
of the past. He means that the past can only be understood in the present
moment, and the present moment is only able to "know" the past via
interpretation of the past. It is this sense of the split between past and
present as well as the perception that the past is known only in the
present (and indeed has fashioned the present, but in ways that can only
be interpreted) that makes the artist acutely aware of his own contemporaneity: everything he knows about the past is known through the
present, and in the present moment all he knows is the past. Eliot writes,
"Someone said: 'The dead writers are remote from us because we *know* so
much more than they did'. Precisely, and they are that which we know"
(*SP*, 40). It is the sense of both the distinctness and the closeness of the
past and the present that allows the artist to move forward. As Piers Gray
puts it, "The historical development of the poet's art is understood as a
constant re-ordering of the experience of the past" (*Poetic Development*,
113). Eliot explains that the artist must "be quite aware of the obvious fact
that art never improves, but that the material of art is never quite the
same. He must be aware that the mind of Europe . . . is a mind which
changes, and that this change is a development which abandons nothing
en route" (*SP*, 39). Therefore, when Eliot begins this essay by discussing
ideas of originality in art and claiming that the truly new piece of poetry
may be the one "in which the dead poets, his ancestors, assert their immortality most vigorously" (*SP*, 38), he emphasizes the dynamic interaction between the past and the present that produces the latest work of art.
An artist who craves spontaneous originality in the present creates art
that exists in a vacuum—it does not belong to the process of development
that Eliot calls the historical sense, and it therefore does not effect real
change. A return to the sources breathes new life into the art of the
present by allowing the artist to see his task in terms that take account of
historical development and change.

Lethaby's understanding of the necessity for change in art and of the
way that this change should take place, stemming from his readings in
anthropology, is remarkably similar. Like Eliot, Lethaby decries contemporary imitations of the past in art: "Old architecture lived because it had
a purpose. Modern architecture, to be real, must not be a mere envelope
without contents" (*Mysticism*, 7). For Lethaby, as for Eliot, the value of
knowing the ritual origins of art is not to attempt to recreate the old

meanings of art for contemporary society. That would not be possible or sensible because there is a gulf separating civilized from primitive societies. The real value for the present of studying the role of art in primitive society is that such a study teaches that art used to be integrally connected to a way of life and it used to reflect, in very real ways, the development of the human mind over time. Understood this way, art is not a mere aesthetic gloss on society, but is essential to its growth. Eliot and Lethaby wish to restore the role of art in society. They wish for change in art because change, taking place out of an understanding of the role of the past in the present, would indicate that art is becoming, once again, fundamental to a society's way of life.

Eliot and Lethaby propose a revolution in art, one that looks to the past to discover how art, ritual in origin, was related to a people's way of life and beliefs about the universe in order to create an art for the present moment that is not mere ornamentation but that is central and vital in the modern world. In short, they propose a role for modern art that looks, Janus-like, in two directions.

SACRED ARCHITECTURE: A TRUE ARCHITECTURE IS BUILT OUT OF THE HEARTS OF ITS BUILDERS

Eliot was always drawn personally, and intellectually, to church buildings. As a young man, he was attracted to churches as sites for tourist curiosity; he later took lunch breaks in the churches of Sir Christopher Wren in London; he campaigned for the preservation of these churches and included two Wren churches in *The Waste Land*;[12] he wrote a commissioned pageant-play for the creation of churches in London's suburbs; and he used the cathedral setting to great effect in his martyr's play, *Murder in the Cathedral*. Always appreciative of the aesthetic and historic value of church buildings, Eliot at first questioned their relevance in modern society and considered how the meaning they symbolized might be translated into secular terms for a secular culture. Increasingly, however, his view of the aesthetic value of churches was subordinated to his growing sense of their importance as sacred places, and he began to complete his earlier appreciation of church architecture from a theological point of view. After his formal reception into the Church of England, the emptiness of churches continued to trouble him, not as a sign of their irrelevance as earlier, but as a symbol of his society's spiritual anemia.

We know that Eliot admired Lethaby and that he had read at least one of the architect's books when he wrote to Lethaby in October 1923. Given the affinity between their formulations of the role of art and of the need for modern art to look to the sources in order to be refashioned for the present moment, it is possible to speculate that Lethaby's understanding of the symbolic significance of architecture would appeal to Eliot's own interest in the role of sacred buildings. Without assuming any kind of wholesale affiliation between the two, it is nevertheless valuable to hypothesize that Eliot's knowledge and appreciation of the work of Lethaby adds a significant layer of complexity to Eliot's responses to church architecture.

In *Architecture, Mysticism and Myth,* Lethaby explains that as the primitive human mind developed the meaning given to structures became increasingly complex until humans decided to build special structures that would embody the relationships between symbol and reality; these buildings would symbolize what humans knew and imagined about the universe, and they were, consequently, sacred. These sacred buildings, says Lethaby, "were the scenes of great ritual dramas, and they were themselves of a magical character" (*Magic,* 90). The act of building a sacred structure was itself "a magic with many rites, from the ceremonial marking out of an auspicious site, and laying the foundation at the right time with due sacrifice, to the consecration at the end" (*Magic,* 90). Church buildings are reminders of the connection between art and ritual that ancient societies embodied in the structures they built.

As Eliot walked around London looking at the churches of Sir Christopher Wren, ecclesiastical architecture might appear representative of a time when humans embodied their religious apprehensions about the universe in buildings. In other words, the church buildings might seem to Eliot to symbolize some vestiges of the mystical mind still lingering, through these structures, in a modern setting. His appreciation of history, and his belief that the primitive mystical mind underlies the modern civilized mind, might have caused him to view church buildings as valuable reminders of the connection that existed in antiquity between art and ritual. However, Eliot noticed that the City churches were largely deserted and were threatened with destruction or disaffection. It would appear that the sacred meaning of these buildings had been lost or had become irrelevant in modern society, and Eliot asks, in *The Waste Land* for instance, what meaning, if any, the empty City churches have in contemporary life. On the one hand they reveal modern dissociation from spiritual ideas about the world, but on the other hand they symbolize perhaps the need for some kind of translation into secular terms of the religious ideas they embody.

As his own spiritual life developed and changed, so too did his responses to church architecture. He became deeply interested in sacredness; Eliot was drawn to church buildings because they symbolized for him human reflections on the relationship between human beings and God. Similarly, the ritual significance of a church building, of its construction and of the rituals taking place weekly or daily within it, appealed to Eliot's sense of the need, in modern society, for a reconnection with meaningful ritual. Churches might represent for the Christian Eliot the ways in which human beings have tried, and continue to try, to express their connection with God through art. His interest developed, in *The Rock* for example, to ask whether a church building is able to bridge the gap between a person's spiritual life and daily life. The importance of a church building was not so much its aesthetic history but its potential to connect modern people to ritual and through ritual to community and to God. By the time he wrote "Little Gidding," Eliot viewed the church building as a site where past and present meet and are unified.

Since Eliot certainly knew at least part of Lethaby's scholarship on the subject of architectural history and would have been able to recognize Lethaby's investment in the work of the same anthropologists who influenced Eliot himself, and since there is such a clear affinity between the ways that Lethaby and Eliot formulated the role of art in society based on their readings in anthropology, it is possible to speculate that Eliot's developing appreciation first of the historic value and later of the sacredness of church buildings is connected, in important ways, to his early reading in anthropology and to the ways in which anthropological thought continued to affect him throughout his career. If it is true, therefore, that knowledge of Lethaby's work contributed to the complexity of Eliot's architectural imagination, then it is very probable that his understanding of church architecture, and the ways he represented it in his poetry and plays, was related to his broader reflections on tradition and ritual in art.

NOTES

1. T. S. Eliot, "The Stones of London," *Criterion* 7, no. 1 (January, 1928): 4.

2. Eliot, *The Letters of T. S. Eliot; Volume II, 1923–1925*, ed. Valerie Eliot (London: Faber and Faber, 2009), 211. Cited hereafter in the text as *Letters*.

3. John Ruskin, "The Nature of Gothic," in *The Stones of Venice Volume II* (Chicago: Belford, Clarke and Co. 1851), 180–81.

4. Quoted by David E. Chinitz, *T. S. Eliot and the Cultural Divide* (Chicago: University of Chicago Press, 2003), 74. Cited hereafter in the text as *Cultural Divide*.

5. Eliot, review of *The Growth of Civilization* and *The Origin of Magic and Religion*, by W. J. Perry, *Criterion* 2, no. 8 (1924): 490.

6. Eliot, quoted in Piers Gray, *T. S. Eliot's Intellectual and Poetic Development, 1909–1922*, (Sussex: Harvester Press, 1982), 122. Cited hereafter in the text as *Poetic Development*.

7. See Robert Crawford, *The Savage and the City in the Work of T. S. Eliot* (New York: Oxford University Press, 1987), 94. See also David Spurr, "Myths of Anthropology: Eliot, Joyce, Lévy-Bruhl," *PMLA* 109 (1994): 268.

8. Eliot, *Selected Prose of T. S. Eliot*, ed. Frank Kermode (London: Faber and Faber, 1975), 178. Cited hereafter in the text as *SP*.

9. See Godfrey Rubens, *William Richard Lethaby: His Life and Work 1857–1931* (London: The Architectural Press, 1986), 65 and 80.

10. William Richard Lethaby, *Architecture, Mysticism and Myth* (New York: George Braziller 1975), 3. Cited hereafter in the text as *Mysticism*.

11. Lethaby, *Architecture, Nature and Magic* (London: Duckworth, 1956), 15. Cited hereafter in the text as *Magic*.

12. Saint Magnus the Martyr was restored by Christopher Wren after the Great Fire of London. Saint Mary Woolnoth was rebuilt by Nicholas Hawksmoor, a pupil and disciple of Wren.

IV

Culture and Religion

ELEVEN

Backgrounds to *The Idea of a Christian Society*: Charles Maurras, Christopher Dawson, and Jacques Maritain

Christopher McVey

Eliot's social criticism and political philosophy continued to evolve over the course of his career, beginning with *The Idea of a Christian Society* (1939) and extending through his involvement in the Moot between 1938 and 1947. When Eliot remarks in 1949, however, that Western liberalism licenses the opinions of the foolish and fosters "a notion of *getting on* to which the alternative is a hopeless apathy,"[1] his critique is really an extension of an early poem, "The Hollow Men" (1925). The problem with the hollow men is not that they choose right, nor that they choose wrong—it is that they do not choose. When Eliot responds to Middleton Murry's description of a tension between Christianity and anti-Christian nationalism, he suggests that "a nationalism which is overtly antagonistic to Christianity is a less dangerous menace for us than a nationalism which professes a Christianity from which all Christian content has been evacuated."[2] Modern society, for Eliot, had become "quiet and meaning-less/ As wind in dry grass" ("The Hollow Men"), a world of cocktail parties and coffee spoons, unreal cities of social and cultural alienation.

Since the 1960s, and perhaps culminating with the work of Anthony Julius in 1995, the animus toward Eliot's intolerance, anti-Semitism, or cultural elitism has continued to grow.[3] It is important not to sweep aside these discussions when reading the poems ourselves, or when teaching them to our students. Yet in *The Idea of a Christian Society*, Eliot is not interested in simply making tradition more meaningful in a pluralistic and secular age, as some scholars have suggested.[4] For Eliot, abstract doctrines—even royalism—were usually the problem, not the solution. As Eliot writes toward the beginning of *Christian Society*, "[s]ome persons have gone so far as to affirm, as something self-evident, that democracy is the only régime compatible with Christianity; on the other hand, the word is not abandoned by sympathizers with the government of Germany. If anybody ever attacked democracy, I might discover what the word means."[5] Though I do not wish to ignore Eliot's problematic representation of Jews throughout his work, it is important to remember Eliot's abhorrence for the Nazis, too. For Eliot, democracy itself had become a somewhat impoverished idea, one that did not "contain enough positive content to stand alone against the forces that [one] dislike[s]— [and that] can easily be transformed by them."[6] Not one to shrug his shoulders at what to many may seem like a purely intellectual conversation, Eliot warns his readers that "if you will not have God (and He is a jealous God) you should pay your respects to Hitler or Stalin."[7] How then, do we reconcile Eliot's own intolerance with his apparent disdain for intolerant systems of government? Is such reconciliation even possible? However we answer that question, I hope to at least make clear that to focus only on Eliot's anti-Semitism is only to tell one part of a much larger story.

Eliot's social critique did not begin with his baptism in the Anglican Church in 1927; rather, the conversion, his later drama and poetry, and his political philosophy are the final realizations of problems he had been wrestling with since his early days at Harvard. Although it is tempting to pivot Eliot's beliefs on the conversion, dismissing Eliot's earlier life in order to give the latter more coherence, it is that earlier life which provides an important staging ground for his work in the 1930s and 1940s. This essay is an attempt to recover and explain a few of the many important backgrounds to Eliot's later political philosophy. In particular, I argue that many of Eliot's ideas can be traced back to three formative, though very different, political or theological thinkers in the early twentieth century: Charles Maurras, Christopher Dawson, and Jacques Maritain. Contextualizing these figures and their respective influences on Eliot's reworking of Monarchism, Christian Humanism, and neo-Thomism, we can chart the critical vocabulary and political vision of Eliot's later social criticism. That Dawson and Maritain, in particular, were extremely influential on Eliot is obvious—Eliot himself names them as formative influences in the preface to *The Idea of a Christian Society*. Russell Kirk's critical biography of Eliot notes, "Of social thinkers in his own time, none influenced Eliot more than Dawson."[8] These influences continued to condition the tone and focus of Eliot's work in the *Criterion*, his involvement in the *Chandos* group in 1934, and most directly in the articles published through the *Christian News-Letter* and almost-decade-long attendence at meetings of the Moot, a small think-tank of Christian elite that met in the late 1930s and early 1940s.[9]

Eliot's 1910–1911 year in Paris probably marked his first direct exposure to Maurrasian ideas, although he had heard of Maurras in Babbitt's classes at Harvard.[10] The *Action Française*, a French Monarchist counterrevolutionary movement born out of the Dreyfus affair, had already been publishing its own newspaper, and one of its chief figures—Pierre Lasserre—had written *Le romantisme français* just a few years earlier. Hulme cites Maurras and Lasserre in "Romanticism and Classicism," where he contrasts a Rousseauistic romantic view, which he defines as the belief that "man, the individual, is an infinite reservoir of possibilities, and if you can so rearrange society by the destruction of oppressive order then these possibilities will have a chance and you will get Progress," with "its exact opposite," the classical view, which holds that "[man] is an extraordinarily fixed and limited animal whose nature is absolutely constant. It is only by tradition and organization that anything decent can be got out of him."[11] As Roger Kojecký describes it, the *Action Française* attempted to define itself in direct opposition to a Rousseauistic point of view, becoming "nationalistic to the point of anti-Semitism, monarchist to a point to which the Duc d'Orléans himself did not go, and called for a return to hierarchical and non-republican 'order' even by means of violence."[12] Hulme believed, as did Ford Madox Ford and Eliot, that an aristocratic elite was necessary to ensure progress or a moral order, as well as to prevent a Hobbesian war of all against all. Monarchy seemed important not simply for the sake of tradition, but for its practical necessity. What anti-Semitic ideas Eliot might have taken from Maurras or from the *Action Française* must be read alongside the general critique of Rousseau's belief in man's innate civility; as Ezra Pound would later note in his critique of "the great mass of mankind," any government "'by the people and for the people' is the worst thing on the face of this earth."[13]

Nancy Hargrove, pointing to some of the riots and disturbances orchestrated by the *Action Française* during Eliot's Parisian year, has argued that Eliot also experienced a temporary conversion to the philosophy of Maurras alongside his conversion to Bergsonism.[14] In "The Idea of a Literary Review" (1926), Eliot echoes the romantic and classical binary articulated by Lassere and Hulme, writing that "the modern tendency is toward something which, for want of a better name, we may call classicism . . . toward a higher and clearer conception of Reason, and a more severe and serene control of the emotions by Reason."[15] Eliot goes on to name six books that seem to him to exemplify this tendency, including Maurras's *L'Avenir de l'intelligence* (1905), Hulme's *Speculations* (1924), and Jacques Maritain's *Réflexions sur l'intelligence* (1924). In 1928 Eliot translated Maurras's "Prologue to an Essay on Criticism" for two issues of the *Criterion*, and he retained a great respect for his literary work, particularly his style—indeed, Eliot dedicated his small book on Dante to Maurras. It is clear, then, that the *Action Française* informed much of Eliot's critique of liberalism.

Eliot's interest in Maurras involved more than a disdain for the uneducated masses, as it did for Pound. As Peter Dale Scott characterizes the *Action Française*, "Maurras argued that the trappings of French Republican democracy had been a façade, behind which industrial and financial interests had vanquished the older landed and aristocratic classes."[16] Maurras justifies this importance of a conservative social order not simply because it would ensure class-structured legacies, but because these structures proved useful in balancing the disorder and greed of unrestricted capitalist systems. Eliot writes that what happened in September of 1938 "was something in which one was deeply implicated and responsible. It was not, I repeat, a criticism of the government, but a doubt of the validity of a civilization. We could not match conviction with conviction, we had no ideas with which we could either meet or oppose the ideas opposed to us."[17] What happened, of course, was Prime Minister Chamberlain's "peace in our time" pact with Hitler, continuing a policy of appeasement in response to German aggression. Eliot himself seems troubled by such a policy, blaming not Chamberlain but the otherwise apathetic response of society as a whole: "Was our society, which had always been so assured of its superiority and rectitude, so confident of its unexamined premises, assembled round anything more permanent than a congeries of banks, insurance companies, and industries, and had it any beliefs more essential than a belief in compound interest and the maintenance of dividends?"[18] One year later Hitler refers back to Chamberlain's agreement as nothing but a "scrap of paper," invading Poland on 1 September 1939.

Indeed, Eliot begins *The Idea of a Christian Society* by commenting that he has no personal vendetta against Democracy as such—but rather, that the term had in England in that particular time become emptied of all pragmatic meaning or conviction. He emphasizes the "negativity" of liberalist Democracy not because it threatens a new social order, but because, according to Eliot, it did the exact opposite. Eliot writes that the Western world has come to stand for "Liberalism" and "Democracy," but his larger point is that these are impoverished banners and rhetorical gestures under which a more sinister, self-interested leviathan lurks:

> By destroying traditional social habits of the people, by dissolving their natural collective consciousness into individual constituents, by licensing the opinions of the most foolish, by substituting instruction for education, by encouraging cleverness rather than wisdom, the upstart rather than the qualified, by fostering a notion of *getting on* to which the alternative is hopeless apathy, liberalism can prepare the way for that which is its own negation: the artificial, mechanized or brutalized control which is a desperate remedy for chaos.[19]

I am not interested in arguing whether Eliot's characterization of liberalism was correct—indeed, I am inclined to think it wasn't. What I wish to point out, though, is that Eliot's Maurrasian point of view must be histor-ically contextualized; it is a response to what he sees as an atrophy in the ability of the masses to engage in politics and culture in any meaningful way. He differed from Maurras because his issues with liberalism or democracy stemmed not only from an anxiety about a threatened set of traditions or the upper class, but rather because he saw modern culture turning into nothing more than a set of capitalist ventures, where work-ers have themselves become a type of commodity, and that all tradition, including religious, scientific, or artistic practice had become, for him, merely products of that commodity culture.

Maurras was an atheist or an agnostic, a demagogue who wanted nothing more than to impose his own will on history and the political avant-garde. Clearly this is not a figure Eliot wanted to lionize, or to model himself after. If Maurras shaped the way Eliot understood and articulated the problem of modern society, then, Jacques Maritain and Christopher Dawson helped to shape Eliot's proposed solution: a Chris-tian Society. Both were Christians, but whereas Maritain was a neo-Tho-mist in the tradition of Aristotle and Aquinas, Dawson was an Augustin-ian. Neo-Thomists believed that human reasoning could always lead back to God, whereas Augustinians emphasized the limits of that reason-ing and the importance of faith. Eliot would balance the pragmatism of the former with the humility of the latter. He first contacted Dawson through Sheed and Ward, Dawson's publishers, in the summer of 1929. In that letter, Eliot praises Dawson's works and asks him to contribute to the *Criterion*, also suggesting that the two should meet.[20] The relationship was highly regarded by Eliot—in the early 1930s, Eliot told an American audience that Dawson was one of the most important political theorists of his generation.[21]

Dawson, born to a privileged upper-middle-class Welsh family in 1889, converted to Roman Catholicism in 1913, influenced in that direc-tion by his tutor, E. I. Watkin, and his deep passion for St. Augustine. During the mid 1920s he began to attempt a massive five-volume world history of culture and religion—noting that "All the events of the last years have convinced me what a fragile thing civilization is and how near we are to losing the whole inheritance. . . . Some new Augustan order must arise to take [the place of monarchies] if Europe is to survive."[22] He would never publish the whole series but, as his biographers note, he spent the greater part of his life publishing sections of it when he could manage consistent work, or when Frank Sheed could encourage him along. Even if Dawson seemed unable to live up to his own aspirations, he was remarkably prolific, publishing over twenty books in the course of his lifetime. An early article, "Catholic Tradition and the Modern State" (1916), clearly resonates as a progenitor for Dawson's later work, and its description of cultural alienation in the modern age suggests why Eliot would be interested in his ideas. Dawson writes:

> An official touches the handle of a great machine, and from every
> corner of an empire millions of men move automatically, with an utter
> suppression of their own individualities, to the fulfillment of one gi-
> gantic task—a task that will bring wounds and deaths to millions, suf-
> fering and privation to all.[23]

In the 1920s, from his involvement with the London LePlay House, Dawson began publishing in the *Sociological Review* for close to a decade,
focusing largely on his own interpretation of Christian Humanism. In
these articles, Dawson seems almost Marxist in his ideas, but as Bradley
Birzer has argued, he was really following the Roman Catholic line of
beliefs as emphasized in papal encyclicals of the nineteenth and twentieth centuries. Dawson lamented the "disaffection of the wage laborer"
who possessed control over neither his work nor its value—the anger of
the laborer against the industrial machine is "rather an attempt to reverse
the subordination of the human to the mechanical and the creative to the
commercial function."[24]

At the end of the 1920s, Dawson and others, including Eric Gill, Stephen Spender, and Jacques Maritain, began meeting at the apartment of
Tom Burns.[25] Though Eliot would come to read Maritain on his own,
especially since *True Humanism* became one of the cornerstones for the
Moot's early meetings, the Chelsea Group had an interest in Maritain's
Art and Scholasticism, since Gill's Ditching circle published the first translation. Both texts were highly influential on Eliot and Jones. David Jones's
own notion of art as an act of sign-making, not unlike the transubstantia-
tion of the host into the body of Christ, was really an extension of the
ideas set out in Maritain's work. Jones—an important modernist writer
who today is more read in England than in America—wrote "three
bloody cheers" next to a passage at the end of Maritain's *Philosophy of Art*,
where Maritain argues,

> Art as such is superior to time and place, it transcends, like the intelli-
> gence, every limitation of nationality. . . . By its very nature and by its
> very object it is universal. But Art has not its home in an angelic intelli-
> gence, it is subjectivised in a soul which is the substantial form of a
> living body; and this substantial form, by its natural need of learning
> and of perfecting itself by degrees and with difficulty, turns the animal
> it inhabits into an animal by nature political. In this way Art is funda-
> mentally dependent on all that city and race, spiritual tradition and
> history bring to the body and the intelligence of mankind.[26]

As Jonathan Miles has suggested, Maritain's ideas helped Jones "to recognize fundamental similarities between such apparently diverse acts as
icing a cake, making a painting, and the celebration of a mass."[27] If Dawson helped Eliot engage the problems of modern society from a political
or sociological angle, Maritain provided a language to describe art's role
in shaping and defining cultural practice.

After Sheed and Ward solidified their alliance with the Chelsea Group, they began to publish a fourteen-volume series concerning contemporary culture, theology, and sociology, entitled Essays in Order. For the first number, Maritain wrote *Religion and Culture,* Dawson soon following with *Christianity and the New Age* in 1931. Dawson was deeply concerned about modernity's fascination with the self and loss of reverence for the divine—the scientific revolution of the sixteenth and seventeenth centuries, along with the rise of capitalism, made man "a subordinate part of the great mechanical system that his scientific genius has created." Eliot echoes many of Dawson's metaphors and predictions when he advocates, in *The Idea of a Christian Society,* that liberalism is not an evil in and of itself, but lacks any pragmatic application because, as Eliot wrote, "it is a movement not so much defined by its end, as by its starting point; away from, rather than towards, something definite."[28] As early as his work at Oxford in 1907, Dawson insisted that religion shaped almost all norms, language, and cultural practices. In other words, religion was not a layer of beliefs and practices that could be carefully peeled away from the culture beneath it, but was rather a constitutive and essential part of all cultural practices. For Dawson, a culture that rejected its religion or believed itself to be fully secular had, as Bradley Birzer has put it, "merely substituted some false religion—most likely an ideology of some kind—for its lost faith."[29]

The *Order* group sought to open further lines of communication between the Catholic and Anglican Churches, even if at the same time it wanted a bolder, less secularized Catholic community. In 1933 Dawson writes to the *Cambridge Review,* noting that "The Catholic conception of society is not that of a machine for the production of wealth, but of a spiritual organism in which every class and every individual has its own function to fulfill and its own rights and duties in relation to the whole."[30] A separation between Church and State was not only illusory for Dawson, but unpractical, just as a rejection of class differences was ignorant and impossible. For the *Order* group, early twentieth-century humanism failed to provide a coherent and enduring ethics or morality that could withstand anything more than cocktail party debate. As Eliot later notes, "[w]hat we are seeking is not a programme for a party, but a way of life for a people: it is this which totalitarianism has sought partly to revive, and partly to impose by force upon its peoples. Our choice now is not between one abstract form and another, but between a pagan, and necessarily stunted culture, and a religious, and necessarily imperfect culture."[31]

As Dawson would later write in the *Tablet,* the impoverished arguments between the Left and Right would lead only to rival extremisms, neither of which could respond adequately to fascism or, more generally, develop a substantive and lasting social structure. Evil had become "depersonalized, separated from individual passion and appetite, and exalted above humanity into a sphere in which all moral values are confused and transformed." For Dawson, the second World War had to be fought on two fronts, each inter-related: England must face its enemies in combat and at the same time "resist the enemy within," which made itself visible in the "subordination of morals to politics." Dawson warned that "the technique of propaganda and psychological aggression can be used by any Power or Party that is bold enough to abandon moral scruples and plunge into the abyss."[32] Eliot would later echo these ideas in *The Idea of a Christian Society*, where he writes that "so far as a man sees the need for converting *himself* as well as the World, he is approximating to the religious point of view. But for most people, to be able to simplify issues so as to see only the definite external enemy, is extremely exhilarating, and brings about the bright eye and the springy step that go so well with the political uniform. This is an exhilaration that the Christian must deny himself."[33] Fascism distracted western Christians from noticing the beam in their own eye. The congeries of banks and the political rhetoric of the day failed to secure a sense of community grounded in shared values and beliefs other than those which it opposed or those which did not seem to serve self-interests. As democracies continued to shift value-systems to accommodate these self-interests, Dawson worried they would eventually be replaced by some form of fascism, instead of communism, since the former was "more able to secure a relatively high degree of political efficiency and economic control without involving the complete destruction of the existing social structure."[34] Eliot insisted that any Christian society, even if it was possible, must be on guard against such pretenses: "And what is worst of all is to advocate Christianity, not because it is true, but because it might be beneficial."[35]

Maritain's philosophical project was one of the centers of the Thomist revival within Catholic intellectual circles. He was originally involved with Maurras and the *Action Française*, anxious to convert those involved, even publishing a pamphlet in 1926 urging priests to take positions in the movement. Yet, with Pope Pius XI officially condemning the movement that December, Maritain broke away to pursue a democratic variety of Catholic social philosophy in 1928.[36] It is important to emphasize how the Augustinian thought of Dawson contrasted with Maritain's neo-Thomism. For Dawson, every philosophy was culturally specific, but the neo-Thomists, to quote Dawson, "ignored the problem of diversity of cultures," and had simply attempted to adapt "Thomism to modern European science or to meeting the challenge of modern systems of philosophy which are themselves purely Western."[37] Dawson reviled twentieth-century democracy, whereas Maritain was eventually pro-liberal and pro-democracy.[38] As Birzer observers, Dawson thought that Maritain's scholarly output declined after 1936, the year in which Maritain declared himself a man of the Left.

Eliot and Dawson both feared that a humanism not tied to orthodox Christianity would become nothing more than an "Ethical Culture Society," as Eliot explains in "Second Thoughts about Humanism," published in 1929. As the thirties moved onward, Dawson continued to develop his anti-Marxist and anti-Capitalist critiques. In particular, Dawson cultivated the view that culture preceded the political system; any attempt to change culture through politics would end in failure or disaster. This is essential for understanding why Eliot believed that a homogeneous Christian society was the only positive answer to totalitarian regimes; the loss of religious faith, for Dawson, meant the eventual destruction of all culture. In *Religion and Culture*, Dawson observed, "The society without culture is a formless society—a crowd or a collection of individuals brought together by the needs of the moment,"[39] and at the conclusion of his second book, *Progress and Religion*, Dawson writes, "Since a culture is essentially a spiritual community, it transcends the economic and political orders. It finds its appropriate organ not in a state, but in a Church."[40] Eliot would not agree with all of Dawson's views, however. Citing *Beyond Politics*, Eliot acknowledges a "close sympathy with Mr. Dawson's aims," but claims that Dawson fails to appreciate the extent to which culture refers to a vast web of interconnected practices organized around certain religious and political convictions; culture, in Eliot's view, was the product, rather than the cause, of a society's moral and religious beliefs:

> I find it difficult to apprehend the meaning of [Mr. Dawson's] "culture" which will have no philosophy (for philosophy, he reminds us, has lost its ancient prestige) and which will not be specifically religious. What, in the kind of society to which we are approximating, will be a "democratic organization of culture"? . . . Unless some useful analogy can be given from the past, I cannot understand [Dawson's point about the] "organization of culture," which appears to be without precedent; and in isolating culture from religion, politics and philosophy we seem to be left with something no more apprehensible than the scent of last year's roses.[41]

For Eliot, culture and religious belief cannot be said to "transcend" economic or political realities; rather, they shape and are shaped by those more general social contexts. Dawson's aim was to privilege spirituality and religious doctrines over, and above the fray of, more general social practices. Eliot's aim was to put spirituality and religious doctrines back into that fray. These ideas would form the bedrock of *Notes towards the Definition of Culture*, where Eliot reminds us of the metaphoricity of that term: "culture is something that must grow; you cannot build a tree, you can only plant it, and care for it, and wait for it to mature in its due time. . . . A political structure is partly construction, and partly growth."[42] Christianity was both a belief and practice that could provide fertile ground for culture to grow, though it could not in itself constitute a

culture. A Christian society must not only believe; it must actively practice and, through those social practices, help individuals understand their
individual roles in a larger social collective.

The Eliot, Dawson, and Maritain connections finally triangulated in
the Oxford Conference on "Church, Community, and State," during July
of 1937. At that conference, Eliot delivered a lecture entitled "The Oecu-
menical Nature of the Church and Its Responsibility towards the World,"
further recasting his synthesis of Dawson's and Maritain's program. As
Kojecký reports, Eliot "referred to the way worship and theology had
been fractured by two forces: on the one hand that containing the three
elements of nationality, race, and language, and, on the other, class or
social group. A right philosophy, Christian or secular, would neither give
an unnatural primacy to race or nation, nor attempt to eradicate these
differences."[43]

Soon after, at the smaller Lambeth conference, Eliot continued to propose the formation of some sort of order or group, largely pushing J. H.
Oldham to take the initiative. Soon they began publishing the *Christian
News-Letter*, attaining almost ten thousand subscribers by the beginning
of 1940. By this time, though, semi-official meetings of the Moot had
already commenced; the first involved about a dozen people from the
Oxford Conference, receiving a letter from Oldham raising the idea of a
Christian order. Dawson himself attended the meeting—as Eric Fenn's
minutes of the meeting relay, Dawson advocated for the formation of a
complete Christian Order, and Eliot responded by arguing that the
strength of Christianity

> was not the hierarchy but local circles and small groups. At present all
> economic tendencies are for the destruction of the local community . . .
> welding people together without local distinction [would] let loose ter-
> rible demonic forces . . . given pseudo-religious sanction.[44]

Preliminary reading for the third Moot, held from January 6–9, 1939, was
Jacques Maritain's *True Humanism* (1938) which argued that the unity of a
Christian civilization would be a minimum one, based not on dogma but
on civil tolerance. By this time, Maritain abhorred totalitarianism—
against Maurras and even perhaps Dawson, this importance of the laity
and local initiative as the main conduit for cultural practices resurfaces
when Eliot writes,

> In any Christian society which can be imagined for the future—in what
> M. Maritain calls a *pluralist* society—my "Community of Christians"
> cannot be a body of the definite vocational outline of the "clerisy" of
> Coleridge: which, viewed in a hundred years' perspective, appears to
> approximate to the rigidity of caste. The Community of Christians is
> not an organization, but a body of indefinite outline; composed of both
> clergy and laity, of the more conscious, more spiritually and intellectu-
> ally developed of both.[45]

Soon after these remarks, Eliot proposes three essential elements for any functional Christian society, clearly reworking and synthesizing the ideas of Maurras, Maritain, and Dawson—A Christian society must (1) have "a hierarchical organization in direct and official relation to the state" (Maurras), (2) "[remain] in direct contact with the smallest units of the community and their individual members" (Maritain), and finally (3) have "an elite clerisy, or scholarly and devout officers, its masters of ascetic theology and its men of wider interests" (Dawson).[46] For the 10 January 1941 meeting of the Moot, Mannheim had produced a paper describing the relationship between the elite and society, and Eliot had suggested that a more organic idea of a nation's culture was required. For a later Moot meeting, Eliot composed an essay entitled "On the Place and Function of the Clerisy," clearly an early version for much of *Notes towards the Definition of Culture*. The Moot would continue to meet until 1947, dissolving itself after the death of an equally important leader for the order, Karl Mannheim.

Eliot's involvement with the Moot spanned nine years, but clearly he had been thinking about the ideas of Maurras, Dawson, and Maritain since the 1920s or even before. To read *The Idea of a Christian Society* or *Notes towards the Definition of Culture* without understanding how and why Eliot articulated the provocative, and often contradictory, ideas of these three figures, or to contend that Eliot's work was merely derivative of them, is to ignore the complex and evolving calculus of Eliot's thought. Eliot continued to reformulate his ideas over the course of the 1930s and 1940s. He remains a moving target. Unfortunately it is the tendency of modern criticism to flatten and homogenize Eliot's later work, as if it constituted a uniform or stable political theory.

As with Eliot's best poetry, his social criticism frequently engenders more problems than solutions. For Eliot, theories and ideologies were only tools that could be used for good as well as for evil. "In our time," Eliot reminds us, "we read too many new books, or are oppressed by the thought of the new books which we are neglecting to read; we read many books, because we cannot know enough people."[47] Eliot implicated himself in his own critique, hoping that in the future there might be less of a need for avant-garde manifestos or political treatises, and more conversation between individuals who cared legitimately for each other, working together to advance social justice. We may not share Eliot's proposed solutions, but we might at least aspire toward his conviction. In an age that must contend with even greater ideologues and an ever-widening polarization of political allegiances, we would do well to continue that conversation today.

TIMELINE

1905	Maurras, *L'Avenir de l'intelligence*.
1910–11	Eliot's year in France.
1912	Hulme publishes "Romanticism and Classicism," citing Maurras and Lasserre.
1913	Dawson converts to Catholicism.
1916	Dawson publishes "Catholic Tradition and the Modern State" in the *Catholic Review*.
1920	The LePlay House founded; Dawson begins involvement with the *Order*.
1924	Hulme, *Speculations*
	Jacques Maritain, *Réflexions sur l'intelligence*
1928	Eliot translates Maurras's "Prologue to an Essay on Criticism" for two issues of the *Criterion*; publishes infamous preface in *For Lancelot Andrewes*.
	The Order Group begins publishing *Order*, only prints four issues, ending in 1929. Dawson publishes in each issue.
1929	Eliot first contacts Dawson through Sheed and Ward, Dawson's publishers.
	Eliot, "Second Thoughts about Humanism"
	Dawson, "The Psychology of Sex and the Catholic Order"
1930	Sheed and Ward begin Essays in Order, edited by Dawson and Burns; Maritain publishes *Religion and Culture* as the first number.
1931	Dawson publishes *Christianity and the New Age* for *Essays in Order*.
1932	Dawson, *Modern Dilemma*
1933	Eliot delivers the Page-Barbour lectures
1934	Tom Burns quits Sheed and Ward.
	Eliot, *After Strange Gods: A Primer on Modern Heresy*
1935	Dawson, *Religion and the Modern State*
1936	Eliot, *Essays Ancient and Modern*
	Maritain's *Integral Humanism*; he declares himself a "man of the Left."

1937	The *New Review* begins.
	July 12: 400 delegates begin a fortnight conference at Oxford on the subject of "Church, Community, and State." On July 16, Eliot delivers "The Oecumenical Nature of the Church and Its Responsibility towards the World."
1938	Lambeth Conferences take place. At Eliot's urging, Oldham begins to organize an order, eventually leading to the *Christian News-Letter* and the Moot.
	Jacques Maritain, *True Humanism*
	The Moot holds first two meetings (April and September), discussing *True Humanism.*
1939	Dawson, *Beyond Politics*
	Eliot, *The Idea of a Christian Society*
1941	Dawson attends Moot meetings again; K. Mannheim presents on the function of the elite.
1944	Eliot writes "On the Place and Function of the Clerisy" in anticipation of the December Moot meeting.
1947	Death of Karl Mannheim; formal dissolution of the Moot
1948	Eliot, *Notes towards the Definition of Culture*

NOTES

1. T. S. Eliot, *Christianity and Culture: The Idea of a Christian Society and Notes towards the Definition of Culture* (New York: Harcourt, Brace, and World, 1949), 12.

2. Ibid., 62.

3. See Anthony Julius, *T. S. Eliot, Anti-Semitism, and Literary Form* (London: Thames and Hudson, 2003); and Christopher Ricks, *T. S. Eliot and Prejudice* (London: Faber, 1988).

4. See, especially, Louis Menand, *Discovering Modernism: T. S. Eliot and His Context* (New York: Oxford University Press, 1987, Revised 2007), 175.

5. Eliot, *Christianity and Culture*, 11.

6. Eliot, *Christianity and Culture*, 50.

7. Ibid., 50.

8. Russell Kirk, *Eliot and His Age: T. S. Eliot's Moral Imagination in the Twentieth Century* (1971; second ed., Wilmington, DE: ISI Books, 2008), 253.

9. Barry Spurr has more recently argued that Eliot had become quickly disaffected with the Moot; however his regard for the meetings changed, Eliot clearly used it as an important forum to develop and refine his own work. See Spurr, *Anglo-Catholic in Religion: T. S. Eliot and Christianity* (Cambridge: Lutterworth Press, 2010), 188–93.

10. See Ronald Schuchard, *Eliot's Dark Angel: Intersection of Art and Life* (New York: Oxford University Press, 1999), 54. For an excellent extended analysis of T. S. Eliot's year studying in Paris, see Nancy Hargrove, *T. S. Eliot's Parisian Year* (University Press of Florida, 2010).

11. T. E. Hulme, "Romanticism and Classicism," in *The Collected Writings of T.E. Hulme*, ed. Karen Csengeri (Oxford: Clarendon, 1994), 61.

12. Kojecký, *T. S. Eliot's Social Criticism* (London: Faber and Faber, 1971), 61.

13. See Pound, [Herman Carl Georg Jesus Maria] "On Certain Reforms and Pass-Times," *Egoist* 1 (Apr. 1914): 130–31; and Louise Blakeney Williams, "'A Certain Discipline': Radical Conservative Solutions," in *Modernism and the Ideology of History* (Cambridge: Cambridge University Press, 2002), 74–90.

14. Hargrove, 45.

15. Eliot, "The Idea of a Literary Review," *Criterion* 4, no. 1 (1926): 5. See also Jason Harding, "Keeping Critical Thought Alive: Eliot's Editorship of the *Criterion*," in *A Companion to T. S. Eliot*, ed. David Chinitz (Malden, MA: Blackwell, 2009), 391.

16. Peter Dale Scott, "The Social Critic and His Discontents," in *The Cambridge Companion to T. S. Eliot*, ed. A. David Moody (Cambridge: Cambridge University Press, 1994), 64.

17. Eliot, *Christianity and Culture*, 51.

18. Ibid., 51.

19. Ibid., 12.

20. T. S. Eliot to Dawson, December 10, 1929, in Box 14, Folder 120, UST/CDC. See Bradley J. Birzer, *Sanctifying the World: The Augustinian Life and Mind of Christopher Dawson* (Front Royal, VA: Christendom Press, 2007), 6.

21. See Birzer, *Sanctifying the World*, 6; and Christina Scott, *A Historian and His World: A Life of Christopher Dawson* (New Brunswick, NJ: Transaction, 1992), 210.

22. Birzer, *Sanctifying the World*, 28–9.

23. Christopher Dawson, "Catholic Tradition and the Modern State," in *Catholic Review* (1916): 24.

24. Dawson, "The Passing of Industrialism," in *Enquiries into Religion and Culture* (London: Sheed and Ward, 1933), 48–53.

25. Paul Robichaud, "David Jones, Christopher Dawson, and the Meaning of History" in *Logos: A Journal of Catholic Thought and Culture* 6, no. 3 (2003): 68–85; and Thomas Dilworth, "David Jones and the Maritain Conversation," in *David Jones: Diversity in Unity: Studies in His Literary and Visual Art* (Cardiff: University of Wales Press, 2000), 51.

26. Quoted in Jonathan Miles, *Backgrounds to David Jones* (Cardiff: University of Wales Press, 1990), 42–3.

27. Miles, *Backgrounds*, 6.

28. Eliot, *Christianity and Culture*, 12.

29. Birzer, *Sanctifying the World*, 76.

30. Dawson, letter to the *Cambridge Review*, 17 February 1933, reprinted in the *Chesterton Review*, 23 (November 1997): 530. Quoted in Birzer, *Sanctifying the World*, 76.

31. Eliot, *Christianity and Culture*, 14.

32. Christopher Dawson, "The Hour of Darkness," *Tablet* (2 December 1939): 625–26. See also Birzer, *Sanctifying the World*, 132.

33. Eliot, *Christianity and Culture*, 75.

34. Dawson, *Religion and the Modern State*, 14.

35. Eliot, *Christianity and Culture*, 46.

36. Kojecký, *T. S. Eliot's Social Criticism*, 65.

37. Dawson, "The Relation of Philosophy to Culture," 7 Sept. 1955, in Box 1, Folder 15, ND/CDAW. Quoted in Birzer, *Sanctifying the World*, 66.

38. James Hitchcock, "Postmortem on a Rebirth: The Catholic Intellectual Renaissance," in *Years of Crisis: Collected Essays 1970–1983* (San Francisco: Ignatius Press, 1985), 203–16.

39. Christopher Dawson, *Religion and Culture* (London: Sheed and Ward, 1949), 48.

40. Dawson, *Progress and Religion* (Washington, DC: Catholic University of America Press, 2001), 192.

41. Eliot, *Christianity and Culture*, 59–60.

42. Ibid., 196–97.

43. Kojecký, *Social Criticism*, 156–57.

44. Quoted in Kojecký, *Social Criticism*, 164.

45. Eliot, *Christianity and Culture*, 34.
46. Eliot, *Christianity and Culture*, 38.
47. Eliot, *Christianity and Culture*, 161.

TWELVE

Between "Absolutism" and "Impossible Theocracy": Hierarchy in Eliot's Anglo-Catholicism

Anderson Araujo

As early as 1917, T. S. Eliot took pains to define the essence of Christianity in a review of R. G. Collingwood's *Religion and Philosophy* (1916), a study of religion as a form of knowledge. Orthodox Christianity "must base itself upon a unique fact," Eliot asserts, "that Jesus was born of a virgin: a proposition which is either true or false, its terms having a fixed meaning."[1] From this basic standpoint, he challenges Collingwood's "insufficient claim" for a philosophy of Christianity hinging on Jesus as a wholly historical figure. Collingwood's evidential approach misemploys history *and* philosophy, forgetting that neither one calls for a transcendent metaphysics. For Eliot, this is no mere quibble. At stake is the truth-value of Christianity. For without a priori transcendence Christianity *qua* revelation would amount to little more than tribal memory, ritual, and myth. Put in Eliotic terms, Christ would be but one among many other Fisher Kings. Nor would the idea of God as the "absolute good will" (Collingwood's phrase) withstand scrutiny if the totality of the universe were to remain, in Eliot's words, "only *in posse*."[2] Yet at the same time Eliot is keen to rest his argument on logical, and not, strictly speaking, theological grounds. His concern here is to draw clear boundaries between the timeless and the temporal, the sacred and the secular.[3] His negation of "historical demands" for Christian historiography also shows, among other things, that long before his conversion to Anglo-Catholicism he had already staked out the path that his faith would later follow.[4] In time, he would anchor his "allegiance to something outside [the self]"[5] onto a

195

transcendent absolute, the "fixed meaning" of his 1917 review. It is Eliot's commitment to this cosmic sense of hierarchy as manifested temporally in the Church that informs the following discussion.

Yet Eliot also strives for a symbiosis between the Word and the world, an economy in which "material knowledge and power is gained without loss of spiritual knowledge and power."[6] However it is read, this is not the zero-sum game of materialist humanism. Eliot's idea of cultural equilibrium entails a constructive dialectic. It seeks to bridge the rifts between the fragmented spheres of culture. His harmonizing project disallows the notion of "non-overlapping magisteria," as paleontologist Stephen J. Gould famously dubs science and religion.[7] For Eliot, such equilibrium could still be found in the "social-religious-artistic complex" of aboriginal societies (*ICS*, 62).[8] But he strips this "complex" of any Rousseauean fantasies, citing the fetishism of "primitive feelings" as the basis for D. H. Lawrence's "aberrations." Here, as elsewhere, excess is the enemy. Eliot felt keenly that the structural kinship between church and state might allow for a creative (if danger-fraught) traffic of ideas in the service of *Kultur*, *Bildung*, and *Geist*, to use Raymond Geuss's capacious definition of culture.[9] In shucking off belief in transcendence, however, post-Enlightenment Western civilization also has lost its spiritual and cultural moorings. In 1948, Eliot would scold post-war Britain, too, for being "unconscious" of the formative role of religion in culture.[10] It is the struggle of a Christian society, then, as he had put it nine years earlier, "to recover the sense of relation to nature and to God" and "the purpose of reascending to origins" (*ICS*, 62). Eliot's Thomistic sense of rank and proportion thus can be said to inform his humanist-classicist concern with order, standards, values, criteria or, in a word, hierarchy.

Jason Harding astutely characterizes Eliot's political philosophy as "based upon an ecclesiastical conception of hierarchy."[11] I draw on Harding's conclusion, while interrogating one-sided readings of Eliot's politics-in-religion and religion-in-politics. These twin concerns have given a polemical edge to Eliot studies at least since Bonamy Dobrée complained to Herbert Read in 1929 that *The Criterion* was a "Religio-Political Organ."[12] In its more extreme forms, Dobrée's binary becomes a rigid interpretive arc. A case in point is Anthony Julius's critique of Eliot's speculations as leaning "toward either the vapid or the eccentric."[13] "Lumping together politics, morals, and religion," Julius writes, "he failed to make necessary distinctions" (208). While it is out of our scope to enter this controversy, Julius's censure beckons commentary. For a start, it largely ignores the ethico-politics of hierarchy that Eliot made much fuss about. In keeping with Julien Benda and José Ortega y Gasset, Eliot turned away from the romantic irrationalism of Bergson and Nietzsche and meticulously charted his spiritual and moral-political evolution. Hence the charges lobbed against Eliot miss the mark. That Julius adduces *For Lancelot Andrewes* and *After Strange Gods* as edge-blurring "problems" further overlooks the intensely self-critical, self-aware nature of Eliot's prose. At times, indeed, no critic can be harsher on the poet than himself.

In *After Strange Gods* Eliot goes to great lengths to revisit his oft-quoted classicist, royalist, and Anglo-Catholic self-rendering in the earlier *For Lancelot Andrewes*.[14] It is worth quoting this less-known passage in full:

> The facility with which this statement has been quoted has helped to reveal to me that as it stands the statement is injudicious. It may suggest that the three subjects are of equal importance to me, which is not so; it may suggest that I accept all three beliefs on the same grounds, which is not so; and it may suggest that I believe that they all hang together or fall together, which would be the most serious misunderstanding of all. That there are connexions for me I of course admit, but these illuminate my own mind rather than the external world; and I now see, the danger of suggesting to outsiders that the Faith is a political principle or a literary fashion, and the sum of all a dramatic posture.[15]

Whence, then, the "lumping together" of Julius's critical caricature? Even if Eliot were guilty of such carelessness, is it not also proper to acknowledge his about-face in the Page-Barbour lectures as a kind of atonement?[16] Consider, too, how the above passage seeks to ensure that religious faith does not become a convenient façade. The chanciness that Julius sees in Eliot's cultural-religious politics fails to take into account the poet's abiding concern with secular and religious instantiations of hierarchy and with establishing "connexions" among them.

The principle of "connexions" can also be said to underwrite Eliot's most sustained critical-literary enterprise, *The Criterion*. As several critics have shown, the journal joined a transnational conversation with American and European periodicals, such as *The Dial, Revista de Occidente, Nouvelle Revue Française, Neue deutsche Beiträge*, and *Europäische Revue*.[17] In 1926 moreover Eliot writes that the new version of *The Criterion* "should exhibit heterogeneity which the intelligent reader can resolve into order" (2).[18] A creative, shape-generative commerce with readers, contributors, and other periodicals undergirds Eliot's critical-aesthetic enterprise. Far from random, his thought is fundamentally cross-disciplinary, cross-cultural, retrospective, experimental, and exploratory. This is not to say of course that it is faultless, as Eliot recognized. I can think of no better metaphor to illustrate the folds and twists of his method of argumentation than the art of origami. Both exhibit seemingly chaotic patterns of development while being directed by some kind of overarching design. Hence nearly every significant enterprise Eliot took up after his conversion in 1927 was inflected by an all-subsuming faith in the Judeo-Christian tradition. That he would nonetheless keep his faith at bay from politics as such bears witness to his awareness of the dangers inherent in such an alliance. Still, Eliot did endeavor to incorporate the structure of a higher order into his cultural politics. To that end he brought a religious rationale to the humanist project articulated by E. R. Curtius in the *Criterion* as meaning "to restore the natural hierarchy of the successive ages of man and the interplay of their functions."[19] In sum, I argue that Eliot's conception of hierarchy found ideal (though not uncritical) instantiation in the Anglo-Catholic movement.

As interrelated discourses, *hierarchy* and *Anglo-Catholicism* provide sufficient warrant for our exploration of both in the context of Eliot's religious conversion. The hyphenated denomination that he would take up in 1927 in itself suggests a dialogic synthesis of sacrament, liturgy, and hierarchy between Anglicanism and Roman Catholicism. It is useful to unpack these heavily-freighted terms so as to situate Eliot's nuanced stance in relation to each. Anglo-Catholicism would conjoin for Eliot "the element of humanism and criticism," as we can infer from his essay on Babbitt, written soon after his conversion.[20] It is, then, the Anglo-Catholic dialectic that he would deem vital in preventing "a Catholicism of despair." The English Church affords a salutary alternative to the ultramontane Catholicism that Babbitt (ventriloquized by Eliot) terms "the hierarchy in communion with the Holy See." Eliot, in contrast, envisions ideal religious experience as the fostering of "*inner* control,"[21] a hedge against autarchic forms of hierarchy, whether political or priestly. His phrase plays off on Babbitt's Emersonian "inner check."[22] However, Eliot chafes at Babbitt's suggestion that humanism void of orthodox religion can effectively rein in egotistic behavior.[23] "[Babbitt] is thus trying to build a Catholic platform out of Protestant planks," Eliot quips.[24] On the face of it, it is little wonder that Eliot would turn away from what he saw as a ramshackle structure, humanism. In its stead, his religio-aesthetic sensibility would come into its own under the aegis of Anglo-Catholicism, a counter-Reformation skeptical of the Establishment and striving for *libertas ecclesiae* ("freedom of the Church"). Eliot would also bring his religious consciousness to bear on his *Kulturkritik*. Hence the need to uncover the origins of his many-sided creed.

Anglo-Catholicism is a knotted-up crux of semantic ambiguity and political resonance. Its origins are associated with a range of labels, such as High Church, Ritualism, Tractarianism, and the Oxford Movement. It would emerge out of the politico-theological ferment of the Oxford Movement in the 1830s. The political origins of the revival of Catholicism in the Church of England that came to be known as the Oxford Movement was codified in the sacral theory of monarchy espoused by Oxford theologians John Keble, John Henry Newman, and Edward Pusey. The early Church's creed marshaled a Toryism underlain by "a romantic, almost mystical reverence for the House of Stuart and that potent symbol, the Royal Martyr, Charles I."[25] Keble's Accession Day Sermon of 1836 cast the office of monarch as representing the "anointed of the Lord, a living, type of the supreme dominion of Jesus Christ."[26] The ideal of royal supremacy is thus threaded into the very fabric of the Anglo-Catholic doctrine of apostolic succession and episcopacy.[27] Not that this meant a blithe endorsement, however. While claiming a Catholic essence for the Church of England, Keble called on the Established Church in his famous assize sermon of 14 July 1833 "to assert its autonomy and to reject encroachments from the State by firmly opposing what might loosely be called Erastianism."[28] Eliot thought likewise. His anti-Erastianism would in time put him at loggerheads with the politics-laden Catholicism of Maurras.

"Erastian" is precisely how Eliot terms the Concordat between the Vatican and Mussolini's regime in a 1928 review-essay in *The Criterion*.[29] Similarly, in 1936, at the height of fascist power—Mussolini annexed Ethiopia that summer—Eliot worries that "ideas of authority, of hierarchy, of discipline and order, applied inappropriately in the temporal sphere, may lead us into some error of absolutism or impossible theocracy."[30] Autocracy and theocracy evidently meet in his mind. It is beyond doubt that he rejected both. However, as Rémi Brague cogently argues, there is no hard-and-fast need "to take 'theocracy' in its usual meaning of the frowned-upon 'government by clerics.'"[31] Rather, Brague suggests an alternate meaning for theocracy as "a regime in which norms are considered to rest on a divine foundation." As such, we, too, still live in a kind of theocracy. Whether the idea of democracy is rooted in a Thomistic conception of "law" or Rousseauean "conscience," both have "theological underpinnings."[32] To this, it is fair to assume, Eliot would assent.

"Impossible theocracy" thus stands for totalitarian rule in ecclesiastical guise. The notion is distinct from the hierarchical idea of the Mosaic *theokratia*, a community governed by God or, in Eliot's neo-Thomistic expression, a polity informed by orthodox Christian principles. Eliot's pairing of "impossible"[33] and "theocracy" suggests ipso facto a form of theocracy that *might* be possible. Eliot, I propose, means to recover the moral-theological dimension of the term. As for the "absolutism" cited above, he probably has in mind, among other things, fascist *Gerarchia*, the corporative structure of the Italian state under Mussolini. Italian fascism's neo-pagan *mythoi* celebrated in spectacular rallies, theatrical rituals, and mass media created an *ersatz* religious experience. Fascism consolidated its motley array of heroic myths with a political theology known as *mussolinismo*, the cult of *Il Duce*. In this quasi-religious liturgy—a carnivalesque parody of the Holy Mass—politics itself becomes, as Eliot puts it, a "muddle."[34] The "alternative of Christianity or paganism," sketched out in the postscript to the *Idea of a Christian Society*[35] once the Munich Agreement had collapsed, could no longer be ignored—it meant war. Conversely, Catholicism appealed to Eliot as a "coherent traditional system of dogma and morals," as he affirms in his 1929 essay on Dante.[36] But rather than choose the Roman Catholic Church, Eliot thinks Anglicanism leaves "some room for divergent opinions over a more hierarchical one that impose[s] uniformity," as Johan Kuin proposes.[37]

Eliot's categorical rejection of totalitarian hierarchy is not meant to suggest that there is an unspannable gap between the state and the church. Rather, he maintains that religious and secular institutions ought to sustain culture without becoming lethally intertwined. The "friction" arising from the interplay of these forces will, ideally, be "highly creative" and lead to "the emergence of several cultural levels" (*NTDC*, 23). Eliot envisions these cultural layers interacting along a vertical or hierarchical axis. In a way, he modernizes the church-state dialectic that Coleridge argues for in *On the Constitution of Church and State* (1829). Coleridge presupposes that each has its proper province, which he calls "ideas," "the most real of all realities."[38] But as Rev. Peter Hinchliff points out, "the 'church' in Coleridge's writing was neither the transcendent theological concept of the ideal Church nor the actual Church of England. It was the sum of all the nation's spiritual resources, including art, science, literature, and scholarship."[39] While Coleridge's conception of "church" might seem fuzzy-edged or even secularized, it differs little, it seems, from the protean conception of "culture" that Matthew Arnold would envisage as a hedge against anarchy.

For Eliot, however, no "sweetness and light" can be sustained over time without the unifying sensibility and traditional authority provided by religion. As he writes in a book review of 1918 in the *Monist*, "The awareness of a group gives us law and morality. The awareness of a supreme spiritual pressure gives us religion."[40] The heteroglossic spaces of irreligious culture serve as paltry substitutes for the "spiritual pressure" of hierarchical structures. The alternative is bleak and disjunctive. "I can connect / Nothing with nothing," sings the third Thames Daughter in *The Waste Land* from the depths of a fragmented psyche, perhaps a symptom of anomie in post-metaphysical culture. In 1926, Eliot praises Ramon Fernandez's withering review of the fiction of Marcel Proust, published in the April 1924 number of the *Nouvelle Revue Française*. Eliot cites in French Fernandez's contention that Proust's fiction "does not create an hierarchy of values, and it manifests from start to finish no spiritual progress."[41]

Eliotic hierarchy may be seen as a kind of "Aquinas-map" (to borrow Ezra Pound's term)[42] to guide a deracinated Western culture back to the heart of light. But Pound's polytheism differed radically from his friend's more conservative faith. The religious roots of Eliot's conceptual-moral scheme may be seen in the etymology of "hierarchy." The term encodes the tripartite angelic orders[43] established by first-century Paulinian convert to Christianity, Dionysius the Areopagite, the first Bishop of Athens. The two main works ascribed to Dionysius by a sixth-century Neoplatonist (known as "Pseudo-Dionysius"), *The Celestial Hierarchy* and *The Ecclesiastical Hierarchy*, establish a parallel between the angelic and clerical ranks, as the titles indicate. Evelyn Underhill's *Mysticism* (1911) (which Eliot read carefully during his last years at Harvard[44]) bears the imprint of Dionysius's mystic theology. Her tiered phases of "mystic consciousness"— "1. Awakening or Conversion; 2. Self-knowledge or Purgation; 3. Illumination; 4. Surrender, or the Dark Night; 5. Union"[45] —would inform Eliot's adherence to Anglo-Catholic doctrine and help to drive him further away from his family's Unitarian faith. Underhill's scheme is also in keeping with the Oxford Movement's recovery of "long-forgotten forms of spiritual discipline," the "revival of the 'religious life' as a recognized path to Christian perfection," and a ritualism that sought to transform Anglican eucharistic worship.[46] As James E. Miller Jr. notes, Eliot's reading of Underhill's book, "and especially her use of Dante in her 'argument,' clearly must be counted as a major factor in his conversion to Anglo-Catholicism some years later."[47]

The Florentine poet would inform Eliot's project to harmonize temporal and spiritual life (*ICS*, 54–5), as Dominic Manganiello and Nunzio Cossu have shown.[48] Eliot was especially indebted to "Dante's conviction of the special providential mission assigned to the Holy Roman Empire as the instrument of world order and peace."[49] Maurras, too, subscribed to Dante. In a nod to this association, Eliot dedicates his 1929 *Dante* to Maurras, with the epigraph from Maurras, "*La sensibilité, sauvée d'elle-même et conduite dans l'ordre, est devenue un principe de perfection.*"[50] Yet it is *ordre*—not *sensibilité*—I propose, that is the keyword here, as Maurras subjects the whims of sensibility to the formal structure provided by a traditional notion of order. Put most generally, Dante and Maurras may be said to have given Eliot's religious thought a local habitation in the idea of hierarchy.

As Roger Kojecký rightly comments, Maurras' concept of hierarchy brought Eliot "into easy association with Catholicism."[51] Be that as it may, the *Anglican* side of Eliot's Catholicism is too often lost sight of, while the influence of Maurras on Eliot can easily be exaggerated. As early as 1919, in the *Athenaeum*, Eliot denounced Maurras' "intemperate and fanatical spirit."[52] In his essay in this section, Ben Lockerd discusses the neglected influence of British Catholic historian Christopher Dawson on Eliot's cultural theory. Dawson brought Eliot to a religious valuation of hierarchical structure and traditional authority, which Maurras had over-politicized. My own concern is to underline what Eliot himself referred to in "Lancelot Andrewes" as the "*English* Catholic Church,"[53] founded as a national institution independent of papal jurisdiction. As Pickering maintains, Anglo-Catholicism "is essentially a British phenomenon."[54]

Eliot evidently rooted his Anglo-Catholic sensibility in an idealized past, though not in the reigns of either Henry VIII or Edward VI. Rather, the "*via media* which is the spirit of Anglicanism was the spirit of Elizabeth in all things," he writes in "Lancelot Andrewes" (179). For Eliot, the

Church at the end of the Elizabethan era was "a masterpiece of ecclesiastical statesmanship" (180). Intellectually, the Church was buttressed by the capacious Renaissance humanism of Andrewes and Richard Hooker. From this Anglo-patristic heritage, it follows that the spirit of Anglicanism entails for Eliot the finest mean between "Papacy and Presbytery" (179). His royalist-inflected appraisal of the Church corresponds, again, with the link that high churchmen (most of whom were ardent royalists) traditionally have drawn between the doctrines, ministry, and sacraments of the Church and "a high Tory doctrine of the state."[55] But lest we impose too bracing a church-state alliance upon orthodox Anglicanism and Anglo-Catholicism, it is worth noting that the High Church supposed "the *interdependence* of church and state, and not the dependence of the church upon the state."[56] Eliot, too, upheld this notion.

As Eliot exhorts in *The Idea of a Christian Society*, the Church's hierarchical organization must have a "direct and official relation to the State" (47). Coincidentally, the *OED* locates the first distinctly political use of "hierarchy" in the English language in Sir Thomas Elyot's *The Boke named The Gouernour* (1531). That Sir Thomas's guide for rulers was influenced by Machiavelli, Plato, and Xenophon, among other sources, attests to its syncretic, classicist-humanist approach to political economy. Eliot, as we know, greatly admired his Tudor ancestor. The concept of "clerisy" that animates *Notes towards the Definition of Culture* arguably fuses Sir Thomas's moral-political with the theological-Thomistic sense of hierarchy.[57] Harding quotes the appeal Eliot made to the Assembly of the Church of England in 1935 to consider "'the fundamental moral laws founded on Christian theology' when examining social and economic problems."[58] It follows that for Eliot the state has much to gain from a political economy informed by Christian principles. And yet, as he cautions in 1939, the hierarchy of the Church itself "is always in danger of corruption and in need of reform from within" (*ICS*, 48). The *via media* that typifies Anglo-Catholicism perhaps stood for Eliot as the last bulwark against the machinations of power, both within and without the Church. The Hobbesean art of government, to be sure, is hardly up to par. As the Third Priest states in *Murder in the Cathedral*, "I see nothing quite conclusive in the art of temporal government, / But violence, duplicity and frequent malversation" (5). Anglo-Catholicism enabled Eliot to rise above the fray of partisan politics and secular ideologies. It is, finally, this anglicized brand of the Church that he would pit against Communist and fascist tyrannies, godless parodies, as it were, of divinely sanctioned forms of hierarchy.

NOTES

1. T. S. Eliot, review of *Religion and Philosophy*, by R. G. Collingwood, *International Journal of Ethics* 27, no. 4 (July 1917): 543. I am indebted to Randall J. Woods's gift of a bound copy of his doctoral dissertation, "'Prufrock' to *The Waste Land*: T. S. Eliot's Periodical Publications, 1915–1922," which contains this review among 166 other articles that Eliot published from 1915 to 1922, most of which had never been reprinted heretofore.

2. That is, "potential," "not actual."

3. The kind of demarcation I propose can be seen as a slight move away from the idea Eliot expressed in a letter of 6 January 1915 to Norbert Wiener, a mathematician at MIT: "Of course one cannot avoid metaphysics altogether, because nowhere can a sharp line be drawn—to draw a sharp line between metaphysics and common sense would itself be metaphysics and not common sense. . . . One cannot, of course, hope to separate Reality from Value" (Eliot, *Letters*, 80).

4. Incidentally, Eliot's literalist reading of the Incarnation narrative echoes Article II of the Church of England, "The Incarnation and Atonement," designed to oppose the "ancient heresies" of historical theology. See E. J. Bicknell, *A Theological Introduction to the Thirty-Nine Articles of the Church of England* (London: Longmans, 1961), 54ff. Article II was based on the Lutheran Confession of Augsburg of 1553.

5. Eliot, "The Function of Criticism," in *Selected Prose of T. S. Eliot*, ed. Frank Kermode (London: Faber and Faber, 1975), 70.

6. Eliot, *The Idea of a Christian Society* (London: Faber and Faber, 1939), 62. Cited hereafter in the text as *ICS*.

7. Gould, "Nonoverlapping Magisteria," *Natural History* 106 (March 1997): 16–22.

8. Cf. Eliot, *Notes towards the Definition of Culture* (New York: Harcourt, 1949), 20–24.

9. Geuss, "*Kultur, Bildung, Geist*," *History and Theory* 35, no. 2 (May 1996): 151–64. Geuss notes that these three words are used in German in place of the English "culture" (153).

10. Eliot, *Notes towards the Definition of Culture* (New York: Harcourt, 1949), 92. First published by Faber in 1948. Cited hereafter in the text as *NTDC*.

11. Harding, *The Criterion: Cultural Politics and Periodical Networks in Inter-War Britain* (Oxford: Oxford UP, 2002), 181. In support of his argument, Harding quotes Eliot's *Criterion* "Commentary" of June 1928: "In the theory of politics, in the largest sense, the *Criterion* is interested so far as politics can be dissociated from party politics, from the passions or fantasies of the moment, and from problems of local and temporary importance."

12. Quoted in Harding, 178.

13. Julius, *T. S. Eliot, Anti-Semitism, and Literary Form* (Cambridge: Cambridge University Press, 1995), 208.

14. Eliot, *For Lancelot Andrewes*, vii. As discussed in Torrens's "Charles Maurras and Eliot's 'New Life,'" *PMLA* (March 1974): 312–22, Eliot cribbed the French thinker's threefold program for *L'Action Française* as *classique, catholique, monarchique*.

15. Eliot, *After Strange Gods: A Primer of Modern Heresy* (London: Faber and Faber, 1934), 27–28.

16. For the purposes of this chapter, I will also avoid discussing the anti-Semitism that Eliot allegedly displays elsewhere in *After Strange Gods*. For a spirited take on this long-standing controversy, one need look no further than the debate hosted in *Modernism/modernity* 10, no. 1 (2003). Prominent figures in this debate included Ronald Schuchard, Marjorie Perloff, David Bromwich, Ronald Bush, Denis Donoghue, Anthony Julius, and James Longenbach.

17. For a sustained discussion of the *Criterion*'s relation to these periodicals see Jeroen Vanheste, *Guardians of the Humanist Legacy: The Classicism of T. S. Eliot's Criterion Network and Its Relevance to our Postmodern World* (Leiden and Boston: Brill, 2007).

18. Eliot, "The Idea of a Literary Review," *New Criterion* 4 (Jan. 1926): 1–4.

19. Curtius, "Restoration of the Reason," *Criterion* 6 (Nov. 1927): 391–92.

20. Eliot, "The Humanism of Irving Babbitt," in *Selected Prose of T. S. Eliot*, ed. Frank Kermode (London: Faber and Faber, 1975), 283.

21. Ibid., 281 (Eliot's italics).

22. See Russell Kirk, "The Enduring Influence of Irving Babbitt," in *Irving Babbitt in Our Time*, eds. George A. Panichas and Claes G. Ryn (Washington, DC: The Catholic University of America Press, 1986): "The disciplinary arts of *humanitas* teach man to put checks upon his will and his appetite. Those checks are supplied by reason—not the private rationality of the Enlightenment, but by the higher reason that grows out of a respect for the wisdom of one's ancestors and out of the endeavour to apprehend the character of good and evil" (21).

23. Cf. Eliot's essay "Religion without Humanism" (1930), where in a conciliatory manner he states that "humanism is in the end futile without religion" but at the other extreme there is "the danger, a very real one, of *religion without humanism*" (105).

24. Eliot, "Humanism of Babbitt," 281.

25. Nockles, *The Oxford Movement*, 72.

26. Quoted in Nockles, 72.

27. See Torrens, 312–22. Eliot famously styled himself in *For Lancelot Andrewes* in 1928 as a "classicist in literature, royalist in politics, and anglo-catholic in religion" (*Lancelot Andrewes*, vii).

28. W. S. F. Pickering, *Anglo-Catholicism: A Study in Religious Ambiguity* (New York: Routledge, 1989), 17.

29. Eliot, "The Literature of Fascism," *Criterion* 8 (December 1928): 280–90.

30. Eliot, *Essays Ancient and Modern* (London: Faber and Faber, 1936), 118.

31. Brague, "Are Non-Theocratic Regimes Possible?" *Intercollegiate Review* 41 (Spring 2006): 11.

32. Brague, 6. While extending the idea of "theocracy," Brague (like Eliot) also complicates the usual Greek-derived meaning of democracy, arguing instead that "our modern so-called 'democracies' are in the last analysis '*laocracies*': their subjects are human beings who are 'free' . . . . *Our* freedom means . . . that we need not obey any authority other than the promptings of our own conscience, which are ultimately expressions of God's concern for the Good of this creation" (9).

33. Is it possible that Eliot also had had in mind "impracticable" (as a cognate meaning of "impossible")? See *OED*, def. A3.

34. Eliot, "The Literature of Fascism," 282.

35. Eliot, *ICS*, 66.

36. Eliot, "Dante," in *Selected Prose of T. S. Eliot*, ed. Frank Kermode (London: Faber and Faber, 1975), 222.

37. Johan Kuin, "Proeve van een apologie: T. S. Eliot als Anglicaan," in *T. S. Eliot; Een Amerikaan in Europa*, ed. W. Bronzwaer (Baarn: Ambo, 1988), 9–45. Translated and paraphrased in Vanheste, 148.

38. Coleridge, *On the Constitution of the Church and State*, vol. 10 of *The Collected Works of Samuel Taylor Coleridge*, ed. John Colmer (Princeton: Princeton University Press, 1969), 18.

39. Peter Hinchliff, "Church-State Relations," in *The Study of Anglicanism*, ed. Stephen Sykes and John Booty (London: SPCK, 1988), 358–59.

40. Eliot, review of *Religion and Science*, by John Theodore Merz, *Monist* 28, no. 2 (April 1918): 319–20.

41. Quoted in Leon Surette, *The Modern Dilemma: Wallace Stevens, T. S. Eliot, and Humanism* (Montreal: McGill-Queen's University Press, 2008), 206.

42. Pound, *The Selected Letters of Ezra Pound*, ed. D. D. Paige (New York: New Directions, 1971), 323.

43. The highest of the three divisions contains seraphs, cherubs, and thrones.

44. Lyndall Gordon, *T. S. Eliot: An Imperfect Life*, 89.

45. Evelyn Underhill, *Mysticism: A Study in the Nature and Development of Man's Spiritual Consciousness*, twelfth ed. (London: Methuen, 1930), 167.

46. Eugene R. Fairweather, Introduction to *The Oxford Movement,* ed. Fairweather (New York: Oxford University Press, 1964), 12.

47. Miller Jr., *T. S. Eliot, The Making of an American Poet* (University Park: Pennsylvania State University Press, 2005), 181.

48. See Nunzio Cossu, "Dantismo Politico-Religioso di Eliot," *Nuova Antologia* 495 (Sept.–Dec. 1965): 181–91, and Dominic Manganiello, *T. S. Eliot and Dante* (London: MacMillan, 1989), 137–46.

49. Manganiello, 143.

50. "Sensibility, saved from itself and subject to order, becomes a principle of perfection" (my translation). Quoted in Torrens, 315.

51. Roger Kojecký, *T. S. Eliot's Social Criticism* (London: Faber and Faber, 1971), 64.

52. Eliot, "Was There a Scottish Literature?" *Athenaeum* 4657 (1919): 680–1.

53. Eliot, "Lancelot Andrewes," in *Selected Prose of T. S. Eliot,* ed. Frank Kermode (Faber and Faber, 1975), 181 (my italics).

54. Pickering, *Anglo-Catholicism: A Study in Religious Ambiguity,* 222.

55. Geoffrey Rowell, *The Vision Glorious: Themes and Personalities of the Catholic Revival in Anglicanism* (Oxford: Oxford University Press, 1983), 3.

56. Edward Norman, *Church and Society in England, 1770–1970: An Historical Study* (Oxford: Oxford University Press, 1976), 33 (my italics).

57. Cf. Kojecký's interpretation of Eliot's concept of clerisy as "influenced by Thomist assumptions of the importance within medieval society of the elite of clerics" (115).

58. Harding, *The Criterion,* 193.

THIRTEEN

Eliot's Christian Sociology and the Problem of Nationalism

Paul Robichaud

T. S. Eliot's search for a specifically Christian solution to the crises of the 1930s reflects in part his understanding of the problem posed by nationalism. He saw the success of nationalism in Europe as the displacement of a religious sense of community into the sphere of politics, animated by all the passion that religion is capable of commanding. If fascism and Nazism had made a religion of the state, Eliot hoped that Britain, particularly England, could aspire to collective purpose and action by recovering an understanding of itself as a spiritual community *as well as* a nation. In a 1941 broadcast, he tells his listeners that "Our ambition to create a Christian Britain is the greatest we can take to ourselves."[1] Eliot wanted to restore the balance between religion and Europe's national cultures, which he thought necessary for a sane and healthy civilization. From this perspective, modern Europe had both lost its religious orientation and invested nationality with a false sense of the sacred. Rediscovering the common religious sources of European culture, while preserving the distinction between religion and national cultures, was for Eliot a necessary step in restoring equilibrium to western civilization. This chapter will consider Eliot's Christian social thought specifically as a response to the rise of extreme nationalism in Europe during the interwar years.

In "East Coker," published in 1940, T. S. Eliot looks back at "Twenty years largely wasted, the years of *l'entre deux guerres.*"[2] His immediate sense of failure is one of failed articulation, in which words themselves defeat intended meaning and expression. The line resonates, however, with a larger sense of cultural failure: the inability of European writers and intellectuals to stop the events that culminated in the Second World War. Eliot's decision to cease publication of *The Criterion* in 1939 stemmed from what he called "a depression of spirits so different from any other experience of fifty years as to be a new emotion."[3] He felt Chamberlain's decision to appease Hitler a moral defeat for Britain, and symptomatic of the bankruptcy of modern western politics. The interwar years which Eliot thought wasted marked the pinnacle of early twentieth-century nationalism, the triumph of irrationality, and totalitarianism in politics. Recent scholarship, such as Jason Harding's work on interwar periodicals, allows us to see Eliot's project in its immediate cultural context, and with a new emphasis on the ways in which it relates to wider historical currents. Eliot intended *The Criterion* to function as a bulwark against the divisions created by the various European nationalisms. In a postwar broadcast on "The Unity of European Culture," he argues that the international cooperation of such journals "should continually stimulate that circulation of influence of thought and sensibility, between nation and nation in Europe, which fertilises and renovates from abroad the literature of each one of them."[4] As editor, Eliot cultivated relationships between *The Criterion* and periodicals in France, Germany, Italy, and Spain. Reflecting on this experience, he concludes that "the existence of such a network of periodicals, at least one in every capital of Europe, is necessary for the transmission of ideas" (*CC*, 193). From Eliot's perspective, *The Criterion* served its function as part of a circulatory system of intercultural exchange that included *La Nouvelle Revue Française*, the *Neue Rundschau*, and the *Neue Schweizer Rundschau*, among many others. This system began to break down in the 1930s, with what Eliot calls "the gradual closing of the mental frontiers of Europe. A kind of cultural autarchy followed inevitably on political and economic autarchy" (*CC*, 194). While Michael North has criticized Eliot's cultural politics as implying "those cultures will be best that have maintained themselves behind the most impermeable barriers," Eliot here identifies such barriers with the undesirable closing of Europe's "mental frontiers."[5]

The *OED* defines *autarchy* as "absolute sovereignty, despotism," with a variant spelling meaning "self-sufficiency, esp. economic," so the word conveys a sense of totalizing political and economic authority appropriate for describing the various communist and fascist regimes in 1930s Europe. Eliot's word choice is significant. Denis Donoghue argues that Eliot's method of analysis is consistently "mythical": "a procedure by which the mind adverts to contingent events but refuses to be intimidated by the local conventions by which they operate; it calls upon a higher system of values by which the immediate event or situation may be judged."[6] The abstract idea of autarchy, with its classical resonance, thus subsumes such contingent and local expressions as Stalinism or National Socialism. In effect, Eliot is appealing to an idea that is meaningful beyond its present and local manifestations, and that will make sense of them. This aversion to modern political discourse as such reflects his belief that such discourse is at the root of Europe's cultural disintegration: "A universal concern with politics does not unite, it divides. It unites those politically minded folk who agree, across the frontiers of nations, against some other international group who holds opposed views. But it tends to destroy the cultural unity of Europe" (CC, 194–5). Such concern with "the cultural unity of Europe" reflects the influence of cultural historian Christopher Dawson, who was similarly concerned with the way nationalist politics were throwing fault lines across western culture.

Like Eliot, Dawson opposed the ways in which nationalism was narrowing the European intellectual horizon. In his practice as a historian, Dawson argued that "the alternative to the nationalist conception of history is the cultural or sociological one which goes behind the political unit and studies that fundamental social unity which we term a culture."[7] His historical methodology has clear affinities with Eliot's own analytical procedure, seeking to go beyond the biased contingency in which nationalist histories are embedded toward an ideal and more objective cultural history. Dawson's central thesis is that the formative period in European history is not the Renaissance, as it is for Burkhardt, or the Enlightenment, as it is for the Whig historians and, more recently, Michel Foucault, but the early Middle Ages. He identifies four major elements in the formation of a common European culture: the Roman Empire; the Catholic Church; the Classical tradition; and the barbarian peoples.[8] European culture is at its healthiest when the legacies of these four elements are properly balanced; modern Europe suffers from an imbalance in which its constituent nations, ultimately derived from settlements of "the barbarian peoples," give priority to their own particularity at the expense of their common Classical and Christian inheritance. In *The Judgement of Nations* (1942), Dawson drew attention to the fact that "[f]or a thousand years the peoples and states of Europe have developed under similar influences and shared a common cultural patrimony."[9] Inspired by Dawson's writings, T. S. Eliot made a similar appeal to "that fundamental social unity" in "The Unity of European Culture," arguing that

> For the health of the culture of Europe two conditions are required: that the culture of each country should be unique, and that the different cultures should recognize their relationship to each other, so that each should be susceptible to the influence from the others. And this is possible because there is a common element in European culture, an interrelated history of thought and feeling and behaviour, an interchange of art and ideas. (CC, 197)

Cultural variety enables individual cultures to benefit from the influence of a multitude of others. The "common element in European culture" balances and enriches the particularism of local cultures for both Dawson and Eliot.

The difficulty with Eliot's "mythic" mode of analysis when applied to politics is its potential to slight the contingent in attempting to discover its meaning through the ideal. This method of detached analysis informed Eliot's editorial practice at *The Criterion*, with serious consequences for the periodical's immediate effectiveness and subsequent critical reputation. Jason Harding offers a realistic assessment:

> *The Criterion*'s 'disinterested' symposial treatment of some pretty unappealing right-wing causes has left it open, in recent debates, to slack charges of 'fascism' and 'anti-Semitism'. In truth, the *Criterion*'s largely dismissive treatment of the violent and abrasive *realpolitik* of inter-war foreign affairs is evidence of a rather painful inability to estimate contemporary social and political forces at their true strength. [10]

In providing "disinterested" analyses of contemporary European problems, *The Criterion* failed to recognize the threat posed by totalitarianism. The mythical procedure of Eliot's reasoning, which acknowledges the contingent but summons the ideal to inform judgments made upon it, is clearly implicated in this failure. Eliot himself recognized this. In *The Idea of a Christian Society*, published before the outbreak of war in 1939, he describes his emotional response to the Munich Crisis as a "feeling of humiliation, which seemed to demand an act of personal contrition, of humility, repentance and amendment; what had happened was something in which one was deeply implicated and responsible" (*CC*, 51). He was "deeply shaken by the events of September 1938, in a way from which one does not recover" (*CC*, 50). Eliot's reaction and decision to suspend publication of *The Criterion* acknowledges the failure of this particular cultural project to restore sanity and moral intelligence to international relations. He took this failure, and his share of responsibility for it, personally.

Eliot's subsequent diagnosis of the dangerous rise of autarchy during the interwar years is, however, corroborated by the Marxist historian E. J. Hobsbawm, who observes that "inter-war economic crises reinforced the self-contained 'national economy' in the most spectacular manner." [11] The rise of increased border controls and high tariffs spurred the withdrawal of foreign investment across Europe, producing "a protectionism so defensive that it came close to a policy short of autarchy, mitigated by bilateral agreements." [12] Against this background of economic and political isolation, which included Britain's 1931 cancellation of Free Trade, Eliot marshaled his forces in the cause of European unity. As early as 1924, he characterized "the present age" as "a singularly stupid one," an "age of a mistaken nationalism and of an equally mistaken and artificial internationalism." [13] Eliot sought to balance these erroneous tendencies by seeking out and presenting ideas with greater historical depth than those promulgated by modern ideologies. The unifying idea of a shared European culture offered the possibility of an alternative international-ism, one rooted in tradition and "the mind of Europe." [14]

Culture in Eliot's view offers the potential to mediate between nation-alities. In *Notes towards the Definition of Culture*, published in 1948, he outlines three levels of culture: individual, "*group* or *class*," and society (*CC*, 93). Eliot understands culture in the widest possible sense, including "all the characteristic activities and interests of a people" (*CC*, 104). While some of these are unique to a particular nation—Eliot cites such English shibboleths as Derby Day and Wensleydale cheese—others may reflect the local development of elements common to Europe as a whole, such as association football or neo-Gothic cathedrals. Eliot's idea of culture, as Richard Shusterman observes, is the logical development of his earlier formulations of tradition and orthodoxy, demanding "a balance of un-consciousness with consciousness, consensual unity with pluralistic ten-sion in order to maintain the desired balance of continuity with change that is necessary for its vigor." [15] This sense of balance is reflected in his binary analysis of European culture as a whole.

Eliot's analysis of western culture ultimately formulates a set of two binaries, that of region/nation and that of nation/civilization, which inter-sect insofar as both region and civilization are in constant tension with nation, and manifest shared cultural values locally and globally. What is the nature of these shared values? For Eliot, shared western values are ultimately religious, but he carefully distinguishes between "primitive societies," in which "no clear distinction is visible between religious and non-religious activities," and "more developed societies" characterized by "a greater distinction, and finally contrast and opposition, between these activities" (*CC*, 141). This conflict between spiritual and secular action is generated by religion itself, which produces a form of conscious-ness acutely aware of conflicting motives and desires within the individ-ual. It is only in the modern unconscious that religion and culture remain identical, and Eliot shrewdly observes the political consequences of the human tendency to "revert" from "the excessive burden" of conscious-ness. He argues that "the tendency towards reversion may explain the powerful attraction which totalitarian philosophy and practice can exert upon humanity. Totalitarianism appeals to the desire to return to the womb" (*CC*, 142). Modern totalitarian politics target the unconscious identity of religion and culture, giving this fusion political expression in the cult of the nation-state. Eliot would agree with Benedict Anderson that nationalism *as such* is best treated "as if it belonged with 'kinship' and 'religion', rather than with 'liberalism' or 'fascism.'" [16] Totalitarian politics invert the proper relationship between religion and culture, which mainly vary in affording different perspectives on human life. In his review of *Notes towards the Definition of Culture*, Christopher Dawson offers a succinct summary of Eliot's postwar position: "a culture is the incarnation of a religion: they are not two different things which may be related to each other, but different aspects of the same thing: one common life, viewed at different levels, or in reference to different ends."[17] Nationality is an important, even determinative feature of culture, but it cannot be an end in itself.

Classical liberalism had attempted to define nationality in ways that would limit the divisive power of religion and ethnicity, theorizing the nation as a secular space, but often in ways that suggest a displaced religious community. The state's gradual absorption of traditionally ecclesiastical functions, such as aiding the poor, combined with the marginalization of religion in public life, opened the way for the nation-state to inspire fanaticism and a near-mystical sense of communal identity. In the nineteenth century, Ernest Renan, for example, answers the question "what is a nation?" by ultimately defining it as "a soul, a spiritual principle."[18] This collective essence is comprised of two elements, "the possession in common of a rich legacy of memories" and "present-day consent, the desire to live together, the will to perpetuate the value of the heritage that one has received in an undivided form."[19] Renan's "consent" and "will" derive from Rousseau's theory of the social contract, and suggest a basis for nationality in conscious choice. His concern is to avoid "ethnographic" or racial definitions of the nation: "a very great error, which, if it were to become dominant, would destroy European civilization."[20] Through the "unificatory agents" of Rome and the Christian Church, "the ethnographic argument was debarred from the government of human affairs for centuries," and Renan expresses his dismay at its emergence in modern times.[21] The social-contractual model of nationality seemed to offer a rational alternative to ethnically inflected definitions, but in practice "a rich legacy of memories" would too often produce an aggressively racist nationalism over the next hundred years. Renan's reduction of the nation to a consensually recognized "spiritual principle" also raises a question for Europe's multi-ethnic states: what if a particular ethnicity does not consent to perpetuate a heritage shared with other ethnicities under the aegis of a nation? Is a nation as collective "soul" coterminous with the boundaries of a nation-state? In the aftermath of the Great War, Woodrow Wilson's benign liberal belief that "all nations had the right to self-determination" would bring these problems to the forefront of international politics.[22]

For T. S. Eliot, a Christian sociology of the nation, rooted in historical experience, offered a way of balancing the claims of the more particular and the more general within western societies. This balance centrally involves the Christian church. As Charles Ferrall notes, Eliot hoped cultural disintegration could be arrested "by maintaining a balance between a religion and its 'sects', that is between Rome and Canterbury and Canterbury and the various Protestant churches and chapels."[23] Ferrall is skeptical of Eliot's program for renewal, but rightly recognizes the Anglican *via media* as a model for his sense of cultural and religious balance. In "Lancelot Andrewes" (1926), Eliot praises the formation of the Elizabethan Church:

> In its persistence in finding a mean between Papacy and Presbytery the English Church under Elizabeth became something representative of the finest spirit of England of the time. It came to reflect not only the personality of Elizabeth herself, but the best community of her subjects of every rank.[24]

The "finest spirit of England" here intersects with "the best community" of English subjects, at precisely the point of achieving a mean between Roman universality and Protestant sectarianism. This "best community" anticipates, in embryonic form, the "community of Christians" Eliot calls for in *The Idea of a Christian Society*. If Eliot here comes close to Renan in defining a nation as "a soul, a spiritual principle," it is significant that he is characterizing the national church, rather than the nation itself. Although the Anglican Church under Elizabeth and James is "a masterpiece of ecclesiastical statesmanship," it is not identical with the state.[25] In Eliot's imagination, it will increasingly provide what Andrew John Miller calls "a transcendental reconciliation of institutional contingency and spiritual purity."[26] The Church of England thus functions as the ideal expression of English spirit and community, transmitting a specifically English form of orthodoxy while remaining institutionally responsive to the demands of English history. As such, the Church brings cultural unity to England. For Eliot, however, the Church of England is the local expression of a universal Church, which in turn has the potential to form a culturally united international community.

In his 1933 address to the Anglo-Catholic Summer School of Sociology, "Catholicism and International Order," Eliot characterizes the *via media* as "a way of mediation, but never, in those matters which permanently matter, a way of compromise."[27] The formula which enabled the Elizabethan Church to negotiate between competing forms of Christianity is offered up as "a way of mediation" in the twentieth century. Eliot's address offers a vision of religious unity that allows for cultural difference: "The only positive unification of the world, we believe, is religious unification; by which we do not mean simply universal submission to one world-wide ecclesiastical hierarchy, but cultural unity in religion— which is not the same thing as cultural uniformity."[28] Neither "simply universal submission" nor "cultural uniformity," Eliot's idea of "cultural unity in religion" is predicated on a Christianized world, but one in which cultural unity is a common faith informing diverse global cultures. As Eliot would later state in *Notes towards the Definition of Culture*, "[t]he ideal reunion of all Christians does not, of course, imply a *uniform* culture the world over: it implies simply a 'Christian culture' of which all local cultures should be variants—and they would and should vary widely indeed" (*CC*, 153). This cultural unity transcends the political divisions between nations, as it did during the European Middle Ages.

Eliot more explicitly addresses the question of Church and State in *The Idea of a Christian Society*. Considering the institutional means through which a Christian society might be realized in England, he argues that only the Church of England "which, by reason of its tradition, its organisation, and its relation in the past to the religious-social life of the people, is the one for our purpose—and that no Christianisation of England can take place without it" (*CC*, 37–8). He nonetheless recognizes that such a Church may be peculiarly vulnerable to the forces of nationalism (*CC*, 41). Paradoxically, Eliot claims this danger can be best avoided by a Church "which shall *aim at* comprehending the whole nation" (*CC*, 43). This inclusiveness allows for civic and religious life to complement each other, avoiding extreme nationalism through its affiliations with the broader Church:

> Unless it has that aim, we relapse into that conflict between citizenship and church-membership, between public and private morality, which today makes moral life so difficult for everyone, and which in turn provokes that craving for a simplified, monistic solution of statism or racism which the National Church can only combat if it recognises its position as part of the Universal Church. (*CC*, 43)

Even though the Church of England is celebrated by Eliot for its English particularity, this particularity needs to be balanced by an awareness of the "Universal Church."

Throughout his writings on Christian sociology, Eliot consistently returns to the need for balance. While rejecting Roman Catholicism as the best mode of Christian organization for Britain, he acknowledges its importance for the Anglican Church as a connection with the sources of European culture. Latin culture is to Anglicanism what Anglican culture is to the dissenting churches: "just as the culture of Protestant dissent would perish of inanition without the persistence of Anglican culture, so the maintenance of English culture is contingent upon the health of the culture of Latin Europe, and upon continuing to draw sustenance from that Latin culture" (*CC*, 149). With a common religious inheritance at its root, Eliot's vision of diverse European cultures drawing sustenance from the same Christian spring challenges the virulent nationalism of the 1930s. While Eliot's mode of political analysis drew him away from historical contingency, his social thought built upon a specifically Christian understanding of the development of European culture. A middle way, modeled on the historical experience of Anglicanism, in which common religious inheritance is balanced by local cultural particularity, seemed to Eliot a necessary measure to restore Europe's political and spiritual equilibrium.

NOTES

1. T. S. Eliot, "Towards a Christian Britain," *The Listener* (10 April, 1941): 575.
2. Eliot, "East Coker," *Collected Poems* (London: Faber, 1963), 202.
3. Eliot, "Last Words," *Criterion* 18 (January, 1939): 274.
4. Eliot, *Christianity and Culture* (New York: Harcourt Brace, 1976), 193. Hereafter cited parenthetically in the text as *CC*.
5. Michael North, *The Political Aesthetic of Yeats, Eliot, and Pound* (Cambridge: Cambridge University Press, 1991), 86.
6. Denis Donoghue, *Words Alone: The Poet T. S. Eliot* (New Haven: Yale University Press, 2000), 219.
7. Christopher Dawson, *The Age of the Gods* (London: Sheed and Ward, 1933), xiii.
8. Dawson, *The Making of Europe: An Introduction to the History of European Unity* (London: Sheed and Ward, 1933), 3–24.
9. Dawson, *The Judgement of Nations* (London: Sheed and Ward, 1942), 35.
10. Jason Harding, *The "Criterion": Cultural Politics and Periodical Networks in Inter-War Britain* (Oxford: Clarendon Press, 2002), 6.
11. E. J. Hobsbawm, *Nations and Nationalism Since 1780: Programme, Myth, Reality,* second ed. (Cambridge: Cambridge University Press, 1992), 132.
12. Ibid.
13. Quoted in Roger Kojecký, *T. S. Eliot's Social Criticism* (New York: Farrar, Straus and Giroux, 1972), 43.
14. Eliot, "Tradition and the Individual Talent," in *Selected Prose,* ed. Frank Kermode (London: Faber, 1975), 39.
15. Richard Shusterman, "The Concept of Tradition: Its Progress and Potential," in *T. S. Eliot,* ed. Harriet Davidson (London: Longman, 1999), 31.
16. Benedict Anderson, *Imagined Communities: Reflections on the Origin and Spread of Nationalism,* rev. ed. (London: Verso, 1991), 5.
17. Dawson, "T. S. Eliot and the Meaning of Culture," in *Dynamics of World History,* ed. John J. Molloy, third ed. (Wilmington, DE: ISI Books, 2002), 113.
18. Ernest Renan, "What Is a Nation?" trans. Martin Thom, in *Nation and Narration,* ed. Homi K. Bhabha (London: Routledge, 1990), 19.
19. Ibid.
20. Ibid., 13.
21. Ibid., 14.
22. Quoted in Margaret Macmillan, *Paris 1919: Six Months That Changed the World* (New York: Random House, 2003), 12.
23. Charles Ferrall, *Modernist Writing and Reactionary Politics* (Cambridge: Cambridge University Press, 2001), 109.
24. Eliot, "Lancelot Andrewes," in *Selected Prose,* ed. Frank Kermode (London: Faber, 1975), 179.
25. Ibid., 180.
26. Andrew Miller, "'Compassing Material Ends': T. S. Eliot, Christian Pluralism, and the Nation-State," *ELH* 67 (2000): 241.
27. Eliot, "Catholicism and International Order," *Christendom: A Journal of Christian Sociology* 3, no. 11 (Sept. 1933): 183–4.
28. Ibid., 177.

FOURTEEN

Beyond Politics: T. S. Eliot and Christopher Dawson on Religion and Culture

Benjamin G. Lockerd

"Eliot's reputation as a critic of society has been worse than his record" — so wrote Roger Kojecký at the beginning of his 1971 book, *T. S. Eliot's Social Criticism*.[1] Some forty years later, the situation has not changed appreciably, for T. S. Eliot's cultural criticism continues to be more maligned than studied. It is not uncommon to hear Eliot accused of having "flirted with fascism" and of having proposed the establishment of a theocratic state. When scholars make such insinuations, they inevitably identify Eliot's views with those of the anti-Semitic French reactionary Charles Maurras. In a well-informed essay, for instance, Kenneth Asher calls Maurras (without qualification) "the source" of Eliot's political ideas, asserting that "from beginning to end, Eliot's work, including both the poetry and the prose, reveals itself to have been shaped by Maurras's advocacy of an endangered Latin tradition and all that it entailed."[2] There is no doubt that Maurras was a major influence on Eliot at an early period, but over time (beginning in the late 1920s) the prime influence on his cultural thought came from a wiser source, the British Catholic historian Christopher Dawson. Maurras raised the banner, as Asher says, of the Latin tradition, but he ultimately rejected the religious core of that tradition. He valued the hierarchical structure and traditional authority of the Catholic Church but was himself a non-believer whose motto was "politique d'abord," politics before all else. In 1926 and 1927, Pope Pius XI placed several of his works on the Index and condemned the *Action Française* movement. Though Eliot at that time wrote an essay in *The*

Criterion in support of Maurras, the latter's influence over him faded. At about the same time, Eliot came to know the work of Dawson, who increasingly became his primary mentor on cultural issues. Dawson, in stark contrast to Maurras, argued that religion is integral to culture. Following Dawson, Eliot maintained that religious consciousness should ideally permeate all the elements of cultural life. However, again following Dawson, he makes it clear that his ideal state would not be a theocracy but would involve a creative tension between church and state. Under Dawson's influence—or perhaps we could say in collaboration with Dawson—Eliot developed a balanced, coherent, and remarkably flexible cultural theory that consistently put forward their contention concerning the necessary integration (but not identification) of civil and spiritual authorities.

The central thrust of Eliot's cultural criticism is to envision the possibility of unifying the cultural life of a people by bringing the religious and civil spheres into dynamic complementarity with each other. As he slowly worked out his cultural theory, Eliot found support for his developing ideas in the writings of Dawson. Kojecký mentions Dawson in passing but does not give him an important role.[3] In fact, only one critic has previously pointed out the importance of Dawson as an influence on Eliot. Russell Kirk, in his 1971 book on Eliot, declares that "Of social thinkers in his own time, none influenced Eliot more than Dawson."[4] Kirk does not develop this important assertion at any length, however, and later Eliot scholars have neglected to follow Kirk's lead and explore Dawson's work in relation to Eliot. This chapter is an attempt to begin that exploration.

Christopher Dawson was born in 1889, just a year after the birth of T. S. Eliot. His father was an Anglo-Catholic, and Dawson later converted to Roman Catholicism. He wrote some twenty books and came to be regarded as one of the leading historians of his time.[5] In a recent book that gives an excellent overview of Dawson's life and work, Bradley Birzer notes that Henry Luce devoted his editorial column in one issue of *Life* (March 16, 1959) to praising Dawson's ideas. Luce went so far as to order copies of Dawson's latest book for all the editors at *Time*.[6] This small incident gives some idea of how prominent—and even popular—the British historian had become by that time. Nevertheless, he never held an academic appointment at one of the leading universities (until, near the end of his life, he became the first Professor of Roman Catholic Studies at Harvard), and after his death in 1970, Dawson's work sank into obscurity. By the end of the century, many of his books were out of print and difficult to find. Perhaps his neglect among academic historians accounts in part for the fact that literary scholars have not taken account of his influence on Eliot.

In the late 1920s, Dawson's first two books were reviewed in Eliot's journal, *The Criterion*.[7] The reviewer, H. J. Massingham, acknowledged the learning and genius of Dawson's work but was not particularly sympathetic to his central ideas. At the end of his review of *Progress and Religion*, Massingham accurately paraphrases Dawson's thesis but rejects it:

> The only way to save modern Europe, writes Mr. Dawson, is to replace the old ideals of material success which have alienated the best minds in the community by the religious impulse. The only trouble is—what does he mean? He seems to mean the restoration of 'historical Christianity', a sufficiently vague term. But the heart of the matter is surely the restoration of human and natural values, an essentially religious concept but one not bound to any particular formula.[8]

Massingham's alternative is hardly less vague, and it is essentially the same as Irving Babbitt's humanism, an approach that both Eliot and Dawson admired but found wanting.

The editor of *The Criterion* clearly had a higher estimate of Dawson's work than his reviewer, for in August of 1929 Eliot wrote to Dawson asking him to contribute an essay. Dawson's response was an article entitled "The End of an Age," which Eliot published in 1930, and in this piece Dawson sums up many of the interpretations of history, philosophy, and culture that he shared with the editor of the journal.[9] The age that was ending, according to Dawson's article, began with Renaissance humanism and developed through Enlightenment rationalism and the French Revolution to the scientific materialism of the late nineteenth century, when "The goal of the Liberal Enlightenment and Revolution had been reached and Europe at last possessed a completely secularized culture." The churches were still given a privileged position, "But they held this position only on the condition that they did not interfere with the reign of Mammon" (387). Not only religion but the very humanism that had inspired the beginning of this age was being pushed aside. Humanism had increasingly cut itself off from the supernatural and now found itself subject to rationalism, empiricism, and skepticism. Its glorification of the individual had paradoxically called forth "the new bureaucratic state" (390). Thus, "humanism by its own inner development is eventually brought to deny itself and to pass away into its opposite" (391). Humanism without religion has come to deny the human, along with the old moral truths based on religious beliefs. Lacking an ability to make any metaphysical claims, European culture has given itself to a mechanistic worldview in which the only choice seems to be between two types of materialism: "The greatest danger here is not that we should actively adopt the Bolshevik cult of Marxian materialism, but rather that we should yield ourselves passively to a practical materialization of culture after the American pattern" (393). The only genuine alternative to a culture founded on mechanistic assumptions is one founded on religious belief. The "reign of the machine . . . can only be conquered by the spiritual power which is the creative element in every culture" (396). Here Dawson introduces one of the keynotes of his historical theory, the claim that it is not only material but spiritual forces that form cultural life.

At the end of his essay, Dawson points to the failure of humanistic individualism but maintains that Marxist collectivism is not (as many intellectuals of the time believed) the only way to prevent a complete atomization of society: "The choice that is actually before us is not be-tween an individualistic humanism and some form of collectivism, but between a collectivism that is purely mechanistic and one which is spiritual" (400). The communal spirit of Christianity may be recovered in "a return to spiritual solidarity" (a phrase prophetic of the Catholic Solidarity movement in Poland that helped end the domination of communism in Eastern Europe sixty years later). Dawson hastens to add that his call for a Christian renewal is not merely nostalgia and "does not necessarily involve a retrogression of culture" but may in fact lead to a genuinely new age of creative activity (400). As in all his writings, he makes it clear that an attempt to return to a medieval order would be foolish; he is calling for a renewal, not a return. This essay is a fine synopsis of Dawson's work, though my summary does not do it justice because much of the value of his writing is in the vast range of his historical references and in his eloquent and metaphorically rich expression. The major points of this essay are also the touchstones of Eliot's cultural criticism, where we find the same history of ideas, the same emphasis on the effects of secularism, and a similar proposal of a renewed integration of Christianity and culture.

Both writers give serious consideration to the ideas of Eliot's old Harvard professor, Irving Babbitt, who opposed the same tendencies and who advocated a type of humanism that acknowledged traditional wisdom as the answer to modern anti-authoritarian humanism.[10] In "The End of an Age," Dawson claims that "the disappearance of the Christian element in humanism has involved the loss of its vital quality" and notes that "this is admitted by the protagonist of the new humanism, Professor Babbitt, who fully realizes that every culture is a spiritual order and that humanism is only possible if we throw over naturalism and return to spiritual principles" (398). Dawson doubts, however, that Babbitt's new humanism will answer, for Babbitt "is unwilling to make the complete return to metaphysical and religious foundations. He prefers a kind of spiritual positivism based on the accumulated moral wisdom of the great historic traditions—Greek, Buddhist and Confucian" (398–99). Babbitt clings to "the critical and individualistic attitude" of the old humanism and distrusts "organized religion," but, in Dawson's view, religion cannot be integral to culture if it is not organized.

Eliot had already expressed a very similar analysis of Babbitt's ideas in "The Humanism of Irving Babbitt" (1927).[11] Eliot strongly agrees with Babbitt's critique (in his book *Democracy and Leadership*) of what he calls the "humanitarian" idea, which projects a sentimental love of humanity but denies the spiritual essence of humanity, thereby devaluing individual human beings and promoting utilitarian solutions that treat humanity as a herd. However, "Mr. Babbitt makes it very clear, here and there throughout the book, that he is unable to take the religious view—that is to say that he cannot accept any dogma or revelation; and that humanism is the *alternative* to religion" (*SE*, 420). Though Babbitt insists on the spiritual dimension and wishes to draw on the collective spiritual wisdom of the ages, he declines the dogmatic claims of any particular religion and is therefore not far enough from the position he is opposing: "the humanitarian has suppressed the properly human, and is left with the animal; the humanist has suppressed the divine, and is left with a human element which may quickly descend again to the animal from which he has sought to raise it" (*SE*, 420–21). Near the end of this piece, however, Eliot expresses a balanced view of the matter that values the critical thinking in Babbitt's humanism. The danger on one side is a collapse into the "humanitarian" idea, but the danger on the other side would be a "collapse . . . into a Catholicism *without* the element of humanism and criticism, which would be a Catholicism of despair" (*SE*, 426). This passage expresses forcefully the tendency in Eliot's thought that counters what might become a call for a simple return to the medieval organization of culture. Dawson, though he distrusts Babbitt's "critical and individualistic attitude," is fundamentally in agreement with Eliot on this crucial point: any simplistic and uncritical attempt to return to the Christian culture of the past would be disastrous.

During the 1930s, Dawson's subsequent books were reviewed in *The Criterion*, and he contributed several reviews and articles.[12] Eliot eventually wrote two books of cultural criticism, and in both he explicitly acknowledged the importance of Dawson's work to his own ideas. In his Preface to *The Idea of a Christian Society* (1939), Eliot acknowledges, "I owe a great deal to a number of recent books," and the first one he names is "Mr. Christopher Dawson's *Beyond Politics*"—followed by books by Middleton Murry and V. A. Demant.[13] In the Preface to *Notes towards the Definition of Culture* nearly a decade later (1948), Eliot writes, "Throughout this study, I recognise a particular debt to the writings of Canon V. A. Demant, Mr. Christopher Dawson, and the late Professor Karl Mannheim."[14] Not surprisingly, given these acknowledgments, Eliot's thinking in these major works of cultural criticism is indeed very close to Dawson's. The historian has worked the ideas out more carefully and consistently than the poet, so reexamining Eliot's pronouncements along with Dawson's tends to clarify what the former was aiming at.

In these works, Eliot argues that culture must be grounded in religion, but he also claims that culture must be grounded in nature, and that nature and religion are intimately related. "We may say," Eliot writes, "that religion, as distinguished from modern paganism, implies a life in conformity with nature. It may be observed that the natural life and the supernatural life have a conformity to each other which neither has with the mechanistic life" (*Idea*, 61). By "modern paganism" he seems to mean secularism. The claim that the natural and supernatural are in conformity may seem surprising but is based on the connection of sacramental religion to physical objects and their symbolic meaning. The "mechanistic life" of the modern world is seen by Eliot as a result of the Cartesian split and the scientific revolution, which have stripped nature of its sanctity and significance, allowing us to manipulate it without limit for our purposes. Eliot goes on to say that "a wrong attitude towards nature implies, somewhere, a wrong attitude towards God," and adds, "it would be well for us to face the permanent conditions upon which God allows us to live upon this planet" (*Idea*, 62). Dawson similarly points out (in his 1949 book *Religion and Culture*) that "During the last century or two the world of culture has grown until it has subjugated the world of nature and pushed back the frontiers of the superhuman spiritual world beyond the boundaries of consciousness." [15] He goes on to speak of "the attitude of the primitive farmer to the earth and the fruits of the earth. However low is the level of his culture, man cannot but recognize the existence of laws and rhythms and cycles of change in the life of nature in which his own life is involved." These are not merely mechanical phenomena but "divine mysteries to be adored with trembling" (*R&C*, 41). Dawson is speaking partly from his own childhood experience in Yorkshire, where "religion was not simply concerned with the pious moralities which held such a prominent place in Victorian books for children, but stood close to that wonderful non-human world of the river and the mountain which I found around me." [16] He is also influenced, as was Eliot, by his profound interest in the new field of anthropology, and he maintains that "primitive man in his weakness and ignorance is nearer to the basic realities of human existence than the self-satisfied rationalist who is confident that he has mastered the secrets of the universe" (*R&C*, 28). The world created by this rationalist sounds remarkably like that of *The Waste Land*: "In so far as he is content to live within this world of his own creation—the artificially lit and hygienically conditioned City of Man—he is living precariously on a relatively superficial level of existence and consciousness, and the higher he builds his tower of civilization the more top-heavy it becomes" (*R&C*, 28). This is Eliot's "Unreal City," with its "falling towers."

The technological age had created a mass culture that both authors found troubling. People in England in this period were congratulating themselves on not being subject to totalitarian regimes such as those in Germany and Russia, but Eliot and Dawson were not so sure that English democracy offered sufficient protection. In *Beyond Politics* (the book Eliot singles out for mention) Dawson insists that

. . . it is not enough for us to repudiate these evils in principle and to congratulate ourselves on the moral superiority of western democracy. For democracy . . . is no safeguard against such things: indeed in so far as democracy involves the standardization and mechanization of culture and the supremacy of the mass over the individual, it is a positive danger.[17]

The "greatest danger that threatens modern civilization," he claims, "is its degeneration into a hedonistic mass civilization of the cinema, the picture paper and the dance hall, where the individual, the family and the nation dissolve into a human herd without personality, or traditions or beliefs" (*BP*, 78–79). Eliot (who liked ragtime, Marie Lloyd, Groucho Marx, and other popular entertainments) might have been a little more favorably disposed toward some elements of popular culture, but he agreed that mass modern culture, for all its claims of individual freedom, tends to reduce humanity to a herd: "the tendency of unlimited industrialism is to create bodies of men and women—of all classes—detached from tradition, alienated from religion, and susceptible to mass suggestion: in other words, a mob. And a mob will be no less a mob if it is well fed, well clothed, well housed, and well disciplined" (*Idea*, 21). The mob Eliot speaks of is precisely what Dawson has in mind when he worries about the possibility of a "democratic totalitarianism." For instance, at the beginning of *Beyond Politics* Dawson writes, "The forces that make for social uniformity and the mechanization of culture are no less strong in England and the United States than in Germany and Italy, so that we might expect to see the rise of a democratic totalitarianism which would make the same universal claims on the life of the individual as the totalitarian dictatorships of the Continent" (*BP*, 3). In an essay published in *The Criterion* (in 1934) entitled "Religion and the Totalitarian State," Dawson speaks at length about the hostility toward religion in both the communist and fascist totalitarian regimes, but he also warns of the possibility of a seemingly benign version that might develop in democratic nations: "the same forces that make for governmental control and social uniformity are at work here also and in the U.S.A." Unlike the fascist and communist systems, "its ideals would probably be humanitarian, democratic and pacific. Nevertheless it will make the same universal claims as the Totalitarian State in Russia and Germany and it will be equally unwilling to tolerate any division of spiritual allegiance. . . . The new state will be universal and omnicompetent. It will mould the mind and guide the life of its citizens from the cradle to the grave."[18] In his 1935 book *Religion and the Modern State*, Dawson puts this view even more strongly:

It may, I think, even be argued that Communism in Russia, National Socialism in Germany, and Capitalism and Liberal Democracy in the Western countries are really three forms of the same thing, and that they are all moving by different but parallel paths to the same goal, which is the mechanization of human life and the complete subordination of the individual to the state and to the economic process.[19]

He adds that there are of course differences and good reasons to prefer Liberal Democracy to the other systems but insists that it cannot be regarded as a "final solution." Britain's strongest hope, Dawson says in *Beyond Politics*, is in its tradition of limited government (*BP*, 13).

The problem of modern secularized and mechanized society is not only its relation to nature but to human nature—a concept that is explicitly rejected by many modern theorists, such as the behavioral psychologists. Eliot decries "The kind of political theory which has arisen in quite modern times" because it "is less concerned with human nature, which it is inclined to treat as something which can always be re-fashioned to fit whatever political form is regarded as most desirable. . . . It too often inculcates a belief in a future inflexibly determined and at the same time in a future which we are wholly free to shape as we like" (*Notes*, 90). This brilliantly captures the modern paradox, the existentialist claim that we are free to reinvent ourselves, coupled with the contradictory materialist doctrine that we have no free will because our behavior is totally determined by outside forces. These are the two horns of the modern dilemma—represented in recent literary criticism by the existentialist freeplay of the deconstructionists on one hand and the reductive deterministic materialism of the Marxists on the other. What they have in common is the assertion that there is no transcendent meaning. The traditional view of human nature has it that we are quite limited beings but that within our sphere we can choose for ourselves. The concept of human nature is fundamental to the philosophy of natural law, which Dawson mentions: "Now behind the philosophic idea of natural law, there is the much older theological idea that law is not a purely political or social creation, but requires a divine sanction and origin in order to make it truly law" (*R&C*, 154). Many modern legal theorists tend to be positivists, assuming that law is always merely an arbitrary cultural creation decided by power politics. The law is thus regarded as infinitely malleable and controlled strictly by the Nietzschean will to power.

The central idea of all Dawson's writing was the integral relationship between culture and religion. He repeatedly expressed his doubt that a completely secular culture could survive. In a chapter of *Religion and Culture* on the priestly class in various cultures, he concludes,

> It is, however, questionable whether a culture which has once possessed . . . a spiritual class or order that has been the guardian of a sacred tradition of culture . . . can dispense with it without becoming impoverished and disorientated. This is what has actually occurred in the secularization of modern Western culture, and men have been more or less aware of it ever since the beginning of the last century. (*R&C*, 106)

Noting that the intellectual class has replaced the priesthood, he maintains that this substitution has been a failure, giving much the same analysis that he had earlier stated in his essay in *The Criterion*:

> For the intellectuals who have succeeded the priests as the guardians of the higher tradition of Western culture have been strong only in their negative work of criticism and disintegration. They have failed to provide an integrated system of principles and values which could unify modern society, and consequently they have proved unable to resist the non-moral, inhuman and irrational forces which are destroying the humanist no less than the Christian traditions of Western culture. (*R&C*, 106)

The relation between religion and culture is the central idea in both of Eliot's books on the subject, too. At the beginning of *Notes towards the Definition of Culture*, for instance, he says, "The first important assertion is that no culture has appeared or developed except together with a religion." (13). He goes so far as to say that a culture is "essentially, the incarnation (so to speak) of the religion of a people" (27) and states explicitly that he means to combat the erroneous idea "that culture can be preserved, extended and developed in the absence of religion" (28). At the end of the book he declares, "I do not believe that the culture of Europe could survive the complete disappearance of the Christian Faith. And I am convinced of that, not merely because I am a Christian myself, but as a student of social biology. If Christianity goes, the whole of our culture goes. Then you must start painfully again, and you cannot put on a new culture ready made" (126). Eliot and Dawson deny that culture can be effectively created, rejecting the Enlightenment notion of social engineering. Religious tradition is experienced as a given, an objective symbolic reality integrally connected with human nature and the natural world, and fundamentally constitutive of (not derivative of) culture.

Dawson argues for the primacy and irreducibility of religion in cultural formation, taking issue with the modern assumption that religion is a by-product of material culture. *The Making of Europe* (1932), his groundbreaking study of the formation of European culture in the Middle Ages (one of the first books, by the way, to acknowledge the importance of Islamic civilization to European culture), begins by declaring that the process of cultural formation in Europe was "not the product of blind material and economic forces."[20] History is often moved, he frequently maintains, by spiritual revelations rather than economic interests. For instance, near the end of *Progress and Religion* (1931), Dawson writes, "Europe is not . . . a group of peoples held together by a common type of material culture, it is a spiritual society which owes its very existence to the religious tradition which for a thousand years moulded the beliefs, the ideals, and the institutions of the European peoples."[21] Here he implicitly contradicts the Marxist claim that all cultural phenomena (including

literature, art, and religion) are merely epiphenomena, entirely reducible
to the material forces that are their foundation (*Grundlage*). Marx writes
in *The German Ideology*, for example, "The phantoms formed in the human
brain are also, necessarily, sublimates of their material life-process, which
is empirically verifiable and bound to material premises."[22] All Dawson's
works assert the opposite, that the spiritual life of human culture creates
its material manifestations:

> We are only just beginning to understand how intimately and pro-
> foundly the vitality of a society is bound up with its religion. It is the
> religious impulse which supplies the cohesive force which unifies a
> society and a culture. The great civilizations of the world do not pro-
> duce the great religions as a kind of cultural by-product; in a very real
> sense the great religions are the foundations on which the great civil-
> izations rest. A society which has lost its religion becomes sooner or
> later a society which has lost its culture. (*P&R*, 232–33)

Cultures are formed, he maintains, not only by material circumstances
but by sudden spiritual insights.[23] For instance, "The experience of Mo-
hammed in the cave of Mount Hira, when he saw human life as transitory as the beat of a gnat's wing in comparison with the splendour and
power of the Divine Unity, has shaped the existence of a great part of the
human race ever since" (*P&R*, 77).

Dawson, with his vast knowledge of all cultures and periods, gives at
one point a striking example of secularized government not from his own
time but from ancient China. He describes a society dominated by "the
new school of Legal Positivists—the Fa Hia—which inspired the brilliant
and ruthless statesmen who created the Empire of Ts'in in the third century B.C. They taught that Virtue is Power and that states acquire Power
not by correct ritual and traditional morality but by the political instru-
ments of war and law" (*R&C*, 169). Dawson notes that "this doctrine of
the Chinese positivists was as completely irreligious as that of any school
of thought in any age or country." What was the result of this experiment? He concludes chillingly, "The application of the principles of the
legal positivists to practical politics produced a predatory imperialism
which deluged China in blood," leaving it to his readers to draw the
analogy with the Nietzschean legal positivists of the modern era (*R&C*,
170).

Another problem both Eliot and Dawson saw with the increasingly
secularized culture of Europe was the tendency to cut itself off from the
past. The progressivist dogma that arose in the Enlightenment regards all
early thought as mere superstition and nonsense. The religious mentality,
on the other hand, regards the traditions of the past as a prime source of
wisdom. Dawson quotes Edmund Burke as saying that society is not an
artificial construct but a spiritual community, "a partnership in all science, a partnership in all art, a partnership in every virtue and in all

perfection. As the ends of such a partnership cannot be obtained in many generations, it becomes a partnership not only between those who are living, but between those who are living, those who are dead and those who are yet to be born" (quoted in *BP*, 25). Eliot uses very similar words when speaking of the central role of the family in society: "But when I speak of the family, I have in mind a bond which embraces a longer period of time than this: a piety towards the dead, however obscure, and a solicitude for the unborn, however remote" (*Notes*, 42). Thus, the historical sense itself tends to be lost in the shift from a traditional to a progressive idea of culture. Eliot had been at pains to promote the importance of the historical sense and of tradition from the earliest period of his career, and these concepts feature, of course, in his famous essay of 1917, "Tradition and the Individual Talent." In Dawson's work he found verification of his own thinking, along with an array of historical examples from all cultures and times.

Both writers argued that every culture will have either a traditional religion or some ideology acting as a religious substitute. Dawson maintained that when a society attempts to become secularized, as the Russian society was doing, the religious impulse will still be powerfully expressed, though in a perverted and destructive manner: "When the prophets are silent and society no longer possesses any channel of communication with the divine world, the way to the lower depths is still open and man's frustrated spiritual powers will find their outlet in the unlimited will to power and destruction" (*R&C*, 83). He saw virtually the same thing happening in the fascist states, asserting that the militaristic brutality of the Nazi state in Germany was secondary to its attempt to replace religion at the core of the culture:

> . . . the essential characteristic of National Socialism is to be found rather in its attempt to create an ideology which will be the soul of the new State and which will co-ordinate the new resources of propaganda and mass suggestion in the interest of the national community. This is the most deliberate attempt that has been made since the French Revolution to fill the vacuum which has been created by the disappearance of the religious background of European culture and the secularization of social life by nineteenth century liberalism. It is a new form of natural religion, not the rationalized natural religion of the eighteenth century, but a mystical neo-paganism which worships the forces of nature and life and the spirit of the race. . . . (*BP*, 81)

Eliot makes the point dramatically in *The Idea of a Christian Society* soon after: "If you will not have God (and He is a jealous God) you should pay your respects to Hitler or Stalin" (*Idea*, 63). It happens that Dawson had the opportunity to lecture the Nazis at the beginning of their regime, for in November of 1932 he spoke at a conference in Rome organized by the Royal Academy of Italy and attended by the recently elected president of

the Reichstag, Hermann Goering. Dawson's talk was provocatively entitled "Interracial Cooperation as a Factor in European Culture," and in it
he offered scathing denunciations of "modern pan-racial theorists . . .
who infuse an element of racial hatred into the political and economic
rivalries of European peoples." One comment of his was aimed directly
at Goering's party: "If we were to subtract from German culture, for
example, all the contributions made by men who were not of pure Nordic
type, German culture would be incalculably impoverished."[24] Christina
Scott (Dawson's daughter and biographer) tells this story and goes on to
say that Goering was called away from the conference not long after
hearing Dawson's talk by a telegram informing him of Von Papen's resignation as Chancellor, which opened the way for Hitler. It makes a great
difference indeed to be aware that Dawson's influence on Eliot's political
thought was at this period superseding that of Maurras, who would become a Vichy collaborationist.

Now, it begins to sound as if Eliot and Dawson favored some sort of
medieval theocratic government, but both reject unequivocally such a
simplification. In *Beyond Politics*, Dawson declares, "it is to-day impossible to return to the undifferentiated unity of mediaeval culture" (*BP*,
20). In almost identical words, Eliot acknowledges that the Christian Society he envisions "can neither be mediaeval in form, nor be modelled on
the seventeenth century or any previous age" (*Idea*, 25). Dawson insists
that religion must be at the heart of a healthy culture, but he warns
against a total identification of religion and culture:

> On the other hand, the identification of religion with the particular
> cultural synthesis which has been achieved at a definite time and space
> by the action of historical forces is fatal to the universal character of
> religious truth. It is indeed a kind of idolatry—the substitution of an
> image made by man for the eternal transcendent reality. If this identifi-
> cation is carried to its extreme conclusion, the marriage of religion and
> culture is equally fatal to either partner. . . (*R&C*, 206)

Eliot states this truth similarly: "We know from our reading of history,
that a certain tension between Church and State is desirable. When
Church and State fall out completely, it is ill with the commonwealth;
and when Church and State get on too well together, there is something
wrong with the Church" (*Idea*, 91). In another passage, Eliot remarks, "it
must be kept in mind that even in a Christian society as well organised as
we can conceive possible in this world, the limit would be that our temporal and spiritual life should be harmonised: the temporal and spiritual
would never be identified" (*Idea*, 54–55). Thus Dawson and Eliot opposed
simplistic solutions to the Church-State tension, regardless of which side
proposed them: they would accept neither the radical secularization of
the political sphere advocated by secular liberalism nor the theocratic
state proposed by some overzealous religious leaders.[25]

Dawson emphasizes that religion is not simply (what it is often called today) an ideology seeking for control of a society. Religion is rather an encounter with the divine, a partial revelation of truths beyond our understanding and control—and thus it can never be a simple political ideology. Christianity came to the Roman Empire, Dawson writes (in phrases that again seem to echo *The Waste Land*), "not as an ideology which should provide a basis for social reconstruction and reform, but as a new light appearing suddenly in a dark place. . . . This new word was of a different order to the philosophies and ideologies of men. It recreated the world from within, silently and irresistibly filling the waste places of the human soul which had been left derelict in the external advance of material civilization" (*BP*, 88–89). These two thinkers agree, then, that religion debases itself if it attempts to dominate civil society entirely. As Dawson puts it near the end of *Beyond Politics*, "The Church is no human society, but she is the channel by which divine life flows into human society and her essential task is the sanctification of humanity as a whole in its corporate as well as in its individual activities" (*BP*, 134).

Nevertheless, Dawson's emphasis on the Church's role in "corporate" (i.e. communal) activities as well as individual ones contradicts a secularist notion that was already frequently asserted in his time—that religion is a purely private matter and should not intrude in the public sphere. This simple-minded solution to the tension between Church and State is firmly rejected by both Dawson and Eliot. The former states (in his typically lively style), "to treat religion as a purely individual and personal matter is to deprive it of actuality and to degrade it to a lower level of value and potency. To keep religion out of public life is to shut it up in a stuffy Victorian back drawing-room with the aspidistras and the antimacassars, when the streets are full of life and youth" (*BP*, 104). A few pages later Dawson asserts, "It is no longer possible for religion to confine itself to the inner world of the individual conscience and private religious experience, any more than it is possible for the State to confine itself to its functions as the guardian of public order" (*BP*, 114). Eliot expresses himself on the subject in nearly identical terms:

> The Liberal notion that religion was a matter of private belief and of conduct in private life, and that there is no reason why Christians should not be able to accommodate themselves to any world which treats them good-naturedly, is becoming less and less tenable. . . . The problem of leading a Christian life in a non-Christian society is now very present to us. . . . It is the problem constituted by our implication in a network of institutions from which we cannot dissociate ourselves: institutions the operation of which appears no longer neutral, but non-Christian. And for the Christian who is not conscious of his dilemma— and he is in the majority—he is becoming more and more de-Christianised by all sorts of unconscious pressure: paganism holds all the most valuable advertising space. . . . In the modern world, it may turn out

that the most intolerable thing for Christians is to be tolerated. (*Idea*, 21–23)

The healthy Christian society must not be a theocratic state, but it must express its Christian principles publicly and legislatively. Eliot goes so far as to say this: "We must abandon the notion that the Christian should be content with freedom of cultus, and with suffering no worldly disabilities on account of his faith. However bigoted the announcement may sound, the Christian can be satisfied with nothing less than a Christian organisation of society—which is not the same thing as a society consisting exclusively of devout Christians" (*Idea*, 33–34). Such a statement is indeed likely to be taken today as merely an expression of bigotry and intolerance, but it should be read in the context of Eliot's repeated insistence that he does not advocate a complete dominance of the civil authority by the religious. He is not imagining a pure, monolithic Christian utopia.

In fact, even as Eliot and Dawson called for the renewal of Christian culture, they acknowledged that if such a renewal were to take place it would not create a perfect society. As Eliot says, "It is very easy for speculation on a possible Christian order in the future to tend to come to rest in a kind of apocalyptic vision of a golden age of virtue. But we have to remember that the Kingdom of Christ on earth will never be realised, and also that it is always being realised; we must remember that whatever reform or revolution we carry out, the result will always be a sordid travesty of what human society should be—though the world is never left wholly without glory" (*Idea*, 59). Perhaps Eliot is thinking partly of mistakes made by his own ancestors attempting to establish a reformed Christian society in New England. In any case, he remembers that his entire conservative approach (which began with the anti-Romantic ideas of Irving Babbitt, Paul Elmer More, and T. E. Hulme) is based on a belief in Original Sin and the imperfectability of mankind—a limitation which applies to religious leaders as well as to secular ones. He fully acknowledges the reality that a religious organization of society, though desirable, cannot perfect human culture and can, at best, create a "sordid travesty" of the ideal society. Dawson states the same caveat: "we have no right to expect that Christian principles will work in practice in the simple way that a political system may work. The Christian order is a supernatural order. It has its own principles and its own laws which are not those of the visible world and which may often seem to contradict them. Its victories may be found in apparent defeat and its defeats in material success" (*BP*, 127). His words here are quite similar to those of Eliot in his 1927 essay on F. H. Bradley: "there is no such thing as a Lost Cause because there is no such thing as a Gained Cause. We fight for lost causes because we know that our defeat and dismay may be the preface to our successors' victory, though that victory itself will be temporary; we fight rather to keep something alive than in the expectation that anything will triumph."[26] Eliot, like Dawson, had too much of the historical sense to fall under the spell of millenarian fantasies.

Eliot sometimes felt it more likely that the religious renewal would not happen and that a new dark age would ensue. We are, he proclaimed, "destroying our ancient edifices to make ready the ground upon which the barbarian nomads of the future will encamp in their mechanised caravans" (*Notes*, 111). Yet he was not without hope even with that prospect: "The World is trying the experiment of attempting to form a civilized but non-Christian mentality. The experiment will fail; but we must be very patient in awaiting its collapse; meanwhile redeeming the time: so that the Faith may be preserved alive through the dark ages before us; to renew and rebuild civilization, and save the World from suicide."[27] Dawson and Eliot were not much inclined toward optimistic predictions of cultural regeneration, but neither were they much inclined to despair. Both believed that the human spirit was naturally given to religious inspiration so that continual spiritual renewal was certain, even in the most unlikely circumstances. At the conclusion of *Religion and Culture*, Dawson urges a reintegration of the material and spiritual forces divorced by the Cartesian dualism of the modern world: "We are faced with a spiritual conflict of the most acute kind, a sort of social schizophrenia which divides the soul of society between a non-moral will to power served by inhuman techniques and a religious faith and a moral idealism which have no power to influence human life. There must be a return to unity — a spiritual integration of culture—if mankind is to survive" (*R&C*, 217).

A fresh examination of Eliot's cultural criticism in light of Dawson's influence requires the correction of some mistaken assumptions commonly found in studies of Eliot's social thought. Eliot has often been regarded as an abstract thinker with little sympathy for the natural world, but it appears that his sacramental theology involved a pervasive sense that the natural and supernatural were integrally connected. He subscribed to a view that would today be called Christian environmentalism. His surprising statement in *The Idea of a Christian Society* is worth quoting again: "a wrong attitude towards nature implies, somewhere, a wrong attitude towards God" (62).

Eliot has also been called a crypto-fascist (and sometimes simply a fascist), but he was, in fact, an early and consistent opponent of fascism. No one who reads his commentaries in *The Criterion* can think of him as a fascist sympathizer, as Russell Kirk and Roger Kojecký showed some time ago and Jason Harding has demonstrated more recently.[28] Eliot objected to fascism, but on religious grounds that also led him to object to communism and to the secular materialism of the western democracies. On the eve of World War II, he writes, "The fundamental objection to fascist doctrine, the one which we conceal from ourselves because it might condemn ourselves as well, is that it is pagan" (*Idea*, 20).

The charge of fascism leveled at Eliot has been maintained largely by exaggerating the influence of Charles Maurras on his political views. Maurras was indeed important to Eliot in his early years. Eliot was introduced while at Harvard to Maurras's ant-Romantic, anti-Revolutionary views by Irving Babbitt, who shared those views. Eliot derived his declaration of royalism, classicism, and Catholicism from Maurras—but also, as Ronald Schuchard shows, from T. E. Hulme.[29] It does not follow, however, that Eliot followed Maurras into the latter's increasingly ugly program of virulent anti-Semitism and incitement of street violence. Asher's insistence that Eliot never distanced himself from Maurras is surely wrong.[30] Peter Dale Scott quotes from a 1919 piece in the *Athenaeum* in which Eliot writes of Maurras's "intemperate and fanatical spirit" and also cites a letter to *TLS* in 1920, in which Eliot agrees with Julien Benda's claim that Maurras is a romantic.[31] In 1927, shortly after adopting Maurras's triple declaration, Eliot strongly qualified his admiration. In "The Humanism of Irving Babbitt" (an essay Asher does not cite), Eliot wishes Babbitt could bring himself to ground his humanism in religious belief: "His influence might thus join that of another philosopher—Charles Maurras—and might, indeed, correct some of the extravagances of that writer."[32] Kojecký quotes an unpublished 1930 letter to the editor of the *Bookman* in which Eliot declared that ". . . there are far grosser positive errors and far greater dangers in the doctrine of Maurras than in that of Babbitt."[33]

Asher cites as evidence of persistent adherence to the Maurrasian program Eliot's 1948 statement calling Maurras "a sort of Virgil who led us to the gates of the temple," failing to put this into the inevitable Dantean context (27). Eliot places Virgil squarely in that context at the end of his lecture to the Virgil Society in 1944. He speaks of Virgil as "the great ghost who guided Dante's pilgrimage: who, as it was his function to lead Dante towards a vision he could never himself enjoy, led Europe towards the Christian culture which he could never know; and who, speaking his final words in the new Italian speech, said in farewell . . . 'Son, the temporal fire and the eternal, hast / thou seen, and art come to a place where I / of myself, discern no further.'"[34] Just as the pagan poet Virgil could lead Dante only to the threshold of the earthly paradise in the *Purgatorio* but no further (after which he was constrained to return to his place in Limbo), Maurras had brought Eliot to the gates of the temple but had remained behind when Eliot entered. Asher's attempt to make Maurras "the source" of Eliot's political thought requires him to misread this statement and to ignore others. In fact there were many other sources—S. T. Coleridge, Irving Babbitt, T. E. Hulme, Paul Elmer More, V. A. Demant, Karl Mannheim, Jacques Maritain, and others—but chief among them in Eliot's mature thought was Christopher Dawson.[35]

In "T. S. Eliot on the Meaning of Culture," a review of *Notes towards the Definition of Culture*, Dawson praises Eliot's clear definition of culture and his insistence that "a culture is the incarnation of a religion."[36] He then emphasizes, however, an Augustinian distinction which must be made between culture and religion, owing to the transcendent nature of religious experience: Dawson writes that "the higher religions, and especially Christianity, involve a certain dualism from the nature of their spiritual claims" (113). He is gently reminding Eliot that while religion is integral to culture it also transcends it. He adds, however, that "No one understands this better than Mr. Eliot, who has done so much to restore to our generation a consciousness of the high tradition of Christian culture" (115). Dawson concludes with a subtle reflection on the paradoxes of nature, religion, and culture: "It is this conception of the intervention of a transcendent divine principle in the life of man which none the less retains its roots in the earth and in the order of nature that renders the history of Christian culture so difficult to investigate and the ideal of Christian culture so hard to realize" (115). Religion, with its roots in nature and its branches reaching into the supernatural spiritual world, exists in between, in a dynamic and complex middle earth, just as human life itself does. The long-maintained discussion of these matters between Eliot and Dawson is the primary context for understanding the fundamental ideas in Eliot's cultural criticism. And the more we read Eliot together with Dawson, the more we will see the depth and the balance of Eliot's meditations on religion and culture.

The central claim Dawson and Eliot made, based on their wide-ranging knowledge of anthropology and history, was that every culture has a cult, some religious system that serves as an ultimate source of value and meaning. As Eliot puts it in the Choruses for the pageant play *The Rock*, "There is no life that is not in community, / And no community not lived in praise of God." They further maintained that even in a fully secularized state there will inevitably be some sort of godless religion, such as the all-encompassing totalitarian ideologies that commanded obeisance and bloody sacrifice in Italy, Germany, and Russia in the 1930s when they were working out these ideas. If the secular ideology took a more benign form in England and America, they predicted that it would nonetheless result in the worship of Mammon and in the increasing domination of the omnicompetent state in a totalitarian democracy, attempting to create (as Eliot puts it in *The Rock*) "systems so perfect that no one will need to be good." Their belief was that a culture could not thrive without a genuine religious commitment at its center, that the eclectic intellectualized spirituality of Babbitt's humanism would be incapable of satisfying that profound need, and that the European experiment in secularism would finally fail to produce a rich and meaningful life for its peoples. Though Dawson and Eliot insisted on the centrality of religion in culture, however, they strongly rejected theocratic solutions, envisioning instead a dynamic tension between church and state in which neither would claim complete authority. Furthermore, they had no illusions about the church, knowing it to be a human and corruptible organization, even if under divine guidance. Critics today are of course free to disagree with their point of view, but it behooves them first to understand it and to admit that it is serious, coherent, rational, and balanced.

NOTES

1. Roger Kojecký, *T. S. Eliot's Social Criticism* (London: Faber, 1971), 11. One work Kojecký has in mind is John R. Harrison's *The Reactionaries: W. B. Yeats, Wyndham Lewis, Ezra Pound, T. S. Eliot, D. H. Lawrence* (New York: Schocken Books, 1967). This book was savaged in a review by Hugh Kenner, "The Sleep Machine," *Triumph* (August, 1967): 32–34. Nevertheless, Harrison's slipshod slanders have endured.

2. Kenneth Asher, "T. S. Eliot and Charles Maurras," *ANQ* 11, no. 3 (Summer, 1998): 20. One exception to this tendency is an excellent piece by Peter Dale Scott, "The Social Critic and His Discontents," in *The Cambridge Companion to T. S. Eliot*, ed. A. David Moody (Cambridge: Cambridge University Press, 1994), 60–76. Scott points out that "In practice Eliot's efforts for a culturally integrated Europe brought the *Criterion* into alliance with critics of Maurras, such as the *Nouvelle Revue Française* of André Gide, Julien Benda, and Jacques Rivière, and in Germany the humanist and classicist scholar Ernst Robert Curtius. . . . Eliot's affinities within l'Action Française were less with the "integral nationalism" of Maurras than with Henri Massis's and Jacques Maritain's vision of a united, federal, Catholic Europe" (64–65). Scott mentions Christopher Dawson's name only in passing, in a list of members of the Moot.

3. Kojecký, 89, 153, 164, 217.

4. Russell Kirk, *Eliot and His Age: T. S. Eliot's Moral Imagination in the Twentieth Century* (Peru, IL: Sherwood Sugden, 1984), 300. First published in 1971. In his book *T. S. Eliot and Ideology* (Cambridge: Cambridge University Press, 1998), Kenneth Asher makes one passing reference to Dawson, while speaking constantly of Maurras. He cites Kojecký once and Kirk not at all.

5. See Christina Scott, *A Historian and His World: A Life of Christopher Dawson* (New Brunswick, NJ: Transaction, 1992).

6. Bradley J. Birzer, *Sanctifying the World: The Augustinian Life and Mind of Christopher Dawson* (Front Royal, VA: Christendom Press, 2007), xix.

7. H. J. Massingham, review of *The Age of the Gods*, by Christopher Dawson, *Criterion* 8, no. 30 (Sept., 1928): 149–53. H. J. Massingham, review of *Progress and Religion*, by Christopher Dawson, *Criterion* 9, no. 34 (Oct., 1929): 146–50.

8. Massingham, review of *Progress and Religion*, 150.

9. Christopher Dawson, "The End of an Age," *Criterion* 9, no. 36 (April, 1930): 386–401. Dawson also sent Eliot an essay that Faber published in 1930 as a booklet, *Christianity and Sex*. See Birzer, xxiii. See also Scott, 93–94.

10. See Birzer, 67.

11. Eliot, "The Humanism of Irving Babbitt," in *Selected Essays* (New York: Harcourt, 1950), 419–28. Cited hereafter as *SE*.

12. Christopher Dawson, review of *Mediaeval Culture*, by Carl Vossler and *New Light on the Youth of Dante*, by Gertrude Leigh, *Criterion* 9, no. 37 (July, 1930): 718–22. Christopher Dawson, review of *Woman and Society*, by Meyrick Booth, *Criterion* 10, no. 38 (Oct., 1930): 176–77. F. McEachran, review of *Christianity and the New Age*, by Christopher Dawson, *Criterion* 10, no. 41 (July, 1931): 750–55. Dawson, "The Origins of the Romantic Tradition," *Criterion* 11, no. 43 (Jan., 1932): 222–48. Dawson, review of *The Great Amphibian*, by Joseph Needham, *Criterion* 11, no. 44 (April, 1932): 545–48. Dawson, "H. G. Wells and History," *Criterion* 12, no. 46 (Oct., 1932): 9–16. F. McEachran, review of *The Making of Europe*, by Christopher Dawson, *Criterion* 12, no. 47 (Jan., 1933): 290–92. F. McEachren, review of *The Modern Dilemma*, by Christopher Dawson, *Criterion* 12, no. 48 (April, 1933): 494–96. Montgomery Belgion, review of *Enquiries into*

Religion and Culture, by Christopher Dawson, *Criterion,* 13, no. 50 (Oct., 1933): 143–46. Dawson, "Religion and the Totalitarian State," *Criterion* 14, no. 54 (Oct., 1934): 1–16. Dawson, review of *Reflections on the End of an Era,* by Reinhold Niebuhr, *Criterion* 14, no. 54 (Oct., 1934). E. W. F. Tomlin, review of *Religion and the Modern State,* by Christopher Dawson, *Criterion* 15, no. 58 (Oct., 1935): 130–37.

13. Eliot, *The Idea of a Christian Society* (London: Faber, 1939), 6. Cited hereafter as *Idea.*

14. Eliot, *Notes towards the Definition of Culture* (New York: Harcourt, 1949), 9. The book combines a series of articles published in 1943 in the *New English Weekly.* Cited hereafter as *Notes.*

15. Christopher Dawson, *Religion and Culture* (London: Sheed and Ward, 1949), 27. Cited hereafter as *R&C.*

16. Dawson, "Memories of a Victorian Childhood," Appendix to Scott, *A Historian and His World,* 230–31.

17. Dawson, *Beyond Politics* (New York: Sheed and Ward, 1939), 49. Cited hereafter as *BP.*

18. Dawson, "Religion and the Totalitarian State," *Criterion* 14, no. 54 (Oct., 1934): 10.

19. Dawson, *Religion and the Modern State* (New York: Sheed and Ward, 1935), xv. Reviewing this book in *The Criterion* (vol. 15, no. 58), E. W. F. Tomlin names Dawson "a historian of the first rank" (133) and says the book must not only be recommended but prescribed (134).

20. Dawson, *The Making of Europe* (Cleveland, OH: Meridian, 1956). 22. First published New York: Sheed and Ward, 1932.

21. Dawson, *Progress and Religion: An Historical Inquiry* (London: Sheed and Ward, 1931), 217. Cited hereafter as *P&R.*

22. Karl Marx, *The German Ideology,* in *The Critical Tradition: Classic Texts and Contemporary Trends,* ed. David H. Richter, second ed. (Boston: St. Martin's, 1998), 391.

23. In his last—and still unpublished—book, Dawson wrote, "The creative force of a culture always comes from . . . the spiritual side . . . the material environment or the material circumstances of life only condition the form of its expression." Quoted by Birzer, 113.

24. Scott, 104–107.

25. Another thinker whose influence on Eliot's social theory has not been considered adequately is Jacques Maritain, and he also warns against a theocratic solution. E. W. F. Tomlin reviews Maritain's *Freedom and the Modern World* along with Dawson's *Religion and the Modern State* in *The Criterion* (vol. 15, no. 58). Tomlin quotes Maritain as saying that it would be fatal "to substitute for the error of Liberalism an opposite error and to erect . . . a Theocratic Church in opposition to or alongside the theocracies of the Collectivist Man" (132).

26. Eliot, "Francis Herbert Bradley," in *Selected Essays* (New York: Harcourt, 1950), 399.

27. Eliot, "Thoughts after Lambeth," *Selected Essays,* 342.

28. Kirk, 155–71. Kojecký, 11–12, 61–62, 127, 139, 186. Jason Harding, *The Criterion: Cultural Politics and Periodical Networks in Inter-War Britain* (Oxford: Oxford University Press, 2002), 177–84.

29. Ronald Schuchard, *Eliot's Dark Angel: Intersections of Life and Art* (New York: Oxford University Press, 1999), 54–61.

30. Kenneth Asher, "T. S. Eliot and Charles Maurras," 20.

31. Scott, 65. See *Athenaeum* 4657 (August 1, 1919): 681. See also *Letters* I, 416.

32. Eliot, "The Humanism of Irving Babbitt," *Selected Essays,* 427.

33. Quoted by Kojecký, 67. Kojecký also quotes from Eliot's letter to the editor published in *Time and Tide* (1953), in which Eliot says of Maurras that "throughout his life he was explicitly a rationalist—a disciple of Comte: and it was precisely his support of the Church solely on political and social grounds that exposed him to ecclesiastical censure and led to the condemnation of the *Action Française* in 1926" (68).

Kojecký's conclusion about Eliot's attitude toward Maurras seems valid: "Despite the show of wide reading he made in the *Criterion* debate on the papal condemnation, he does not appear to have studied the political writings of Maurras particularly closely. Always aware of Maurras's excesses, he primarily valued his literary work, and in a general way the rationalistic élitism and royalism" (223).

34. Eliot, "What Is a Classic," *On Poetry and Poets* (London: Faber, 1957), 70–71.

35. As Birzer states (xxiii), "it would be difficult if not impossible to find a scholar who influenced Eliot more." It is significant that Maurras's name comes up only once in Birzer's entire book on Dawson, and then in a letter of Dawson's saying he "had no sympathy whatever" for Maurras (quoted by Birzer, 11). Clearly, Dawson and Maurras were not similar Catholic social thinkers, but rather represented antagonistic schools of thought.

36. Dawson, "T. S. Eliot on the Meaning of Culture," *The Month* 1 (March 1949); reprinted in *Dynamics of World History*, ed. John J. Mulloy (Wilmington, DE: ISI Books, 2002), 113.

V

Contemporaries

FIFTEEN

Poetry and Religion in George Santayana and T. S. Eliot

James Seaton

A review of the ideas on poetry and religion of T. S. Eliot's one-time teacher George Santayana illuminates Eliot's own stance. Santayana's thought, expressed with clarity and literary elegance, was one of the alternatives Eliot rejected in working out his own ideas. Santayana's philosophy of art and religion was for Eliot one of the roads not taken, and in understanding Santayana's perspective one also comes to understand better the road Eliot did take. Santayana and Eliot were apparently never personally close, and their recorded comments about each other are not always particularly friendly. Santayana's biographer John McCormick describes their relationship as "long, uneasy, and always tenuous."[1] McCormick notes that Eliot remembered Santayana's lectures as "soporific," but protests that "on all other evidence than T. S. Eliot's, Santayana as a lecturer and presence at Harvard was anything but soporific" (99). On the other hand, Santayana once described Eliot as "an amateur Catholic," displaying, in his biographer's words, "the intolerance of the born Catholic for the convert" (417). Eliot praised Santayana's *Three Philosophical Poets* in his 1926 Clark Lectures, saying it was "too little read, though one of the most brilliant of Mr. Santayana's works," but he immediately observed that Santayana's interest and, Eliot implies, his brilliance, lay in philosophy rather than literary criticism: "But I think the effect of Mr. Santayana's book is a little too clearly to *trancher les genres*. As a philosopher he is more interested in poetical philosophy than in philosophical poetry."[2]

Nevertheless, Eliot and Santayana agreed on a number of key literary issues. One important shared idea may have been the source of a good deal of the tension between the two. In the concluding essay of *Interpretations of Poetry and Religion* (1900), "The Elements and Function of Poetry," Santayana, after acknowledging that "the substance of poetry is, after all, emotion," emphasized that a poet's "glorious emotions . . . must at all hazards find or feign their correlative objects."[3] Santayana's language reappears, slightly rephrased, in Eliot's famous pronouncement that "The only way of expressing emotion in the form of art is by finding an 'objective correlative'; in other words, a set of objects, a situation, a chain of events which shall be the formula of that particular emotion."[4] Whether Eliot derived this formula from Santayana is uncertain, but it is certain that the one-time student never acknowledged the contribution of his former professor to one of those "notorious phrases, which" — Eliot said in a 1956 lecture — "have had a truly embarrassing success in the world."[5] Eliot's silence undoubtedly played its part in increasing the distance between the two.[6]

Yet the phrase occurs in a controversial essay in which Eliot's position, outrageous to many, was close to Santayana's own. In "Hamlet and His Problems," Eliot scandalized the English literary world by declaring that "so far from being Shakespeare's masterpiece, the play is most certainly an artistic failure," adding that "probably more people have found *Hamlet* a work of art because they found it interesting, than have found it interesting because it is a work of art."[7] Eliot found that the play provided no "objective correlative" for Hamlet's emotion, an emotion "in *excess* of the facts as they appear" [italics in original].[8] In his own 1908 introduction to the play, Santayana does not call it an "artistic failure," but he does point out that it is based on "a violent and somewhat absurd fable" and offers a reason why English and American audiences might find Hamlet interesting despite or rather because of the hero's "incoherence" and the confusion or "disarray" of the play's world-picture:

> In Hamlet our incoherent souls see their own image; in him romantic potentiality and romantic failure wears each its own feature. In him we see the gifts most congenial and appealing to us reduced to a pathetic impotence because of the disarray in which we are content to leave them.[9]

Both Santayana and Eliot rejected literary and philosophical romanticism, and both broke with the consensus of the English-speaking world in preferring Dante to Shakespeare. Attempting to explicate the relation between poetry and religion, Eliot wrote in the preface to the 1928 edition of *The Sacred Wood* that he preferred "the poetry of Dante to that of Shakespeare . . . because it seems to me to illustrate a saner attitude towards the mystery of life."[10] In the last essay of the volume Eliot returned to the comparison, once again arguing for the superiority of Dante over Shakespeare. Dante, Eliot asserts, provides "the most comprehensive, and the most *ordered* [italics in original] presentation of emotions that has ever been made," while Shakespeare exhibits or analyzes emotions in isolation, without relation or hierarchy between them: "Shakespeare takes a character apparently controlled by a simple emotion, and analyses the character and the emotion itself. . . . Dante, on the other hand, does not analyse the emotion so much as he exhibits its relation to other emotions."[11] This contrast parallels Santayana's argument that "The Absence of Religion in Shakespeare" (the title of a chapter in *Interpretations of Poetry and Religion*) prevents the playwright, despite his genius, from giving us "all that the highest poet could give."[12] Homer and Dante, Santayana observes, "gave us man with his piety and the world with its gods." Their poetry presented "man in his relations, surrounded by a kindred universe in which he fills his allotted place. He knows the meaning and issue of his life, and does not voyage without a chart." In contrast, "Shakespeare's world . . . is only the world of human society. . . . He depicts human life in all its richness and variety, but leaves that life without a setting, and consequently without a meaning" (95). Santayana argues that lack of a definite philosophy or religion is not only an intellectual but a literary limitation; some definite view of the nature of things "is an aesthetic no less than a logical demand. . . . Without it the imagination cannot fulfill its essential function or achieve its supreme success" (100–1). Santayana offers an historical explanation for this limitation that sounds very much like Eliot's celebrated thesis that "in the seventeenth century a dissociation of sensibility set in, from which we have never recovered."[13] Santayana speculates in similar terms about a seventeenth century "divorce between the fullness of life on the one hand and the depth and unity of faith on the other":

> In Shakespeare's time and country, to be religious already began to mean to be Puritanical; and in the divorce between the fullness of life on the one hand and the depth and unity of faith on the other, there could be no doubt to which side a man of imaginative instincts would attach himself. A world of passion and beauty without a meaning must seem to him more interesting and worthy than a world of empty principle and dogma, meager, fanatical, and false. It was beyond the power of synthesis possessed by that age and nation to find a principle of all passion and a religion of all life. (161)

Opposing the kinds of grandiose claims made by romantic heresiarchs from Percy Shelley to Harold Bloom, Santayana and Eliot both believed that in general orthodoxy, with its tendency to encourage the union of thought and feeling, is superior to heresy, with its tendency to promote "the dissociation of sensibility." "Orthodoxy is My Doxy," the title of a subchapter of Russell Kirk's perceptive critical biography, *Eliot and His Age*,[14] rightly emphasizes Eliot's affinity not for conformity but for tradition, memorably affirmed in his most important essay on literature, "Tradition and the Individual Talent." [15] For both Eliot and Santayana, Dante represented the great example of the advantages of orthodoxy for poetic genius. In contrast, Eliot argued, in the chapter preceding the concluding essay on Dante in *The Sacred Wood*, that the poetry of William Blake suffers from its lack of "a framework of accepted and traditional ideas which would have prevented him from indulging in a philosophy of his own." [16] The resulting "crankiness" and "eccentricity," betraying "a certain meanness of culture," has the effect of stifling Blake's very real and impressive poetic gifts, in Eliot's view. [17] (There are many who regard Blake as a great spiritual teacher as well as poet, but if one takes seriously such Blakean aphorisms as "Sooner murder an infant in its cradle than nurse unacted desires," [18] "crankiness" or "eccentricity" sound like very mild epithets.) For his part, Santayana reaffirmed the superiority of orthodoxy to heresy in a variety of contexts. In *Interpretations of Poetry and Religion* he declared roundly that "to a person sufficiently removed by time or by philosophy from the controversies of sects, orthodoxy must always appear right and heresy wrong" (39). In a later essay Santayana explained that "heresies are systems that inherit all the claims of orthodoxy with only a part of its resources." [19] Heresies, philosophical or religious, may very well capture a part of the truth, Santayana concedes, but they mistake the part for the whole, and in insisting on their particular truth neglect or distort the lessons of human experience preserved and passed on, perhaps precariously and contradictorily, by a capacious orthodoxy.

The humanism of Irving Babbitt, Santayana's Harvard colleague and Eliot's teacher at Harvard, was criticized by the two in similar terms. Both argued that only a religion could have the social and even the intellectual authority Babbitt claimed for humanism. Humanism, Eliot argued "is auxiliary to and dependent upon the religious point of view." Indeed, the humanist outlook was not so much the result of pondering the wisdom of the ages as "a product—a by-product—of Protestant theology in its last agonies." [20] Santayana made very much the same argument in "The Genteel Tradition at Bay," suggesting that Babbitt's success in arousing public controversy was actually a sign of "the demise of the genteel tradition, though by a death more noble and glorious than some of us had looked for." If the American humanists really wanted to "reestablish our moral sentiments on foundations more solid than tradition or gentility," Santayana warned that they had no choice except to "reinstate a settled belief in a supernatural human soul and in a precise divine revelation." [21] For Eliot humanism without religion could never be a major moral or intellectual force but would remain "merely the state of mind of a few persons in a few places at a few times." [22] Religious belief, in contrast, is the typical human response to life on earth, and remains an option under any and all circumstances. Thus Santayana comments, "If all the American humanists had become Catholics like Newman, or even like Mr. T. S. Eliot, I should understand the reason" (194). On the other hand, there seems no circumstance under which humanism could take the place of Catholicism, Christianity, or any other religion. Santayana's question answers itself: "can the way of Matthew Arnold and of Professor Norton be the way of life for all men for ever?" (193).

One can understand why Russell Kirk was able to subtitle the first edition of *The Conservative Mind* "From Burke to Santayana" and later change the subtitle to "From Burke to Eliot" without radically altering his account of the tradition he was claiming and reaffirming—and reinvigorating. Yet there are also important differences between Santayana and Eliot, differences that do something to explain why Russell Kirk eventually found T. S. Eliot the more suitable exemplar of twentieth-century conservatism. The most important difference has to do with religion, and with the relation of religion to poetry. Throughout his career Santayana reaffirmed the thesis the fictional Professor Godfrey St. Peter, the main character of Willa Cather's 1925 novel *The Professor's House*, offers to a student in the course of responding to a question about the importance of science. St. Peter answers "No, Miller, I don't myself think much of science as a phase of human development. . . . Art and religion (they are the same thing, in the end, of course) have given man the only happiness he has ever had."[23] Professor St. Peter must have been reading Santayana. On the first page of the preface to his *Interpretations of Poetry and Religion*, Santayana declares the idea that underlies all his "interpretations": "religion and poetry are identical in essence, and differ merely in the way in which they are attached to practical affairs. Poetry is called religion when it intervenes in life, and religion, when it merely supervenes upon life, is seen to be nothing but poetry" (3). In the closing paragraph of the book Santayana reaffirms and clarifies his thesis, emphasizing that by "in essence" he means "at their best": "Poetry raised to its highest power is then identical with religion grasped in its utmost truth" (172).

Eliot, of course, rejected any attempt, whether by Matthew Arnold, George Santayana, or anybody else, to identify religion with literature. In his preface to the 1928 edition of *The Sacred Wood* he is willing to call poetry an "amusement," albeit a "superior amusement,"[24] thus anticipating Stanley Fish's thesis in a 6 January 2008, *New York Times* column that the humanities, including literature "cannot be justified except in relation to the pleasure they give to those who enjoy them." Fish and Eliot, of course, make their similarly provocative statements for opposed reasons. Fish is delighted to tell anybody who will listen that "the only honest answer" to a question about the deeper significance of anything is "none whatsoever," since Fish sees to it that his universe has no depth.[25] In contrast Eliot's willingness to call poetry an "amusement" betrays the seriousness with which he regards the error involved in calling it "something still more false" (viii-ix). Eliot rejects claims that poetry might mean "the inculcation of morals, or the direction of politics; and no more is it religion or an equivalent of religion, except by some monstrous abuse of words" (ix). For Eliot, attempts to conflate religion with art or anything else were reminders of the bad old days of the late nineteenth century when "Religion became morals, religion became art, religion became science or philosophy; various blundering attempts were made at alliances between various branches of thought."[26]

Santayana, who made one of those attempts, considered the notion that the ultimate reality was something other than matter to be "mythical physics" or just "bad physics."[27] He took it for granted that religious dogmas were fictions, to be judged for their ability to provide moral insight and formulate meaningful ideals. Unlike many other non-believers, however, let alone other philosophical materialists, Santayana believed that orthodox religion, Christianity in particular and, even more specifically, Catholic Christianity, provides real moral insight wiser and more penetrating than the supposedly more enlightened views of its secular critics. For Santayana the traditional doctrines of the Catholic Church are factually false but symbolically true. He defended the "doctrine of eternal rewards and punishments" in all its rigor,[28] arguing that "the harshness of the doctrine of eternal judgment is . . . a consequence of its symbolic truth" (62). Modern humanitarianism prefers, of course, the theory that all are saved and hell is empty; Santayana points out that the logical consequence of this comforting doctrine is that the choices one makes on earth are unimportant, since they all lead to the same result: "If every one is ultimately saved, there is nothing truly momentous about alternative events: all paths lead more or less circuitously to the same end" (65). The reality of human life, however, is far different. One does not require revelation to prove "moral distinctions" are real: "A cool philosophy suffices to show us that moral distinctions exist, since men prefer some experiences to others and can by their action bring these good and evil experiences upon themselves and upon their fellows" (63). Every choice we make in daily life affirms the belief that "some things are really better than others" (64). Every choice we make, once made, cannot be changed. In this life at least "every loss is irretrievable" (64) and, similarly, joy, however brief, cannot be retroactively canceled. The choices human beings make are significant and, once made, cannot be unmade. The notion that all are saved is pleasant but sentimental—bad poetry. On the other hand, "the doctrine of eternal rewards and punishments is . . . an expression of moral truth" (66).

Santayana, it should be noted, did not attempt to argue, as the Catholic Modernists of his time and religious liberals past and present have argued or intimated, that belief in the symbolic truth of religious doctrines is comparable to or equivalent with religious faith. He did not try to pass himself off as a believing Catholic, and he advised the Church to reject attempts to modernize itself by compromising with intellectuals who only believed, as he did, in Christian doctrines if "taken in a purely symbolic or moral sense" (29), but who, unlike him, wished to be considered good Catholics.[29] He warned against acceding to the intellectual fashions of the day, observing "for an idea ever to be fashionable is ominous, since it must afterwards be always old-fashioned" (48). Santayana the materialist philosopher encouraged the Church to remain true to its ancient teaching: "In a frank supernaturalism, in a tight clericalism, not in a pleasant secularization, lies the sole hope of the church. Its sole dignity also lies there. It will not convert the world; it never did and it never could. It will remain a voice crying in the wilderness; but it will believe what it cries, and there will be some to listen to it in the future, as there have been many in the past" (49).

For himself, Santayana practiced a spiritual discipline that he called, following Spinoza, "seeing things under the form of eternity."[30] As Eliot underwent a conversion experience that led him to Christianity, Santayana experienced what he calls in his autobiography a *metanoia*, a "change of heart," a "disintoxication" from the things of the world. Santayana's *metanoia* was not a dramatic event brought about "by any one crisis or conjunction of events" but a response to "the very nature of existence, when this had been honestly faced and frankly admitted."[31] He had learned that the only source of certain happiness is the life of the spirit:

> I had not been ravaged by any hostile fate; my heart had simply uttered a warning against its own weakness. It had said to me: Cultivate imagination, love it, give it endless forms, but do not let it deceive you. Enjoy the world, travel over it, and learn its ways, but do not let it hold you. Do not suffer it to oppress you with craving or with regret for the images that you may form of it. You will do the least harm and find the greatest satisfactions, if, being furnished as lightly as possible with possessions, you live freely among ideas. To possess things and persons in idea is the only pure good to be got out of them; to possess them physically or legally is a burden and a snare. (427–8)

"Let us be content to live in the mind," advised Santayana at the conclusion of his famous lecture on "The Genteel Tradition in American Philosophy."[32] Against the American feeling that thought is only for the sake of action, Santayana insisted that "reflection is itself a turn, and the top turn, given to life."[33] Oliver Alden, the hero of Santayana's best-selling novel *The Last Puritan*, has a moment of insight paralleling Santayana's *metanoia*, though prompted by an occasion very different, one assumes, from any that Santayana himself ever confronted. A prostitute embraces him, but she has bad breath, having just eaten sardines and cucumber salad (it's a Friday, and she is a Catholic). Any feelings of lust on Oliver's part are followed by "a shiver of loathing." The two emotions neutralize one another, opening the way to "a far-reaching clearness such as they say comes to ecstatic philosophers and to drowning men." Oliver suddenly achieves a transcendent feeling of "calm, just, deliberate charity, under-standing all things, forgiving all things, and willingly draining the cup of truth to the dregs, as it were in atonement for the blind sin of existence. A bottomless sadness, a bottomless peace, seemed to possess him."[34]

The evocation of Paul's praise of love or charity in the thirteenth chapter of First Corinthians points to Santayana's belief that the kind of insight Oliver attains and the kind of *metanoia* he himself experienced are in full accord with the teaching of the Christ of the Gospels as interpreted by a "sympathetic humanist and unprejudiced man of letters," as he describes himself in his 1946 book *The Idea of Christ in the Gospels*.[35] In "Modernism and Christianity" Santayana had mocked contemporary liberalizers who identified their own ideas with primitive Christianity: "Thus Professor Harnack, not to mention less distinguished historians, makes the original essence of Christianity coincide — what a miracle! — with his own Lutheran and Kantian sentiments" (18–19). Yet Santayana himself, after more than 250 pages of analysis in the later work, comes to the conclusion that "the idea of Christ in the Gospels" represents an ideal that he himself has already formulated in terms of his own philosophy: "the intrinsic ideal of spirit; that is to say, the acme of disinterested intelligence and disinterested love" (253). Santayana understands that the idea of Christ that he finds in the Gospels is not the Christ of faith. It is closer to the "radically mystical and gnostic doctrine" whose acceptance, he acknowledges, would have been "a suicidal step" (49) for the church.

Santayana's idea of Christ is not the Christ to whom believers pray, just as the change of heart or *metanoia* that he underwent differs from the conversion experience that Harry experiences in *The Family Reunion* or Celia in *The Cocktail Party* or, one suspects, that Eliot himself underwent in his path to Christianity. Harry does not know where he will go in following "the bright angels," but he thinks he might undertake "a care over lives of humble people."[36] After Celia undergoes "the process by which the human is/ Transhumanised," she goes to Kinkanja, where she is ultimately "crucified/ Very near an ant-hill" when she refuses to leave "a handful of plague-stricken natives/ Who would have died anyway," in Edward Chamberlayne's words.[37] Eliot himself did what he could to redeem the time, to recover and give meaning in a secular age to Christian faith and "the idea of a Christian society."[38] Santayana, on the other hand, contemplated the end of Christianity with philosophic resignation: "A flood of barbarism from below may soon level all the fair works of our Christian ancestors . . . Romantic Christendom — picturesque, passionate, unhappy episode — may be coming to an end. Such a catastrophe would be no reason for despair."[39] For Santayana living in the mind meant taking the stance of a detached observer, to whom all things are merely objects of contemplation and therefore sources of intellectual pleasure. Eliot had his objections to Irving Babbitt's crusading humanism, but he could not share the attitude flaunted in Santayana's rhetorical question to the humanists: "Why not frankly rejoice in the benefits, so new and extraordinary, which our state of society affords? We may not possess those admirable things which Professor Norton pined for, but at least (besides football) haven't we Einstein and Freud, Proust and Paul Valery, Lenin and Mussolini?"[40]

Despite occasional lapses, Santayana's literary criticism, his philosophy of life, and his conception of the spiritual life, as well as his analyses of the United States and the modern world, are all well worth study and reflection. In part just because Santayana wrote as a detached observer without solutions to offer or advice to give, his writings retain their freshness and their relevance. An awareness of Santayana's thought is also valuable as a means of better understanding the poetry and ideas of his student and contemporary, T. S. Eliot. Because of their similarities but especially because of their differences, an awareness of Santayana's conception of the life of the spirit and the relations between poetry and religion can enrich and clarify our understanding of Eliot's attitudes about spirituality, poetry, and religion.

NOTES

1. John McCormick, *George Santayana: A Biography* (New York: Paragon, 1988), 415. Following quotations from this work in this paragraph are cited by page number in the text.

2. T. S. Eliot, *The Varieties of Metaphysical Poetry: The Clark Lectures at Trinity College, Cambridge, 1926 and The Turnbull Lectures at the Johns Hopkins University, 1933*, ed. Ronald Schuchard (London: Faber and Faber, 1993), 48–9. Eliot drew on his 1926 Clark Lectures for the 1933 Turnbull Lectures but often revised and sometimes changed his emphasis. In 1933 Eliot's characterization of *Three Philosophical Poets* was more favorable. The book is now not merely "brilliant" only in comparison to Santayana's other works but unconditionally "brilliant and admirable." In the later lecture Eliot emphasizes his agreement with Santayana, leaving possible objections unstated: "I think that on the whole I agree with Mr. Santayana's definition of 'philosophical poetry'" (251).

3. George Santayana, *Interpretations of Poetry and Religion*, ed. William G. Holzberger and Herman J. Saatkamp Jr. (Cambridge, MA.: MIT Press, 1989), 276, 277.

4. T. S. Eliot, "Hamlet and His Problems," *Selected Essays* (New York: Harcourt, 1964), 124–5.

5. T. S. Eliot, "The Frontiers of Criticism," *On Poetry and Poets* (New York: Noonday, 1961), 117.

6. John McCormick observes that "As editor of *The Criterion* . . . and as a director at Faber & Faber, Eliot was in professional touch with all manner of writers, but not with Santayana." McCormick's explanation for Eliot's "coolness" is at least plausible: "His professional coolness more than likely resulted from an intellectual debt which he never acknowledged, and which Santayana well knew he had not acknowledged. The origins of that debt rested in both men's conviction that romantic individualism was a blight and an evil. Eliot's debt was not incurred by that shared conviction, but by his influential and widely discussed theory of the 'objective correlative.'" McCormick, *George Santayana: A Biography*, 416.

7. T. S. Eliot, "Hamlet and His Problems," 123–4.

8. Ibid., 125.

9. George Santayana, *"Hamlet,"* in *Essays in Literary Criticism of George Santayana*, ed. Irving Singer (New York: Scribner's, 1956), 135–6.

10. T. S. Eliot, Preface to the 1928 Edition, *The Sacred Wood; Essays on Poetry and Criticism* (New York: Barnes and Noble, 1960), x.

11. T. S. Eliot, "Dante," *The Sacred Wood*, 168.

12. George Santayana, "The Absence of Religion in Shakespeare," *Interpretations of Poetry and Religion*, 100. Following quotations from this work are cited by page number in the text.

13. T. S. Eliot, "The Metaphysical Poets," *Selected Essays of T. S. Eliot*, 247.

14. Russell Kirk, *Eliot and His Age: T. S. Eliot's Moral Imagination in the Twentieth Century*, second ed. (Wilmington, DE: ISI Books, 2008). "Orthodoxy Is My Doxy" is the second subchapter of Chapter 4, "A Criterion in a Time of Hollow Men."

15. T. S. Eliot, "Tradition and the Individual Talent," *The Sacred Wood*, 47–59.

16. T. S. Eliot, "Blake," *The Sacred Wood*, 157–58.

17. Ibid., 157.

18. William Blake, "The Marriage of Heaven and Hell," *Poems of William Blake*, ed. W. B. Yeats (London: Routledge and Kegan Paul, 1905), 182.

19. George Santayana, "Philosophical Heresy," in *Obiter Scripta: Lectures, Essays and Reviews*, ed. Justus Buchler and Benjamin Schwartz (New York: Scribner's, 1936), 95.

20. T. S. Eliot, "The Humanism of Irving Babbitt," *Selected Essays*, 422.

21. George Santayana, "The Genteel Tradition at Bay," in *The Genteel Tradition: Nine Essays by George Santayana*, ed. Douglas L. Wilson (Lincoln, NE: University of Nebraska Press, 1998), 167–68. Following quotations from this work in this paragraph are cited by page number in the text.

22. T. S. Eliot, "The Humanism of Irving Babbitt," *Selected Essays*, 421.

23. Willa Cather, *The Professor's House* (New York: Vintage, 1973), 67, 69.

24. T. S. Eliot, Introduction to the 1928 Edition, *The Sacred Wood*, viii. Following quotations from this work in this paragraph are cited by page number in the text.

25. Stanley Fish, "Will the Humanities Save Us?" *New York Times*, January 6, 2008. Online at http://fish.blogs.nytimes.com/2008/01/06/will-the-humanities-save-us/.

26. T. S. Eliot, "Arnold and Pater," *Selected Essays*, 393.

27. George Santayana, *Reason in Science*, Volume V of *The Life of Reason* (New York: Dover, 1983), 103, 168.

28. George Santayana, "The Poetry of Christian Dogma," *Interpretations of Poetry and Religion* (Cambridge, MA: MIT Press, 1989), 66. Following quotations from this work are cited by page number in the text.

29. George Santayana, "Modernism and Christianity," in *Winds of Doctrine* (New York: Charles Scribner's Sons, 1937), 44. Following quotations from this work are cited by page number in the text.

30. George Santayana, *Three Philosophical Poets* (New York: Doubleday Anchor, 1953), 170.

31. George Santayana, *Persons and Places: Fragments of Autobiography* (Cambridge, MA: MIT Press, 1986), 426. The following quotation from this work in this paragraph is cited by page number in the text.

32. George Santayana, "The Genteel Tradition in American Philosophy," *The Genteel Tradition: Nine Essays by George Santayana*, 64.

33. George Santayana, *Character and Opinion in the United States* (New Brunswick, NJ: Transaction, 1991), 3.

34. George Santayana, *The Last Puritan: A Memoir in the Form of a Novel*, ed. William G. Holzberger and Herman J. Saatkamp Jr. (Cambridge, MA: MIT Press, 1994), 531.

35. George Santayana, *The Idea of Christ in the Gospels or God in Man: A Critical Essay* (New York: Scribner's, 1946), 5. The following quotations from this work in this paragraph are cited by page number in the text.

36. T. S. Eliot, *The Family Reunion* (New York: Harcourt, 1966), 111.

37. T. S. Eliot, *The Cocktail Party* (New York: Harcourt, 1978), 147, 175.

38. T. S. Eliot, *The Idea of a Christian Society*, in *Christianity and Culture* (New York: Harcourt, 1968).

39. George Santayana, *Character and Opinion in the United States*, xliii.

40. George Santayana, "The Genteel Tradition at Bay," 163.

SIXTEEN

"A Long Journey Afoot": The Pilgrimages toward Orthodoxy of T. S. Eliot and Paul Elmer More

David Huisman

In a letter to Paul Elmer More in early August 1929, T. S. Eliot wrote, apropos of the reaction to his announcement in *For Lancelot Andrewes* of his "general point of view" as "classicist in literature, royalist in politics, and Anglo-Catholic in religion,"[1] that "[m]ost critics appear to think that my catholicism is merely an escape or an evasion, certainly a defeat. . . . But it [is] rather trying to be supposed to have settled oneself in an easy chair, when one has just begun a long journey afoot."[2] To this important letter we will return; for now, I wish to observe, first, that the long journey to which it refers, far from *beginning*, was reaching something closer to its midpoint, albeit with a surer sense of direction and a new resolve; and, second, that More himself had played a significant role in bringing Eliot this far. Indeed, More's relationship to Eliot was somewhat that of a foster father, supplying the intellectual and spiritual exemplar Eliot never found in Henry Ware Eliot; somewhat that of a Virgil to Dante, pointing the way toward a higher vision while himself resting short of the goal. Eliot, expressing a dislike for "the worn and soiled phrase 'spiritual pilgrimage'"—a phrase he would nevertheless soon use again in reference to More—found in his life's work "an analogy with my own journey."[3]

The analogy is inexact, in that while More and Eliot traveled in tandem, as often as not they were out of step. More, for example, confessed to "coldness to Dante,"[4] and found modernist poetry, including Eliot's, unintelligible, though he grudgingly admitted that *Ash-Wednesday* was closer than the earlier poems to Eliot's critical classicism and, moreover, that it was expressive of a religious sensibility they now shared. Still, More detected in *Ash-Wednesday* a "disharmony between subject and mode of expression" that warranted the pejorative "Cleft Eliot."[5] We may speculate that *Four Quartets* would have met with More's approval, but only "Burnt Norton" was published during his lifetime, less than a year before his death in March 1937 at seventy-two. Perhaps it was a sense of their mixed closeness and remoteness that led Eliot, in his last letter to More on his deathbed, to describe More's spiritual biography as "oddly, even grotesquely, more like my own, so far as I can see, than that of any human being I have known."[6]

Before focusing on some key aspects of this complex relationship, it may prove useful to detour into one of the myriad topics on which More wrote in a lifetime of literary, philosophical, and theological speculation. It will serve—as many of those writings would—as a context within which to view the spiritual journeys of Eliot and his mentor. Although we have no direct evidence that Eliot read More's essays on American literature in the eleventh series of the Shelburne Essays, *A New England Group and Others*, "Henry Adams" and "Emerson" would have been of interest to a poet keenly aware of his New England heritage and the religious evolution which eventuated in his being brought up, as he commented in his review of John Middleton Murry's *Son of Woman*, "outside the Christian Fold, in Unitarianism."[7]

In the concluding paragraph of the essay on Adams—"a cousin of ours," as Eliot referred to him in a letter to his mother—More places Adams near the end of the tradition of religious decay that commenced with the Puritan founders, but dares to hope that the tradition might yet be redeemed:

> If we regard Adams's scholarship, his imagination, his verbal dexterity, his candor, his cynical vivacity, his range of reflection, we must give him a high place in the American literature of the past generation. . . . But one winces a little at acknowledging that the latest spokesman of the Adamses and of New England ends his career in sentimental nihilism. . . . The tragedy of Adams's education is that of a man who could not rest easy in negation, yet could find no positive faith to take its place. From one point of view he may appear to be the most honest and typical mind of New England in its last condition; yet withal some manlier voice, some word of deeper insight that yet faces the facts of life, we must still expect to hear from the people of Mather and Edwards and Channing and Emerson.[8]

The "last condition" to which More refers is diagnosed earlier in the essay:

> This breed of New England, of whom [Adams] was so consciously a titled representative, had once come out from the world for the sake of a religious and political affirmation . . . to confirm which they were

ready to deny all the other values of life. For the liberty to follow this affirmation they would discard tradition and authority and form and symbol and all that ordinarily binds men together in the bonds of habit. But the liberty of denying may itself become a habit. . . . By a gradual elimination of its positive content the faith of the people had passed from Calvinism to Unitarianism, and from this to free thinking, until in the days of our Adams there was little left to the intellect but a great denial. (*NEG*, 123)

More then quotes the well-known passage from *The Education of Henry Adams* in which Adams reflects, as throughout the book, in the third person, on the "mild Deism" in which he had been reared:

Of all the conditions of his youth which afterward puzzled the grown-up man, this disappearance of religion puzzled him most. . . . The religious instinct had vanished, and could not be revived. . . . [T]hat the most intelligent society, led by the most intelligent clergy, in the most moral conditions he ever knew . . . should have persuaded itself that all the problems which had convulsed human thought from earliest recorded time, were not worth discussing, seemed to him the most curious social phenomenon he had to account for in a long life. (quoted in *NEG*, 124)

To his credit, More acknowledges, Adams could not acquiesce in the "serene indifference to evil" exhibited by his complacent forbears, a complacency which More traces to Emerson, who, he says, "had found no difficulty in combining skepticism with an intuition of pure spirituality, though . . . to maintain his inner vision intact he shut his eyes resolutely on the darker facts of nature" (*NEG*, 135). This "intuition," which would soon eventuate in the "volatile and heady liquid known as Emersonianism" (*NEG*, 74), More finds, among other places, in Emerson's *Journals*, through which "runs this thread of self-communion, the poetry, it might be called, of the New England conscience deprived of its concrete deity and buoying itself on gleams and suggestions of eternal beauty and holiness" (*NEG*, 73).

The transcendental faith, More observes in the essay on Emerson, was the product of "a great movement that was sweeping over the world" (*NEG*, 82). Romanticism's "new emancipation of the emotions" had little use for theological dogmas such as Original Sin, and no interest, as Emerson famously announced to his congregation at the Second Unitarian Church of Boston, in the Sacrament of the Lord's Supper. "Emerson's suave displacement of the person of Jesus for the 'chorus of thought and hopes' in any human soul," More writes, marked the distance he and the New England Unitarians had traveled from the Calvinism of the Pilgrim Fathers (*NEG*, 75). In terms that recall fellow New Humanist Irving Babbitt's critique of romanticism, More describes how Puritan emancipation and individualism led to "the elevation of enthusiasm above judgment, of emotion above reason, of spontaneity above discipline, and of unlim-

ited expansion above centripetal control" (*NEG*, 82). Emerson's "blind-
ness to the reality of evil was not of his strength," More concludes, "it
was of his weakness. . . . He is preeminently the poet of religion and
philosophy for the young; whereas men as they grow older are inclined
to turn from him, in their more serious needs, to those sages who have
supplemented insight with a firmer grasp of the whole of human nature"
(*NEG*, 93–94).

Readers for whom that last sentence rings a distant bell might turn up
the Preface to the second edition of *The Sacred Wood*: "If I ask myself . . .
why I prefer the poetry of Dante to that of Shakespeare," Eliot writes, "I
should have to say, because it seems to me to illustrate a saner attitude
towards the mystery of life."[9] Indeed, as we will see, More's moral critique had already had a significant impact upon the *first* edition, altering
its contents and shifting Eliot's perspective on its ostensibly formalist
agenda: "I discovered," he writes in 1928, having "grown older" intellectually than the interval between editions would seem to account for,
"that what had happened in my own mind, in eight years, was not so
much a change or reversal of opinions, as an expansion or development
of interests."[10] Indeed, the "expansion or development" had begun even
earlier, impelled in part by Eliot's encounter with More.

Born a generation apart, More and Eliot shared the cultural background of their native St. Louis.[11] Taking his baccalaureate degree from
Washington University (founded by Tom's grandfather, Rev. William
Greenleaf Eliot), More taught for four years at Smith Academy (also
founded by Rev. Eliot). Although his tenure there did not overlap Tom's
student days, Eliot comments, "if he had remained there a few years
longer, he would have taught me Greek as he had taught my brother"
("PEM" 373). Both families had backgrounds in England: More's ances-
tral middle name is believed to derive from John Aylmer, Bishop of London in the mid-sixteenth century; Eliot's ancestor Andrew emigrated
from East Coker, Somerset, a century later. To be sure, their ecclesiastic
backgrounds were not the same: the Mores were Presbyterians, his father
an elder and Sunday school superintendent. The Eliots were Unitarians,
the aforementioned Rev. William Greenleaf, whom Emerson once commended as "the Saint of the West,"[12] a presence young Tom was
"brought up to be very much aware of" though he had died a year before
Tom's birth.[13]

That is to say, to revert to the analysis quoted earlier from More's
essay on Adams, More's and Eliot's roots were only a field apart in the
depleted soil of American Protestantism, the erosion of which had begun
with the New England transcendentalists, but which, on the banks of the
Mississippi, had not yet reached its "final condition"—the "sentimental
nihilism" and "denial" More attributes to Adams.[14] Eliot, in a review of
The Education which anticipated More's essay by a year, traces Adams's
skepticism to "the Boston doubt: . . . a product, or a cause, or a concomi-

tant, of Unitarianism," which, though "it is not destructive . . . is dissolvent." Alluding to the "austere grandeur" of Emerson's pulpit declension of the Communion, Eliot says that in Adams's case, the Boston skepticism became destructive: "Wherever this man stepped, the ground did not simply give way, it flew into particles. . . . he could believe in nothing."[15]

According to Eliot's memoir of More in the *Princeton Alumni Weekly,* "More's work was forced on my attention" for the first time in Babbitt's course in French criticism during his senior year at Harvard, when he also met More himself at a reception given by the Babbitts. Yet, he states, it was not until The Greek Tradition started to appear in 1917 and 1921, that More began to have any importance for him ("PEM" 373). In point of fact, he had reviewed More's *Aristocracy and Justice* in July 1916, in the course of the review indicating familiarity with earlier volumes of the Shelburne Essays, *Aristocracy* being the ninth. The review is most interesting in its anticipation of themes and phrases that echo in Eliot's poems and prose for decades to come: "two points of view which are really complementary and which flourish in the same soil" is rephrased in "Little Gidding" III: "There are three conditions which often lock alike / Yet differ completely, flourish in the same hedgerow."[16] Dante's phrase *l'anima semplicetta,* quoted from *Purgatorio* 16, returns in "Animula," in which the simple soul "Issues from the hand of God" into a world where it must cope with "the imperatives of . . . desire and control." Eliot's concern is the extremes to which uncontrolled desire leads: in the review, materialist utilitarianism versus sentimental humanitarianism; in "Little Gidding," attachment to self, things, and persons versus detachment from the same. Thus, "in order to be good, in order to be human, [the soul] requires *discipline: Onde convenne legge per fren porre"* ("Therefore laws were needed as a curb"). This line, also from canto 16, will reappear in the first two of Eliot's essays on Dante in 1920 and 1929. Eliot continues: "The fundamental beliefs of an intellectual conservatism, that man requires an askesis, a *formula* to be imposed upon him from above" and that the drift of romanticism, with its "impatience against all restraint" and faith in "the undisciplined imagination and emotions," must be resisted—these beliefs Eliot finds writ large everywhere in More.[17]

While Eliot values what he calls More's revolutionary philosophy and his moral emphasis, it would be some time before he worked out—albeit never to his complete satisfaction—the proper role of a moral standpoint in literary criticism. In keeping with his insistence, in the period prior to the publication of *The Sacred Wood,* upon the strictly *aesthetic* nature of genuinely *literary* criticism, Eliot is not willing to grant More the status of literary critic, a status denied even to the "cultural" critic Matthew Arnold, who "went for game outside of the literary preserve altogether" (*SW,* xiii). For only the critic actively engaged in the creation of literary art merits that title:

Mr. More is not . . . in the strictest sense, a literary critic. . . . One does not find those flashes of insight which arise in the comments of one creative artist upon another. . . . If he possessed . . . an overpowering aesthetic appreciation . . . Mr. More would not be what he is—one of the most interesting *moralists* of the present time.[18]

Much the same view of More is set forth in "The Local Flavour," published in December 1919:

Most critics have some creative interest—it may be, instead of an interest in any art, an interest (like Mr. Paul More's) in morals; but an interest in morals will not produce sound criticism of art. Consequently, we may say that the only valuable criticism is that of the workman. . . . Criticism is not an independent practice, but the by-product of some other activity.[19]

But when the article was reprinted in *The Sacred Wood* just a year later, a significant shift in Eliot's view of the function of criticism and of More's moral stance had taken place, for everything from "but an interest in morals will not produce sound criticism" onwards had been deleted. Eliot thereby not only retracts his denial of More's status as a creative critic and mutes his call for the workman-critic; he reverses the point about More's interest in morals, which is now cited as an alternative credential of the genuine *literary* critic.

In "A Note on the American Critic," unpublished prior to *The Sacred Wood*, Eliot reiterates that "More is primarily a moralist, which is a worthy and serious thing to be," but wishes that More were "free from a mystical impulse which occasionally gets out of . . . hand" (*SW*, 41). Emerging here is a hint of what was to become one of Eliot's consuming preoccupations for the next two decades and beyond: his search for the best way to bring precise moral—and indeed, theological—concerns to bear upon the evaluation of literature. The "expansion or development of interests" he would speak of in the 1928 Preface has already begun to make its presence felt in 1920. It was Babbitt who would challenge Eliot to "come out into the open" in 1927,[20] but it was More a decade earlier who prompted him to recognize that his iconoclastic formalism was inadequate to the challenges inherent in the "age of Arnold," when the decline of common assumptions about man and his place in the world leads the critic to look to literature for values formerly supplied by religion. Only by making his extra-literary commitments explicit can the critic practice a criticism not prone to subvert literature into a substitute for religion. Ironically, the very concern for the integrity of poetry, that poetry should be valued "as poetry and not another thing," the concern which initially prompted Eliot to adopt a formalist "aesthetic" position, soon led him to see that formalism as only *part* of "a larger and more difficult subject . . . that of the relation of poetry to the spiritual and social life of its time," as he states in the 1928 Preface. Recalling the theme of

Russell Kirk's *Eliot and His Age,* we may say that only when the "moral imagination" is acknowledged and exercised in its full scope is the aesthetic imagination free to go about its proper work, unencumbered by the forlorn hope of an Arnold, a Pater, or an I. A. Richards that "poetry is capable of saving us" now that religion no longer can. "[I]t is like saying," Eliot retorts, "that the wall-paper will save us when the walls have crumbled."[21]

This recognition of the need to hold moral and aesthetic critical standpoints in creative tension is an important impetus in the development of Eliot's intellectual outlook, an outlook which More's philosophic dualism did much to stimulate and structure. I refer to Eliot's often misunderstood concept of orthodoxy and heresy, his promulgations of which were to gain him few friends in the literary world and beyond. Orthodoxy consists, for Eliot, not in adherence to a central truth, centrifugal deviation from which is heresy, as in the controlling metaphor of Babbitt's humanism, but in the steady state of equilibrium in which two truths—the humanity and the divinity of Christ, to cite a fundamental Christian dogma—hold each other in tension, overemphasis on either constituting heresy. So it must be in this life, until, in the language of *Four Quartets,* "At the still point of the turning world," "the tongues of flame are infolded / Into the crowned knot of fire / And the fire and the rose are one."

It is this structure which undergirds Eliot's call for "orthodoxy of sensibility."[22] In the letter to More quoted at the outset, just prior to the sentence denying that his catholicism is an escape, evasion, or defeat, he describes what such a sensibility would entail:

> What I should like to see is the creation of a new type of intellectual, combining the intellectual and the devotional—a new species which cannot be created hurriedly. I dont [*sic*] like either the purely intellectual Christian or the purely emotional Christian—both forms of snobism. The co-ordination of thought and feeling . . . seems to me what is needed.[23]

The word "purely" is the key here: co-ordination of thought and feeling is the only defense against "pure"—that is, heretical—intellectualism and emotionalism.

Here again, More stands in the near background, for the unifying theme of his philosophical and theological work is his condemnation of all forms of absolutism. In his review of More's *The Demon of the Absolute* in 1929, referring to the title essay, Eliot writes:

> The essay is a protest against certain modern tendencies in art and in philosophy, and it is to these tendencies that the author opposes his dualism. The demon of the absolute is for Mr. More the spirit of heresy in all things: the human craving for unification which will push any theory to the extreme.[24]

He then notes that More's "dualism is remarkably similar to the theory of discontinuity put forth by the late T. E. Hulme," and quotes at length from Hulme on the "theory of gaps." As Ronald Schuchard has demonstrated, it was "Hulme of Original Sin" (Wyndham Lewis's *soubriquet*) who "show[ed] Eliot that Original Sin was the basic element of the classical compound."[25] Eliot's linking of Hulme and More should not come as a surprise to those familiar with More's analysis of the Transcendentalists' "serene indifference to evil" noted above, and particularly of Emerson, who "shut his eyes resolutely on the darker facts of nature."

It was over issues such as the metaphysical nature of God and of evil that More and Eliot sparred in the nearly eight years of their correspondence, sometimes accusing each other—heatedly but always in good humor—of exotic heresies and far-fetched apostasies.[26] Responding to More's letter of 9 July 1930, Eliot, purportedly trembling under what he deemed More's "excommunication," calls upon him to demonstrate *his* orthodoxy and to declare how much of orthodox theology he refuses.[27] Yet, throughout their cut-and-thrust exchanges, Eliot regarded More's religious position as close to his own. In a letter to Allen Tate about the time of the *Demon* review, he comments that in their face-to-face conversations, he had found More to be nearer to Catholic orthodoxy than he had come to expect on the basis of reading *Christ the Word,* and that he expected More to receive the sacraments before he died.

Eliot's hopes for his mentor were not to be fulfilled. Austin Warren, friend of both Eliot and More, observes regarding the latter's spiritual quest that in the process of writing about Plato and the impact of Platonic dualism on Christianity in The Greek Tradition, More

> found himself a Christian and an Anglican. To the Episcopal Church as offering a liturgical mode of worship, More had been attracted . . . when he was still creedless and vaguely religious. Now he found himself gradually being converted from religiosity to belief, finding in the Incarnation the fulfillment of the Platonic hope and in the Eucharist a center for incarnational worship.

Yet, Warren observes,

> [i]t is characteristic of More that he arrived at his Catholic Faith on Protestant principles—that is, instead of making a single act of assenting faith, he proceeded to bear his critical weight upon each dogma and practice in turn. Thus, though he was able, in some sense, to affirm his belief in each article of the Apostles' Creed, he took it upon himself to decide which should be taken literally and which symbolically.[28]

The same point had been made by Eliot, when, reviewing More's posthumously published apologia, *Pages from an Oxford Diary,* he says that More's "faith remains to the end rather personal and individualistic," indeed, "downright heterodox, as in his treatment of the Doctrine of the Eucharist."[29] The perplexing irony of More's pilgrimage, which he recounts in "Marginalia," published a few months before his death, and in the Oxford diary, is that, like Emerson, he did not

> personally care to be a partaker in the Communion. I am satisfied, I even prefer, to remain in undisturbed contemplation as a spectator, leaving the active role to the priest, whose function and duty it is. So sitting, and watching, and hearing, and meditating, I seem to be brought very close to the heart of the creating and redeeming God, carried for a season into the hidden world of spiritual forces.

He concludes, in words that might have been penned by Emerson:

> [S]ometimes from the clear radiance of morning on the dewy fields coming into the candle-light of the altar, and surrendering myself to the spell of the ancient liturgy, I have known an emotion deeper than tears, stronger than any doubt, beyond all expression in words.[30]

To trace in detail the spiritual biography that brought More, the compiler and author of *Anglicanism: The Thought and Practice of the Church of England*, and, in Eliot' words, "more Anglican than the Anglicans" ("PEM" 373), to emulate Emerson's polite refusal of the Eucharist and to decline Confirmation, would be beyond the scope of this inquiry. A comprehensive overview would assess the enduring impact on More's thought of his youthful "adventure . . . [in] the religious philosophy of India," where he was attracted to Buddhism's "creedless faith," which "included no omnipotent God as Creator and Ruler, nor had any apparatus of Platonic Ideas or of an eternal heaven and hell."[31] Still, that Eliot, whose poems often reflect his own Harvard excursion into Sanskrit literature and Patanjali's metaphysics, should attest to More's heterodoxy, their spiritual kinship notwithstanding, calls for some attempt to account for the divergence of their paths.

When, in Warren's words, More "decided to die as he had so long lived, in the anteroom of the Church, in the Porch of the Temple,"[32] it is as if—to alter the Virgil-Dante analogy with which we began—More chose to remain with his beloved Plato on the farther shore of classical paganism rather than abandon him for the Christian faith his dualistic idealism had anticipated and enriched. Actually, to put it this way would be to understate More's view of the historical relationship. In *The Christ of the New Testament*, he credits the Hellenizing of Christianity with having mitigated the "harmful effects" of Paul's Messianic eschatology and rabbinical theology, with its "doctrine of predestination and grace, faith and law."[33] And while these "legalistic elements" would reappear in Tertullian and Augustine and "burst out with devastating malignity in the theology of Luther and Calvin,"

> in the main Christianity passed with the fourth Gospel into the wide stream of Greek thought, while bringing to that Tradition its own vital contribution; henceforth we have to study the mutual assimilation of

the faith of Jesus with the Idealism of Plato. . . . Christianity to become a world religion had to be translated into the universal and more spiritual terms of Greek intuition. . . . So far as Jesus' consciousness of his divine nature transcended the limits of Messianism it was already implicitly Greek and not Hebrew. It remained for John . . . under the influence of Hellenistic philosophy to lay hold of those sayings of Jesus which expressed his relation to the Father in general language, and so to fulfil the hidden purpose of the Master, hidden partly perhaps even to himself. Thus only could the accomplishment of prophecy become the universal revelation of God to man.[34]

But More's Hellenized deity bears the scars of a crisis forced by the very dualism which underlay his whole project of philosophical and theological speculation. In "Marginalia" he relates how, from the Sunday when as a youth he entered a church sanctuary a Calvinist and departed an agnostic, he rejected any dogma with the least taint of absolutism.[35] Thus the bedrock of Calvin's systematic theology, the sovereignty of God, whom, in More's view, only "the hyperbole of reverence" names "the Almighty" (*POD*, XXI), was anathema: "that definition of God as the absolute unconditioned Cause of all things" constituted for More "an undigested and undigestible mass" in "the old inherited faith of Calvin," with its otherwise "noble aspect, maintaining an authority over the conscience, and lending a logical consistency to the fluctuating world of the spirit" (23). Presumably, it was this "noble aspect" whose gradual elimination by the generations succeeding the Pilgrim Fathers led inevitably to "the last condition" More had diagnosed in the case of Henry Adams. Left unexamined by More is how this "positive content" might have flourished in a climate "deprived of its concrete deity"; how, in other words, the drift toward Unitarianism More lamented could have been averted if God's sovereignty had been compromised in a Manichaean standoff with Necessity. W. Norman Pittenger, friend and critic of More, observes of his "finite God":

> More came to a belief in a Being who is in some sense limited. . . . God is working with some intractable necessity, perhaps some downward drag in things, even some pre-existent material; He is more like an artificer than a creator . . . who out of His very self brings forth that which is other than Himself. To some degree it was the problem of evil which brought More to this conclusion.[36]

Such a conception of God could not but have implications for More's understanding of the Incarnation, the basic tenet of his faith—"any true philosophy of God demands the Incarnation" (*POD*, XXI)—and of the Eucharist. In the Incarnation, More holds, God reveals himself "as a person implicated, morally at least, in the consequences of His acts. . . . In some sense the imperfection of the creature is the weakness of the creator; no amount of sophistical theology can avoid the shuddering conclusion that tracks the causes of evil back to the first Cause of all" (*POD*, XXII). God also reveals himself as the redeemer; not, however, in victory over death and sin in the Resurrection, but in Promethean expiation of his cosmic *mea culpa*:

> If there be any meaning in the tragic end of the Incarnation, if the Cross have any cosmic significance, it must be simply this, that God as the Author of an imperfect world, so through his suffering made himself voluntarily its redeemer. . . . We know that until now the whole creation groaneth and travaileth together, waiting for its release, and I believe that on Calvary the great *peripeteia* took place. On that day the demands of Necessity were satisfied, the awful responsibility was acknowledged, the debt of creation was paid. (*POD*, XXIII)

Thus it might be said that for More, the self-described Patripassionist,[37] the *original* Original Sin was not man's first disobedience but God's flawed act of creation, and that with Christ the Son, he must pay for "the failure of His own handiwork and somehow [redeem] the evil of the world by participating in the penalties of imperfection" (*POD*, XXIV). As for the bodily Resurrection of Christ, it must be regarded as the work of the "mythopoeic imagination": "The Gospel story of the risen Christ, beautiful though it may be in some respects, lowers the spiritual life to a semimaterialism which has left an unfortunate trail in religion; it ought to be surrendered as pure superstition, or, at the least, interpreted symbolically."[38] Seen in this light, the Eucharist becomes something quite different from the communal celebration of the perfect vicarious sacrifice of the Lamb of God for the sins of the world, and the elements of bread and wine become only material testaments to that "lowered" spiritual life.

It could only have been with sadness that, upon reading the manuscript of *Pages from an Oxford Diary* in 1929, Eliot had to accept that More's long-evolving unorthodoxies had become settled convictions.[39] When he reviewed the posthumously published book in 1937, he honored More for the "solitary road" his pilgrimage had taken, but also confronted the fact of his self-imposed isolation from the Church:

> [T]he man who can go on [from praising Anglicanism for affirming the Real Presence and the mystery of the Eucharist] to say "Nor do I personally care to be a partaker in the Communion" has surely some cardinal error fundamental to his whole doctrine of the Eucharistic Sacrifice. And one cannot help feeling that—as is not surprising in a lonely and self-taught theologian—More had an inadequate conception of the divine nature of the Church as the Living Body of Christ.[40]

In the final analysis, of course, a man's theology cannot fully account for his faith; personal and perhaps intangible factors play their part. In their last exchange (as More's "Marginalia" and Eliot's appreciative letter in response might be characterized), there is an additional clue to More's reversion to something like the Boston doubt, a clue which leads us back to St. Louis and to what Eliot identified as the "antiquated and provincial American Presbyterianism" against which More rebelled in his youth.[41] In "Marginalia," More writes: "I have often wondered what line my experience might have taken had I been brought up in a form of belief and practice of worship from which the office of the imagination and of the aesthetic emotions had not been so ruthlessly evicted" (24–25). More's reflection stirred similar thoughts in his fellow Missourian. In that last letter, after remarking upon the "grotesque" resemblance of their spiritual biographies, Eliot quotes back to More his sentence about the eviction of the imagination and emotions, and confesses to the same speculation about his own upbringing.

If we conclude, as Eliot implicitly must have, that More's was not the "manlier voice" he hoped would redeem the faith of Emerson and Adams from its "last condition," we may nevertheless endorse the high tribute paid him by his grateful student and friend. "One is always aware," Eliot wrote in his Princeton memoir, "of the sincerity, and in the later works the Christian humility . . . of the concentrated mind seeking God." And we might wish to add Eliot's handwritten postscript to the last letter, perhaps as much a petition on behalf of his dying friend as an offering of gratitude for aid on his own journey: "May one say, under the guidance of the Holy Spirit?"

NOTES

1. Eliot, *For Lancelot Andrewes: Essays on Style and Order* (London: Faber, 1928), vii.

2. Quoted in Roger Kojecký, *T. S. Eliot's Social Criticism* (New York: Farrar, 1971), 74.

3. Eliot, "Paul Elmer More," *Princeton Alumni Weekly* 37 (1937): 373. Cited hereafter in text as "PEM."

4. Quoted in Arthur Hazard Dakin, *Paul Elmer More* (Princeton: Princeton University Press, 1960), 289.

5. More, "The Cleft Eliot," review of *Selected Essays*, by T. S. Eliot, *Saturday Review of Literature* (12 Nov. 1932): 233, 235. Rpt. in *T. S. Eliot: A Selected Critique*, ed. Leonard Unger (New York: Rinehart, 1948), 28.

6. Quoted in John D. Margolis, *T. S. Eliot's Intellectual Development 1922–1939* (Chicago: University of Chicago Press, 1972), 145.

7. Eliot, review of *Son of Woman: The Story of D. H. Lawrence*, by John Middleton Murry, *Criterion* 10 (1931): 771.

8. More, *A New England Group and Others*, Shelburne Essays 11 (Boston: Houghton, 1921), 140. Cited hereafter in text as *NEG*.

9. Eliot, *The Sacred Wood: Essays on Poetry and Criticism*, second ed. (London: Methuen, 1928), x.

10. Ibid., vii.

11. See Herbert Howarth, *Notes on Some Figures behind T. S. Eliot* (Boston: Houghton, 1964), chapter 2, especially his discussion of the St. Louis Movement.

12. Ralph Waldo Emerson, letter to Lidian Emerson, 31 Dec. 1852. *The Letters of Ralph Waldo Emerson*, ed. Ralph L. Rusk, vol. 4 (New York: Columbia University Press, 1939), 338.

13. Eliot, *To Criticize the Critic and Other Writings* (New York: Farrar, 1965), 44.

14. Discussing Babbitt's conflation of humanism and religion, Eliot comments that "[h]is humanism is . . . (to my mind) alarmingly like very liberal Protestant theology of the nineteenth century; it is, in fact, a product—a by-product—of Protestant theology in its last agonies." "The Humanism of Irving Babbitt," in *Selected Essays* (New York: Harcourt, 1950), 422. On the impact of "the decay of Protestantism" on contemporary writers, see *After Strange Gods: A Primer of Modern Heresy* (New York: Harcourt, 1934), 41.

15. Eliot, "A Sceptical Patrician," review of *The Education of Henry Adams*, by Henry Adams. *Athenaeum* (23 May 1919): 361–62.

16. Quotations from *Four Quartets* are from *The Complete Poems and Plays* (New York: Harcourt, 1962).

17. Eliot, "An American Critic," review of *Aristocracy and Justice*, by Paul Elmer More, *New Statesman* (24 June 1916): 284.

18. Ibid.

19. Eliot, "The Local Flavour," review of *Literary Studies*, by Charles Whibley, *Athenaeum* (12 Dec. 1919): 1333.

20. Eliot, *To Criticize the Critic*, 15.

21. Eliot, "Literature, Science, and Dogma," review of *Science and Poetry*, by I. A. Richards, *Dial* 82 (1927): 243.

22. Eliot, *After Strange Gods*, 40.

23. Quoted in Kojecký, 74.

24. Eliot, "Mr. P. E. More's Essays," review of *Demon of the Absolute*, by Paul Elmer More, *Times Literary Supplement* (21 Feb. 1929): 136.

25. Ronald Schuchard, *Eliot's Dark Angel: Intersections of Life and Art* (New York: Oxford University Press, 1999), 55.

26. In 1931, More wrote to friends that Eliot said he was "looking forward to long evenings" with More, "enlivened by whiskey and tobacco and countercharges of heresy." For his part, More relished the thought of "convict[ing] a devout Anglo-Catholic of heresy" (quoted in Dakin 299). For a useful overview of the correspondence and what it reveals about the two men, see R. A. Harries, "The Rare Contact: A Correspondence between T. S. Eliot and P. E. More" *Theology* 75 (1972): [136]–44.

27. More's letter is quoted in Dakin (290–92); Eliot's reply is dated 10 August 1930. See Robert Shafer, *Paul Elmer More and American Criticism* (New Haven: Yale University Press, 1935), 260–61, for a succinct list of dogmas More discarded in his effort to spike the guns of what he characterized as the "purely humanitarian view of Christianity" of Strauss and Schweitzer, while at the same time largely accepting the "solid results" regarding the literary and historical problems of the Biblical text that emerged from the higher criticism. See More, *The Christ of the New Testament*, The Greek Tradition, vol. 3 (Princeton: Princeton University Press, 1924), viii.

28. Austin Warren, *Connections* (Ann Arbor: University of Michigan Press, 1970), 147–50.

29. Eliot, "An Anglican Platonist: The Conversion of Paul Elmer More," review of *Pages from an Oxford Diary*, by Paul Elmer More, *Times Literary Supplement* (30 Oct. 1937): 792.

30. More, *Pages from an Oxford Diary* (Princeton: Princeton University Press, 1937), XXX. Cited hereafter as *POD* (unpaginated; numerals refer to chapter numbers). Illustrating how Emerson's "faith in the inner power grew out of the Puritan distrust of traditional rites and institutions," More cites the opening lines of his poem "The Problem" (*NEG* 84): "I like a church; I like a cowl; / I love a prophet of the soul; / And on my heart monastic aisles / Fall like sweet strains, or pensive smiles: / Yet not for all his faith can see / Would I that cowlèd churchman be."

31. More, "Marginalia," *American Review* 8 (1936): 26.

32. Warren, 150.

33. More, *Christ of the New Testament*, 284.

34. Ibid., 286–88.

35. More, "Marginalia," 23–24.

36. W. Norman Pittenger, *Theology and Reality: Essays in Restatement* (Greenwich, CT: Seabury, 1955), 228.

37. On More's Patripassionism and related theological views, see his letter to Eliot of 20 May 1930 (quoted in Dakin, 289), Eliot's reply of 2 June 1930 (quoted in Margolis, 143–44), and More's reply of 9 July 1930 (quoted in Dakin, 290–92). See also More's letter to C. S. Lewis of 29 November 1934 (quoted in Dakin 358–60).

38. More, *Christ of the New Testament*, 274, 271.

39. Eliot advised More that while Faber and Gwyer would take anything with More's name on it, they were unlikely to publish the book anonymously, as More wished (letter to More, Shrove Tuesday 1928 [i.e., 1929]). Eliot attempted—obviously without success—to place it with another publisher. A fortnight before he died, More slightly revised the text for publication by Princeton University Press (Dakin, 386).

40. Eliot, "An Anglican Platonist," 792.

41. Ibid.

SEVENTEEN

C. S. Lewis's Appreciation of T. S. Eliot

Charles A. Huttar

Writers on C. S. Lewis—including some scholars to whom we are indebted for significant insights into his life and work—often uncritically perpetuate a falsehood that has long distorted the scholarship, describing his attitude toward Eliot (at least until late in his life) with words like "antipathy," "bête noire," "pathological" dislike, even "arch enemy" and "hate."[1] The phenomenon is not confined to Lewis studies. John Shaw-cross has made the general observation that there tends to be "a persistence of past interpretations and 'facts'" even when newer scholarship "has created revisions of those supposed 'facts' and provided significant additions."[2] There are, to be sure, voices that speak in a more nuanced fashion, and the garden of Lewis scholarship has flourishing blooms. Yet, as in any garden, weeds are hard to eradicate. For this reason, although some of the points that follow have been made already in scattered publications and in other contexts, it seems desirable to assemble them here, along with new material, in a brief chapter focused on this single topic. I hope to show that while Lewis disagreed with Eliot fundamentally in some matters of critical judgment,[3] there is no basis for using such emotion-laden terms as I have quoted, especially when his remarks are understood in context; and there is much evidence—too often overlooked, it appears—for concluding that, on the whole, his attitude toward Eliot and his work was quite favorable.

It is necessary to keep in mind that we are dealing with a nearly fifty-year span of Lewis's intellectual life, and his opinions are far more likely to have developed than to have remained static. (We will also observe some shifting in Eliot's stance over a similar period.) We must begin by identifying several distinct issues. What did Lewis think of Eliot as a person? What did he think of the trends in poetry with which Eliot's name was associated, and third, of the cultural and religious movements in which Eliot figured? Fourth, what did he think of Eliot's views as a critic? Finally, what did he think of the creative work of Eliot as a literary artist?

Regarding the first of these questions, Lewis's attitude toward Eliot as a person, it is acknowledged that once the two came into close association as members of a church commission,[4] friendship developed. The Eliots and the Lewises, both recently wed, lunched together, and Lewis tried to arrange a second such meeting but schedule conflicts prevented it. Lewis described his labors on the commission as "delightful work with delightful colleagues,"[5] and letters written in his final years display his cordiality toward Eliot.[6] It is less well recognized that a mutually respectful personal relationship began, as we shall see, considerably earlier, and that Lewis had made overtures in that direction earlier still.

Granted, it was not always so. Early in his career Lewis wanted to be remembered, above all, as a poet. He had published his first volume of verse while still an undergraduate, and other work was in progress—but all in a style that was rapidly passing out of fashion. The American expatriates Pound and Eliot represented new trends that he considered dangerous, not merely as a threat to his own ambitions but on reasoned critical grounds. In the 1920s Lewis and some friends concocted schemes to lampoon what they considered the vacuous pretentiousness of the vers libre then in vogue. One of these involved trying to get *The New Criterion*, of which Eliot was editor, to publish parodies of the modern style in poetry, then triumphantly exposing the hoax.[7] Eliot was then thirty-seven and wielded power in the literary establishment, Lewis ten years younger and relatively powerless, but high-spirited. It is reasonable to think of this as a passing phase. And it should be noted that, according to Lewis's biographer Walter Hooper, there is no evidence that the parodies were ever submitted.[8] In any case, the target was not Eliot himself but the literary movement of which, for Lewis, he had become a symbol.[9] Thus we are concerned here with the second of the questions I have listed.

What Lewis in all seriousness did ask the *Criterion* a few years later to consider publishing was his essay "The Personal Heresy in Criticism," developing ideas in critical theory that he believed were in line with Eliot's own.[10] For two events occurred about this time that are of great importance for our story. In 1928 Eliot, who had been raised in a rather secularized Unitarian tradition, publicly declared his new adherence to Christian belief—specifically, Anglo-Catholic belief. In 1931 Lewis, brought up in a Church of Ireland parish of which his grandfather was the rector, but where the preaching of Christian essentials appears to have been rather bland,[11] returned to Christian faith after a youthful period of outspoken atheism. After Eliot's conversion his poetry took a new direction, most notably in the themes he explores, a direction that Lewis after *his* conversion could appreciate and that, as we shall see, removed the basis for some of his earlier objections. It may well be that Lewis's "rooted antipathy" to Eliot was "hard to shake off,"[12] but he did try to shake it off—helped perhaps by the change Walter Hooper describes: "With his conversion, that little hard core of worldly ambition, evident on almost every page of his diary [and, as we have seen, partly responsible for the animus exhibited earlier], seems to have dropped into oblivion"—a point that Lewis's close friend J. R. R. Tolkien has confirmed.[13] He still could be outspoken, in the banter of conversation or in private letters, when hasty composition or the dynamics of personal exchange can easily account for overstatements that an outside observer might incautiously take at face value.[14] But Lewis's long-time friend Roger Lancelyn Green assures us that "though [he] sometimes overstated his opinions in conversation, he never rushed them into print."[15]

Sometimes the target was not so much Eliot as the cultural movements with which he was identified. To one correspondent in 1934 Lewis wrote: "Beware of the people (Maritain in your Church, and T. S. Eliot in mine) who are at present running what they call 'neo-scholasticism' as a fad."[16] In print, Lewis was careful to avoid any personal attack.[17] The satire in *The Pilgrim's Regress* (1933) was veiled by allegory. What the Three Pale Men of Book 6 have in common, according to Lewis's later marginal additions, are "Counter-romanticism" and "Negativism."[18] Mr. Neo-Angular, the only theist among them, does not strictly speaking represent an individual but a group, a "set" who wanted, Lewis thought, to "make of Christianity itself one more high-brow, Chelsea, bourgeois-baiting fad"—adding that "T. S. Eliot . . . sums up the thing I am fighting against."[19] Ten years later, Lewis's view had mellowed considerably. Prefacing a new edition in 1943 he apologized for the book's "uncharitable temper" and regretted the "bitterness" of his attack on various contemporaries, among them "Neo-Scholastics, and some who wrote for *The Criterion*," who "seemed to me to be condemning what they did not understand."[20]

Lewis's other comments on Eliot in the 1930s and 1940s relate to either Eliot's pronouncements as a critic—the fourth of the five issues I have identified—or his poetry. Lewis's style in debate was always marked as much by generosity toward his opponent as by vigor of attack,[21] and whenever he explicitly challenged Eliot's literary opinions he always juxtaposed remarks about Eliot's work that were affirmative and conciliatory. In his Shelley lecture, Lewis's main aim was to reverse Eliot's canonization of Dryden at Shelley's expense, but he agreed with some things Eliot had said about Dryden and he stressed what he considered views they held in common: a respect for classicism, a Christian outlook that would reject a Shelleyan sort of spirituality, and a high valuation of

Dante.[22] Lewis appears now, in the late 1930s, to be jumping at opportunities to align himself with Eliot. After citing Eliot's view of the *Paradiso* he adds: "I think the same—and since it is so pleasant to agree, let me add irrelevantly that I think as he does about the *Bhagavad-Gita*."[23] In discussing Shelley's *Epipsychidion* Lewis returns to a distinction made in *The Personal Heresy* and calls Eliot to his aid, speaking of the "problem with which Mr Eliot has been much occupied . . . of the relation between our judgement on a poem as critics, and our judgement as men on the ethics, metaphysics, or theology presupposed or expressed in the poem."[24] The distinction is important: it will appear again when we consider Lewis's comments on Eliot's poetry. Early in his British Academy lecture on *Hamlet* he disagrees with Eliot's labeling the play "an artistic failure"; however, he accepts Eliot's view that Shakespeare did not make Hamlet's motives clear and, citing with approval Eliot's comment that *Hamlet* is "interesting," he bolsters his own interpretation by an appeal to "Eliot's own method in poetry."[25] In his 1941 lectures on Milton, Lewis undertakes to rebut "a recent remark" by Eliot but starts with this disclaimer: "If I make Mr Eliot's words the peg on which to hang a discussion of this notion, it must not, therefore, be assumed that this is, for me, more than a convenience, still less that I wish to attack him *quâ* Mr Eliot. Why should I? I agree with him about matters of such moment that all literary questions are, in comparison, trivial." Such matters were not limited to their self-identification as Christians but went well beyond the basic creedal elements that Lewis would later call "mere Christianity."[26] A 1943 letter from Lewis to Eliot captures the spirit of these friendly disagreements: "I hope the fact that I find myself often contradicting you in print gives no offence: it is a kind of tribute to you—whenever I fall foul of some widespread contemporary view about literature, I always seem to find that you have expressed it most clearly. One aims at the officers first in meeting an attack!"[27] But for all that, he did appreciate Eliot's skill as a critic: when invited in 1948 to give a radio talk on Charles Williams's novels, he replied, "T. S. Eliot would do it better."[28] In the same year Lewis observed in a talk before the Dante Society that "one aspect of [Dante's] imagery" is an "almost sensuous intensity about things not sensuous." It would be going too far to say that Lewis here alludes to Eliot's famous 1921 remark about the "immedia[c]y" for Donne of thought and feeling, before a "dissociation of sensibility set in" later in the seventeenth century, but arguably Lewis had (by whatever route) come by this time, and possibly much earlier, to agree with Eliot's analysis.[29]

In *A Preface to "Paradise Lost"* Lewis undertook to defend Milton against several recent detractors, Eliot among them. Eliot said that Milton, though undeniably a great poet, was in some important ways not "a *good* poet," and therefore had had a "bad influence," one "against which we still have to struggle."[30] After a short chapter in his *Preface* (pp. 9–11) refuting Eliot's claim that only the best practicing poets could speak with authority as critics of poetry, Lewis addressed Eliot's strictures on Milton—failure in "visual imagination" (Eliot 158), the pursuit of sonority at the expense of thought (159-61, 163-64), and departure from "conversational language" in blank verse (161) as it had been modeled by Shakespeare and his successors. He did so mainly by an appeal to the decorum of the epic genre, though he also claimed for Milton's verse visual and intellectual achievements greater than Eliot would allow.[31]

In 1947 Eliot returned to the subject, acknowledging Lewis's contributions to a degree that seems not yet to be fully appreciated. Not only does he refer to Lewis explicitly (Eliot 168–69), but in saying that "the *errors of our times* have been rectified by vigorous hands" (165, emphasis added) and in granting the need to acknowledge the prejudices of one's age (167), he alludes obliquely to Lewis's reiterated warnings of the dangers, in any age, of accepting uncritically the assumptions that belong to the spirit of that age (see, for example, *Preface* 54–56, 61–63). Eliot's readiness now to find value in the scholar's kind of criticism (166) suggests that he has found Lewis's chapter persuasive (though Lewis is not named); so also when Eliot opines that "a more vivid picture of the earthly Paradise would have been less paradisiacal" (178; cf. Lewis, *Preface* 47) or when he speaks of "Milton as, outside the theatre, the greatest master in our language of freedom within form" (183; cf. Lewis, *Preface* 79–80). In addition, Eliot's choice to single out for praise, among Milton critics, Lewis's friend Charles Williams, whose "prolegomenon to *Comus*" is "the best" (166), may glance at the similar praise that Lewis accorded Williams in dedicating his *Preface* to him.

These remarks—or, we may even say, concessions—shed a new light, I believe, on what Eliot is reported to have said to Lewis when they first met (over tea at the Mitre Hotel in Oxford, brought together by Williams). According to a third-party report it was an awkward meeting; still, in Eliot's remark that he considered *A Preface to "Paradise Lost"* Lewis's "best book" we may have an intimation of the conciliatory stance he would adopt in the Milton lecture of 1947. The third party present who found the remark merely embarrassing would have had no way of knowing that two years previously, Eliot and Lewis had had an exchange of letters about Lewis's *Preface*.[32] Lewis himself jotted down this memorandum: "Mr. Eliot has asked me not to write about his literary criticism. Very well. I obey."[33] The biographers' idea that "beyond that, [Lewis] seems to have put Eliot out of his mind till they met years later under more congenial circumstances" (Green and Hooper 224) is surely mistaken, for within a month Lewis was inviting Eliot to contribute to a memorial festschrift honoring Williams (who had just died suddenly and unexpectedly). Eliot at first agreed and even settled on a topic, Williams's plays, but was, finally, to Lewis's considerable disappointment, not able to do so.[34]

But the story of Lewis's continued engagement with Eliot's criticisms arguably does not end there, though his next move, following Eliot's 1947 lecture, was very indirect. In that lecture Eliot, though obliquely acknowledging points made in Lewis's *Preface*, essentially repeats his charge concerning Milton's "bad influence"—however, with some qualifications and with a narrower focus. He is careful to point out that he offers his criticism not as a scholar but as a practitioner of poetry (ignoring a possible third sort of critic, the common reader).[35] "The scholar's interest," he says, "is in the permanent, the practitioner's in the immediate. The scholar can teach us where we should bestow our *admiration* and *respect:* the practitioner should be able . . . to make an old masterpiece actual, give it contemporary importance, and persuade his audience that it is interesting, exciting, enjoyable, and *active*" (166, Eliot's emphasis). That is said of the practicing poet *qua* critic. Then Eliot proceeds to the main question, that of Milton's "technical" influence on "the writer of poetry in our own time" (171). He explicitly sets aside, as unprovable, his earlier judgment concerning Milton's bad influence in prior centuries and the prediction that his influence could never be good (172; cf. 157). He does *not* give up the idea that "the study of Milton could be . . . only a hindrance" to poets of the generation of *The Waste Land* (182). But times change, and now, twenty-five years later, "the study of his verse might at last be of benefit to poets" (181).

Eliot's so-called recantation[36] is usually thought to have closed that exchange. But although Lewis had been enjoined from writing further about Eliot's criticism, he found another way to have the last word. The next year, 1948, he published in *Punch* a Christmas poem, "The Turn of the Tide," a reshaping of Milton's *Nativity Ode.* In this way he takes up Eliot's hint that it has become possible, again, to imitate Milton with profit; and he demonstrates how it can be done. One should not be dogmatic, of course, about an author's "intention," but I suggest that "The Turn of the Tide" might be viewed as a response to Eliot, conciliatory in nature—an offering, one might say, of a test case for Eliot's dictum that practicing poets may now approach Milton "without danger, and with profit" (Eliot 183). But Eliot's concern was with Milton as a model for technique— "the language, the syntax, the versification, the imagery" (171). Eliot did not talk about theme, except for repeated efforts to distance himself from particular features of Milton's theology, yet theme is the primary point of contact between Lewis's poem and Milton's. Lewis also had an eye to technique, however, and he found in Milton positive guidance for imagery and for versification, though in neither case was he a simple imitator. His choice of a model other than *Paradise Lost,* one having a complex stanza form, leaves unaddressed Eliot's worries about the influence in particular of Miltonic blank verse. As to language and syntax, and rhetoric as well (another of Eliot's concerns [161]), Lewis departed significantly from Milton's example. In "The Turn of the Tide,"

Lewis implicitly identified aspects of Milton's achievement which would be impossible, or inadvisable, for a twentieth-century poet to emulate — for example, the overt theologizing — and set these aside. He retained what he considered timeless, most notably the profoundly Christian conception (however indirectly stated) that at the Deity's taking of human form the world's history took a turn for the better. And thus (to borrow Eliot's phrasing) he "ma[d]e an old masterpiece actual" (Eliot 166) for contemporary readers.[37]

Finally, what did Lewis think of Eliot's poetry? One thing is clear, that whatever his critical judgments, he cannot be charged with failure to understand it. Negative comments may still be found among Lewis's private remarks, but there is also clear evidence that he read Eliot with insight and even appreciation.[38] Derek Brewer, one of his pupils in the late 1940s, reports that Lewis "greatly admired" Eliot's work. He had enjoyed a performance of *Murder in the Cathedral* that he attended, he acknowledged in print Eliot's artistic power in the portrayal of evil, he drew on an observation of Eliot's about English taste, he quoted a line in *The Dry Salvages* that seemed to him perceptive, he alluded to lines in *The Waste Land* that he must have found evocative, in *That Hideous Strength* he adapted phrasing from "Fragment of an Agon" (I believe attention has not yet been called to this borrowing), he spoke of his "debt to Mr. Eliot's poetry" and included Eliot in a short list of poets whose work he found "enrich[ing]" and "congenial," and he praised "the penitential quality of [Eliot's] best work." When Eliot found himself unable to meet the deadline for his planned essay in the Williams festschrift, Lewis asked whether he might instead "have a *poem* ready" that could be included — not necessarily one having "any special connection with Charles Williams." All these citations come from the mid-1930s onward.[39]

That Lewis did not accord Eliot's poetry uncritical adulation should be neither surprising nor objectionable. From early days, his objections to the modernist movement — for which, we recall, the name of Eliot was a synecdoche — were threefold: the forsaking of traditional prosody, a (to him) willful obscurity that at worst could cloak having nothing to say, and a celebration of squalor that he considered morally irresponsible. These are the errors of the "Dirty" and "Lunatic Twenties" that he caricatured in Book 3 of *The Pilgrim's Regress* (52–54). Most of his negative comments on Eliot's poetry refer to the work of that period or earlier; Eliot's post-conversion poetry was less open to these criticisms.

On Eliot's prosody Lewis had little if anything to say. The problem of obscurity in poetry he addressed in an analytic way in an essay on Charles Williams's poetry, and by then — the late 1940s — he was painting with a much finer brush. He distinguished four kinds of obscurity, in what may be (though he does not so specify) diminishing order of badness. The fourth kind — the least unacceptable — arises from "unshared background," and he draws on Williams and on Eliot's *The Waste Land* to illustrate it. Within this category there are gradations, ranging from things that the reader ought to know, might properly be expected to catch, such as Eliot's allusions to Dante and Shakespeare, down to things that are less clearly a part of even a well-educated person's equipment: Jessie Weston and the Tarot deck are the examples Lewis gives. Where to draw the line between this category and the third, "privatism"—alluding to information that is not at all public ("the colour of your nurse's hair, the jokes of your preparatory school," and so on) which no reader, "however sensitive and generally cultivated," could be supposed to know—is difficult to judge. But privatism, except in poetry addressed to a narrow coterie, is "a reckless undermining of the very conditions in which literature can flourish." Lewis doubts whether Williams crossed that line; on Eliot he does not, here, express an opinion.[40]

Some light is shed on this question by Lewis's several references to a 1919 poem by Eliot, "A Cooking Egg." The best known of these was in his Cambridge inaugural lecture in 1954, in which he cited a symposium published the preceding year in *Essays in Criticism*. Seven experienced scholars of poetry, he said, exhibited "not the slightest agreement among them as to what [the poem] means."[41] This was not an attack on Eliot as such. It was merely an illustration of Lewis's point that one feature of a radical shift in culture since the early nineteenth century was what he perceived as a new fashion of obscurity in the arts. The symposium was current when he was working on his lecture and therefore handy for use.[42] But the point Lewis made is not very different from what Donald Davie said a few years later: "This rather trivial poem does not deserve all the attention that has been lavished on it. . . . perhaps deserves nothing better than the fate which has come upon it—to be the occasion of a sustained critical wrangle" with "several distinguished critics falling out about what the poem means."[43] A letter to Dorothy L. Sayers indicates that he believed Eliot did, in "A Cooking Egg," cross the line into privatism. The most obscure of its allusions, he wrote, "were, and were known by Eliot to be, the privities of a single, contingent human life."[44] Not all Eliot scholars would disagree.[45]

Lewis's third concern was more on ethical than esthetic grounds, for he believed a critic should rightly be concerned with a poem's moral stance as well as its technical execution: there is a "larger world where literary laws must yield to laws logical and ethical."[46] We have noted already, in Lewis's comments on Shelley's *Epipsychidion*, his concern with this issue. He held a high view of persons' responsibility for the effects of their actions, and he saw no reason artists should be exempted. He would apply the principle not only to effects intended by the poet but also to side effects in the responses of readers which have been insufficiently guarded against. And he considered a "cardinal problem of much of Mr Eliot's poetry . . . whether it is possible to distinguish poetry about squalor and chaos from squalid and chaotic poetry." Eliot's Sweeney he offered as an example.[47] He agreed with C. Day Lewis in rejecting the idea that "the right answer to a disintegrated civilization is a disintegrated poem."[48] Along similar lines he wrote to Paul Elmer More, "I must be content to judge his work by its fruits, and I contend that no man is fortified against chaos by reading the *Waste Land*, but that most men are by it infected with chaos." To say otherwise, he argues, is to "confus[e] . . . poetry that represents disintegration and disintegrated poetry. The *Inferno* is not infernal poetry: the *Waste Land* is."[49]

But Lewis's fullest critique in this vein is on a passage in an early work of Eliot's, one that first appeared in book form the year Lewis went up to Oxford, "The Love Song of J. Alfred Prufrock." On several occasions he commented negatively on a particular passage in it, and writers on Lewis have sometimes supposed that he simply misread or failed to appreciate the poem. I am convinced that this is not the case.

It is the opening simile that draws Lewis's criticism. In a letter to Kathryn Farrer he inveighed against

> a widespread tendency in modern literature which strikes me as horrid: I mean, the readiness to admit extreme uses of the pathetic fallacy in contexts where there is nothing to justify them and always of a kind which belittles or "sordidises" . . . nature. Eliot's evening "like a patient etherised upon a table" is the *locus classicus*. I don't believe one person in a million, under any emotional stress, wd. see evening like that. And even if they did, I believe that anything but the most sparing admission of such images is a v. dangerous game. To invite them, to recur willingly to them, to come to regard them as normal, surely, poisons us?[50]

Lewis knew perfectly well, I think, that Eliot would not advocate or even tolerate our regarding such an image as normal. The famous simile tells us nothing about sunsets, nor is it meant to; it tells us a great deal about the *abnormal* state of J. Alfred. Perhaps Lewis is right that in real life that particular likeness would not occur to one in a million, yet Eliot's art persuades us that it is precisely what his fictional Prufrock, who as a type is not *that* rare, would think of. It is an objective correlative for the way Prufrock feels about himself, and Prufrock is always, even in the presence of natural beauty, thinking or feeling about himself. It is his malaise.[51] With this in mind, it must be admitted that Lewis's phrase "nothing to justify them" in the letter quoted above is going a bit far: the simile has a clear and proper function in the poem. In all likelihood he would, in a public version, have corrected that misstatement. What we do have in print is Lewis's description in *A Preface to "Paradise Lost"* of Prufrock's simile as "a striking picture of sensibility in decay,"[52] which suggests that he understood Eliot's strategy.

But he also knew what other contemporaries were making of it: "I have heard" this comparison, he writes, "praised, nay gloated over, not" for its poetic aptness "but because it was so 'pleasantly unpleasant.'"[53] In other words, the Eliot passage may well have been, as Lewis says, a classic expression of a widespread attitude that he finds objectionable, yet without itself, properly read in context, advocating that attitude. Lewis did not so misread it, but other readers did, especially dilettantes caught up in the moral revolution of the between-war years; and for that he held Eliot responsible.[54]

He also tried to combat these effects. The context of his comment in the lectures on Milton was Lewis's argument that "stock responses" need, in this day and age, to be cultivated, not undermined. His antagonist in this debate was not Eliot but I. A. Richards, whose writings on literature and its psychological effects enjoyed considerable influence. Richards believed that good poetry should encourage readers to set aside habitual responses, which he considered stereotypes. But for Lewis, the free play of experience which Richards advocated could too easily lead to responses not more refined but exquisitely perverse. Lewis argued instead for attitudes and emotional responses grounded in "such memories, associations, and values as are widely distributed among the human family in space and time"—grounded, in short, in what Lewis called "the *Tao.*" He valued the belief—now in danger of being lost—"that objects did not merely receive, but could *merit,* our approval or disapproval, our reverence, or our contempt."[55]

These ideas provide the background necessary for understanding Lewis's 1954 poem "A Confession," which begins:

> I am so coarse, the things the poets see
> Are obstinately invisible to me.
> For twenty years I've stared my level best
> To see if evening—any evening—would suggest
> A patient etherized upon a table;
> In vain. I simply wasn't able.[56]

It is astonishing how many otherwise astute readers assume that the "I" of the poem is Lewis, speaking straightforwardly. We don't need to insist that the speaker is a different character, like Browning's duke or Spanish monk. But he is clearly a fiction: if Lewis (for we do find the idea elsewhere: not "one in a million . . . would see"), then a Lewis adopting a pose, just as Socrates did in some of his conversations and thereby gave his name to a type of irony. The persona strategically, exaggeratedly belittles himself, confident that the values he favors can win the field on their own and he has only to keep out of the way. He presents himself as a failure, a "dunce," "coarse," and even as an inept reader of Eliot. He apologizes for his own associative responses—evening as a ship's final departure, the moon as a reminder of our precarious existence, "dull things" like peacocks, honey, and so on, names like Athens and Jerusalem that he somehow finds evocative (Lewis here may be trying to restore the positive associations of these ancient centers of civilization whose decay Eliot had lamented in *The Waste Land* [line 374]). Cowed by the authorities of high culture, he accepts that his own "stock responses" must of course be inferior to those of "the poets." And this pretended failure drives *us* to affirm the value of those things in a way that more direct, positive assertion would not do. The rhetoric is that of understatement, and Lewis is a master of it.

One reason I am convinced that Lewis read "Prufrock" with understanding and appreciation is that traces of its influence appear, in a way that is not argumentative but imaginative, in his fictional work *The Great Divorce* (1946).[57] I am not saying that Lewis consciously followed "Prufrock" as a model in the way that he followed Milton's *Nativity Ode*. But we know that he read it, and Lewis's writings abundantly exemplify the creative fermentation that could take place in his famously retentive memory. There may also be a more specific connection. Lewis most likely knew Charles Williams's suggestion that in reading Eliot we "experience" a depiction of "Hell varied by intense poetry," in other words a Hell that includes "*refrigeria,*" places where "we refresh ourselves." Williams's allusion to that patristic concept, one that Lewis also knew and was thinking about weaving into a story, might have called Lewis's attention to the possible use he could make of "Prufrock."[58] For it is precisely the ancient idea of the *refrigerium* that provides the underlying premise of Lewis's dream fantasy that finally appeared in the mid-1940s: that the inhabitants of Hell are offered an occasional respite in the form of an excursion to more pleasant surroundings, where they are met by people they have known in life and encouraged to stay. For those who do stay, the place becomes the outskirts of Heaven and the trip proves to have been the start of a journey to greater heights of self-realization and bliss.[59] But most, too committed to the illusory selves they have fashioned, choose instead to return on the bus to Hell.

As Grover Smith has observed, Prufrock "is in hell,"[60] and the opening scene of Lewis's story resembles in significant ways the imagery of Eliot's poem:

> I seemed to be standing in a bus queue by the side of a long, mean street. Evening was just closing in and it was raining. I had been wandering for hours in similar mean streets, always in the rain and always in evening twilight. Time seemed to have paused on that dismal moment when only a few shops have lit up and it is not yet dark enough for their windows to look cheering. And just as the evening never advanced to night, so my walking had never brought me to the better parts of town. However far I went I found only dingy lodging houses, small tobacconists, hoardings from which posters hung in rags, windowless warehouses, goods stations without trains, and bookshops of the sort that sell *The Works of Aristotle*. I never met anyone. But for the little crowd at the bus stop, the whole town seemed to be empty.[61]

The bus queue as an image of waiting, mingling despair and hope, may look ahead to the theme of waiting in Samuel Beckett's work. But the resemblances to "Prufrock" catch our attention, in spite of the "drizzle" that contrasts with Eliot's gorgeous sunset. Consider Prufrock's twilight wandering in "half-deserted streets" in a squalid quarter of a smoky, foggy city with cheerless "window-panes," his "go[ing] at dusk through narrow streets," and the "lonely men in shirt-sleeves, leaning out of windows"[62] —their presence inferred by the smoke rising from their pipes. Like Lewis's narrator, Prufrock presents himself as seeing no-one in his wandering. The persons who occupy his thoughts evoke anxiety when he considers how they will victimize him, or merely ignore him, behaving somewhat as the characters in the queue in the long second paragraph of Lewis's narrative. Later details enforce these parallels. The "grey town" of Lewis's Hell has "more and more empty streets," "sad streets," "lonely streets,"[63] peopled by wraiths whose self-centeredness paralyzes any ability to choose their own good when it is placed before them, or even to recognize it. One of the forms their damnation takes, in Lewis's story of the dwarf and the tragedian,[64] may be compared to Prufrock's self-dramatization, constantly imagining scenes in which he might take part and (especially) ruminating on what roles he might play on stage: not the martyred John the Baptist (an allusion to Oscar Wilde's play *Salome*[65]) and not Hamlet, though perhaps some less exalted Shakespearean role[66] —here perhaps is a glimmer of potentially saving self-knowledge.

But even before getting to the anesthetized patient, Lewis would have noticed Eliot's epigraph, the quotation from Dante's *Inferno*.

> If I thought my reply were meant for one
> who ever could return into the world,
> this flame would stir no more; and yet, since none—
> if what I hear is true—ever returned
> alive from this abyss, then without fear
> of facing infamy, I answer you.[67]

In these lines Guido da Montefeltro in the Circle of the Fraudulent decides to tell Dante his story, since he thinks there is no danger of its going farther. Ironically, the deceiver is deceived. Dante is not dead, as he supposes, but will return above ground and broadcast this very tale (the fictitious Dante, the traveler, here merging into Dante the poet) in a work designed, at least in part, to teach virtue by warning of the effects of vice. Alongside this Eliot introduces a further irony, setting the ostensible aim of the *Inferno* over against the futility of such warnings, as taught in Jesus' story of the rich man and Lazarus: "If they will not listen either to Moses or to the prophets, they will not be convinced even if someone should rise from the dead."[68] Prufrock understands this lesson of futility. He declines the role of prophet (line 83), and even if he were able "to say: 'I am

Lazarus, come from the dead, / Come back to tell you all,'" he foresees the probable rejection and asks, "Would it have been worth while[?]"[69]

In *The Great Divorce* Lewis provides a multiplicity of Lazarus figures, not one, and he does not refer explicitly to Dante, Eliot, or Christ; yet Dante certainly, and Eliot very probably, were so lodged in his memory that each played a part in his creative process. The role of revealer returned from the dead, which Christ's parable disallows and Prufrock disbelieves, is assumed in Lewis's story first by the Bright People who come down from the mountains to try to help the busload of visitors understand the choices before them. By an ingenious device, Lewis gets around the plain dominical teaching that such efforts are futile. Unlike the rich man's hedonistic brothers, the ghosts in Lewis's story have already died. One would think their first-hand experience of emptiness in the afterlife might make them readier to accept a second chance.[70] In nearly every case, they fail: the ghosts remain committed to the false values by which they shaped their lives and "will not be convinced even" by truths uttered from beyond the grave. Secondly, the narrator of Lewis's story, one who like Dante relates the adventures he had in a dream, has returned symbolically from the dead to "tell all" in this very narrative. Whether this message of warning will prove futile, as it would for the rich man's brothers in the parable, is left open: it depends on how each one who hears the message—that is, each reader of *The Great Divorce*—responds.

By now it should be clear, I hope, that the question of what Lewis thought about Eliot is far too complex to be couched in extreme terms such as "pathological" or "arch enemy." Differences between the two men certainly existed, though in the course of his life Lewis, raised in Church of Ireland Protestantism, moved more and more toward an Anglo-Catholic sensibility, at least in some areas of belief and practice.[71] Yet simple formulas are tempting, and, human nature being what it is, I suspect that it will be a while before the garden is weed-free.

NOTES

1. Some of this may perhaps be explained as an overreaction to the tendency toward hagiography that has sometimes been perceived in popular writings about Lewis, from which scholars understandably want to distance themselves. But to discern and even sympathize with possible motives behind the dissemination of an untruth is still not to excuse it.

2. John T. Shawcross, *Rethinking Milton Studies* (Newark: University of Delaware Press, 2005), 9. A case in point is the brief appendix, "T. S. Eliot and C. S. Lewis," that appears in a recent book by Barry Spurr, *"Anglo-Catholic in Religion": T. S. Eliot and Christianity* (Cambridge: Lutterworth, 2010), 254–56. Despite his apparently total reliance on outmoded scholarship (Humphrey Carpenter's 1979 book *The Inklings*)—far from typical of his excellent book as a whole—Spurr has some intuitions that are worth consideration regarding Eliot's possible role in Lewis's "journey towards Catholic faith and practice" (254) as well as the role of Charles Williams (255); and he closes

with a reminder (alluding to *Little Gidding*) of the part played by divine grace in the healing of personal relationships. Still, his neglect of later studies that have significantly modified Carpenter's pronouncements and of primary texts such as Lewis's letters to Eliot (available in the *Collected Letters* since 2007) unfortunately perpetuates old errors and confirms Shawcross's observation.

3. The famous friendship between Lewis and Owen Barfield amply testifies to Lewis's ability to maintain personal regard independently of intellectual disagreement. See Lewis, *Surprised by Joy: The Shape of My Early Life* (New York: Harcourt, Brace and World, 1955), 199–200.

4. Commission to Revise the Psalter (see Walter Hooper, *C. S. Lewis: A Companion and Guide* [New York: Harper, 1996], 91–94, 654). Lewis's respect for Eliot's contributions in this work is reported by Derek Brewer ("The Tutor: A Portrait," in *C. S. Lewis at the Breakfast Table and Other Reminiscences*, ed. James T. Como [New York: Macmillan, 1979], 50). The two did not always agree, Eliot resisting alterations to the old Prayer Book version that were favored by Lewis (Hooper 93; possible examples appear in Lewis, *Collected Letters*, ed. Walter Hooper, 3 vols. [New York: Harper, 2004–07; cited hereafter as *CL*], 3:1222, 1228; but it is not certain), but there were also clear instances when Lewis found Eliot persuasive (see *CL*, 3:1346, 1594; in the first of these two letters Lewis compliments Eliot on his linguistic sensitivity). For a fuller account of Lewis's work on the Commission see George Musacchio, "C. S. Lewis, T. S. Eliot, and the Anglican Psalter," *Seven: An Anglo-American Literary Review* 22 (2005): 45–59.

A project was afoot in 1947 that might have brought Lewis and Eliot together then—a "very badly need[ed] . . . new, frankly high-brow periodical *not* in the hands of the Left" (*CL*, 2:757, Lewis's emphasis)—but nothing came of it (2:772).

5. Quoted in William Griffin, *C. S. Lewis: A Dramatic Life* (San Francisco: Harper and Row, 1986), 429.

6. See *CL*, 3:1063, 1069, 1251, 1345–46. Compare Lewis's remark to a friend in 1963 that after becoming acquainted with Eliot "I loved him" (quoted by Hooper, *CL*, 2:1030).

7. *All My Road before Me: The Diary of C. S. Lewis 1922–1927*, ed. Walter Hooper (San Diego, New York, London: Harcourt Brace Jovanovich, 1991), 409–18. See also Hooper, *Companion*, 171–72; *CL*, 3:1503.

8. Private conversation, June 2009.

9. An earlier scheme, which Lewis, still an undergraduate, described in a 1920 letter to his father, was directed more specifically against "the tendencies called 'Vorticist'" (*CL* 1:492), a movement not strictly aligned with Eliot (cf. Donald Davie, "Pound and Eliot: A Distinction," in *Eliot in Perspective: A Symposium*, ed. Graham Martin [London: Macmillan; New York: Humanities Press, 1970], 63) despite some similarities.

10. See *CL*, 3:1521–23 and, for Eliot's ideas, his advocacy in 1919 of an "Impersonal theory of poetry" in "Tradition and the Individual Talent" (*Selected Essays*, new ed. [New York: Harcourt Brace, 1950], 7). This episode is discussed more fully in my "C. S. Lewis, T. S. Eliot, and the Milton Legacy: The *Nativity Ode* Revisited," *Texas Studies in Literature and Language*, 44 (2002): 337–38. Walter Hooper is mistaken, I think, in inferring (*CL*, 2:157n) that Eliot rejected Lewis's essay and Lewis replied by asking, in effect, that he reconsider. As I read the second letter, Eliot apparently had wondered whether Lewis's essay was a stand-alone piece and had asked if Lewis might wait several more months for a decision, or, if he chose, submit the essay elsewhere. Lewis in reply requested clarification about the delay and explained more fully his larger critical scheme in which this would be the first chapter. In the event Lewis did publish the essay elsewhere, and it eventually became the first chapter in a quite different book (see note 17 below).

An interesting study could, and perhaps needs to, be made, I believe, cataloguing the numerous ways in which Lewis's and Eliot's views are aligned, or at least compatible, not only on matters of literary criticism and critical theory but on more general philosophical issues. Such a study would extend back to the period before their respective conversions, a period during which each was profoundly influenced by British Idealism. It is, of course, beyond the scope of the present essay; a good start, however, has been made by Brian Barbour, "Lewis at Cambridge," *Modern Philology* 96 (1999): 444.

11. See Lewis, *Surprised by Joy*, 33–34, and *CL*, 2:702.

12. A. N. Wilson, *C. S. Lewis: A Biography* (New York and London: Norton, 1990), 99.

13. Hooper, Preface to Lewis's *Selected Literary Essays* (Cambridge: Cambridge University Press, 1969), xvii (the diary referred to ends in 1927). Tolkien, as cited by Wilson, 118. See also *CL*, 2:684. Even before his conversion, when Lewis wrote at the behest of a Magdalen College club inviting Eliot to speak, his added note—"it will give me great pleasure if you will dine with me in hall before the meeting and be my guest in College for the night"—seems not wholly in accord with the legend about Lewis's supposed antipathy (*CL*, 3:1518).

14. Such is the caution that must be exercised in interpreting Lewis's remarks to Paul Elmer More in 1935 (*CL*, 2:163–64), to E. R. Eddison in 1942 (2:536), to Dorothy L. Sayers in 1945 (quoted by James Brabazon, *Dorothy L. Sayers: A Biography* [New York: Charles Scribner's Sons, 1981], 235), or to fellow-Inklings in 1947 (W. H. Lewis, *Brothers and Friends: The Diaries of Major Warren Hamilton Lewis*, ed. Clyde S. Kilby and Marjorie Lamp Mead [San Francisco: Harper and Row, 1982], 209).

15. Roger Lancelyn Green and Walter Hooper, *C. S. Lewis: A Biography* (New York: Harcourt Brace Jovanovich, 1974), 138.

16. *CL*, 2:142. The context is relevant: Lewis is answering a question about reliable scholarly sources on scholastic theology and philosophy. A similar statement appears in another letter about the same time, but in a different context and with more detailed development (*CL*, 2:134–35). In contrast to Lewis's disapproval here of a cultural movement he considered a "fad," note his defense of Eliot a few years later against an attack on his personal motives. Lewis admonished his correspondent that "we've no right to assume" Eliot was only "looking for . . . the 'new and strange'" when he converted to Anglo-Catholicism; "he might have embraced this belief because he thought it *true*" (*CL*, 2:443).

17. A passage from an essay by Lewis first appearing in 1934 might be claimed as an exception (E. M. W. Tillyard and C. S. Lewis, *The Personal Heresy: A Controversy* [London: Oxford University Press, 1939], 3). But Tillyard's rebuttal (31-32) was accepted by Lewis in his next response: in effect, he retracted the charge and indicated that his quarrel was not with Eliot per se but with a threatening tendency in criticism, of which he had taken a remark by Eliot—untypical, as he now acknowledges—as an illustration (49).

18. Lewis, *The Pilgrim's Regress: An Allegorical Apology for Christianity, Reason and Romanticism*, third ed. (1943; rpt. Grand Rapids, MI: Eerdmans, 1958), 98, 99.

19. Lewis's later comment to a friend, quoted in Green and Hooper, *Biography*, 130. "Catholic" and "scholastic" are the terms Neo-Angular uses to describe himself (*Regress*, 98). On "bourgeois-baiting" compare note 46 below.

20. *Regress*, 5, 10.

21. See, for example, Lewis's letter to the *Times Literary Supplement* (29 November 1947, 615; quoted by Barbour, "Lewis at Cambridge" 459n.; also in *CL*, 3:1577-78) endorsing F. R. Leavis's praise of A. J. A. Waldock's *Paradise Lost and Its Critics*—a book that attacks Lewis's views.

22. Lewis, "Shelley, Dryden, and Mr Eliot," in *Rehabilitations and Other Essays* (1939), rpt. in *Selected Literary Essays*, 189, 191, 203, 208.

23. Ibid., 203.

24. Ibid., 203. Lewis may possibly be alluding here to the "proposition" Eliot had put forward in *Essays Ancient and Modern*: "Literary criticism should be completed by criticism from a definite ethical and theological standpoint" (*Selected Essays* 343). Developing this point a few pages farther, Eliot (now several years since his conversion) says, "I am not sure I have not had some pernicious influence myself" (351). See also note 35 below.

25. Lewis, *Hamlet: The Prince or the Poem?* (Proceedings of the British Academy 28, 1942), rpt. in *They Asked for a Paper* (London: Bles, 1962), 55, 65, 69, 68.

26. They shared a commitment to a relatively high Anglicanism. Lewis, for example, grew into a deep sense of the centrality of the Eucharist (far less common in the mid-century Church of England than it is today), was comfortable with the doctrine of Purgatory and the practice of prayers for the dead, and adopted the habit of regular auricular confession to a priest as well as other spiritual disciplines associated with Anglican monasticism (see Lyle W. Dorsett, *Seeking the Secret Place: The Spiritual Formation of C. S. Lewis* [Grand Rapids, MI: Brazos, 2004], especially pp. 83–99). Clearly both Eliot and Lewis moved a long way from their religious origins, American Unitarianism and Ulster Protestantism respectively, and in notably parallel directions. "If I make Mr Eliot's words the peg": Lewis, *A Preface to "Paradise Lost"* (London: Oxford University Press, 1942), 9; "mere Christianity": Lewis, "On the Reading of Old Books" (1944), rpt. in *God in the Dock*, ed. Walter Hooper (Grand Rapids, MI: Eerdmans, 1970), 201 (Lewis borrowed the phrase from the seventeenth-century divine Richard Baxter).

27. *CL*, 2:557 (punctuation corrected following the original, Bodl. MS. Eng. lett. 220/ 2, fol. 182 [23 February 1943]). "I hardly ever write a book without showing him [Eliot] one of his errors," he would say in 1945 (quoted by Brabazon, 235). In the letter to Eliot, after the passage quoted, Lewis adds that he is glad Eliot agrees with him about Virgil, and in a postcard a fortnight later he mentions agreeing with Eliot about Charles Williams and about *Paradise Lost* resembling other Renaissance poetry in having something of the grotesque (*CL*, 2:561–62). Later still he assures Eliot of his agreement on other criticisms of Williams's work—the "obscurity" of his poetry ("[I] used to tell him he ought to be birched for it") and that his "plays, as plays, are much the least valuable part of his work" (*CL*, 2:656, 710).

28. *CL*, 2:891. On the other hand, in 1942 he advised *Time and Tide* not to send Eliot *The Forgiveness of Sins* (a rather idiosyncratic theological study) to review: "He couldn't understand one word of C. W.'s book" (*CL*, 3:1545).

29. Lewis, "Imagery in the Last Eleven Cantos of Dante's 'Comedy,'" in *Studies in Medieval and Renaissance Literature*, ed. Walter Hooper (Cambridge: Cambridge University Press, 1966), 93; Eliot, "The Metaphysical Poets," in *Selected Essays*, 247. Eliot mentions Dante among earlier poets who "possessed a mechanism of sensibility" akin to that of the Metaphysicals.

To conclude this survey of Lewis's views on Eliot as a critic, we may note that Lewis also, in an essay published in 1948, stated his agreement with an observation of Eliot's about Kipling ("Kipling's World," rpt. in *They Asked for a Paper*, 91).

30. T. S. Eliot, *On Poetry and Poets* (New York: Noonday, 1961), 157 (emphasis Eliot's). This collection includes "Milton I" (156–64), previously published under the title "A Note on the Verse of John Milton" (*Essays and Studies* 21 [1936]: 32–40), and "Milton II" (pp. 165–83), a revised version of his *Milton* (Oxford: Oxford University Press, 1947), the British Academy lecture. Scattered through Eliot's criticism are many other comments on Milton, appreciative as well as derogatory, and there are echoes of Milton in his poetry. For an overview covering 1919–1947 see E. P. Bollier, "T. S. Eliot and John Milton: A Problem in Criticism," *Tulane Studies in English* 8 (1955): 165–92.

31. For a detailed account of the points on which Lewis spoke in opposition to Eliot, F. R. Leavis, and others, see Charles A. Huttar, "Milton," in *Reading the Classics with C. S. Lewis*, ed. Thomas Martin (Grand Rapids, MI: Baker, 2000), 163–65, 169–70. Lewis did not at this point directly address the question of Milton's influence: that would have involved an excursion into recent literary history. As he explained to Eliot after the book was published, "to discuss your *Note* in detail was not part of my aim" (*CL*, 2:556).

32. Eliot's remark: Green and Hooper, *Biography*, 223–24; exchange of letters: see *CL*, 2:556–57. Here Lewis tried to clear up a misunderstanding regarding what he had and had not said about Eliot. (Eliot's side of the correspondence is not extant, or else not yet available for perusal.) Lewis added, "Charles Williams is always promising (or threatening!) to confront us with each other [to] hammer all these matters out."

33. Green and Hooper, *Biography*, 224.

34. See *CL*, 2:650, 655, 658, 700, 703, 704, 709, 710. The volume appeared in 1947 as *Essays Presented to Charles Williams*, ed. C. S. Lewis (Oxford University Press).

35. This focus in Eliot's concept of criticism was implied in a much earlier essay: "The important critic is the person who is absorbed in the present problems of art, and who wishes to bring the forces of the past to bear upon the solution of these problems" (*The Sacred Wood: Essays in Poetry and Criticism*, second ed. [London: Methuen, 1928], 37–38). Eliot did, however, in a different context, allow a critical role for ordinary readers: "We should all try to be critics, and not leave criticism to the fellows who write reviews ("Religion and Literature," in *Selected Essays* 349). Critical alertness is especially important for Christian readers, he says, considering the prevailing secularist and naturalistic outlook of most modern literature (351; see Eliot's whole developed argument, 347–54). His concern here regarding the influence of the *Zeitgeist* is paralleled in many statements by Lewis.

36. Bollier argues effectively against the implications of this term and for the consistency of Eliot's underlying critical principles.

37. This paragraph greatly condenses my detailed account of Lewis's poem which appears on pp. 326–35 of the article cited in note 10. "The Turn of the Tide" may be found in Lewis, *Poems*, ed. Walter Hooper (London: Bles, 1964), 49–51.

38. His copy of Eliot's *Poems 1909–1925*, minimally annotated, is in the Lewis collection at the Marion E. Wade Center, Wheaton, IL. Private remarks: see *CL*, 2:424, 429, 684, 1030; 3:342, 469, 1293.

39. Brewer, "The Tutor," 50. *Murder*: George Sayer, *Jack: C. S. Lewis and His Times* (San Francisco: Harper and Row, 1988), 155. Portrayal of evil: Lewis, *The Allegory of Love*, rev. ed. (London: Oxford University Press, 1938), 271. Taste: Ibid., 303; I think Joe R. Christopher is mistaken in viewing this as an attack on Eliot ("Modern Literature," in Martin [above, note 31] 259). *Dry Salvages*: Lewis, *Preface*, 59 (in a lecture delivered the same year as Eliot's poem was published). *Waste Land*: see Lionel Adey, *C. S. Lewis: Writer, Dreamer, and Mentor* (Grand Rapids, MI: Eerdmans, 1998), 206. "Fragment of an Agon": see Lewis, *That Hideous Strength* (New York: Macmillan, 1946), 199, where the mad scientist Filostrato speaks of "Birth and breeding and death." "Debt . . . congenial": Lewis, *Personal Heresy*, 63, 102. "Penitential": Lewis, *Preface*, 133. Williams festschrift: *CL*, 2:704 (Lewis's emphasis). For Stephen Medcalf certain other passages in Lewis's late prose suggest the degree to which he read and absorbed the *Four Quartets*: see Medcalf's "Language and Self-Consciousness: The Making and Breaking of C. S. Lewis's Personae," in *Word and Story in C. S. Lewis*, ed. Peter J. Schakel and Charles A. Huttar (Columbia: University of Missouri Press, 1991), 143, 144.

40. Lewis, "Williams and the Arthuriad," in *Arthurian Torso*, ed. C. S. Lewis (London: Oxford University Press, 1948), 188–90.

41. *De Descriptione Temporum* (Cambridge University Press, 1955), rpt. in *They Asked for a Paper*, 19. The controversy over the meaning of "A Cooking Egg" began with an essay by F. W. Bateson, "The Function of Criticism at the Present Time," *Essays in Criticism* 3 (Jan. 1953): 1–27. Bateson and several other critics continued to offer alternative readings of the poem in "The Critical Forum: 'A Cooking Egg,'" *Essays in Criticism* 3 (July 1953): 345–57. Bateson and I. A. Richards had the final word in "'A Cooking Egg': Final Scramble," *Essays in Criticism* 4 (Jan. 1954): 103–8.

42. Compare his more general remarks on the modern aesthetic of obscurity, in a letter written about eight months before his Cambridge lecture: "I'm sick of our Abracadabrist poets. What gives the show away is that their professed admirers give quite contradictory interpretations of the same poem" (*CL*, 3:449).

43. Davie (above, note 9) 74–75. Davie believed, however, that "the discussion was not so pointless as has been made out," since a follow-up in a later issue of the same periodical showed "real progress" (75), and he went on to offer his own reading of the poem (76–78).

44. *CL*, 3:595.

45. See, for example, Grover Smith, who cites several critics in his *T. S. Eliot's Poetry and Plays: A Study in Sources and Meaning*, Phoenix ed. (Chicago: University of Chicago Press, 1960), 48; Lyndall Gordon, *T. S. Eliot: An Imperfect Life* (Chicago: American Library Association, 1982), 108n. A critical position widely accepted today, however, is, despite obvious parallels to aspects of the poet's first thirty years, that he has distanced himself and contrived that all personal background in the poem belongs to the fictional character who is the speaker: see Russell Elliott Murphy, *Critical Companion to T. S. Eliot* (New York: Facts on File, 2007), 130. Possibly Lewis's response would be that, if so, it is a teasingly unfinished, not fully realized bit of fiction, and thus represents another of his four kinds of obscurity.

46. *Personal Heresy*, 64. The context is a brief discussion of a passage in Eliot's *Rock* choruses about "decent godless people"—the nine lines in question may be found on p. 36 of *Heresy*—which Lewis thought perhaps marred by pride and lack of charity. Lewis returns to the point on p. 69. His concern is related, I think, to the charge of "bourgeois-baiting" mentioned above.

This statement should not be taken to imply that Lewis had no concern for what he called an "aesthetic conscience"; simply that he could not allow aesthetics to trump ethics. See his 1946 letter to Sayers, *CL*, 2:728.

47. "Shelley," 199, 202. Compare Lewis in *Personal Heresy* 106 on poems that "succeeded in communicating moods of boredom and nausea that have only an infinitesimal place in the life of a corrected and full-grown man."

48. C. Day Lewis, *The Poetic Image* (London: Jonathan Cape, 1947), 117, as quoted by G. Rostrevor Hamilton, *The Tell-Tale Article: A Critical Approach to Modern Poetry* (London: William Heinemann, 1949), 57, and underlined by Lewis in his copy of Hamilton's book (Marion E. Wade Center, Wheaton, IL).

49. *CL*, 2:163. Note how Lewis's diction in 1935 anticipates that of C. Day Lewis in 1947.

50. *CL*, 3:426–27.

51. The point is well expressed by Cleanth Brooks, "Teaching 'The Love Song of J. Alfred Prufrock,'" in *Approaches to Teaching Eliot's Poetry and Plays*, ed. Jewel Spears Brooker (New York: MLA, 1988), 80.

52. Lewis, *Preface*, 55.

53. Ibid.

54. Relevant to this point is the letter to Paul Elmer More mentioned above, in which Lewis picks up on More's comment on Eliot—"a great genius expending itself on the propagation of irresponsibility"—and indicates his agreement at least with the second part (*CL*, 2:163).

55. Lewis in *Personal Heresy*, 147; Lewis, *The Abolition of Man*, second ed. (London: Bles, 1945), 17, 15 (Lewis's emphasis). The ideas in this paragraph are developed more fully in my essay "A Lifelong Love Affair with Language: C. S. Lewis's Poetry," in *Word and Story*, 97–103.

56. Lewis, *Poems*, 1. First published in *Punch* only months after the letter to Farrer from which I have quoted, under the title "Spartan Nactus"; the new title is Lewis's own—just before his death, he was preparing a volume of collected verse for publication. See Walter Hooper's preface in his edition of Lewis's *Collected Poems* (London: HarperCollins, 1994).

57. Much of what follows is drawn from the more extended treatment in my "C. S. Lewis's Prufrockian Vision in *The Great Divorce*," *Mythlore* 22, no. 4 (Spring 2000): 4-12. I am grateful to the editor of *Mythlore* for permission to reuse and reshape it.

58. Williams, "T. S. Eliot," in *Poetry at Present* (Oxford: Clarendon Press, 1930), 166, 171. Weaving into a story: Hooper, *Companion*, 279–80. If Lewis had not already read Williams's essay on Eliot in the early 1930s, he would almost certainly have read it once they became friends.

59. And the Hell where they had lodged then turns out to have been Purgatory. Compare Williams's remark specifically about "Prufrock": "Can this hell be rather the place of purgation?" (173).

60. Smith, 17.
61. Lewis, *The Great Divorce* (New York: Macmillan, 1946), 11.
62. Lines 4–7, 15–16, 70, 72.
63. *Divorce,* 18–19, 67, 116.
64. Ibid., 109–19.
65. Also, conceivably, to Jesus Christ, of whom King Herod heard rumors that he was John the Baptist *returned from the dead* (Luke 9:7). Such an association would ironically magnify the presumption of Prufrock's posturing, present even in his feeling the need to deny it.
66. Lines 111–19.
67. Dante, *Inferno* 27.61–66. The translation is Allen Mandelbaum's (Berkeley: University of California Press, 1980).
68. Luke 16:31, Jerusalem translation.
69. Lines 83, 94–95, 90.
70. The idea of such a *post mortem* chance is not taught in the New Testament, but Lewis alludes (*Divorce* 66) to its one example in Dante (*Purgatorio* 10.73–93; *Paradiso* 20.106–17), the legend of the Emperor Trajan's redemption.
71. See note 26.

EIGHTEEN

Eliot for David Jones

Thomas Dilworth

Eliot may be the greatest American poet of the twentieth century. David Jones is certainly the greatest native British poet of the century. Eliot was an important influence on Jones as a poet, and he was helpful to him personally and professionally. Jones was, in turn, clarifying for Eliot intellectually. Jones regarded Eliot as a great man but limited in ways that reflect Eliot's values and sensibility. Their shared doctrinally Catholic[1] Christianity was a bond but also a matter of difference since Jones was a Catholic and Eliot was not. Whether or not Eliot felt this difference, Jones did. It was aggravated for him by Eliot's sensibility being (as he thought) abstractly philosophical, while his own was historical and philosophically realistic. Jones and his Catholic friends would have put it this way: Eliot increasingly sided with Plato; Jones remained faithful to Aristotle. The shared values and interests of Eliot and Jones and their affection for one another comprised the ground against which this difference figures.

David Jones was raised in the evangelical Anglicanism of his father but shared with his mother High-Church sympathies. His conversion to Catholicism began in the trenches. While scavenging for wood near the front line in 1917, he came upon a shed in which a Catholic Mass was in progress. For him the sight was numinous. It seemed to involve a closeness between participants unlike anything he had experienced at the Anglican Office of Holy Communion.[2] He began conversing with the Catholic chaplain of his regiment, Fr. Daniel Hughes, a Jesuit who had won the Military Cross for bravery under fire, and Jones became, he said, at this time "inside, a Catholic." After the war he met Fr. John O'Connor, who, in 1921, arranged for him to visit Eric Gill at his Catholic commune of craftsmen near Ditchling.

A discussion with Gill during Jones's second visit completed his conversion. Gill argued that, of all the Churches only the Catholic Church (1) had its origin in New Testament times, (2) professed to be universal in membership, and (3) claimed absolute authority in moral and religious matters. Valid or not, he said, no other Church makes these claims. Gill then drew three triangular shapes and asking Jones to pick the triangle. In one, the lines did not quite meet at one corner, a second was even more disconnected, and the third consisted of lines joining to make angles. Pointing to the last, Jones said that he liked that one. Gill said, "I didn't ask which you preferred. It's not a question of one better than the others. The others are not triangles at all. Either it's a triangle or it's not." There was only one.[3] It was the Catholic Church, the non-triangles being the other Churches. Jones decided to enter the Catholic Church.

The appeal of Catholicism was, especially for him, historical. He was aware of the Anglican apologetical claim of continuity with the ancient Celtic Church in Britain and familiar with Anglican emphasis on the antipathy at the end of the sixth century between the Celtic "'ancient paths' and the 'Roman obedience' of Canterbury," but he realized that there had been no such disunity earlier, when Britain was a diocese of the prefecture of Gaul. As he later put it, Celtic Christianity is "as Roman in origin as the Welsh dragon."[4] Moreover, all we know of Jesus was historically mediated by the Church, which was then "the Churches of the Eastern Orthodox as well as the Catholic Ch of the West."[5] For him, the message included its medium.

Becoming a Catholic had been difficult for him because, according to a non-Catholic artist who knew him, "he felt considerable anxiety about whether he was doing the right thing and where the truth really lay."[6] He was not a Catholic merely by preference, not even for historical-imaginative or aesthetic reasons. Unlike Huysmans, Dowson, Johnson, and Wilde, Jones did not enter the Church as though it was a museum that preserved what would otherwise be "the lost beauty of the ages." Neither was faith, for him, reducible to specific doctrines. Belief and disbelief in doctrine involve, he thought, a large amount of subjective feeling, which he distrusted. He became and remained a Catholic out of conviction that the Catholic Church was "real" as none other was. He had sensed this reality in 1917 in Fr. Daniel Hughes— "a 'reality' absent in C. of E. parsons." He felt it in the chant during high Mass at Westminster Cathedral, so different from the "elegant, sophisticated but unreal sung Evensong at Kings College Cambridge." He sensed it in a bunch of "pretty ghastly & woefully ignorant Irish workmen," one of whom asked to borrow a rosary in order to perform a penance after going to confession. It was what Jones called "the reality, . . . the thing that seldom or ever seemed quite there among the many, many different kinds of Protestants I've known."[7] This "reality" allowed him to accept, "the Catholic cult because it appeared to make sense of the incomprehensible otherness" of Christianity.[8] For him, the liturgies of the two Churches contrasted significantly. Returning from a C. of E. wedding on 19 September 1946, he writes to Harman Grisewood, "this Anglican thing preserves something—but God! how it dates—the 'as by law established' comes through *whatever* they do."[9] At this time, Catholics were forbidden to attend non-Catholic liturgies, a prohibition Jones ignored.

While believing that the Catholic Church is the true church, he was ecumenical in a pre-ecumenical age. He regarded the counciliar statement that "there is no salvation outside of the Church" as nonsense. And he wrote to a friend that, as for "piety, sincerity, goodness, knowledge of the Scriptures and the Fathers and deep devotion to the Passion & effectual grace," there was more of these in many of the Protestants he knew "than in most Catholics."[10]

Although he never attended grammar school, his understanding of his faith was highly sophisticated. A voracious reader, he knew Church history. He was well grounded in various theological traditions through discussions in the 1920s and 1930s with Dominicans at Ditchling and at Blackfriars in Oxford, with the Jesuits at Campion Hall, and with the Benedictines on Caldey Island and at Prinknash. From 1927 till the outbreak of the Second World War, he also participated in an ongoing informal seminar at the Chelsea house of his friend Tom Burns, a friend and devotee of Jacques Maritain and an editor for the Catholic publishing house Burns (no relation) and Oates. Meetings occurred on Saturdays, beginning at lunch, continuing long into the night, and resuming on other weekday evenings. The participants were mostly young Catholics, many of them university students. The eldest in the group were the historian Christopher Dawson and his friend the philosopher E. I. Watkins. In many respects Dawson was, when present, the leader of the group, which I call the Chelsea Group, in contradistinction to the Bloomsbury Group, which was predominantly atheist and sympathetic to Soviet Russia.

Jones became especially close to Dawson, whose conversation was, for him, breathtaking in scope, depth, and clarity. Jones read most of what Dawson wrote.[11] And they would meet and converse apart from the others. The character of their conversations is evident in one that occurred in May 1942 at Dawson's London flat. They had both read John Cowper Powys's *Owen Glendower* and, Jones records in a letter, "chuckled together about things in it." They then went on to speak about the resurgence of "torture, the police-state & Co." and religion. Dawson said that Catholics were becoming more institutional "and mechanical," moving away from "the age of [Baron] von Hügel, the 'belief' in the Holy Ghost, in the subtlety of where truth resides" towards "a belief in effecting things by organisation & formulas"—"in short that 'propaganda' is universally dominant in the Ch as outside it & once you yielded *internally* to the propagandist attitude y're sunk." They discussed the Catholic condemnation of Luther's statement that the burning of heretics is offensive to the Holy Spirit—a statement that, they agreed, was obviously true. "Yet rather than make this admission," Catholic apologists "go in for all kinds of beatings about the bush to justify Papal absurdity—all of which is a pity & *quite* irrelevant to the truths of the Cath. Religion."[12]

Guided by the principle of the unity of all human experience, the Chelsea Group conducted cultural-intellectual explorations of all aspects of life: theological, cultural, historical, philosophical, artistic, moral, literary, political, and psychological. Regardless of cultural or temporal context, every experience was, they believed, of integral importance to every other experience. Everything had its place in a comprehensive, basically Christian synthesis, which they sought to understand. Central to this doctrine was Maritain's assertion that "every unison, or every harmony, every concord, every friendship and every union whatsoever between beings comes forth from the divine Beauty . . . which likens all things to one another, and calls them all unto itself."[13] The basic hypothesis of the group was a Christian-humanist analogue to the Unified Field Theory in physics, about which Einstein first published in 1928. The chief cultural fruits of these discussions would be: the magazine *Order,* edited by Tom Burns, and its successors *Collosseum* and *The Changing World,* edited by Bernard Wall; the BBC Third Program, the cultural channel, first organized and run by Harman Grisewood; and Jones's *The Anathemata* (1952), his cultural *summa,* which W. H. Auden considered (and I agree) the greatest long poem of the twentieth century.

Jones and Eliot first met in 1930. The occasion was lunch in Tom Burns's Chelsea flat.[14] Only the three of them were present. Eliot was forty-two years old. Jones was thirty-five and already recognized as one of the best living British engravers and painters. When, "in 1926 or '7," he had read *The Waste Land,* he felt the full impact of its combination of Spenglerian theme and anthropological myth and said to himself "That's it!"—the first literary work to be entirely modern in content and form.[15] It became his favourite modern literary work until he read, in 1930, what would be the Anna Livia chapter of *Finnegans Wake. The Waste Land* would influence the final section of the long poem he was currently writing. This was an epic poem in free verse and non-verse concerning seven months of his experience in the trenches culminating in the battle of the Somme. The poem already had its title, *In Parenthesis.*

After their first meeting, Eliot and Jones saw nothing of one another for several years. Jones suffered a nervous breakdown and spent the mid-1930s in Sidmouth, where he wrote the introduction and notes for *In Parenthesis* and revised the text. In 1936 he submitted the typescript to Richard de la Mare, his primary contact at Faber, and Eliot read it in typescript. He immediately considered it "a work of genius."[16] This was the real beginning of friendship between them. Jones had his first private conversation with Eliot in early July 1937 and found him "so quiet and unpretentious to talk with."[17]

Jones became one of Fabers' prominent writers in 1938 when *In Paren-thesis* won the Hawthornden Prize, then the only important British liter-ary award. But the relationship was never merely professional. From fairly early on, Eliot was at ease in Jones's company. This is suggested by his confiding that a favourite song of his was "Casey Jones," which he sang to himself in the morning while shaving.[18] Eliot probably told Jones this after reading *In Parenthesis*, in which British soldiers sing "Casey Jones" to drown out Germans singing Christmas carols. Their relation-ship became closer when Jones returned to live in London in 1939, and it warmed during the Blitz, which intensified most friendships between people living in London. Eliot was at the height of his fame and relatively inaccessible. They met privately only about three times a year. Occasion-ally Jones would seek out Eliot in his office in Russell Square. Usually they met for lunch at the Garrick Club or, occasionally, at the Russell Hotel. And they saw each other at meetings of the Virgil Society, of which they were founding members. Each sometimes phoned the other though there is no indication until very late that Jones had Eliot's home telephone number.

It was not until September 1951 that friendship became close. Until then Jones addressed Eliot in his letters as "Tom E." or "T.S.E." From 4 October 1951 it became simply "Tom." Eliot initially addressed Jones as "My Dear Davy"—which is affectionate, American, but condescending. Jones was nobody's "Davy." His best friends called him David or Dai, names Eliot began to use in 1951. On Eliot's part, the reason for increased intimacy seems to have been Eliot's awareness of the nature and scope of the new long poem Jones was writing.

When Eliot heard that this work, *The Anathemata*, was ready for sub-mission, he arranged for lunch on 8 October 1951 at the Garrick Club, so that Jones could hand him the typescript personally and they could talk about it.[19] The next day Eliot writes that his first quick inspection of the book confirms his expectations, and that he is sure it will be accepted for publication. Afterward he read it more carefully, and later he remembers that his sense "on first reading it, was of being in a state of excitement sustained to the end."[20] Eliot's positive response was a relief to Jones, who had "had no idea" what his reactions might be.[21] The poem is 'diffi-cult' in the modernist style and richly allusive—the sort of thing Eliot would be expected to appreciate, but which was not necessarily easier for him to comprehend than for anyone else. Eliot especially liked Jones's Preface to the poem,[22] possibly because he was sure he fully understood it. The others in the firm reacted less enthusiastically, and Eliot apologeti-cally offered a ten percent royalty and no advance, saying the book would be expensive to produce and would not have wide appeal. At this time Jones was living in abject poverty, and Eliot realized that the offer was not a good one. In conversation he may have implied that the others in the firm were less enthusiastic than he was. Certainly Jones himself thought that "without Tom, *The Anathemata* would probably not have been accepted" for publication.[23] With its publication David Jones joined the first rank of living writers. Eliot implies this in his 1961 preface to the first American edition of *In Parenthesis* when he associates him with Pound, Joyce, and himself.[24]

Before the book's publication, Jones had several meetings with Eliot and liked him more with each meeting. He found him "a withdrawn character . . . an astonishing fusion of something youthful & something immeasurably old & wise." Jones was especially impressed at how "incredibly hard" Eliot worked at Faber in addition to traveling to lecture, and doing his creative work.[25]

Eliot himself wrote the advertising blurb for *The Anathemata*. First he asked Jones for a brief description of the poem, and received five closely written foolscap pages in which Jones says among other things that the work "in a sort of way . . . presumes to be a *kind* of epic" and that "perhaps the bloody book is like a kind of 'lucky dip' in a bran-tub in a church bazaar. Chaps will have to be satisfied with what they may happen to pull out."[26] The blurb was not Jones's genre.

Writing more concisely, Eliot describes the work as "a *testimony*, and also a kind of *testament*, an inventory of what the author has inherited, what he has acquired, and what he has to bequeath of spiritual possessions." Jones strongly objected to the last two words, but Eliot, in consultation with someone he calls the firm's blurb expert, decided to retain the words so that the sentence they conclude would not go flat.[27] This difference of opinion suggests the difference between them which I mentioned at the onset. Eliot liked spirituality as a concept; Jones distrusted it—and a 'spiritual possession' is probably an oxymoron.

After the publication of *The Anathemata*, Eliot proposed that Jones publish a collection of essays. I remember David Jones saying "Tom had asked me to put out a book of collected pieces I had done and I didn't want to, because I didn't want to do the work involved in going back over the things. But he said, 'No, it is a good idea and you *should* do it, and you'll be glad about it after.'"[28] Harman Grisewood agreed to do the editing, so Jones acquiesced, and the result is *Epoch and Artist* (1959)—a book Harold Rosenberg praised as containing "some of the most acutely relevant writing on contemporary form and value to have appeared in years."[29]

In discussion with the Chelsea Group, Jones had developed an original theory of culture, which informs *The Anathemata* and influenced Eliot. The principal element of this theory is a distinction between utility and gratuity, the basic categories of motive. Utility has only one value, efficiency. In contrast, gratuitous acts and objects symbolize various human values. A screwdriver is utile; a birthday cake is gratuitous. Utility defines civilization; gratuity characterizes culture. In Jones's view the balance between these psychological polarities is a diagnostic gauge by which culture-phases may be analyzed and compared. For example, the modern West rhymes with imperial Rome because, in both, utility is emphasized to the near exclusion of gratuity. Consequently we live in a culturally impoverished civilization. Jones expounded to Eliot this theory, which informed their conversations about western culture. They agreed about the displacement of the arts in an increasingly technological society and believed that civilization was entering a new dark age. Eliot told him about his plans for a book, which would eventually be published as *Notes towards the Definition of Culture*.[30] Jones's theory influences this work, in which Eliot warns of the increasing dominance of technology and its exclusive virtue of efficiency. Jones read it when first published as a series of essays in the *New English Weekly*. He thought it "*Really* good & serious & on the spot & balanced & true."[31] A few days later, Kenneth Clark invited him and Eliot to dinner in his flat. During the meal Jones was able to express his appreciation for these essays. He enjoyed them "enormously," and thought the most recent "the only completely good & serious & accurate statement of all that which has appeared at all since the war began. . . . It really says things of a fundamental nature that need very badly to be said" and "is certainly about the only thing *I've* seen for a very long while with which I find myself in unqualified agreement." The main point, as Jones expressed it, is "that *in the end* you can't have the things the intelligentsia call 'culture' unless you have a real 'culture' underneath—I am absolutely certain about that. . . . It is the *central* problem of our time & is a problem common to *all* the groups now struggling—it is deeper than all else I think & the least understood."[32]

Eliot's interest in Jones's prose was a natural extension of their conversations. The first piece of unpublished writing Jones seems ever to have shown Eliot—at lunch in August of 1943—was the typescript of a long essay entitled "Art in Relation to War and our Present Situation." Eliot took it home, read it and wrote that he liked it but thought there was too much in it, and that it should eventually be transformed into a book though not at the expense of Jones's present creative work. He added that as an essayist Jones was carrying on the work of Eric Gill—though he realized that Jones was not Gill and had his own point of view. He also suggested that Jones rewrite the essay as juxtaposed fragments after the manner of Pascal's *Pensées*. Jones kept this letter by itself in a special manila envelope marked "N.B."—perhaps because the advice to write in fragments had immediate influence on *the Anathemata*, which is subtitled "fragments of an attempted writing."[33]

The Anathemata, which is set during the consecration of the Mass, reflects Jones's devotion to the Mass, which he regarded as "a supreme artform," consisting of "juxtaposed forms in relationship . . . which centuries of usage had perfected." For him, becoming and remaining a Catholic was largely a matter simply of attending Mass. As often as not, the per-

formance was bad, but the written and choreographed form-and-mean-
ing, to which the personal and subjective was subordinated, was the
paradigm of symbols. Because everything else was, he thought, an ap-
proximation or precursor of the Eucharist or of the Passion which the
Eucharist makes present, the Mass contained and interpreted legend,
myth, and pagan ritual. It was for him the centre or apex of a continuity
of all art works throughout time.[34] It contradicted for him "the ludicrous
division" between abstract and non-abstract art "for nothing could ... be
more 'abstract' than the Mass, or *less 'realistic'* or *more 'real.'*" He considered the Mass to be the greatest of the works of art he loved and continuous with them.[35] Speaking with Eliot about the Mass as the ultimate
artwork, he mentioned his admiration for *The Shape of the Liturgy* by
Gregory Dix, an Anglo-Catholic Benedictine monk and liturgical scholar.
Eliot knew Dix and promised to introduce them, but Dix died before he
could.[36]

Other subjects they spoke about and agreed on are suggested in a
letter in which Jones asks whether Eliot heard a talk on "The Dying God"
by Victor White, O.P. on the Third Programme:

> It greatly rejoiced my heart that the whole business of the identity of
> *pattern* between our Xtian Passiontide rites & the immemorial rites of
> earlier cultures and the factual story as related in the Gospels and
> much that the findings of contemporary psychology have discovered in
> the individual, should at *last* have been frankly & clearly expressed &
> given its proper perspective. There was probably nothing new in his
> exhortations for you or me.[37]

In religious matters Jones was in fairly substantial agreement with the
Anglo-Catholic Eliot.

They did not agree about everything, however. While Eliot praised
Dante above all other writers, Jones thought Dante was too idealistic and
abstract and that Beatrice should have been more believably human.[38]
Eliot admired the poetry of St. John of the Cross, which Jones "could
never get into." Jones suspected that Eliot liked the Spanish mystic because, he said, "he thought it was the thing to do."[39]

According to Grisewood their chief disagreement was over Milton.
Jones whole-heartedly endorsed the early essay by Eliot (1936), in which
Eliot regards Milton as theologically, morally and psychologically repug-
nant, and claims that, because his sensibility was exclusively auditory or
musical, Milton wrote an artificial language devoid of visual precision or
tactility. The result, said Eliot, was a serious deterioration of the language. Jones thought, furthermore, that Milton's puritanical abhorrence
of the flesh confused his art—so that Satan embodies so much of what is
positive about man yet is damned, while, by comparison and only to the
extent that he is believable at all, Milton's Messiah is a milksop. Eliot and
Jones discussed all this. When Eliot published his second essay on Milton

in 1947, he sent Jones a copy. In the new essay, Eliot reverses his earlier negative judgment. He sees Milton's invention of a new language as a mark of greatness, and praises his mastery of structure in syntax and overall design and his ability to work in "large musical units." This, writes Eliot, makes him "the greatest master of free verse in the language." Astonished at this turnabout, Jones was convinced that Eliot had sold out to the English establishment, which had always esteemed Milton. He told Grisewood, "By God, they've got hold of him."[40] He was too diffident, too accommodating, Jones thought, and was now (he thought, rightly or wrongly) a creature of the establishment.[41] Jones disliked the English establishment, including the Anglican clerical hierarchy. He complains to Grisewood about English politicians being even more boring than American politicians, a characteristic he discerned as well, in their different spheres, in the Royal Academy and the Church of England.[42] About his own aversion to Milton, Jones remained adamant, although in conversation with Eliot he argued with some deference. In 1957 Jones writes to him: "I *still* think *Milton I* is ok. I see the point of *Milton II*, but I think *Milton I* has permanent truths that still need much ramming home."[43]

In 1952 Jones entered into a long correspondence with Fr. Desmond Chute, a friend since 1921 at Ditchling and now a friend of Ezra Pound in Rapallo. The correspondence enabled Chute to write a review of *The Anathemata*, which Jones liked so much he handed it to David Bland at Faber to read and then pass on to Eliot. Then he remembered that Chute praises the poem as "more Catholic than *Four Quartets*" and wrote to Bland to hold it back, for fear the comment would irritate Eliot, but Bland replied that he had already sent the review on to Eliot, who liked it.[44]

Jones may have agreed with Chute's judgment, understanding "more Catholic" as less abstract, more involving the physical and psychological, more realistic in the Aristotelian, Thomistic sense. He later writes, "I may be wrong but I have a feeling that in T.S.E's late poetry especially the 'religious' ones, superb as they are, the concrete images are less—the feeling is more 'conceptual' or something. In the earlier ones culminating in *The Waste Land* concrete images are held up more than in the later ones."[45]

Jones admired Eliot and felt warmly affectionate toward him, but his affection seems hedged with a slight reserve. With friends and acquaintances Jones was informal and relaxed; Eliot was inhibited, less forthcoming. Grisewood told me that, with Eliot, Jones could not be as "jolly and unbuttoned" as he habitually was with friends. He "had rather best-behaviour relationships with Eliot."

In conversation with others, Jones praised Eliot's generosity, his wit, and his beautiful grey eyes. But he was irritated by what he saw as Eliot's puritanical streak. Jones said that while he himself was "prodigal" and wasted his "substance on taxis,"

Tom always took the tube. He didn't believe in spending money need-
lessly. By that time he probably didn't even have to work at Fabers. On
leaving the Garrick Club once I suggested a taxi to Fabers. He refused.
We could have talked longer but no.

During the war the firms organized fire-watching teams. It was
very nice watching for fires. Because of the blackout, you could see the
stars. Tom was on Fabers' team. I once proposed we talk the next night
and he said no, that he had to watch that evening. "So much the better,
I don't mind where we talk." He said no, that he had a system whereby
he could get through several books while watching—he was a reader
for Fabers. He said he made it a policy never to break from routine
except for something extraordinary. I said, "Well, this is extraordinary
enough—we'll have a good talk about poetry." He said no.

Then, as if to repair whatever dent he may have made in Eliot's reputation, Jones added, "He was quite funny when he'd had a few drinks.⁴⁶

Jones remembered Eliot as a "darling man, the soul of kindness and
helpfulness." But he was also "cagey":

he could cut you off sharply and refuse to talk about something. Once
at the Garrick Club I introduced the topic of Browning and how his
poems were the start of it all, bringing together the colloquial thing and
the poetic thing, you know, and he turned to the waiter and said,
"Bring Mr Jones another cup of coffee."

Jones recalled on another occasion praising the poetry of G. K. Chesterton, saying that while the style is no good, there is a wise thought in
almost every line. "*The Ballad of the White Horse*, for example, is very
good." Eliot replied that "old Chesterton reminded him of a cabman
beating himself to keep warm."⁴⁷ Jones was frequently put off by Eliot's
inability to achieve ease of cordiality and by the abrupt clampdowns by
which Eliot deadened or terminated conversation.⁴⁸ But Jones was not
gainfully employed, like Eliot, and was under no pressure to economize
on time. For Jones a conversation with a friend ought to (and often did)
last five or six hours.

When they met, he would tell Eliot war anecdotes. Eliot talked about
his acquaintances Joyce, Pound, and Wyndham Lewis. "Let's go see old
Lewis," he said, but Jones, who had met Lewis and found him uncongen-
ial, declined.⁴⁹ Certainly they spoke about Joyce's writing, about Hopkins's poetry, about the metaphysical poets, whom they both admired,
about the sculptor Eric Gill—a close friend of Jones and someone whose
work Eliot admired.

After Eliot remarried, Jones was occasionally invited to lunch with the
Eliots in their Kensington flat. (Lunch was easier than supper for Jones,
who lived and worked in a rented room in Harrow-on-the-Hill and had
to ride the underground for an hour to get into the center of London.) In
1960 he went to sign a large inscription he had given the Eliots in 1958 as
a belated wedding present. It was subsequently hung in the front hall of

their flat. At least once he was their guest for Christmas dinner—the only other guest being Valerie's mother. His entrance to the inner circle is indicated by Eliot entrusting him with his home telephone number.[50]

In the later years of their friendship, Jones and Eliot talked about the growing reaction against modernism, which became apparent to both of them after the war. In 1948 Jones writes to Eliot that he finds "both with regard to painting & writing the *younger* generations are almost oblivious of certain things that one imagined had been more or less thrashed out with great pain & difficulty twenty or so years ago." And he wonders whether it isn't always the case that "certain salutary discoveries or re-discoveries . . . seem to be misunderstood or lost before they have had a chance to bear proper fruit." Then he supposes that in our late civilizational phase, "the extreme eclecticism & the rapidity of change" explain this loss of insight.[51] Eliot and Jones agreed in seeing this change as a serious falling off in the standard of literature and criticism. But, although he would never have hinted it to Eliot, Jones thought that Eliot himself was caught up in the general decline.

I remember Jones saying that he liked Eliot's early poems best, the ones written "when he wasn't well off" (and he added, "it figures, doesn't it"). Jones could recite "The Hollow Men" by heart. The only poems by Eliot that he positively disliked were "Tom's awful poems about cats" which he thought were "embarrassing!"[52] He admired *Four Quartets*. In fact, he writes that his appreciation of modern literature "stops short at somewhere round about T.S.E.'s *Four Quartets.*"[53] He acquired each of the quartets as it came out, and exclaims in a letter to Eliot, "*How good* they are!"[54] He kept from Eliot his one serious critical reservation, which he discussed with Grisewood, to whom he writes about "East Coker": "I've read it once or twice again. It really has some lovely poetry in it I must say but I feel our original criticism on that one point stands— but it's good, very."[55] The point of objection is disclosed in a later letter, in which he regrets the current adulation of "subjective vision" even by his friend "dear Bertie R[ead]," and he adds, "at *bottom* it's the trouble with Tom E. also. In fact, in one form or another, it holds the field. At base, I suppose it is this subjectivism that separates them *all* from Joyce."[56] At the time, this was an acute observation. Now, over a half century later, it is a critical commonplace to stress the subjective feeling that pervades Eliot's writing.

It remains debatable whether or to what extend Eliot partook of what Jones saw as a general lapse of aesthetic sensibility. This lapse, if it is that, reached its nadir, in his lifetime, in confessional poetry and has since collapsed further into the dubious aesthetics of postmodernism. In any case, despite his debt to *The Waste Land,* Jones's aesthetics differed somewhat from Eliot's. He remained true in his allegiance to the objectivist or realist tradition he saw as extending from Aristotle, through Aquinas to

James Joyce and the Neo-Thomism of the Dominicans and Jacques Maritain—this had been the philosophical core of Jones's Catholicism.

Jones's own attitude toward the general change in sensibility was sharpened because he saw it, no doubt rightly, as one of the reasons for the limited reception of *The Anathemata*. He writes to Grisewood with Eliot in mind:

> It could all be so different if just one or two chaps (I will not mention names) had refused to give an inch, had stood by the guns. As it is, the lesser chaps, such as myself, can make no impression at all I feel. This may sound a subjective or silly moan. But there is a kind of thing about the arts where one has to have a kind of corporate something—some sort of response from certain kinds of chaps, or it gets very hard. Not that one doubts what one is trying to do, but it is a bit shaking when combined currents flow more & more against the kind of direction one feels to be the *only* direction that's worth while.[57]

About objectivity Jones had written in his introduction to *The Anathemata*: "the workman must be dead to himself while engaged upon the work, otherwise we have that sort of 'self-expression' which is as undesirable in the painter or the writer as in the carpenter, the cantor, the half-back, or the cook."[58]

He had first acquired this conviction from post-impressionist art theory immediately after the First World War. His conviction had been initially confirmed by Eric Gill, by his reading of Maritain, and subsequently by Eliot himself, who had concluded "Tradition and the Individual Talent" by saying, "The emotion of art is impersonal." Jones would never have put it that way. The artist has to care intensely about the subject or content of his art, but however strong his feeling, it must not render the finished work in any degree private or subjective. To the end Jones remained an entrenched modernist—after the model of Joyce, whom he regarded as the greatest modern writer.

If Eliot had changed with the times, he had not changed so much as to lose Jones's genuine appreciation, and not enough to escape the wrath of the counter revolutionaries. When these included Eliot among their targets, Jones would commiserate. In 1957 he wrote Eliot to say:

> I've followed with increasing perturbation, depression and dislike such things as the *Litt. Sup.* article on Joyce's letters and then the one on Wyndham L[ewis] and the correspondence that followed. It is as though the whole nature, intention & interior feeling of most of the creativity of our time is *already* entirely misunderstood, misinterpreted, or, worse, deliberately misrepresented. . . . I think your *Waste Land*, for example, is as 'contemporary' in form & content as when it was written *only more so.* . . .[59]

In his reply, Eliot writes characteristically that while he objects to being one of the victims of such reviewers, he is much more disturbed by the decline of the *Literary Supplement*, which seems to him to represent a deterioration of morals and manners (24 Oct 1956). It may seem a prissy thing to say, but Eliot was quite right. During this period, reviewers for the *TLS* were anonymous and often incompetent.

It was not until Eliot was safely dead, of course, that he became a primary target of the new subjectivism in its most moralistic form. When the edition of the drafts of *The Waste Land* was published in 1971, an anonymous reviewer declared that "Eliot's poetry gives offence" and cannot cease to do so until "Eliot the man is made to emerge from the shadows among which he concealed himself" (*TLS* 10 December). "*Appalling* stuff," Jones calls it; "apart from all sorts of beastliness there [is] the primal & central heresy that you can't assess a work of *poiesis* unless you are acquainted with the maker's mode of life."[60]

As Jones would be the first to stress, he owed Eliot a great deal. Eliot had not 'discovered' David Jones—not, certainly, in the sense in which he had discovered W. H. Auden and Vernon Watkins. But more than anyone else, including Jones himself, Eliot had promoted Jones's writing. He had been personally responsible for the publication of *The Anathemata*. He had written letters supporting Jones for inclusion in the Civil List Pension in 1954 and for the Bollingen Prize in 1963. After the appearance of *The Anathemata*, he had publicized Jones as a writer "of major importance."[61]

Although Jones had read all Eliot's poetry and drama and much of his critical writing, he was influenced importantly only by *The Waste Land*. All Jones's poetry involves the theme of the Waste Land—though for Jones the theme belonged to Malory before Eliot. Like Eliot's *The Waste Land*, all Jones's poetry uses allusions to establish mythic, historic, and literary parallels, and his long poems are accompanied by explanatory notes. The fragmented, open form of *The Anathemata* is clearly indebted to *The Waste Land*. Not that Jones's poetry reads anything like imitation Eliot. In fact, it entirely expresses Jones's aesthetic sensibility—like all great poetry, it is uniquely distinctive of its author.

Tom Burns told me that they were "very much on the same wave length, they were looking in the same direction." Jones "had a boundless respect and affection for Eliot" and "Eliot had an immense regard for David as a poet and as a man."[62] There was considerable sympathy between them. Both (Eliot for most of the years Jones knew him) were bachelors. Both had suffered emotionally. Both were hypochondriacs in the sense of suffering exaggeratedly from frequent genuine illnesses and exchanged sincerely felt, mutual commiseration. Harman Grisewood told me of being asked to lunch by Eliot in 1962 to discuss what might be done about Jones's poverty (with the monetary help of friends, Jones lived in a single rented room) and his health, particularly his being prescribed the tranquillizer Nembutal, to which Eliot had been addicted a decade earlier.

Imaginatively and intellectually Jones was not a disciple of Eliot. Although they were in basic agreement about art, culture, and religious values, Jones had come to most of his own conclusions long before reading or meeting Eliot, and his ideas and interests were fully developed by the time their acquaintanceship became friendship. Jones had reached aesthetic maturity by 1928, and not as a poet but as a visual artist. In this respect his imaginative development was independent of the influence of any writer. And although Eliot's example—along with those of Hopkins, Joyce, and St. John Perse among modern writers—helped him make the transition from visual to literary art, he remains, as a writer, distinctly himself. In the blurb he wrote for *The Anathemata*, Eliot regards him as "a wholly unclassifiable author."

Their religion united them, and their difference in affiliation was minimized by both of them. Jones considered himself a member of a universal Church extending back to Jesus. That was true of Eliot's religion but not, Jones thought, Eliot's Church. Politeness precluded Jones from ever mentioning this.

On 4 January 1965, David Jones switched on his radio to catch the late news bulletin, which was almost over. He heard only a few words in a familiar voice and then the announcer concluding, "That was Mr. Auden paying tribute to Mr. T. S. Eliot who died this evening." To Jones the news was "an awful blow."[63] He had just received a Christmas card from the Eliots and had not known that his friend had been ill. In the weeks and months that followed, Jones increasingly felt that an era had ended. Eliot's work and personality had dominated the literary and critical world for over thirty-five years. Joyce had been a greater artist; Pound, in the years before the war, a more energetic propagandist; but for Jones as for most people old enough to remember, it had been the era of Eliot. Jones had also loved the man. Now he missed him.

NOTES

1. Those whom Protestants, Anglicans, and Anglo-Catholics regard as "Roman Catholics" refer to themselves simply as Catholics and to their Church as the Catholic Church.
2. Jones quoted by René Hague, *David Jones* (Cardiff: University of Wales Press, 1975), 58; Jones, *Dai Greatcoat* (London: Faber, 1980), 248; letter to René Hague, 9–15 July 1973; Jones in conversation with Tony Stoneburner, written record 5 May 1966.
3. Eric Gill, "Responsibility" (1925), in *Art-Nonsense and Other Essays* (London: Cassel, 1929), 131; *Manchester Guardian* (2 November 1972); see Gill, *Autobiography* (New York: Devin-Adair, 1961), 188; Jones related the meaning of Gill's triangles to William Blissett and me in conversation in 1971 or 1972.
4. Jones, to the *Times*, unpublished, nd.
5. David Jones to Harman Grisewood, 9 October 1971.
6. Jones in conversation with Ray Howard Jones in the 1950s, interviewed by the author 11 September 1989.
7. Jones to Grisewood, 10 June 1964.

8. Ibid.

9. Jones to Grisewood, 20 September 1946.

10. Jones to Grisewood, 10 June 1971.

11. At the time of his death, Jones owned the following works by Dawson (acquired in the year of publication unless otherwise noted): *The Age of the Gods* (1928, given him for his birthday, 1929, by B.H., probably Barbara Hepworth), *Progress and Religion* (1929, acquired 1932), *Christianity and Sex* (1930), *Christianity and the New Age* (1931), *Enquiries into Religion and Culture* (1933, acquired 1934), *Edward Gibbon* (1934), *Beyond Politics* (1939), *Religion and Culture* (1948), *Medieval Essays* (1953, acquired 1954), *The Formation of Christendom* (1967), *The Dividing of Christendom* (1971), *The Gods of Revolution* (1972). When his cousin Maurice Bradshaw left in 1931 for the Anglican missions in Borneo, Jones gave him a present of a book by Dawson, probably *Progress and Religion*. Dawson sent Jones a copy of *The Wind and the Rain* V (Spring 1949), containing his memoirs of childhood, "Tradition and Inheritance."

12. To Grisewood, 1 June 1942.

13. Jacques Maritain, *The Philosophy of Art*, trans. John O'Connor (Ditchling, England: St. Dominic's Press, 1923), 45.

14. David Jones to Valerie Eliot, 5 January 1965, draft. I am grateful to the trustees of the estate of David Jones for permission to quote from the poet's unpublished correspondence and to Valerie Eliot for copies of Jones's letters to her late husband.

15. On 4 June 1971, Jones said this to William Blissett and me. For Blissett's memories of these and other visits, see *The Long Conversation* (Oxford: Oxford University Press, 1981).

16. Eliot, "A Note of Introduction," *In Parenthesis*, by David Jones (London: Faber, 1961), vii.

17. David Jones, Letter to Laurence Binyon, 13 July 1937.

18. Jones in conversation with author, 31 August 1972.

19. Eliot to Jones, 26 September 1951.

20. The advertising blurb on *The Anathemata*, which Eliot wrote for the Faber catalogue, 1952.

21. Jones to Eliot, 6 November 1951.

22. Eliot to Jones, 8 January 1952.

23. Jones, in conversation with author, 24 Aug 1972.

24. Eliot, "A Note of Introduction," *In Parenthesis*, by David Jones (New York: Chilmark Press, 1961), vii-viii.

25. Jones to Helen Sutherland, 11 September 1952.

26. Jones to Eliot, 5 January 1952.

27. Eliot to Jones, 18 March 1952.

28. Jones, in conversation with author, 24 August 1972.

29. Harold Rosenberg, "Aesthetics of Crisis," *New Yorker* (22 August 1964): 114–22.

30. Jones to Sutherland, 2 December 1948.

31. Jones to Tom Burns, 6 May 1943.

32. Jones to Sutherland, 14 May 1943.

33. Eliot to Jones, 19 August 1943.

34. Jones to Sutherland, 14 May 1943.

35. Jones to Grisewood, 3 October 1971. These included the Parthenon, the Venus of Melos, the Lindisfarne Gospel, the west portal of Charles Cathedral, Palestrina's setting of the Good Friday liturgy, the *Dies Irae*, Botticelli's *Primavera*, Cezanne's *Card Players*, and Joyce's *Finnegans Wake*.

36. Jones, *Letters to a Friend*, ed. Aneirin Talfan Davies (Swansea: Christopher Davies, 1980), 30.

37. Jones to Eliot, 22 November 1951.

38. Jones to Grisewood, 5 April 1973.

39. Jones in conversation with author, 4 June 1971.

40. Grisewood interviewed by the author, 5 October 1987.

41. Ibid.

42. Jones to Grisewood, 12 August 1956.
43. Jones to Eliot, 17 October 1957.
44. Jones to Grisewood, 10 August 1953.
45. Tony Stoneburner, 12–16 August 1968.
46. In conversation with author, 24 August 1972.
47. Jones, in conversation with author, 9 September 1972, 24 August 1972.
48. Grisewood, interviewed by the author, 4 Oct 1987.
49. Jones, in conversation with author, 4 June 1971.
50. Eliot to Jones, 2 August 1961.
51. Jones to Eliot, 15 February 1948.
52. Jones in conversation with author, 24 August 1972.
53. Jones to Grisewood, 22 May 1962.
54. Jones to Eliot, 25 November 1952.
55. Jones to Grisewood, 13 April 1940.
56. Jones to Grisewood, 10 January 1954.
57. Jones to Grisewood, Tues., St Thomas Martyr, 1953
58. David Jones, *The Anathemata* (London: Faber, 1952), 12.
59. Jones to Eliot, 17 October 1957.
60. Jones to Grisewood, 17 December 1971.
61. Eliot, *Dockleaves* 6, no. 16 (Spring 1955): 23.
62. Burns, interviewed by the author, 13 June 1988.
63. Jones to René Hague, 6 January 1965.

Bibliography

Ackroyd, Peter. *T. S. Eliot.* London: Hamish Hamilton, 1964.

Adey, Lionel. *C. S. Lewis: Writer, Dreamer, and Mentor.* Grand Rapids, MI: Eerdmans, 1998.

"A French Romantic." *Times Literary Supplement* 976 (30 September 1920): 625–26.

Airaudi, Jesse T. "Finding the Stairs Lit: Contemporary Architecture's Return to Tradition, and the Relevance of *The Waste Land* at the Fin de Millénaire." *Yeats Eliot Review* 16, no. 2 (1999): 2–17.

Anderson, Benedict. *Imagined Communities: Reflections on the Origin and Spread of Nationalism.* Rev. Ed. London: Verso, 1991.

Anson, Peter F. *Bishops at Large.* London: Faber, 1964.

Aquinas, Thomas. *Commentary on Aristotle's "De Anima."* Translated by Kenelm Foster and Silvester Humphries. New Haven: Yale University Press, 1951.

———. *On the Unity of the Intellect Against the Averroists.* Translated by Beatrice H. Zedler. Milwaukee, WI: Marquette University Press, 1968.

———. *Summa Contra Gentiles.* 4 Vols. Translated by A. C. Pegis, et al. Notre Dame, IN: University of Notre Dame Press, 2001.

Aristotle. *De Anima.* Translated by J. A. Smith. Vol. 3 of *The Works of Aristotle*, edited by W. D. Ross. 12 vols. Oxford: Clarendon, 1930.

———. *Nicomachean Ethics.* Translated by W. D. Ross. Vol. 9 of *The Works of Aristotle*, edited by W. D. Ross. 12 vols. Oxford: Clarendon, 1930.

———. *De Poetica.* Translated by Ingram Bywater, Vol. 10 of *The Works of Aristotle*, edited by W. D. Ross. Oxford: Clarendon, 1946.

———. *Politica.* Translated by Benjamin Jowett. Vol. 10 of *The Works of Aristotle*, edited by W. D. Ross. Oxford: Clarendon Press, 1921.

Arnault, Michel. "L'Oeuvre de Charles-Louis Philippe." *Nouvelle Revue Française* (February 1910): 141–61.

Arnold, Matthew. *Prose Works.* 11 vols. Ed. R. H. Super. Ann Arbor: University of Michigan Press, 1961–1977.

Asher, Kenneth. "T. S. Eliot and Charles Maurras." *ANQ* 11, no. 3 (1998): 20–30.

———. *T. S. Eliot and Ideology.* Cambridge: Cambridge University Press, 1995.

Auden, W. H. *The Complete Works. Prose Volume 1: 1926-1938.* Edited by Edward Mendelson. Princeton: Princeton University Press, 1996.

———. "A Contemporary Epic." *Encounter* 2, no. 2 (February 1954): 67–71.

Augustine. *Confessions.* Translated by R. S. Pine-Coffin. Harmondsworth, England: Penguin, 1984.

Averroes, *Cordubensis Commentarium Magnum in Aristotelis De Anima Libros.* Edited by F. Stuart Crawford. Cambridge, MA: The Medieval Academy of America, 1953.

Bailey, Simon. *A Tactful God: Gregory Dix, Priest, Monk, and Scholar.* Leominster: Gracewing, 1995.

Baillie, John and Hugh Martin, Eds. *Revelation.* London: Faber and Faber. 1937.

Barbour, Brian. "Lewis at Cambridge." *Modern Philology* 96 (1999): 439–84.

Bars, H. *Maritain en notre temps.* Paris, 1959.

Bateson, F. W. "The Function of Criticism at the Present Time." *Essays in Criticism* 3 (Jan. 1953): 1–27.

Bateson, F. W., et al. "The Critical Forum: 'A Cooking Egg.'" *Essays in Criticism* 3 (July 1953): 345–57.

Bateson, F. W. and I. A. Richards. "'A Cooking Egg': Final Scramble." *Essays in Criticism* 4 (Jan. 1954): 103–8.

Beaubourg, Maurice. "Notes." *Nouvelle Revue Française* (February 1910): 290–98.

Belgion, Montgomery. Review of *Enquiries into Religion and Culture,* by Christopher Dawson. *Criterion,* 13, no. 50 (Oct. 1933): 143–46.

Benda, Julien. *Belphégor: essai sur l'esthétique de la présente société française.* 1918. Reprint, Paris: Émile-Paul frères, 1924.

———. *The Betrayal of the Intellectuals.* Translated by Richard Aldington. Boston: Beacon Press, 1955.

Bergonzi, Bernard. "Eliot's Cities." In *T. S. Eliot at the Turn of the Century,* edited by Marianne Thormählen, 59–76. Lund, Sweden: Lund University Press, 1994.

Bessière, Jean. "Mémoire et temporalité de la ville." In *Mémoire des villes,* edited by Yves Clavaron and Bernard Dieterle, 403–18. Saint-Etienne, France: Université de Saint-Etienne, 2003.

Bicknell, E. J. *A Theological Introduction to the Thirty-Nine Articles of the Church of England.* 1919. Reprint, London: Longmans, 1961.

Birzer, Bradley J. *Sanctifying the World: The Augustinian Life and Mind of Christopher Dawson.* Front Royal, VA: Christendom Press, 2007.

Blake, William. "The Marriage of Heaven and Hell." In *Poems of William Blake,* edited by W. B. Yeats, 176–94. London: Routledge and Kegan Paul, 1905.

Blissett, William. *The Long Conversation.* Oxford: Oxford University Press, 1981.

Bollier, E. P. "T. S. Eliot and John Milton: A Problem in Criticism." *Tulane Studies in English* 8 (1955): 165–92.

Bottum, Joseph. "What T. S. Eliot Almost Believed." *First Things* no. 55 (1995): 25–30.

Boyd, John D. "*The Dry Salvages*: Topography as Symbol." *Renascence* 40 (1998): 265–81.

Brabazon, James. *Dorothy L. Sayers: A Biography.* New York: Charles Scribner's Sons, 1981.

Bradbury, Malcolm. "*The Calendar of Modern Letters*: A Review in Retrospect." *The London Magazine* 1, no. 7 (October 1961): 37–47.

Brague, Rémi. "Are Non-Theocratic Regimes Possible?" *Intercollegiate Review* 41 (Spring 2006): 3–12.

Bray, Suzanne. "Disseminating Glory: Echoes of Charles Williams in the Works of T. S. Eliot." *Seven: An Anglo-American Literary Review* 14 (1997): 59–73.

Brewer, Derek. "The Tutor: A Portrait." In *C. S. Lewis at the Breakfast Table and Other Reminiscences,* edited by James T. Como, 41–67. New York: Macmillan, 1979.

Brooker, Jewel Spears. *Mastery and Escape: T. S. Eliot and the Dialectic of Modernism.* Amherst: University of Massachusetts Press, 1994.

Brooks, Cleanth. "Teaching 'The Love Song of J. Alfred Prufrock.'" In *Approaches to Teaching Eliot's Poetry and Plays,* edited by Jewel Spears Brooker, 78–87. New York: Modern Language Association, 1988.

Bush, Ronald. "But Is It Modern? T. S. Eliot in 1988." *The Yale Review* 77, no. 2 (March 1988): 193–206.

Carpenter, Humphrey. *The Inklings: C.S. Lewis, J.R.R. Tolkien, Charles Williams, and Their Friends.* New York: Ballantine, 1978.

Cather, Willa. *The Professor's House.* 1925. Reprint, New York: Vintage, 1973.

Catholicity: A Study in the Conflict of Christian Traditions in the West. Westminster: Dacre Press, 1947.

Chace, W. M. *The Political Identities of Ezra Pound and T. S. Eliot.* Palo Alto: Stanford University Press, 1973.

Chesterton, G. K. *Charles Dickens.* Vol. 15 of *The Collected Works of G.K. Chesterton.* San Francisco: Ignatius Press, 1989.

Childs, Donald. *T. S. Eliot: Mystic, Son and Lover.* New York: St. Martin's, 1997.

Chinitz, David E. *T. S. Eliot and the Cultural Divide.* Chicago: University of Chicago Press, 2003.

Christopher, Joe R. "Modern Literature." In *Reading the Classics with C. S. Lewis,* edited by Thomas Martin, 245–64. Grand Rapids, MI: Baker, 2000.

Clarke, Graham. *T. S. Eliot: Critical Assessments, IV: The Criticism and General Essays.* London: Christopher Helm, 1990.

Coffey, P. *Epistemology, Or the Theory of Knowledge: An Introduction to General Metaphysics.* 2 Vols. Gloucester, MA: Peter Smith, 1958.

Coghill, Nevil. "An Essay on the Structure and Meaning of the Play." In *The Cocktail Party,* edited by Nevil Coghill, 237–91. London: Faber and Faber, 1974.

Coleridge, S. T. *On the Constitution of the Church and State.* Vol. 10 of *The Collected Works of Samuel Taylor Coleridge,* edited by John Colmer. Princeton: Princeton University Press, 1969.

Compagnon, Antoine. "Maurras critique." *Revue d'histoire littéraire de la France,* 105, no. 3 (July 2005): 517–32.

Copeau, Jacques. "L'Enquête d'Agathon sur 'Les jeunes gens d'aujourd'hui.'" *Nouvelle Revue Française* (November 1912): 929–35.

Copleston, Frederick, S.J. *A History of Philosophy.* 9 vols. New York: Doubleday, 1985.

Cossu, Nunzio. "Dantismo Politico-Religioso di Eliot." *Nuova Antologia* 495 (Sept.–Dec. 1965): 181–91.

Crawford, Robert. *The Savage and the City in the Work of T. S. Eliot.* New York: Oxford University Press, 1987.

Cunningham, A. "Continutiy and Coherence in Eliot's Religious Thought." In *Eliot in Perspective,* edited by Graham Martin, 217–25. London: Macmillan, 1970.

Curtius, E. R. "Restoration of the Reason." *Criterion* 6 (Nov. 1927): 389–97.

Dakin, Arthur Hazard. *Paul Elmer More.* Princeton: Princeton University Press, 1960.

Dante. *De Monarchia.* Translated by Donald Nicholl. New York: Noonday Press, 1947.

———. *The Divine Comedy I: Hell (L'Inferno).* Translated by Dorothy L. Sayers. Harmondsworth, England: Penguin, 1971.

———. *The Divine Comedy II: Purgatory (Il Purgatorio).* Translated by Dorothy L. Sayers. Harmondsworth, England: Penguin, 1988.

———. *The Divine Comedy III: Paradise (Il Paradiso).* Translated by Dorothy L. Sayers and Barbara Reynolds. Harmondsworth, England: Penguin, 1969.

———. Dante. *The Divine Comedy.* Translated by Allen Mandelbaum. 3 vols. Berkeley: University of California Press, 1980–82.

———. *Dante's 'Vita Nuova': A Translation and an Essay.* Translated by Mark Musa. Bloomington: Indiana University Press, 1973.

D'Arcy, M. C. "The Thomistic Synthesis and Intelligence." *Criterion* 6 (September 1927): 210–28.

Davie, Donald. "Anglican Eliot." In *Eliot in His Time: Essays on the Occasion of the Fiftieth Anniversary of "The Waste Land,"* edited by A. Walton Litz, 181–96. Princeton: Princeton University Press, 1973.

———. "Pound and Eliot: A Distinction." In *Eliot in Perspective: A Symposium,* edited by Graham Martin, 62–82. New York: Humanities Press, 1970.

Dawson, Christopher. *The Age of the Gods.* London: Sheed and Ward, 1933.

———. *Beyond Politics.* New York: Sheed and Ward, 1939.

———. "Catholic Tradition and the Modern State." *Catholic Review* (1916): 24–35.

———. "Christianity and Sex." *Enquiries into Religion and Culture.* Freeport, NY: Books for the Libraries Press, 1968: 259–91.

———. "The End of an Age," *Criterion* 9, no. 36 (April, 1930): 386–401.

———. "H. G. Wells and History." *Criterion* 12, no. 46 (Oct, 1932): 9–16.

———. "The Hour of Darkness." *The Tablet* (1939): 625–26.

———. *The Judgement of Nations.* London: Sheed and Ward, 1942.

———. *The Making of Europe.* 1932. Reprint, Cleveland: Meridian, 1956.

———. "Memories of a Victorian Childhood." Appendix to *A Historian and His World,* by Christina Scott. New Brunswick, NJ: Transaction, 1992: 230–31.

———. "The Origins of the Romantic Tradition." *Criterion* 11, no. 43 (Jan., 1932): 222–48.

———. *Progress and Religion: An Historical Inquiry.* 1931. Reprint, Washington: Catholic University of America Press, 2001.

———. "The Psychology of Sex and the Catholic Order." *Order: An Occasional Catholic Review* 1 (1929): 79–82.

———. *Religion and Culture*. London: Sheed and Ward, 1949.

———. *Religion and the Modern State*. New York: Sheed and Ward, 1935.

———. "Religion and the Totalitarian State." *Criterion* 14, no. 54 (Oct., 1934): 1–16.

———. Review of *The Great Amphibian*, by Joseph Needham. *Criterion* 11, no. 44 (April, 1932): 545–48.

———. Review of *Mediaeval Culture*, by Carl Vossler, and *New Light on the Youth of Dante*, by Gertrude Leigh. *Criterion* 9, no. 37 (July, 1930): 718–22.

———. Review of *Reflections on the End of an Era*, by Reinhold Niebuhr. *Criterion* 14, no. 54 (Oct., 1934).

———. Review of *Woman and Society*, by Meyrick Booth. *Criterion* 10, no. 38 (Oct., 1930): 176–77.

———. "T. S. Eliot on the Meaning of Culture." In *Dynamics of World History*, edited by John J. Mulloy, 109–115. Wilmington, Delaware: ISI Books, 2002. Originally published in *The Month* 1 (March, 1949).

Day, Robert A. "The 'City Man' in *The Waste Land*: The Geography of Reminiscence." *PMLA* 80 (1965): 285–91.

De-la-Noy, Michael. *Michael Ramsey*. London: Collins, 1990.

DeLeontibus, Gaetano. *Charles Maurras's Classicising Aesthetics and Politics: Aestheticization of Politics*. New York: Peter Lang, 2000.

Demant, V.A. *Christian Polity*. London: Faber, 1936.

———. *Religion and the Decline of Capitalism*. London: Faber, 1952.

———. *Theology of Society*. London: Faber, 1947.

Dettmar, Kevin J. H. "'An Occupation for the Saint': Eliot as a Religious Thinker." In *A Companion to T. S. Eliot*, edited by David E. Chinitz, 363–75. Chichester: Wiley-Blackwell, 2009.

Dilworth, Thomas. *David Jones: Diversity in Unity: Studies in His Literary and Visual Art*. Cardiff: University of Wales Press, 2000.

Dix , Gregory. *The Question of Anglican Orders*. Westminster: Dacre Press, 1945.

———. *The Shape of the Liturgy*. Westminster: Dacre Press, 1946.

Dobrée, Bonamy. "T. S. Eliot: A Personal Reminiscence." In *T. S. Eliot: The Man and His Work*, edited by Allen Tate, 65–88. London: Chatto and Windus, 1967.

Donoghue, Denis. *Words Alone: The Poet T. S. Eliot*. New Haven: Yale University Press, 2000.

Dorsett, Lyle W. *Seeking the Secret Place: The Spiritual Formation of C. S. Lewis*. Grand Rapids, MI: Brazos, 2004.

Eliot, T. S. *After Strange Gods, A Primer of Modern Heresy*. London: Faber and Faber, 1934.

———. "The Aims of Poetic Drama," *Adam* International Review, no. 200 (November, 1949): 10–16.

———. "An American Critic." Review of *Aristocracy and Justice*, by Paul Elmer More. *New Statesman* (24 June 1916): 284.

———. "An Anglican Platonist: The Conversion of Paul Elmer More." Review of *Pages from an Oxford Diary*, by Paul Elmer More. *Times Literary Supplement* (30 Oct. 1937): 792.

———. "Arnold and Pater." In *Selected Essays*. New York: Harcourt, 1950.

———. "Blake." In *The Sacred Wood: Essays on Poetry and Criticism*, 151–8. London: Methuen, 1928. First published 1920 by Methuen.

———. "Books of the Quarter." *Criterion* 4 (October, 1926): 751–57.

———. "Catholicism and International Order." In *Essays Ancient and Modern*. London: Faber, 1936. Originally published in *Christendom* 3 (Sept., 1933): 171–84.

———. *Christianity and Culture: The Idea of a Christian Society* and *Notes towards the Definition of Culture*. New York: Harcourt, Brace, and World, 1949.

———. *The Cocktail Party, A Comedy*. London: Faber and Faber, 1950.

———. *Collected Poems*. London: Faber, 1963.

————. "A Commentary." *Criterion* 4 (April, 1926): 221–23.

————. "A Commentary." *Criterion* 4 (October, 1926): 628–29.

————. "A Commentary." *Criterion* 5 (January, 1927): 1–6.

————. "A Commentary." *Criterion* 5 (June, 1927): 283–86.

————. "A Commentary." *Criterion* 6 (September, 1927): 193–96.

————. "A Commentary: Stones of London." *Criterion* 7 (January, 1928): 1–4.

————. "A Commentary." *Criterion* 13 (April, 1934): 451–54.

————. *The Complete Poems and Plays*. London: Faber and Faber, 1969.

————. "A Contemporary Thomist." *The New Statesman* (29 December 1917): 312–13.

————. "Dante." In *The Sacred Wood: Essays on Poetry and Criticism*, 159–71. London: Methuen, 1928. First published 1920 by Methuen.

————. "Dante." In *Selected Prose of T. S. Eliot*, edited by Frank Kermode, 205–30. Faber and Faber: 1975. First published 1929 by Faber.

————. "Eeldrop and Appleplex, I," *Little Review* 4, no. 1 (May, 1917): 7–11.

————. *Essays Ancient and Modern*. London: Faber and Faber, 1936.

————. *The Family Reunion, A Play*. New York: Harcourt, Brace and Company, 1939.

————. *For Lancelot Andrewes: Essays on Style and Order*. London: Faber and Gwyer, 1928.

————. "Francis Herbert Bradley." In *Selected Essays*. New York: Harcourt, 1950.

————. "The Frontiers of Criticism." In *On Poetry and Poets*, 113–31. New York: Noonday Press, 1961.

————. "The Function of Criticism." In *Selected Prose of T. S. Eliot*, edited by Frank Kermode, 68–76. Faber and Faber, 1975.

————. "Hamlet and His Problems." In *Selected Essays 1917–1932*. New York: Harcourt, Brace, 1932. First published in *Athenaeum* 4665 (26 Sept. 1919): 940–41.

————. "The Humanism of Irving Babbitt." In *Selected Prose of T. S. Eliot*, edited by Frank Kermode. Faber and Faber, 1975. First published in *Forum* 80 (July 1928): 37–44.

————. *The Idea of a Christian Society*. London: Faber and Faber, 1939.

————. "The Idea of a Literary Review." *New Criterion* 4 (Jan., 1926): 1–4.

————. "The Idealism of Julien Benda." *The Cambridge Review* 49 (6 June 1928): 485–88.

————. Introduction to *All Hallows Eve*, by Charles Williams. 1948. Reprint, Grand Rapids, MI: Eerdmans, 1981: ix–xviii.

————. Introduction to *Leisure: The Basis of Culture*, by Joseph Pieper. Translated by Alexander Dru. London: Faber and Faber, 1952.

————. *Inventions of the March Hare: Poems 1909–1917*. Edited by Christopher Ricks. New York: Harcourt, 1996.

————. "Lancelot Andrewes." *Selected Prose of T. S. Eliot*. Edited by Frank Kermode. Faber and Faber, 1975.

————. "Last Words." *Criterion* 18 (January, 1939): 269–75.

————. "The Lesson of Baudelaire." *Tyro* (Spring 1921): 4.

————. *The Letters of T. S. Eliot: Vol. 1, 1898–1922*. Edited by Valerie Eliot. San Diego: Harcourt Brace Jovanovich, 1988.

————. *The Letters of T. S. Eliot*. Vol. 1. Second edition. Edited by Valerie Eliot and Hugh Haughton. New York: Harcourt, 2009.

————. *The Letters of T. S. Eliot: Vol. 2, 1923–1925*. Edited by Valerie Eliot and Hugh Haughton. London: Faber and Faber, 2009.

————. "The Literature of Fascism." *Criterion* 8 (December, 1928): 280–90.

————. "Literature, Science, and Dogma." Review of *Science and Poetry*, by I. A. Richards. *Dial* 82 (1927): [239]–43.

————. "The Local Flavour." Review of *Literary Studies*, by Charles Whibley. *Athenaeum* (12 Dec. 1919): 1332–33.

————. "The Metaphysical Poets." In *Selected Essays 1917–1932*. New York: Harcourt, Brace, 1932.

————. "The Modern Dilemma: Christianity and Communism." *Listener* 7, no. 166 (March 16, 1932): 382–83.

————. "Mr. Middleton Murry's Synthesis." *Criterion* 6 (October, 1927): 340–47.
————. "Mr. P. E. More's Essays." Review of *Demon of the Absolute,* by Paul Elmer More. *Times Literary Supplement* (21 Feb. 1929): 136.
————. *Murder in the Cathedral.* London: Faber and Faber, 1935.
————. "A Note of Introduction." In *Parenthesis,* by David Jones. London: Faber, 1961. vii–viii.
————. "A Note on *In Parenthesis* and *The Anathemata.*" *Dock Leaves* 6, no. 16 (Spring 1955): 21–23.
————. *Notes towards the Definition of Culture.* 1948. Reprint, New York: Harcourt, 1949.
————. *On Poetry and Poets.* New York: Noonday, 1961.
————. "Paul Elmer More." *Princeton Alumni Weekly* 37 (1937): 373–74.
————. "Preface to the 1928 Edition." In *The Sacred Wood: Essays on Poetry and Criticism.* London: Methuen, 1928.
————. "Religion without Humanism." In *Humanism and America: Essays on the Outlook of Modern Civilisation,* edited by N. Foerster, 105–12. New York: Farrar and Rinehart, 1930.
————. "A Reply to Mr. Ward." *Criterion* 7, no. 4 (June, 1928): 84–88.
————. Review of *The Growth of Civilisation,* and *The Origin of Magic and Religion,* by W. J. Perry. *The Criterion* 2, no. 8 (1924): 489–91.
————. Review of *A Manual of Modern Scholastic Philosophy. International Journal of Ethics,* 28 (Oct., 1917): 137–38.
————. Review of *Reason and Romanticism,* by Herbert Read, and *Messages,* by Ramon Fernandez. *Criterion* 4 (October, 1926): 751–57.
————. Review of *Religion and Philosophy,* by R. G. Collingwood. *International Journal of Ethics* 27, no. 4 (July 1917): 543.
————. Review of *Religion and Science,* by John Theodore Merz. *Monist* 28, no. 2 (April, 1918): 319–20.
————. Review of *Son of Woman: The Story of D. H. Lawrence,* by John Middleton Murry. *Criterion* 10 (1931): 768–74.
———— [unsigned]. Review of *Three Reformers,* by Jacques Maritain. *Times Literary Supplement* (8 November 1928): 818.
————. *The Sacred Wood: Essays on Poetry and Criticism.* London: Methuen, 1920.
————. "A Sceptical Patrician." Review of *The Education of Henry Adams,* by Henry Adams. *Athenaeum* (23 May 1919): 361–62.
————. *Selected Essays.* New York: Harcourt, 1950.
————. *Selected Essays 1917–1932.* New York: Harcourt, 1932.
————. *Selected Prose of T. S. Eliot.* Edited by Frank Kermode. London: Faber and Faber, 1975.
————. *To Criticize the Critic and Other Writings.* New York: Farrar, 1965.
————. "Thoughts After Lambeth." In *Selected Essays.* New York: Harcourt, 1950.
————. "Towards a Christian Britain." *The Listener* (10 April, 1941): 574–75.
————. "Tradition and the Individual Talent." In *The Sacred Wood: Essays on Poetry and Criticism.* London: Methuen, 1920. Originally published in *The Egoist* 6 (Sept., 1919): 54–5.
————. "The Twelfth Century." *Times Literary Supplement* (11 August 1927): 542.
————. *The Use of Poetry and the Use of Criticism.* Cambridge: Harvard University Press, 1964.
————. *The Varieties of Metaphysical Poetry.* Edited by Ronald Schuchard. New York: Harcourt, 1993.
————. "War Paint and Feathers." *Athenaeum* 4668 (1919): 1036.
————. "Was There a Scottish Literature?" *Athenaeum* 4657 (1919): 680–1.
————. "What Is a Classic?" In *On Poetry and Poets.* London: Faber, 1957.
Ellis, Steve. *The English Eliot: Design, Language and Landscape in "Four Quartets."* New York: Routledge: 1991.
————. *T. S. Eliot: A Guide for the Perplexed.* London: Continuum, 2009.

Emerson, Ralph Waldo. *The Letters of Ralph Waldo Emerson.* Edited by Ralph L. Rusk. Vol. 4. New York: Columbia University Press, 1939.

Every, George. "The Way of Rejections." In *T. S. Eliot: A Symposium,* edited by Richard March and Tambimuttu, 181–88. London: Editions Poetry, 1948.

Faber, Geoffrey. *Oxford Apostles: A Character Study of the Oxford Movement.* Harmondsworth, England: Penguin, 1954.

Fabrègues, J. de. *Charles Maurras et son Action Française.* Paris, 1966.

Fairweather, Eugene R. Introduction to *The Oxford Movement.* New York: Oxford University Press, 1964. 3–15.

Ferrall, Charles. *Modernist Writing and Reactionary Politics.* Cambridge: Cambridge University Press, 2001.

Fish, Stanley. "Will the Humanities Save Us?" *New York Times,* January 6, 2008.

Fletcher, John Gould. Review of *Art et Scolastique* and *The Philosophy of Art,* by Jacques Maritain. *Criterion* 11 (1929): 346–49.

Forster, E. M. *Howards End.* Harmondsworth, England: Penguin, 1985.

———. *Selected Letters of E.M. Forster.* Edited by Mary Lago and P. N. Furbank. Vol. 1. Cambridge, Mass.: Belknap Press, 1985.

Frye, Northrop. *T. S. Eliot: An Introduction.* Chicago: University of Chicago Press, 1981.

Gardner, Helen. "The Landscapes of T. S. Eliot." *Critical Quarterly* 10 (1968): 313–30.

Garman, Douglas. "A Reply to *The Criterion.*" *The Calendar of Modern Letters* 4 (July 1927): 154–55.

Gentile, Emilio. "Fascism as Political Religion." *Journal of Contemporary History* 25 (May–June 1990): 229–51.

Geuss, Raymond. "*Kultur, Bildung, Geist.*" *History and Theory* 35, no. 2 (May, 1996): 151–64.

Gide, André. "L'Amateur de M. Remy de Gourmont." *Nouvelle Revue Française* (April, 1910): 425–37.

———. *Charles-Louis Philippe.* Paris: Éditions Athéna, 1922.

———. *Dostoevsky.* London: J. M. Dent and Sons, 1925.

———. *Journals: 1889–1913.* Translated by Justin O'Brien. New York: Alfred A. Knopf, 2000.

Gide, André and Paul Claudel. *Correspondance 1899–1926.* Edited by R. Mallet. Paris: Gallimard, 1949.

Gill, Eric. *Art-Nonsense and Other Essays.* London: Cassel, 1929.

———. *Autobiography.* New York: Devin-Adair, 1961.

Gilson, Étienne. *Dante and Philosophy.* Translated by David Moore. Gloucester, MA: Peter Smith, 1968.

Goldie, David. *A Critical Difference: T. S. Eliot and John Middleton Murry in English Literary Criticism, 1919–1928.* Oxford: Oxford University Press, 1998.

Goodheart, Eugene. *The Failure of Criticism.* Cambridge: Harvard University Press, 1978.

Gordon, Lyndall. *Eliot's Early Years.* New York: Farrar, 1977.

———. *T. S. Eliot: An Imperfect Life.* New York: Norton, 1999.

Gould, Stephen J. "Nonoverlapping Magisteria." *Natural History* 106 (March, 1997): 16–22.

Gray, Piers. *T. S. Eliot's Intellectual and Poetic Development, 1909–1922.* Sussex: Harvester Press, 1982.

Green, Roger Lancelyn, and Walter Hooper. *C. S. Lewis: A Biography.* New York: Harcourt Brace Jovanovich, 1974.

Greene, Edward J. H. *T. S. Eliot et la France.* Paris: Boivin, 1951.

Griffin, William. *C. S. Lewis: A Dramatic Life.* San Francisco: Harper and Row, 1986.

Grogin, R. C. *Bergsonian Controversy in France.* Calgary: University of Calgary Press, 1988.

Gross, Harvey. "The Figure of St. Sebastian." *The Southern Review* 21 (Autumn, 1985): 974–84.

Hague, René. *David Jones.* Cardiff: University of Wales, 1975.

Hamilton, G. Rostrevor. *The Tell-Tale Article: A Critical Approach to Modern Poetry.* London: William Heinemann, 1949.

Harding, Jason. *The "Criterion": Cultural Politics and Periodical Networks in Inter-War Britain.* Oxford: Oxford University Press, 2002.

———. "'The Just Impartiality of a Christian Philosopher': Jacques Maritain and T. S. Eliot." In *The Maritain Factor,* edited by Rajesh Heynickx and Jan De Maeyer. Leuven: Leuven University Press, 2010.

———. "Keeping Critical Thought Alive: Eliot's Editorship of the *Criterion.*" In *A Companion to T. S. Eliot,* edited by David Chinitz. Malden, MA: Blackwell, 2009.

Hargrove, Nancy. *Landscape as Symbol in the Poetry of T. S. Eliot.* Jackson: University Press of Mississippi, 1978.

———. *T. S. Eliot's Parisian Year.* Tallahassee: University Press of Florida, 2009.

Harries, R. A. "The Rare Contact: A Correspondence between T. S. Eliot and P. E. More." *Theology* 75 (1972): [136]–44.

Harrison, Jane Ellen. *Ancient Art and Ritual.* London and New York: Oxford University Press, 1913.

Harrison, John R. *The Reactionaries: W. B. Yeats, Wyndham Lewis, Ezra Pound, T. S. Eliot, D. H. Lawrence.* New York: Schocken Books, 1967.

Hawkins, Peter. *Dante: A Brief History.* Oxford: Blackwell, 2006.

Hebert, A. G., ed. *The Parish Communion.* London: S.P.C.K., 1939.

Hewes, Henry. "T. S. Eliot at Seventy." In *T. S. Eliot: The Contemporary Reviews,* edited by Jewel Spears Brooker, 567–70. Cambridge: Cambridge University Press, 2004. First published in *Saturday Review* 41 (13 Sept. 1958): 30–32.

Higgins, Bertram. "Art and Knowledge." *The Calendar of Modern Letters* 4 (April, 1927).

Hinchliff, Peter. "Church-State Relations." In *The Study of Anglicanism,* edited by Stephen Sykes and John Booty, 351–63. London: SPCK, 1988.

Hitchcock, James. "Postmortem on a Rebirth: The Catholic Intellectual Renaissance." In *Years of Crisis: Collected Essays, 1970–1983.* San Francisco: Ignatius Press, 1985.

Hobsbawm, E. J. *Nations and Nationalism since 1780: Programme, Myth, Reality.* Second ed. Cambridge: Cambridge University Press, 1992.

Hooper, Walter. *C. S. Lewis: A Companion and Guide.* New York: Harper, 1996.

———. Introduction to *The Collected Poems of C. S. Lewis,* edited by Walter Hooper. London: Harper Collins, 1994. ix–xviii.

———. Preface to *Selected Literary Essays,* by C. S. Lewis. Cambridge: Cambridge University Press, 1979. vii–xx.

Howarth, Herbert. *Notes on Some Figures behind T. S. Eliot.* Boston: Houghton, 1964.

Hulme, T. E. "Romanticism and Classicism." In *The Collected Writings of T.E. Hulme,* edited by Karen Csengeri. Oxford: Clarendon, 1994.

———. *Speculations.* London: Kegan Paul, 1924. Reprint, New York: Routledge and Kegan Paul, 1987.

Huttar, Charles A. "C. S. Lewis, T. S. Eliot, and the Milton Legacy: The *Nativity Ode* Revisited." *Texas Studies in Literature and Language* 44 (2002): 324–48.

———. "C. S. Lewis's Prufrockian Vision in *The Great Divorce.*" *Mythlore* 22, no. 4 (Spring, 2000): 4–12.

———. "A Lifelong Love Affair with Language: C. S. Lewis's Poetry." In *Word and Story in C. S. Lewis,* edited by Peter J. Schakel and Charles A. Huttar, 86–108. Columbia: University of Missouri Press, 1991.

———. "Milton." In *Reading the Classics with C. S. Lewis,* edited by Thomas Martin, 161–86. Grand Rapids, MI: Baker, 2000.

Hylson-Smith, Kenneth. *High Churchmanship.* Edinburgh: T and T Clark, 1993.

Jain, Manju. *T. S. Eliot and American Philosophy.* New York: Cambridge University Press, 1992.

James, William. *Writings 1902–1910.* New York: Library of America, 1987.

Johnson, Malcolm. *Bustling Intermeddler? The Life and Work of Charles James Blomfield.* Leominster: Gracewine, 2001.

Jones, David. *The Anathemata.* London: Faber, 1954.

———. *Dai Greatcoat*. London: Faber, 1980.

———. *In Parenthesis*. London: Faber, 1961.

———. *Letters to a Friend*. Edited by Aneirin Talfan Davies. Swansea: Christopher Davies, 1980.

Julius, Anthony. *T. S. Eliot, Anti-Semitism, and Literary Form*. Cambridge: Cambridge University Press, 1995.

Kazin, Alfred. *God and the American Writer*. New York: Knopf, 1997.

Kearns, Cleo McNelly. "Religion, Literature, and Society in the Work of T. S. Eliot." In *The Cambridge Companion to T. S. Eliot*, edited by A. David Moody, 77–93. Cambridge: Cambridge University Press, 1994.

———. *T. S. Eliot and Indic Traditions: A Study in Poetry and Belief*. Cambridge: Cambridge University Press, 1987.

Ker, Ian. *John Henry Newman: A Biography*. Oxford: Clarendon Press, 1988.

Kim, Hee-Sung. "Automatons in Modern Metropolis." *Journal of the T. S Eliot Society of Korea* 14, no. 2 (2004): 99–127.

Kirk, Russell. *The Conservative Mind: From Burke to Santayana*. Chicago: H. Regnery, 1953. The seventh edition is entitled *The Conservative Mind: From Burke to Eliot*. Chicago: Regnery, 2001.

———. *Eliot and His Age: T. S. Eliot's Moral Imagination in the Twentieth Century*. Second ed. Wilmington DE: ISI Books, 2008. First edition, New York: Random House, 1971.

———. "The Enduring Influence of Irving Babbitt." In *Irving Babbitt in Our Time*, edited by George A. Panichas and Claes G. Ryn, 17–26. Washington, D.C.: The Catholic University of America Press, 1986.

Knowles, Sebastian D. G. *A Purgatorial Flame: Seven British Writers in the Second World War*. Philadelphia: University of Pennsylvania Press, 1990.

Koffeman, Maaike. *Entre Classicisme et Modernité*. Amsterdam: Rodopi, 2003.

Kojecký, Roger. *T. S. Eliot's Social Criticism*. London: Faber and Faber, 1971.

Kuin, Johan. "Proeve van een apologie: T. S. Eliot als Anglicaan." In *T. S. Eliot: Een Amerikaan in Europa*, edited by W. Bronzwaer, 9–45. Baarn: Ambo, 1988.

Laforgue, Jules. *Poems*. Translated by Peter Dale. London: Anvil, 2001.

Larbaud, Valéry. "Charles-Louis Philippe: In Memoriam." *Phalange* (January, 1910): 13.

Lawrence, D. H. *Phoenix II: Uncollected, Unpublished, and Other Prose Works by D.H. Lawrence*. Edited by Warren Roberts and Harry T. Moore. New York: Viking, 1968.

Lethaby, William Richard. *Architecture, Mysticism and Myth*. 1891. Reprint, New York: George Braziller, 1975.

———. *Architecture, Nature and Magic*. 1928. Reprint, London: Duckworth, 1956.

———. *Londinium: Architecture and the Crafts*. London: Duckworth, 1923.

Levy, W. T. and Victor Scherle. *Affectionately, T. S. Eliot*. N.Y.: Lippincott, 1968.

Lewis, C. Day. *The Poetic Image*. London: Jonathan Cape, 1947.

Lewis, C. S. *The Abolition of Man*. Second ed. London: Bles, 1945.

———. *All My Road before Me: The Diary of C. S. Lewis 1922–1927*. Edited by Walter Hooper. San Diego: Harcourt Brace Jovanovich, 1991.

———. *The Allegory of Love*. Rev. ed. London: Oxford University Press, 1938.

———. *The Collected Letters of C. S. Lewis*. Edited by Walter Hooper. 3 vols. New York: HarperSanFrancisco, 2004–07.

———. *De Descriptione Temporum*. Cambridge: Cambridge University Press, 1955. Reprinted in *They Asked for a Paper*, 9–25, and in *Selected Literary Essays*, 1–14.

———. *The Great Divorce*. New York: Macmillan, 1946.

———. "Hamlet: The Prince or the Poem?" in *They Asked for a Paper*, 51–71. Originally published as the Annual Shakespeare Lecture of the British Academy. London: H. Milford, 1942.

———. "Imagery in the Last Eleven Cantos of Dante's 'Comedy.'" In *Studies in Medieval and Renaissance Literature*, edited by Walter Hooper, 78–93. Cambridge: Cambridge University Press, 1966.

———. "Kipling's World." In *They Asked for a Paper*, 72–92.

————. "On the Reading of Old Books." In *God in the Dock,* edited by Walter Hooper, 200–07. Grand Rapids, MI: Eerdmans, 1970. Originally published as the introduction to Athanasius, *The Incarnation of the Word of God,* translated and edited by a religious of C.S.M.V. London: Bles, 1944.

————. *The Pilgrim's Regress: An Allegorical Apology for Christianity, Reason and Romanticism.* Third ed. 1943. Reprint, Grand Rapids, MI: Eerdmans, 1958.

————. *Poems.* Edited by Walter Hooper. London: Bles, 1964.

————. *A Preface to "Paradise Lost."* London: Oxford University Press, 1942.

————. *Selected Literary Essays.* Edited by Walter Hooper. Cambridge: Cambridge University Press, 1969.

————. "Shelley, Dryden, and Mr Eliot," in *Selected Literary Essays,* 187–208. Originally published in *Rehabilitations and Other Essays.* London: Oxford University Press, 1939.

————. *Surprised by Joy: The Shape of My Early Life.* New York: Harcourt, Brace and World, 1955.

————. *That Hideous Strength: A Modern Fairy-Tale for Grown-ups.* New York: Macmillan, 1946.

————. *They Asked for a Paper.* London: Bles, 1962.

————. "Williams and the Arthuriad." In *Arthurian Torso,* edited by C. S. Lewis, 91–200. London: Oxford University Press, 1948.

Lewis, W. H. *Brothers and Friends: The Diaries of Major Warren Hamilton Lewis.* Edited by Clyde S. Kilby and Marjorie Lamp Mead. San Francisco: Harper and Row, 1982.

Lowe, Peter. "Prufrock in St. Petersburg: The Presence of Dostoevsky's *Crime and Punishment* in T. S. Eliot's 'The Love Song of J. Alfred Prufrock.'" *Journal of Modern Literature* 28, no. 3 (2005): 1–24.

Macmillan, Margaret. *Paris 1919: Six Months That Changed the World.* New York: Random House, 2003.

Manganiello, Dominic. *T. S. Eliot and Dante.* London: MacMillan, 1989.

Margolis, John D. *T. S. Eliot's Intellectual Development 1922–1939.* Chicago: University of Chicago Press, 1972.

Maritain, Jacques. *Art and Scholasticism and the Frontiers of Poetry.* Translated by Joseph W. Evans. Notre Dame, IN: University of Notre Dame Press, 1974.

————. *The Degrees of Knowledge.* Translated by Gerald B. Phelan. Notre Dame, IN: University of Notre Dame Press, 1995.

————. *The Philosophy of Art.* Translated by John O'Connor. Ditchling: St Dominic's Press, 1921.

————. "Poetry and Religion." Part 1. Translated by F. S. Flint. *The New Criterion* 5 (January, 1927): 7–22.

————. "Poetry and Religion." Part 2. Translated by F. S. Flint. *The New Criterion* 5 (May, 1927): 214–30.

————. *Pourquoi Rome a parler.* Paris, 1927.

————. *Primauté du Spirituel.* Paris, 1927.

————. *Réflexions sur l'intelligence.* Paris, 1924.

————. *Three Reformers.* London: Sheed and Ward, 1928.

Maritain, Jacques, and Raïssa Maritain. *Oeuvres Complètes.* 17 Vols. Fribourg: Éditions Universitaires, 1984.

Martin, Graham, ed. *Eliot in Perspective.* N.Y.: Humanities Press, 1970.

Mascall, E. L. *Saraband: The Memoirs.* Leominster: Gracewing 1992.

Massingham, H. J. Review of *The Age of the Gods,* by Christopher Dawson. *Criterion* 8, no. 30 (Sept., 1928): 149–53.

————. Review of *Progress and Religion,* by Christopher Dawson. *Criterion* 9, no. 34 (Oct., 1929): 146–50.

Massis, Henri. *Maurras et notre temps.* Paris, 1961.

Massis, Henri, and Alfred de Tarde. *Les jeunes gens d'aujourd'hui.* Edited by Jean-Jacques Becker. Paris: Imprimerie Nationale, 1995.

Maurras, Charles. *Anthinéa: d'Athènes à Florence.* Paris: Champion, 1920.

———. *L'Avenir de l'intelligence*. Paris: Albert Fontemoing, 1905.

———. *Dictionnaire politique et critique*. Ed. Pierre Chardon. Paris: À la cité des livres, 1932.

———. *Enquête sur la monarchie* ("édition définitive"). Paris: Nouvelle Librairie nationale, 1925.

———. *Prologue d'un essai sur la critique*. Paris: La Porte étroite, 1932. Originally published in the *Revue Encyclopédique Larousse, 1896*.

Mazzotta, Giuseppe. *Dante's Vision and the Circle of Knowledge*. Princeton: Princeton University Press, 1993.

McCearney, J. *Maurras et son temps*. Paris, 1977.

McCormick, John. *George Santayana: A Biography*. New York: Knopf, 1987.

McEachran, F. Review of *Christianity and the New Age*, by Christopher Dawson. *Criterion* 10, no. 41 (July, 1931): 750–55.

———. Review of *The Making of Europe*, by Christopher Dawson. *Criterion* 12, no. 47 (Jan., 1933): 290–92.

———. Review of *The Modern Dilemma*, by Christopher Dawson. *Criterion* 12, no. 48 (April, 1933): 494–96.

McKinley, Marlene Marie. "'To Live from a New Root': The Uneasy Consolation of *All Hallows' Eve*," *Mythlore* 59 (Autumn, 1989): 13–17.

Medcalf, Stephen. "Language and Self-Consciousness: The Making and Breaking of C. S. Lewis's Personae." In *Word and Story in C. S. Lewis*, edited by Peter J. Schakel and Charles A. Huttar, 109–44. Columbia: University of Missouri Press, 1991.

Menand, Louis. *Discovering Modernism: T. S. Eliot and His Context*. Rev. ed. New York: Oxford University Press, 2007.

Mercier, Désiré-Joseph, Cardinal, et al. *A Manual of Modern Scholastic Philosophy*. 2 Vols. Translated by T. L. Parker and S. A. Parker. London: Kegan Paul, Trench, Trubner, and Co., 1919.

Milbank, Alison. *Dante and the Victorians*. Manchester: Manchester University Press, 1998.

Miles, Jonathan. *Backgrounds to David Jones: A Study in Sources and Drafts*. Cardiff: University of Wales Press, 1990.

Miller, Andrew John. "'Compassing Material Ends': T. S. Eliot, Christian Pluralism, and the Nation-State." *ELH* 67 (2000): 229–55.

Miller, James E., Jr. *T. S. Eliot, The Making of an American Poet, 1888–1922*. University Park: The Pennsylvania State University Press, 2005.

Montemaggi, Vittorio. "'La Rosa in che il verbo divino si fece': Human Bodies and Truth in the Poetic Narrative of the *Commedia*." In *Dante and the Human Body: Eight Essays*, edited by John C. Barnes and Jennifer Petrie, 159–94. Dublin: Four Courts Press, 2007.

Moody, A. D. "The Mind of Europe." In *T. S. Eliot at the Turn of the Century*, edited by M. Thormählen. Lund, Sweden: Lund University Press, 1994.

More, Paul Elmer. *The Christ of the New Testament*. Vol. 3 of *The Greek Tradition*. Princeton: Princeton University Press, 1924.

———. "The Cleft Eliot." Review of *Selected Essays*, by T. S. Eliot. *Saturday Review of Literature* (12 Nov. 1932): 233–35. Reprinted in *T. S. Eliot: A Selected Critique*, edited by Leonard Unger, 24–29. New York: Rinehart, 1948.

———. "Marginalia." *American Review* 8 (1936): 1–30.

———. *A New England Group and Others*. Vol. 11 of *Shelburne Essays*. Boston: Houghton, 1921.

———. *Pages from an Oxford Diary*. Princeton: Princeton University Press, 1937.

Mourre, M. *Charles Maurras*. Paris, 1953.

Murata, Tatsuo. "Buddhism in T. S. Eliot." *The Modern Schoolman* 73, no. 1 (1995): 40–46.

Murphy, Russell Elliott. *Critical Companion to T. S. Eliot*. New York: Facts on File, 2007.

Murry, John Middleton. "Towards a Synthesis." *Criterion* 5 (June, 1927): 294–313.

Musacchio, George. "C. S. Lewis, T. S. Eliot, and the Anglican Psalter." *Seven: An Anglo-American Literary Review* 22 (2005): 45–59.

Newman, John Henry. *Apologia pro Sua Vita: Being a History of His Religious Opinions.* New York: Sheed and Ward, 1946.

———. *An Essay in Aid of a Grammar of Assent.* Notre Dame, IN: University of Notre Dame Press, 1979.

———. *The Idea of a University.* Edited by Frank M. Turner. New Haven: Yale University Press, 1996.

———. *Works.* 39 vols. London: Longmans, 1897.

Nietzsche, Friedrich. "On Truth and Lies in a Nonmoral Sense." Translated by Daniele Brazeale. *Philosophy and Truth: Selections from Nietzsche's Notebooks of the Early 1870s.* Atlantic Highlands, N.J.: Humanities Press, 1979.

———. *The Will to Power.* Translated by Walter Kaufmann and R. J. Hollingdale. London: Weidenfeld and Nicolson, 1968.

Nockles, Peter Benedict. *The Oxford Movement in Context: Anglican High Churchmanship, 1760–1857.* Cambridge: Cambridge University Press, 1994.

Noh, Jeo-Yong. *"Action Française Condemnation" and Other Essays.* Seoul, Korea: Brain House, 2003.

Nolte, E. *Der Faschismus in seiner Epoche.* Munich, 1971.

Norman, Edward. *Church and Society in England, 1770–1970: An Historical Study.* Oxford: Oxford University Press, 1976.

North, Michael. *The Political Aesthetic of Yeats, Eliot, and Pound.* Cambridge: Cambridge University Press, 1991.

Olney, James, ed. *T. S. Eliot: Essays from the Southern Review.* Oxford: Clarendon Press, 1988.

O'Sullivan, Richard. Review of *The Intellectualism of St. Thomas,* by Pierre Rousselot. *Criterion* 15 (April, 1936): 563–65.

Parrinder, Geoffrey. *Jesus in the Qur'an.* London: Faber, 1965.

Pascal, Blaise. *Pensées and Other Writings.* Translated by Honor Levi. Oxford: Oxford University Press, 1995.

Percy, Walker. "The Holiness of the Ordinary." In *Signposts in a Strange Land.* New York: Farrar, Straus and Giroux, 1991.

Perinot, Claudio. "Jean Verdenal: T. S. Eliot's French Friend." *Annali di Cà Foscari* 35, nos. 1–2 (1996): 265–75.

Perl, Jeffrey. *Skepticism and Modern Enmity.* Baltimore: Johns Hopkins University Press, 1989.

Philippe, Charles-Louis. *Bubu of Montparnasse.* Translated by Laurence Vail. New York: Avon, 1948.

———. "Lettres de Jeunesse de Charles-Louis Philippe." *Nouvelle Revue Française* (April, 1911): 582–606.

Pickering, W. S. F. *Anglo-Catholicism: A Study in Religious Ambiguity.* London and New York: Routledge, 1989.

Pittenger, W. Norman. *Theology and Reality: Essays in Restatement.* Greenwich, CT: Seabury, 1955.

Pope, John C. "Prufrock and Raskolnikov Again: A Letter from Eliot." *American Literature* 18 (1947): 319–21.

Pound, Ezra. "Cavalcanti." In *Literary Essays of Ezra Pound,* edited by T. S. Eliot, 149–200. New York: New Directions, 1968.

———. [Herman Carl Georg Jesus Maria] "On Certain Reforms and Pass-Times." *Egoist* 1 (Apr., 1914): 130–31.

———. *The Selected Letters of Ezra Pound.* Edited by D. D. Paige. New York: New Directions, 1971.

Prior, Arthur N. Review of *The Philosophy of St. Bonaventure,* by Étienne Gilson. *Criterion* 18 (October, 1938): 141–43.

Ray, Marcel. "L'Enfance et la Jeunesse de Charles-Louis Philippe." *Nouvelle Revue Française* (February, 1910): 169–94.

Read, Herbert. "Books of the Quarter." *Criterion* 4 (January, 1926): 189–93.

Reckitt, Maurice. *As It Happened.* London: Dent, 1941.

———. *Maurice to Temple.* London: Faber, 1947.

———. *Prospects for Christendom.* London: Faber, 1945.

Renan, Ernest. "What Is a Nation?" Translated by Martin Thom. In *Nation and Narration*, edited by Homi K. Bhabha, 8–22. London: Routledge, 1990.

Rendel, Christian. "C. S. Lewis und T. S. Eliot." *Inklings: Jahrbuch für Literatur und Ästhetik* 6 (1988): 55–63.

La Révolution d'abord et toujours! Leaflet, August 1925.

Richards, Philip S. Review of *True Humanism*, by Jacques Maritain. *Criterion* 18 (January, 1939): 329–33.

Ricks, Christopher. *T. S. Eliot and Prejudice.* London: Faber, 1988.

Ridler, Anne. Introduction to *The Image of the City and Other Essays*, by Charles Williams. Oxford: Oxford University Press, 1970: ix–lxxii.

Robert, Marthe. *Roman des origines et origines du roman.* 1972. Reprint, Paris: Gallimard, 1985.

Roberts, Michael. *T. E. Hulme.* London: Faber, 1938.

Robichaud, Paul. "David Jones, Christopher Dawson, and the Meaning of History." *Logos: A Journal of Catholic Thought and Culture* 6, no. 3 (2003): 68–85.

Rosenberg, Harold. "Aesthetics of Crisis." *The New Yorker* (August 22, 1964): 114–22.

Rowell, Geoffrey. *The Vision Glorious: Themes and Personalities of the Catholic Revival in Anglicanism.* Oxford: Oxford University Press, 1983.

Royère, Jean. "Remy de Gourmont et André Gide." *Phalange* (October, 1910): 372–76.

Rubens, Godfrey. *William Richard Lethaby: His Life and Work 1857–1931.* London: The Architectural Press, 1986.

Ruskin, John. *The Stones of Venice.* Vol. 2. Chicago: Belford, Clarke and Co., 1851.

Santayana, George. "The Absence of Religion in Shakespeare." In *Interpretations of Poetry and Religion*, edited by William G. Holzberger and Herman J. Saatkamp Jr., 91–101. *Interpretations of Poetry and Religion* first published in 1900 by Charles Scribner's Sons.

———. *Character and Opinion in the United States.* New Brunswick, New Jersey: Transaction, 1991.

———. "The Elements and Function of Poetry." In *Interpretations of Poetry and Religion*, edited by William G. Holzberger and Herman J. Saatkamp Jr., 151–72. *Interpretations of Poetry and Religion* first published in 1900 by Charles Scribner's Sons.

———. "The Genteel Tradition at Bay." In *The Genteel Tradition: Nine Essays by George Santayana*, edited by Douglas L. Wilson, 153–96. Lincoln, NE: University of Nebraska Press, 1998.

———. "The Genteel Tradition in American Philosophy." In *The Genteel Tradition: Nine Essays by George Santayana*, edited by Douglas L. Wilson, 37–64. Lincoln, NE: University of Nebraska Press, 1998.

———. *The Idea of Christ in the Gospels or God in Man: A Critical Essay.* New York: Charles Scribner's Sons, 1946.

———. *The Last Puritan: A Memoir in the Form of a Novel.* Edited by William G. Holzberger and Herman J. Saatkamp Jr. Cambridge, Massachusetts: MIT Press, 1994. First published in 1935 by Constable Publishers in Great Britain.

———. "Modernism and Christianity." In *Winds of Doctrine: Studies in Contemporary Opinion.* Vol. 7 of *The Works of George Santayana.* New York: Charles Scribner's Sons, 1937: 24–49. *Winds of Doctrine* first published in 1913 by Charles Scribner's Sons.

———. *Persons and Places: Fragments of Autobiography.* Edited by William G. Holzberger and Herman J. Saatkamp Jr. Cambridge, Massachusetts: MIT Press, 1994. First published in 1963 by Scribner's.

———. "Philosophical Heresy." In *Obiter Scripta: Lectures, Essays and Reviews*, edited by Justus Buchler and Benjamin Schwartz, 94–107. New York: Charles Scribner's Sons, 1936.

————. "The Poetry of Christian Dogma." In *Interpretations of Poetry and Religion*, edited by William G. Holzberger and Herman J. Saatkamp Jr., 51–72. *Interpretations of Poetry and Religion* first published in 1900 by Charles Scribner's Sons.

————. *Reason in Science*. Vol. 5 of *The Life of Reason*. New York: Dover, 1983. First published in 1906 by Charles Scribner's Sons.

————. *Three Philosophical Poets*. New York: Doubleday Anchor, 1953. First published in 1910 by Harvard University Press.

Sayer, George. *Jack: C. S. Lewis and His Times*. San Francisco: Harper and Row, 1988.

Sayers, Dorothy L. *Further Papers on Dante*. London: Methuen, 1957.

Schloesser, Stephen. *Jazz Age Catholicism: Mystic Modernism in Postwar Paris, 1919–1933*. Toronto: University of Toronto Press, 2005.

Schuchard, Ronald. *Eliot's Dark Angel: Intersections of Life and Art*. New York: Oxford University Press, 1999.

————. "T. S. Eliot as an Extension Lecturer, 1916–1919." *Review of English Studies* 25 (May, 1974): 163–73.

Schwartz, Sanford. *The Matrix of Modernism: Pound, Eliot, and Early 20th Century Thought*. Princeton, NJ: Princeton University Press, 1985.

Scott, Christina. *A Historian and His World: A Life of Christopher Dawson*. New Brunswick, NJ: Transaction, 1992.

Scott, Peter Dale. "The Social Critic and His Discontents." In *The Cambridge Companion to T. S. Eliot*, edited by A. David Moody, 60–76. Cambridge: Cambridge Univ. Press, 1994.

Sencourt, Robert. *T. S. Eliot: A Memoir*. New York: Dodd, Mead, 1971.

Shafer, Robert. *Paul Elmer More and American Criticism*. New Haven: Yale University Press, 1935.

Sharp, Tony. *T. S. Eliot: A Literary Life*. New York: St. Martin's, 1991.

Shawcross, John T. *Rethinking Milton Studies*. Newark: University of Delaware Press, 2005.

Shusterman, Richard. "The Concept of Tradition: Its Progress and Potential." In *T. S. Eliot*, edited by Harriet Davidson, 23–61. London: Longman, 1999.

Skaff, William. *The Philosophy of T. S. Eliot: From Skepticism to a Surrealist Poetic 1909–1927*. Philadelphia: University of Pennsylvania Press, 1986.

Smith, Carol. *T. S. Eliot's Dramatic Theory and Practice*. Princeton: Princeton University Press, 1963.

Smith, Grover. *T. S. Eliot's Poetry and Plays: A Study in Sources and Meaning*. Chicago: University of Chicago Press, 1956. Second edition, 1974.

Souday, Paul. "Charles-Louis Philippe: *La Mère et l'Enfant*." *Le Temps* (June 29, 1911).

Southam, B. C. *A Student's Guide to the Selected Poems of T. S. Eliot*. Fifth ed. London: Faber and Faber, 1990.

Sparrow-Simpson, W. J. *The History of the Anglo-Catholic Revival from 1845*. London: George Allen and Unwin, 1932.

Spencer, Philip. *Politics of Belief in Nineteenth-Century France*. London: Faber, 1954.

Spurr, Barry. *"Anglo-Catholic in Religion": T. S. Eliot and Christianity*. Cambridge: Lutterworth Press, 2010.

Spurr, David. "Myths of Anthropology: Eliot, Joyce, Lévy-Bruhl." *PMLA* 109 (1994): 266–80.

Stanford, Derek. "Mr. Eliot's New Play." In *T. S. Eliot: The Contemporary Reviews*, edited by Jewel Spears Brooker. 573–75. Cambridge: Cambridge University Press, 2004. First published in *Contemporary Review*, no. 194 (1958): 199–201.

Stead, C. K. *Pound, Yeats, Eliot and the Modernist Movement*. New Brunswick, NJ: Rutgers University Press, 1986.

Steiner, George. *In Bluebeard's Castle: Some Notes towards the Redefinition of Culture*. London: Faber and Faber, 1971.

Surette, Leon. *The Modern Dilemma: Wallace Stevens, T. S. Eliot, and Humanism*. Montreal: McGill-Queen's University Press, 2008.

Takayanagi, Shun'ichi. "T. S. Eliot, Jacques Maritain, and Neo-Thomism." *The Modern Schoolman* 73 (November, 1995): 71–90.

Tate, Allen. "Postscript by the Guest Editor." In *T. S. Eliot: The Man and His Work*, edited by Allen Tate, 389–93. New York: Dell, 1966.

Tate, Allen, ed. *T. S. Eliot: The Man and His Work*. New York: Dell, 1966.

Tetreault, James. "Parallel Lines: C. S. Lewis and T. S. Eliot." *Renascence* 38 (1986): 256–69.

Thérive, André. "Poètes: F. P. Alibert." *L'Opinion* 15 (October, 1922): 200–208.

———. "Poètes: Paul Valéry." *L'Opinion*, 15 (September, 1922): 1095–1108.

Thibaudet, Albert. "L'esthétique des trois traditions" (First part). *La Nouvelle Revue Française* 9 (January, 1913): 5–42.

———. "L'esthétique des trois traditions" (Second part). *La Nouvelle Revue Française* 9 (March, 1913): 355–93.

———. *Trente ans de vie française, I: Les Idées de Charles Maurras*. Paris: Éditions de La Nouvelle Revue française, 1920.

Thormählen, Marianne. "The City in *The Waste Land*." In *The Waste Land: A Norton Critical Edition*, edited by Michael North, 235–40. New York: W.W. Norton, 2001.

Thorold, Algar. Review of *L'Esprit de la Philosophie Médiévale*, by Étienne Gilson. *Criterion* 13 (October, 1933): 169–70.

Tillyard, E. M. W., and C. S. Lewis. *The Personal Heresy: A Controversy*. London: Oxford University Press, 1939.

Tomlin, E. W. F. Review of *Religion and the Modern State*, by Christopher Dawson, *Freedom in the Modern World*, by Jacques Maritain, and *Preface to a Christian Sociology*, by Cyril E. Hudson. *Criterion* 15 (October, 1935): 130–37.

———. *T. S. Eliot: A Friendship*. London: Routledge, 1988.

Torrens, James. "Charles Maurras and Eliot's 'New Life.'" *PMLA* 89, no. 2 (March, 1974): 312–22.

Underhill, Evelyn. *Mysticism: A Study in the Nature and Development of Man's Spiritual Consciousness*. 1911. Twelfth ed. London: Methuen, 1930.

———. Review of *La Théologie Mystique de Saint Bernard*, by Étienne Gilson. *Criterion* 14 (January, 1935): 340–42.

Vanheste, Jeroen Franciscus. *Guardians of the Humanist Legacy: The Classicism of T. S. Eliot's Criterion Network and its Relevance to our Postmodern World*. Leiden and Boston: Brill, 2007.

Van Steenbergen, F. *Aristotle in the West*. Louvain: Nauwelaerts, 1955.

Warren, Austin. *Connections*. Ann Arbor: University of Michigan Press, 1970.

Watson, G. *Politics and Literature in Modern Britain*. London, 1977.

Weatherby, H. L. "Two Medievalists: Lewis and Eliot on Christianity and Literature." *Sewanee Review* 78 (1970): 330–47.

Weber, E. *The Action Française*. Palo Alto: Stanford University Press, 1962.

Willey, Basil. *Nineteenth-Century Studies: Coleridge to Matthew Arnold*. Harmondsworth, England: Penguin Books, 1964.

Williams, Charles. *All Hallows' Eve*. Grand Rapids: Eerdmans, 1982.

———. *Collected Plays*. London: Oxford University Press, 1963.

———. *Descent into Hell*. Grand Rapids: Eerdmans, 1980.

———. *The Descent of the Dove: A Short History of the Holy Spirit in the Church*. London: Longmans, 1939.

———. "A Dialogue on Mr. Eliot's Poem" (review of *Four Quartets*). *The Dublin Review* 212 (April, 1943): 114–22.

———. *The Figure of Beatrice: A Study in Dante*. London: Faber and Faber, 1943.

———. *He Came Down from Heaven*. London: Heineman, 1938.

———. *The Image of the City and Other Essays*. Oxford: Oxford University Press, 1970.

———. *Outlines of Romantic Theology*. Edited by Alice Mary Hadfield. Grand Rapids: Eerdmans, 1990.

————. "T. S. Eliot." In *Selected Modern English Essays: Second Series*, edited by H. S. M[ilford], 278–87. World's Classics. London: Oxford University Press, 1932. Originally published in *Poetry at Present* (Oxford: Clarendon Press, 1930).

Williams, Louise Blakeney. *Modernism and the Ideology of History*. Cambridge: Cambridge University Press, 2002.

Wilson, A. N. *C. S. Lewis: A Biography*. New York: Norton, 1990.

Woods, Randall J. "'Prufrock' to *The Waste Land*: T. S. Eliot's Periodical Publications, 1915–1922." PhD diss., Northwestern University, 2007. ProQuest (PQDT 3255920).

Zabarella, Jacobi. *De Rebus Naturalibus in Aristotelis Libros "De Anima."* Venice, 1605.

Index

Psichari, Ernest, 105
Puritanism, 26, 39, 49n6, 241, 245,
    252–253, 263n30, 292–293
Pusey, Edward, 20, 138–139, 198

Ramsey, Michael (archbishop of
    Canterbury), 33, 46, 53
rationalism, 54, 101, 105, 111, 113, 219
Read, Herbert, 18, 100, 107, 109, 132,
    134, 196
realism (philosophical), 16, 101–106,
    110
Reckitt, Maurice, 46–47
Reeves, Ambrose (bishop of
    Johannesburg), 41, 53
Reformation, 50n19, 54–55
Renan, Ernest, 62, 70, 212–213
Rice, Stanley, 17
Richards, I. A., 6, 257, 274, 281n41
Richards, Philip S., 114
Ricks, Christopher, 12, 71
Ridler, Anne, 145
ritual, 11, 21, 36–38, 41, 45, 105,
    167–175, 195, 198–199, 226, 292
Roberts, Michael, 47, 51n23
Rosenberg, Harold, 290
Rousseau, Jean-Jacques, 4, 50n14, 108,
    181, 196, 199, 212
royalism, 40, 84–85, 95, 124, 125, 180,
    232. *See also* monarchy
Royce, Josiah, 167
Rubenstein, Ida, 65
Ruskin, John, 166–167, 169
Russell, Bertrand, 91
Ryle, Gilbert, 35

sacraments, 36–37, 55, 56, 105, 113, 146,
    160n19, 198, 202, 222, 231, 253, 258
Sainte-Beuve, Charles-Augustin, 85
salvation, 55, 61, 66–72, 135, 147, 151,
    157, 287
Santayana, George, 24, 106, 239–247
Sayers, Dorothy, 148–151, 272
Schloesser, Stephen, 105, 108
Schofield, W. H., 59
Scholasticism, 15, 101, 105, 184. *See also*
    Neo-Scholasticism
Schuchard, Ronald, 2, 16, 20, 203n16,
    232, 258

Scott, Christina, 228
Scott-Hall, William Edward (bishop of
    Winchester), 43
Shakespeare, William, 24, 47, 240–241,
    254, 268–269, 272, 276
Sharp, Tony, 1
Shawcross, John, 265
Shaw, George Bernard, 41
Shelley, Percy Bysshe, 151, 241,
    267–268, 272
Skaff, William, 6–7
Smith, Grover, 66, 275
Smyth, Rev. C. H., 34, 54
Somerset, Vere, 42
Sorel, Georges, 91
Souday, Paul, 69
Speaight, Robert, 45
Spencer, Herbert, 46
Spender, Stephen, 184
Spengler, Oswald, 39, 288
Spurr, Barry, 2, 16, 22, 27, 191n9, 277n2
Stalin, Joseph, 6, 50n14, 180, 208, 227
Stead, C. K., 7–8
Stead, Rev. William Force, 37, 42, 133
Streeter, Rev. B. H., 42

Tarde, Alfred de, 61–62
Tawney, R. H., 46–47
Temple, William, 47, 113
Tertullian, 259
theocracy, 24, 199–202, 217–218,
    228–230, 233, 235n25
Thérive, André, 224
Thibaudet, Albert, 15, 80, 84–86
Thirty-Nine Articles of the Christian
    Faith, 38, 132
Thomas Aquinas, Saint, 16, 19, 99–112,
    116n54, 121–122, 123, 130n34, 183,
    200, 295. *See also* Thomism; Neo-
    Thomism
Thormählen, Marianne, 163
Thorold, Algar, 110
Tolkien, J. R. R., 267
Tomlin, E. W. F., 104, 107, 114, 235n19,
    235n25
Torrens, Rev. James, 203n14
totalitarianism, 188, 208, 210–211; and
    democracy, 222–223; and religion,
    23, 185, 187, 199–200, 233

About the Contributors

Anderson D. Araujo (HBA, MA, University of Toronto; PhD, University of Western Ontario) is assistant professor of English at the University of British Columbia, Okanagan campus. He has published articles on avant-garde movements of the 1910s, in particular Imagism, Vorticism, and Futurism. He has also published articles on Ezra Pound's poetry and the literary nonfiction of Virginia Woolf. He is currently producing an annotated edition of Pound's *Guide to Kulchur*, as well as writing a monograph on the cultural politics of Eliot, Pound, and Wyndham Lewis in the years between the world wars.

Hazel Atkins (BA, Huron University College, University of Western Ontario; MA, University of Ottawa; PhD, University of Ottawa) is currently a part-time professor in the Department of English at the University of Ottawa. She has published several articles on T. S. Eliot and Dorothy L. Sayers, and she is a regular contributor to the T. S. Eliot Society's annual meetings and newsletter.

William Blissett (BA, University of British Columbia; MA, PhD, University of Toronto) is emeritus professor of English in the University of Toronto. He is a fellow of the Royal Society of Canada and author of *The Long Conversation: A Memoir of David Jones* and of many articles on Edmund Spenser, William Shakespeare, Ben Jonson, William Morris, G. K. Chesterton, Literary Wagnerism, T. S. Eliot, and David Jones. He gave the Memorial Lecture at the T. S. Eliot Society meeting in St. Louis in 2006.

William C. Charron is professor of philosophy at Saint Louis University. For the past twenty-three years he has been editor of *The Modern Schoolman: A Quarterly Journal of Philosophy*. His scholarly interest in T. S. Eliot commenced upon reading in 1989 the poet's doctoral dissertation in philosophy. He has published work on Eliot and Bradley, and also on Eliot and Kant. He has also edited and annotated, with J. C. Marler, Eliot's papers on Plato and Aristotle.

Thomas Dilworth teaches English Literature at the University of Windsor and is a fellow of the Royal Society of Canada. He is the author of *The Shape of Meaning in the Poetry of David Jones* (1988), *Reading David Jones* (2008), and *David Jones in the Great War* (2013). He has edited Jones's *Inner*

Necessities: The Letters of David Jones to Desmond Chute (1984), *Wedding Poems* (2002), *The Rime of the Ancient Mariner* (2005), and *The Letters of Gertrude Stein and Virgil Thomson* (2011).

David Huisman (BA, Calvin College; MA, PhD, University of Michigan) is professor of English Emeritus at Grand Valley State University. He has published articles on nuclear war fiction and on T. S. Eliot, including the article on *Little Gidding* in *The Facts on File Companion to British Poetry, 1900 to the Present.* "If You Came This Way," his slide show on the landscapes of *Four Quartets*, has been presented at conferences in the United States and at Little Gidding, England. He has served as secretary of the T. S. Eliot Society.

Charles A. Huttar (AB, Wheaton College; MA, PhD, Northwestern University) is professor of English emeritus at Hope College in Holland, Michigan. He is coeditor of *Word and Story in C. S. Lewis* (1991) and other essay collections; editor of *Imagination and the Spirit* (1971), and author of several articles on the Inklings as well as on Milton, Shakespeare, Herbert, Donne, and other poets of the Early Modern period. He was a founding member of the Conference on Christianity and Literature and served as its president, 1966–1968. He is a member of the Guild of Scholars of the Episcopal Church.

Benjamin G. Lockerd (BS, University of Wyoming; MA, University of Toronto; PhD, University of Connecticut) is professor of English at Grand Valley State University in Grand Rapids, Michigan, where he has received the alumni association's Outstanding Educator Award. He is the author of *The Sacred Marriage: Psychic Integration in "The Faerie Queene"* (1987) and *Aethereal Rumours: T. S. Eliot's Physics and Poetics* (1998), as well as articles on Eliot and on Renaissance literature. He also wrote the introduction to a new edition of Russell Kirk's book *Eliot and His Age*. He has served as president of the T. S. Eliot Society.

Dominic Manganiello (BA, McGill; DPhil, Oxford) is a professor of English Literature at the University of Ottawa. He is the author of *Joyce's Politics* (1980) and *T.S. Eliot and Dante* (1989), and coauthor of *Rethinking the Future of the University* (1998). Although he has written extensively on canonical modern authors and the culture of modernism, his recent work has also focused on a group of writers that includes, among others, G. K. Chesterton, Dorothy L. Sayers, J. R. R. Tolkien, C. S. Lewis, Charles Williams, Evelyn Waugh, and their return to the Middle Ages as a quest to locate the roots of Western culture. His current book-length project, *Making Dante New*, accordingly examines the nature of the high-level reception twentieth-century writers accorded *The Divine Comedy*.

William Marx (BA, MA, PhD, University of Paris-Sorbonne) is professor of comparative literature at the University of Paris Ouest Nanterre La Défense and an honorary fellow of the Institut universitaire de France. His books, whose translations have been published in many languages, include *Naissance de la critique moderne: la littérature selon Eliot et Valéry* (2002), *L'Adieu à la littérature: histoire d'une dévalorisation* (2005), *Vie du lettré* (2009), for which he was awarded the Montyon Prize of the Académie française, and *Le Tombeau d'Œdipe: pour une tragédie sans tragique* (2012). He edited, among other collections of essays, *Les Arrière-gardes au XXᵉ siècle* (2004), and also coedited seven volumes of Paul Valéry's *Cahiers 1894–1914* (1997–2012).

Christopher McVey (MA, University of Virginia) is a doctoral candidate in English literature at the University of Wisconsin-Madison. His dissertation, "This Storm We Call Progress: Spatial Form as Modernist and Postcolonial Historiography," examines modernist and postcolonial writers who spatialize history in ways that counteract linear, teleological narratives of progress. He is an active member in the T. S. Eliot Society and was the Fathman Young Scholar Award recipient for the 2010 annual meeting.

John Morgenstern recently completed his doctorate at the University of Oxford. His dissertation, "'Making Up His Own Mind': T. S. Eliot's Formative Year in 1910–1911 Paris," reframes figures central to Eliot's early intellectual biography in light of the literary, religious, artistic, and political controversies that he witnessed during his student year in France. While revising his dissertation for monograph publication, he has started research on a second project, tentatively titled *Line for Line: Henri Matisse and Modern Poetry*. He is currently visiting assistant professor at Clemson University.

Lee Oser teaches religion and literature at the College of the Holy Cross, in Worcester, Massachusetts. His most recent books are *The Ethics of Modernism: Moral Ideas in Yeats, Eliot, Joyce, Woolf, and Beckett; The Return of Christian Humanism: Chesterton, Eliot, Tolkien, and the Romance of History;* and the novels *Out of What Chaos* and *The Oracles Fell Silent.*

Paul Robichaud (BA, MA, University of Western Ontario; PhD, University of Toronto) is associate professor and chair of English at Albertus Magnus College in New Haven, Connecticut. His publications include *Making the Past Present: David Jones, the Middle Ages, and Modernism* (2007), and essays on Hugh MacDiarmid, James Joyce, and Geoffrey Hill.

James Seaton (BA, University of Illinois; MA, PhD, University of Iowa) is professor of English at Michigan State University. He is the author of *A*

Reading of Vergil's Georgics (1983), *Cultural Conservatism, Political Liberalism* (1996), and *Literary Criticism from Plato to Postmodernism: The Humanistic Alternative* (2014), as well as many essays and reviews in publications such as *The Wall Street Journal, The Weekly Standard, The American Scholar,* and *Yale Journal of Law and Humanities.* He is the editor of *The Genteel Tradition in American Philosophy and Character and Opinion in the United States* by George Santayana (2009) and coeditor *of Beyond Cheering and Bashing: New Perspectives on The Closing of the American Mind* (1992).

Shun'ichi Takayanagi (BA, Sophia University; MA, Gonzaga University; PhD, Fordham University) is a member of the Society of Jesus. He is professor emeritus at Sophia University and has published three studies on Eliot in Japanese. He has also translated Northrop Frye's *Myth and Metaphor* and *Creation and Recreation.* He is a former president of the T. S. Eliot Society in Japan. His most recent article on Eliot was published in *The International Reception of T. S. Eliot.* He edited a collection of essays on T. S. Eliot, *Modern and Yet Anti-Modern,* published in Japanese in 2010.

James Matthew Wilson (BA, University of Michigan; MA, University of Massachusetts, Amherst; MFA and PhD, University of Notre Dame) is assistant professor in the Department of Humanities and Augustinian Traditions at Villanova University. He is the author of a book of poems, *Four Verse Letters* (2010), and of *Timothy Steele: A Critical Introduction* (2012), in addition to many essays, poems, reviews, and scholarly articles.